Nurturing Faith Commentary, Year A, Volume 1
Lectionary Resources for Preaching and Teaching: Advent, Christmas, Epiphany

Nurturing Faith Commentary, Year A, Volume 2
Lectionary Resources for Preaching and Teaching: Lent, Easter, Pentecost

Nurturing Faith Commentary, Year A, Volume 3
Lectionary Resources for Preaching and Teaching: Season after Pentecost, Proper 1–14

Nurturing Faith Commentary, Year A, Volume 4
Lectionary Resources for Preaching and Teaching: Season after Pentecost, Proper 15–29

*

Nurturing Faith Commentary, Year B, Volume 1
Lectionary Resources for Preaching and Teaching: Advent, Christmas, Epiphany

Nurturing Faith Commentary, Year B, Volume 2
Lectionary Resources for Preaching and Teaching: Lent, Easter, Pentecost

Nurturing Faith Commentary, Year B, Volume 3
Lectionary Resources for Preaching and Teaching: Season after Pentecost, Proper 1–14

Nurturing Faith Commentary, Year B, Volume 4
Lectionary Resources for Preaching and Teaching: Season after Pentecost, Proper 15–29

*

Nurturing Faith Commentary, Year C, Volume 1
Lectionary Resources for Preaching and Teaching: Advent, Christmas, Epiphany

Nurturing Faith Commentary, Year C, Volume 2
Lectionary Resources for Preaching and Teaching: Lent, Easter, Pentecost

Nurturing Faith Commentary, Year C, Volume 3
Lectionary Resources for Preaching and Teaching: Season after Pentecost, Proper 1–14

Nurturing Faith Commentary, Year C, Volume 4
Lectionary Resources for Preaching and Teaching: Season after Pentecost, Proper 15–29

# Nurturing Faith Commentary

## Year A, Volume 2

Lectionary Resources for Preaching and Teaching:
Lent, Easter, Pentecost

## TONY W. CARTLEDGE

*Nurturing Faith Commentary* is sponsored
by a generous gift from Bob and Pat Barker.

© 2022
Published in the United States by Nurturing Faith, Macon, GA.
Nurturing Faith is a book imprint of Good Faith Media (goodfaithmedia.org).
Library of Congress Cataloging-in-Publication Data is available.

ISBN: 978-1-63528-190-3

Unless otherwise indicated, all scripture citations come from the New Revised Standard Version (NRSV).

# Contents

# Publisher's Preface

Moreore than a decade in the making, *Nurturing Faith Commentary* is unique in its intent and content. Anyone seeking to teach, preach, and/or learn from a broad swath of carefully explored biblical texts will find this to be a reliable, helpful, and treasured resource.

Tony Cartledge brings the mind of a scholar, the heart of a pastor, and the writing skills of an experienced author to this extensive yet accessible multi-volume resource. Rooted in a trusted weekly Bible study, lessons are provided for every possible Sunday of the Christian Year.

Following scripture texts as found in the three-year cycle designated by the Revised Common Lectionary, these lessons are both scholarly and applicable.

The purpose of these Bible studies goes beyond gaining knowledge — although the insights are plentiful — to discovering the inspiration and fresh possibilities for living out biblical truth in one's daily experiences and spheres of influence.

The many years of excellent work in which Tony poured himself into writing thoughtful, weekly Bible studies now form the basis of these volumes. These lessons reflect his wisdom, interpretive skills, diligence, and humility that never prescribe how others are to think and believe.

"Nurturing Faith" is more than just the overall title of this multivolume resource. Learning is seen as the road to redemption and transformation by an individual encountering not just facts, but a living God.

Each week, Tony's lessons have impacted individuals and classes of all shapes and sizes in seeking to learn and apply biblical truths. Having these volumes easily at hand will provide access to a multitude of ideas, insights, and illustrations for those heeding the call to equip disciples to more faithfully follow in the ways of Jesus.

A unique mark of these lessons is the way readers and listeners are treated respectfully and intelligently regardless of their backgrounds. The lessons are never dumbed down to the point of ignoring known scholarly findings.

Yet the purpose is not to impress, but to communicate. Though a Bible scholar and teacher of note, Tony seeks to convey biblical insights effectively rather than using language exclusive to the scholarly community.

When it comes to sharing helpful insights from biblical scholarship with his readers, Tony — intentionally using double negatives for effect — has often said: "I'll never not tell you something I know if it's relevant."

This honest and appreciated approach contrasts with a long history of Bible study curriculum providers that "hand-cuff" writers and therefore "mind-cuff" learners with narrow doctrinal and marketing parameters.

In contrast, *Nurturing Faith Commentary* has no such restrictions — allowing for the freedom of both writer and readers to question, pray, seek, disagree, or apply whatever arises from the exploration of these ancient texts.

The Nurturing Faith approach to Bible study does have a lens, however. It is based on the belief that Jesus is God's fullest revelation, the Living Word through whom all else is filtered in a search for truth.

These insightful and inspiring lessons are a gift — coming from the sharp mind and generous spirit of a minister-scholar who helps us dig more deeply into the rich soil of truth formed by the many layers of experiences, reflections, and stories compiled in what we know and value as the Bible. Dig in!

John D. Pierce
Executive Editor/Publisher
Good Faith Media

# Introduction

The 12 volumes of *Nurturing Faith Commentary* are the product of a committed desire to provide quality Bible study for Christians who come to the scripture with open minds and a desire to go beneath a surface reading. Our goal has been to provide pastors, teachers, and other Bible students with both academic and pastoral insights in approachable language.

The project began in early 2011, when John Pierce, editor of what is now *Nurturing Faith Journal*, envisioned the idea of including a weekly Bible study in the print version of the journal, along with additional resources provided online. The studies were to be based on texts from the Revised Common Lectionary and use the New Revised Standard Version as the primary text. Use of the lectionary had become increasingly common in worship among progressive Baptists, who had been our primary audience, but resources for Bible study were lacking.

With many years of experience as a pastor, academician, professor, writer, and editor, I was asked to take on the challenge of writing these studies. With some trepidation, I accepted, and the first studies appeared in the July 2011 issue of *Baptists Today*. The studies have continued now for more than a decade, even as the newspaper-style *Baptists Today* morphed into the magazine format of *Nurturing Faith Journal and Bible Studies*.

For those who subscribe to the journal, additional resources are available online, including detailed insights through "Digging Deeper," helps for troublesome issues through "The Hardest Question," a weekly video in which I offer a summary of the lesson, plus additional teaching resources for youth and adults prepared by other writers. In this resource, Digging Deeper and The Hardest Question are incorporated into print.*

As years of publication and lectionary cycles piled up, we thought it fruitful to update and compile these lessons in a convenient format for teachers, preachers, or others who rely on helpful Bible studies, especially when lectionary based. That, plus the addition of many new commentaries for texts not previously covered, is now coming to fruition in a 12-volume set of Bible studies, with four volumes for each of the three lectionary years.

The project is a massive undertaking, and we are grateful to all who have contributed time, energy, and finances to the project.

---

*All photos used in Digging Deeper and The Hardest Question, unless otherwise indicated, are by Tony Cartledge.*

# Using This Resource

The Revised Common Lectionary (RCL), devised by a consortium of Protestant and Catholic representatives on the Consultation of Common Texts, was published in 1992. Since then, it has become a standard resource for both Roman Catholics and mainline Protestants.

The lectionary contains hundreds of texts chosen to reflect a progressive study of primary texts in the Bible, along with texts representative of the church year. It follows a three-year cycle known as "Year A," "Year B," and "Year C," then repeats the cycle, using the same texts. Year A relies mainly on Matthew for the gospel readings, while Year B focuses on Mark, and Year C draws mainly from Luke. Selections from the gospel of John are scattered through the three years.

Most days on the lectionary calendar include four readings. These typically follow a pattern of one reading from the Old Testament narratives, prophets, or wisdom; one text from Psalms; one text from the New Testament gospels; and one text from the epistles. Exceptions are many, especially during the Season after Pentecost, when most Sundays include two additional readings as options.

The RCL includes texts for both Sunday worship and other special days. *Nurturing Faith Commentary* focuses on texts for Sundays rather than every "feast day" on the church calendar, many of which are not observed through active services, especially in Protestant churches. We do include texts chosen for New Year's Day, Epiphany, and All Saints' Day, however, because sometimes they fall on Sunday.

A small handful of optional texts from the Apocrypha or "Deuterocanonicals," which are regarded as scripture by Roman Catholics, appear in the lectionary. Given that I write as a Protestant and our audience is mainly Protestant, apocryphal texts are not included in this resource.

The studies in these volumes are not dated, because we want them to be useful in any calendar year, and no year contains all the potential Sundays. Persons who use the text for preaching and teaching may easily consult online and print resources for the specific dates associated with each lectionary Sunday. (Vanderbilt University's library provides an ideal resource at https://lectionary.library.vanderbilt.edu.)

The RCL sometimes uses the same texts on multiple Sundays. When those occur, the study for that text will be printed only once per volume, with appropriate notes to indicate where it may be found if it is indicated on multiple Sundays.

Lectionary texts follow the church year rather than the calendar year, beginning with Advent, the four Sundays prior to Christmas day. Three optional sets of texts are provided for use on Christmas Eve or Christmas Day. These are sometimes referred to as "Christmas 1, 2, and 3," or as "Proper 1, 2, and 3" for Christmas. The first three potential Sundays after Trinity Sunday are also called "Proper 1, 2, and 3," so in this resource we will use the terms "Christmas 1, 2, and 3."

For the sake of completeness, we include studies for all three Christmas options in Volume 1. Many churches hold Christmas Eve services, and Christmas Day sometimes falls on Sunday.

One or two Sundays may follow Christmas, depending on the number of Sundays between Christmas Day and Epiphany. Texts for the second Sunday after Christmas are rarely used and always the same. Studies on those texts are also provided in Volume 1. The texts are sometimes similar to texts for New Year's Day.

Epiphany is celebrated with special texts on January 6, which commonly occurs during the week, but studies on these texts are also included in this resource because Epiphany sometimes occurs on a Sunday. Ministers also sometimes choose to use texts for Epiphany on the Sunday nearest January 6.

The season of Epiphany may include from four to nine Sundays before concluding with Transfiguration Sunday. The number of weeks depends on the date of Easter, which moves about on the calendar, likewise affecting the dates of Ash Wednesday and the beginning of Lent. The last few weeks of Epiphany aren't used in each cycle, but they are included for the sake of those years that do have them. Their location is in Volume 3 of each year, as will be explained below.

Lent always includes six Sundays, concluding with Palm Sunday, which can be celebrated with texts focusing on Jesus' entry to Jerusalem, or on the following passion. Both are provided.

The Season of Easter has seven Sundays leading up to the day of Pentecost, 50 days after Easter.

The first Sunday after Pentecost is always Trinity Sunday. Depending on the calendar, from 23 to 29 Sundays follow Pentecost, ending on the last Sunday before Advent. These are called "Proper" Sundays. The RCL handles the dilemma of differing calendars by starting at the end with Proper 29 as the Sunday before Advent, then working backward. In this system, the texts for Proper 7 through Proper 29 appear in each year's cycle. Texts for Proper Sundays 1–6 are not always used, but are provided for those calendar years in which they appear.

Since Epiphany 6–9 and Proper 1–4 are the least likely to occur, they share the same texts: Epiphany 6 = Proper 1, Epiphany 7 = Proper 2, Epiphany 8 = Proper 3, and Epiphany 9 = Proper 4. Studies for these Sundays are included in Volume 3 for each year, which begins the Season after Pentecost, with their location noted in Volume 1, which contains lessons for the Season of Epiphany.

The number of "Sundays after Pentecost" for a given "Proper" Sunday is different from year to year, so in this resource they will be designated by the "Proper" number, which can be coordinated with each year's number of "Sundays after Pentecost," which will vary.

Texts, especially from the psalms, are often short and designed more for liturgical reading than for individual study. Even so, all texts receive full treatment in Bible study form.

Readers familiar with the RCL know that texts are often chopped and spliced for liturgical reading, which isn't always ideal for a connected Bible study. In many of those cases, the Bible study in these volumes will expand the RCL selection to provide greater context and continuity. Texts listed in the Table of Contents, with each lesson/ commentary, and in the index, are based on the actual text examined, which may be longer than the RCL text, but not shorter.

The basic outline of the series is as follows, for each of the three cycles:

Volume 1 – Advent through Epiphany
Volume 2 – Lent through Pentecost
Volume 3 – Season after Pentecost (Propers 1–14)
Volume 4 – Season after Pentecost (Propers 15–29)

# Abbreviations

| | |
|---|---|
| BCE | Before the Common Era |
| cf. | confer |
| ch., chs. | chapter, chapters |
| cp. | compare |
| CE | Common Era |
| CEB | Common English Bible |
| CSB | Christian Standard Bible |
| e.g. | for example |
| et. al. | and others |
| etc. | and others |
| f., ff. | the following verse, verses |
| HCSB | Holman Christian Standard Bible |
| KJV | King James Version of the Bible |
| LXX | Septuagint |
| MT | Masoretic Text |
| NASB95 | New American Standard Bible, 1995 edition |
| NASB20 | New American Standard Bible, 2020 edition |
| NET | New English Translation of the Bible |
| NET2 | New English Translation, 2nd edition |
| NIV11 | New International Version, 2011 edition |
| NJPS | New Jewish Publication Society |
| NRSV | New Revised Standard Version of the Bible |
| RCL | Revised Common Lectionary |
| v., vv. | verse, verses |

# First Sunday in Lent

## First Reading
## Genesis 2:15-17, 3:1-19*

# Making Choices

*So when the woman saw that the tree was good for food, and that it was a delight to the eyes, and that the tree was to be desired to make one wise, she took of its fruit and ate; and she also gave some to her husband, who was with her, and he ate. (Gen. 3:6)*

Was it really Eve's fault? Would sin never have entered the world if Eve had not chosen to eat from a forbidden tree and share it with Adam? Would none of their descendants have ever chosen to do wrong?

No, we can't blame our own sin on the story found in Genesis 3: the author responsible for the story was making the point that humans have sinned from the beginning. Whether we regard Adam and Eve as historical characters or literary metaphors, the lesson is the same: humans have always been tempted to step out of bounds, and are always prone to do so. **[Original sin]**

It's not surprising that the lectionary uses this text for the first Sunday of Lent, a season of repentance. The reading for the day includes only the beginning of the story, however. We will profit more from a longer look.

### Asking questions
### (2:15-17, 3:1-6)

The book of Genesis begins with two starkly different but equally inspiring creation stories (Gen. 1:1-2:4a and 2:4b-25), both of which describe God's creation of the earth and of humankind as being good in every way.

Both accounts portray humans as the crown of God's creation, but the following story suggests that they constitute a thorny crown.

Genesis 3 is commonly known as the story of "the Fall," though the word "fall" does not appear in the story, nor does

> **Original sin?** Some people who interpret Genesis 3 literally argue that, because the "first" people chose to disobey God, the stain of sin became an automatic heritage, and all their descendants are thus "born in sin." Sin grows from bad choices, however, not one's innate nature, and we can't blame our choices on Eve.
>
> The notion of original sin derives from Paul's argument in Rom. 5:12-21, in which he combined the story of Adam and Eve with developing ideas from apocryphal works such as the Wisdom of Solomon and Second Esdras. Paul's interpretation became dominant in the emerging theology of the church, but it is not the only way of understanding or interpreting the story.

"sin." The notion of a "fall" from original perfection is more at home in Greek philosophy than the Hebrew Bible.

Despite the prominence of this story in much Christian teaching, the remainder of the Old Testament never refers to it, suggesting that it was hardly known among most Hebrews, and therefore not especially important to them. Most of the Hebrew Bible defines obedience or disobedience in terms of covenant stipulations defined in Deuteronomy. The prophets often criticized Israel's worship of other gods or failure to keep the law, but they never mentioned Adam and Eve or the serpent's temptation: they believed, and rightly so, that every person is responsible for his or her own sin. **[Questions]**

The story is a narrative continuation of Genesis 2, a charming creation story rife with metaphors and with special attention to the creation of a man and a woman

---

*This study covers Gen. 2:15-17 and 3:1-19. Genesis 3:8-15 is also the first reading for Year B, Proper 5.*

> **Questions:** We learn by asking questions, and the Bible is filled with them. Did you ever wonder why people typically dislike snakes, for example, or why snakes crawl on their bellies? Did you ever wonder why men dominate women in most societies? Have you ever wondered why life often seems uncertain and full of unrewarded labor? Have you pondered big questions such as "Why must people die?" and "Why is there evil in the world?"
>
> The ancient Hebrews had questions, too, and often employed etiological stories to explain the origin of certain customs, place names, or beliefs. Genesis 3 is a prime example of this, a memorable story that attempts to answer questions.

whose names are symbolic of humankind. The Hebrew word "*adam*" is a generic term meaning "man" or "humankind," and the word is used with the direct article (*ha-'adam*, "the man") until Gen. 4:25, the first time *adam* appears as a name. The name we render as "Eve" is *chavvah*, which means "life" or "living one," but she is not given the name until Gen. 3:20. Prior to that she is called "the woman" (*ha-'ishshah*).

As in ch. 2, God appears in human form in ch. 3, walking in the garden and talking to the man and woman.

The fourth character in the story is a talking serpent. Despite our common notions of the serpent as being sinister, evil, or identified with the devil – all much later interpretations – that is not the story's point of view. Indeed, the serpent is not only a part of God's good creation, but also the cleverest of all the wild creatures "that the LORD God had made" (3:1). The serpent is not described as evil, but shrewd. The word *'arum* can vary in meaning from "cunning" (negative) to "prudent" (positive).

Tradition leads us to think of the serpent as a tempter who deceived the woman in hopes of leading her astray. In the story, however, the serpent functions as a prompt for Eve to have thoughts of her own, and those thoughts led her to want more than God had allowed, to the point of questioning the rules.

The story says God had told the man not to eat from the "tree of the knowledge of good and evil" before the woman was created (2:15-17, 21-22). The reader is required to assume that the man had passed on God's instruction to the woman – and perhaps added a few of

his own. The command in 2:17 says only that "you shall not eat" from the tree upon penalty of death, but the woman's response to the serpent expands the prohibition: "but God said, 'You shall not eat of the fruit of the tree that is in the middle of the garden, nor shall you touch it, or you shall die'" (3:3).

One could argue that God was the real tempter, the one who intentionally planted a most desirable fruit tree in the garden and then declared it off limits. The serpent's questions led the woman to realize that God was holding back knowledge from them, knowledge with great appeal.

The serpent likewise questioned whether the woman would really die if she ate of the fruit. Modern readers might note a logical inconsistency: newly created and in the freshness of a perfect garden, the woman would never have encountered death. That did not concern the narrator, who wrote from the perspective of people who knew death all too well.

The woman was curious, as we would be: she wanted to understand more of life and of what God knew (vv. 4-5). "Good and evil" should probably be understood as a merism, a literary device that names two opposite poles but includes everything between. Thus, "the knowledge of good and evil" could imply far more than discerning right from wrong. [**Gods guarding knowledge**]

Was it worth the risk?

As the story is told, the woman would have known no more of evil than of death, but she wanted to know more of what God knew.

Would we have been any less curious?

> **Gods guarding knowledge:** Other ancient cultures also portrayed the gods as jealously guarding their knowledge and trying to keep it from humans. In the Sumerian and Babylonian versions of the flood story, for example, the council of the gods did not want humans to know the flood was coming, but the god variously known as Enki/Ea gave a surreptitious warning to Ziusudra/Utnapishtim, who took the hint and built an ark.
>
> In the Greek myth of Prometheus, the high god Zeus was outraged when Prometheus revealed the secret of fire to humans, thus speeding their development. As punishment, Prometheus was bound to a rock where a vulture would eat his liver, which would then regenerate so the process could be repeated day after day.

As she thought about it, the text says the woman saw that the tree was "good for food, a delight to the eyes, and to be desired for making one wise" (v. 6). Everything about the mysterious fruit was appealing and consequences were uncertain, so she chose to take the risk and eat. The man, who had been with her all along, appears to have given the matter little thought. When she offered the fruit to him, the text says only that "he ate."

The old tradition that the forbidden fruit was an apple goes back to medieval interpretations of the story, when the only Bible used by the church was written in Latin, in which the words for "evil" and for "apple" could both be spelled *malum*. The Latin expression "good and evil" was *bonum et malum*, so it was natural for Latin readers to think of an evil apple.

Artists popularized the idea in paintings. The biblical text offers no hint as to what the fruit was, other than that it was appealing to the eye, good to eat – and forbidden.

## Passing the buck
### (3:7-13)

After risking that first taste, according to the story, the pair did gain new knowledge, but it came in the form of shame. Previously, the man and woman had been naked, but not ashamed (2:25). Now their sense of guilt came in a perception that nakedness was no longer acceptable. They covered their genitals with leafy skirts, according to the story, but could not hide their actions (v. 7).

Some scholars see this account as a "coming of age" story in which the man and woman lost their innocence, clothed themselves, and entered adulthood. In that sense, they were not unlike Enkidu, an important character in the Babylonian Gilgamesh epic. When the gods first put Enkidu on earth, he ran and ate with the animals until he met a prostitute who slept with him, then taught him to wear clothes and eat from the table. Afterward, he anointed himself with oil and declared himself human. The story in Genesis also has clear sexual overtones in the sense of genital shame, though no sexual activity is mentioned until after the two were expelled from the garden (4:1).

The man and woman were still trying to hide when they heard Yahweh walking in the garden that evening, asking "Where are you?" (vv. 8-9). The couple knew they

had done wrong, but neither wanted to accept responsibility. When God confronted the man, he blamed both the woman and God: "The *woman*, whom *you* gave to be with me, she gave me fruit from the tree, and I ate" (v. 12).

The woman also sought to avoid culpability: "The *serpent* tricked me, and I ate" (v. 13b). Only the serpent had no one to blame. Or, as pundits sometimes observe, it didn't have a leg to stand on.

The story is a metaphorical testimony that humans have sinned from the beginning and have always tried to hide their sin or deny responsibility for it. Paul's later implication that "the one man, Adam" was responsible for human sin (Rom. 5:12) sounds like a further attempt to shift the blame for our failures to someone else, but Paul also understood that "all have sinned and fall short of the glory of God" (Rom. 3:23).

Does this sound familiar? Haven't we sought to deny our wrongdoing, blame it on others, or offer countless rationalizations? Don't we also know what it is like to feel shame and separation when confronted by our bad choices and actions?

The story is not all bad news. God did not leave the man and the woman in hiding, but pursued them with concern and gave them an opportunity to repent: *"Where are you?"*

## A painful judgment
### (3:14-19)

Part of the storyteller's purpose is to offer a divine explanation for various aspects of life as it was experienced in the ancient world.

Why does a snake have no legs? Because God cursed it, saying "upon your belly you shall go, and dust you shall eat all the days of your life" (v. 14).

Why are humans so inclined to fear snakes and desire to kill them? Because God said "I will put enmity between you and the woman, and between your offspring and hers; he will strike your head, and you will strike his heel" (v. 15). [**The first gospel?**]

Why is it that women must suffer so much in giving birth? It was because God said "I will greatly increase your pangs in childbearing, in pain you shall bring forth children" (v. 16a).

**The first gospel?** Gen. 3:15 is sometimes called the *proto-evangelium* ("first gospel") because Catholic teaching saw in it the seed of the gospel: that the serpent (as Satan) would one day cause pain and suffering for Eve/Mary's offspring Jesus by "striking his heel," but that Christ would conquer Satan by smiting his head. The original author would have been agog that such an interpretation would ever be given to his words. His intention was not to prophesy of a future savior, but to explain present circumstances.

Why then would women allow themselves to get pregnant again and be dominated by men? Because God said, "yet your desire shall be for your husband, and he shall rule over you" (v. 16b). For the ancients, it was common to see a divine cause for most things.

The writer of the story in Genesis 3 understood that God had created humans to live in joyful unity, but that ideal had become corrupted. Men came to dominate women in society, even though it was unfair and painful for them.

Conservative Christians who believe men should be in authority over women continue to cite this ancient story as a supposed divine justification for female submission without acknowledging that it was not God's first intention.

The man also faced consequences for disobeying the rules. Food would no longer be easy to come by. The man would have to toil in hot sun and hard soil while battling weeds and thorns to raise crops from the earth (vv. 17-18).

Moreover, humans would not live in the sacred garden forever, as the writer believed God intended. The decision to follow their own way would lead to a hard life and a certain death: "By the sweat of your face you shall eat bread until you return to the ground, for out of it you were taken; you are dust, and to dust you shall return" (v. 19). [Hebrew humor]

The connection of a serpent with the loss of eternal life also appears in the epic of Gilgamesh and his quest for eternal life. After Gilgamesh traveled far, a man named

**Hebrew humor:** Note the author's wry humor: while the serpent is condemned to crawl on his belly and eat dust (v. 14), the man and woman are to die and return to dust (v. 19)—thus becoming snake food!

Utnapishtim, the hero of the Babylonian flood story, told him of a plant from the sea floor that could renew life. Gilgamesh dove and obtained the plant, but planned to try it out on an older person before eating it himself. When he put it down while bathing in a forest pool, a snake slithered from the grass and ate the plant. The serpent then shed its skin, giving the appearance of new youth, and crawled away. Thus, Gilgamesh lost his hope of immortality.

Things looked bad for Adam and Eve, but the narrator did not believe God had given up on humans. In an act of compassion, Yahweh made garments of skin for them (v. 21). It is natural to assume this means that living blood would have been shed in response to human sin. It would not be the last time.

When we look at this story through a Jesus-centered lens, we are reminded that Christ offers forgiveness for our sins, but also calls us to obedience. Following Jesus is not a matter of avoiding forbidden information, but of gaining both knowledge and wisdom as we learn to love God and to love others as God loves us.

### The Hardest Question
### Was the serpent of Genesis 3 the devil?

Modern readers commonly identify the serpent of Genesis 3 as the devil, but that idea is alien to the story. In fact, much of what many people believe about Satan did not develop until after most of the Old Testament was written – especially the concept of Satan as a supernaturally powerful adversary of God.

Even in Job, it is a misnomer to speak of "Satan." The character who questions the ground of Job's faith is described as a member of the heavenly court who assists God in observing humankind. He is not called by a proper name there, but a title: *ha-sātān*, which means "the accuser." Only once in the Old Testament, in the Chronicler's postexilic revision of Israel's history, is the name "Satan" used without the definite article (1 Chron. 21:1), and even there it seems to have in mind a heavenly servant of God: the action attributed to Satan in 1 Chron. 21:1 is said to have been God's doing in 2 Sam. 24:1.

Ancient Hebrews feared evil spirits or demons, but the concept of the devil as an enemy of God emerged only after the exile, almost certainly influenced by the dualistic nature of Zoroastrianism characteristic of the Persians, who ruled Israel for the first 200 years after exiles began to return from Babylon. Zoroastrians worshiped a benevolent god named Ahura Mazda, who was opposed by his evil brother Ahriman, who created things such as snakes and demons and showed up every thousand years to wreak havoc.

The notion of an evil supernatural being who opposed God began to appear in Jewish writings around the first and second centuries before Christ, as reflected in the apocryphal Book of Wisdom, which says "for God created us for incorruption, and made us in the image of his own eternity, but through the devil's envy death entered the world, and those who belong to his company experience it" (Wis 2:23-25, NRSV).

This became a common idea in Judaism, and both Jesus and New Testament writers spoke in the accepted vocabulary of the day, which included demons and an evil power named Satan. Much later, the Apocalypse of John (also known as the Book of Revelation) described the one called "the Devil and Satan" as "the great dragon, the ancient serpent" (Rev. 12:9, 20:2). Some later interpreters projected that backward, arguing that the serpent of Genesis 3 should be identified as Satan despite its clear description as a crafty creature made by God. The author of this story had no such thing in mind.

One particularly egregious error has gained undue popularity: the notion that Satan is an angel gone rogue who was thrown out of heaven and then grew in power to rival God is not biblical at all. The much-misunderstood account of "Lucifer" being cast out of heaven is an obvious misinterpretation of Isaiah 14, a taunt song in which Isaiah clearly celebrated the death of a Babylonian king who had proudly thought of himself as a god associated with the morning star. The Hebrew term is composed of three words, and could be translated literally as "shining one, son of the dawn," a title the king may have attributed to himself. The early Greek translation known as the Septuagint (abbreviated LXX) translated this with the term *heōsphoros*, which could mean "morning star." In the late fourth century CE, when the Catholic church father Jerome translated the Bible into Latin, he rendered "morning star" as *lucifer,* a combination word (from *lux*, "light," and *ferous,* "to bear" or "to carry"). Classical Roman thought called Venus "Lucifer" when it appeared in the morning, and "Vesper" when it appeared in the evening. In iconography, it was often portrayed as a man carrying a torch. Over time, a word that simply meant "light bearer" came to be capitalized and treated as the personal name "Lucifer" – far from the intent of Isaiah, who would have had no concept of a personal devil, and who was taunting a Babylonian king.

The late Jewish tradition in the apocryphal book of 1 Enoch 6–36 muddied the water further with its expansion of the story in Gen. 6:1-4 that claims certain "sons of God" chose to come to earth and have sex with human women, giving rise to giants, and were cast out of heaven as a result.

Today, the popular concept of Satan owes far more to Dante Alighieri's 14th century *Inferno* and John Milton's *Paradise Lost* (1667) than to the Bible.

## Second Reading
## Psalm 32*

# The Hope of Forgiveness

*Many are the torments of the wicked, but steadfast love surrounds those who trust in the LORD. (Ps. 32:10)*

Forgiveness: it's amazing. Only those who have experienced it know the incredible feeling of sweet relief that comes from having a burden of guilt lifted and tossed away.

Marriages, friendships, and even workplaces suffer when hurt feelings or grudges fester and foam, but words of forgiveness can clear the slate and restore joyful relationships.

Today's text is about the kind of forgiveness we need even more: the forgiveness that comes from God. All of us have sinned. We know that. The season of Lent constantly reminds us of how we can accumulate a laundry list of shortcomings ranging from hurtful words and harmful habits to serious breaches of morality or ethics.

Sometimes our failures may seem so run-of-the-mill that we don't notice them, while others may run so counter to our upbringing or personal expectations that they have a devastating impact on our sense of self-worth.

Whether sparked by a gradual distancing of our hearts from God or by a major violation of our own values, the weight of guilt can become oppressive. Bearing a heavy load of shame or self-reproach can lead to psychological and physical ailments.

Today's text reminds us of the freedom and joy that comes from experiencing divine forgiveness, and it's a reminder that all of us could use.

### The voice of wisdom
### (vv. 1-2)

Psalm 32 is one of many associated with David, and the first of 13 Psalms that are labeled as a "Maskil," a word that defies a neat definition. It can't refer to a very specific type of psalm, because the 13 examples fall into different categories. A form of the word appears as an active verb in v. 8, meaning "I will instruct you" (or "Let me teach you"). Perhaps we could best think of Maskil as indicating "a meditation" or "an insightful psalm." The NET focuses on the poem's literary merit, and calls it a "well-written psalm."

The psalm contains elements of both wisdom (vv. 1-2, 9-10) and thanksgiving (vv. 3-8, 11). Thus, we will approach the text as a psalm of thanksgiving or testimony (vv. 3-7), framed by instructive or wisdom elements (vv. 1-2, 8-10). The concluding verse, which some scholars think may have been added later, concludes with a joyous postscript. **[Structure]**

---

**Structure:** The main body of Psalm 32 can be considered as a *chiasmus*, a literary term describing a structure in which a sequence of elements is repeated in reverse order. The following example is adapted, with minor changes, from Peter C. Craigie, *Psalms 1–50*, vol. 19, Word Biblical Commentary (Word Books, 1983), 265.

Superscription

| Part I | (1) Wisdom (vv. 1-2) | A |
| | (2) Thanksgiving (vv. 3-5) | B |
| | | |
| Part II | (1) Thanksgiving (vv. 6-7) | B' |
| | (2) Wisdom (vv. 8-10) | A' |

Conclusion (v. 11)

---

*Psalm 32 is also read in Year C on the Fourth Sunday in Lent, Proper 6, and Proper 26.*

**Terms of in-sin-ment:** The terms used in vv. 1-2 are similar, but not identical. The word translated as "transgression" is *pesha'*, which suggests rebellion or wrongdoing that could be directed against God, other nations, or individuals. The general word for sin is *chāthâ*, which describes an offense against someone or turning away from the right path (the *ch* is pronounced as a rough "k," as in "loch"). "Iniquity" translates the word *'awôn*, which can also be rendered as "guilt" (as in v. 5). "Deceit" (*rĕmîyyâ*) describes a more specific category of sin, though one could argue that any exercise of evil is inherently deceptive.

Hebrew poetry typically employs two or more lines that repeat or expand upon the same thought. This psalm follows that pattern, beginning with a pair of matched beatitudes, each consisting of two parallel lines. Each of the four lines employs a different word to indicate rebellion against God, as the psalmist bemoans his "transgression," "sin," "iniquity," and "deceit" (vv. 1-2).

While one could argue for fine points of distinction between the Hebrew terms, there is no need: We know how it feels to transgress against God, to sin against others, to harbor iniquity in our hearts, and to practice deceit in dealing with God, others, or ourselves. **[Terms of in-sin-ment]**

We know what it is like to fall short, to do wrong, and to feel somehow overcome with evil. It's not a good feeling, so our tendency is to deny our failures, lower our standards, and pretend that all is well and good. In relating to other people, we may throw up barriers or multiply deceptions, actions that undermine healthy relationships.

Sooner or later, the darkness inside haunts us, or our duplicity toward others catches up with us, and we feel the burden of our wrongdoing. We need forgiveness, and we know that we won't be truly happy until we find it. The opening two verses, in the style of Israel's wisdom teachers, affirm the peace and release of one whose sinful encumbrance has been lifted.

## The voice of experience
### (vv. 3-7)

The psalmist had experienced such soulful deliverance, and he turned to a personal testimony of sin and forgiveness (vv. 3-5).

Some scholars believe a copyist's error left something missing from v. 3, because the expected structure of two couplets contains only three elements. It's quite possible, however, that the psalmist intended to begin with a triplet of related thoughts: (1) while he held silence and refused to confess his sin, (2) his sense of well-being imploded, (3) causing moans of distress throughout the day. **[Moaning and groaning]**

Those who remain silent when confession is needed tend to bottle up their sense of guilt and shame, and sooner or later it will manifest itself in distress, whether vocalized or not.

The psalmist described his own condition with the expression "my bones wore out." We know what it is like to be emotionally worn down by inner turmoil. Medical studies and personal experience alike have shown a direct connection between stress – especially negative stress – and our physical or psychological health.

Carrying a perpetual burden of sin and guilt can do more than make us feel worn out: it can literally make us more susceptible to physical ailments and prone to self-defeating behaviors.

It's not surprising, then, that the psalmist saw a direct connection between his strength-sapping symptoms and the convicting hand of God that left him feeling like dry weather corn parched by intense summer heat (v. 4).

In time, the enervating toll of internal drought had its effect, prompting a spiritual wake-up call that led the psalmist to confess his failures and seek forgiveness. Note again the multiplicity of words to describe his wrong-doing: "Then I acknowledged my *sin* to you, and I did not

**Moaning and groaning:** Some commentators are bothered by an apparent disconnect between "keeping silence" in the first line and "groaning" in the third stich of v. 3. The word translated as "groaning" typically means "to roar" – as in the roaring of a lion, the din of crashing waters, or the racket of a mob.

The verb also carries the connotation of ruin, however: the roaring of a lion, of rushing waters, or an unruly crowd can lead to considerable devastation. When used of an individual who feels a sense of personal ruin, the word could suggest groaning or crying out in distress. Another example can be found in Ps. 38:8: "I am utterly spent and crushed; I groan because of the tumult of my heart."

hide my *iniquity*. I said 'I will confess my *transgressions* to the LORD,' and you forgave the *guilt* of my *sin*" (v. 5).

The word translated as "forgave" is a common Hebrew term that means primarily "to take" or "to lift." Its idiomatic usage in this context envisions God lifting and taking away the burden of one's sin and guilt, leaving the penitent free to stand tall and celebrate the sense of release and a renewed relationship with God.

We might expect the psalmist to launch into a paean of praise for the joy of forgiveness, but he has already connected happiness with absolution in vv. 1-2. Instead, in v. 6 he turns evangelist, calling for all the faithful to turn to God in prayer so even "the rush of mighty waters" will not reach them in times of distress.

The intriguing turnabout in metaphors from desiccating heat to rushing waters and the lack of connection to penitence, along with the rather non-poetic nature of v. 6, have led some scholars to regard it as a later insertion.

That might be the case, but if the occasion for prayer could be connected to the psychological strain of guilt described in vv. 3-4, the verse fits the context as a reminder that God is a refuge whether one is threatened by drought, flood, or a metaphorical equivalent.

With v. 7, the psalm takes another turn, directly addressing God as a "hiding place" in which the author is preserved from trouble (or distress) and surrounded "with glad cries of deliverance."

After experiencing the misery that accompanied the silent attempt to hide his sin from God, the psalmist discovered the joyful freedom that came from trusting God as a hiding place for his deepest failures and fears.

The psalmist's testimony should challenge us to ask whether we find ourselves hiding *from* God, or hiding *in* God.

### The voice of instruction
### (vv. 8-11)

Verse 8 brings a bit of a conundrum. Some readers see it as a response to the psalmist, promising further instruction, but it is more likely that the author, emboldened by personal experience, offers to coach the reader on a proper relationship with God, literally, "the way you should go."

And what is the advice? Don't be like a stubborn horse or mule who has to be turned with a bit and bridle

> **Love and grace:** The word translated as "steadfast love" (*chesed*) is often connected in the Bible with God's patience and grace toward a sinful people, as in God's self-declaration in Exod. 34:6: "The LORD, the LORD, a God merciful and gracious, slow to anger, and abounding in steadfast love and faithfulness …" (see also Num. 14:18-19; Deut. 5:10; Neh. 9:17; Ps. 25:6-7, 51:1; and others).

to keep it on the proper course (v. 9). Perhaps the psalmist had in mind the pain that accompanied his earlier period of stubborn silence, thinking of his suffering as the bit by which God had restrained his wandering and turned him back to the path of penitence.

The wicked suffer all manner of torments, he concluded, but those who trust in Yahweh find themselves surrounded by the steadfast love of God (v. 10). **[Love and grace]**

Those who experience the grace that comes through God's steadfast love are prepared to respond to the psalm's closing call to "Be glad in the LORD and rejoice, O righteous, and shout for joy, all you upright in heart" (v. 11).

What has been *our* experience? Have we ever known in our hearts that things weren't right with God, but found ourselves reluctant to do anything about it? We may have stood to sing joyful hymns, but we didn't feel any joy. We stumbled over the words to "Have thine own way" because we knew we were not following God's way. We may have known the spiritual dryness that the psalmist described in v. 4.

Has there been a time when the burden of guilt led us to turn away from our unfaithfulness and pray for forgiveness? Have we sensed the refreshing joy of forgiveness the psalmist talked about, so that we were able to worship more freely?

Or, do we still find ourselves in the spiritual desert, knowing that the life-giving water of forgiveness is available, but we're still holding back?

Let's not forget the psalmist's advice – it has to do with the stubbornness of a mule.

### The Hardest Question
### What does "Selah" mean?

Verses 4, 5, and 7 all conclude with the word "Selah," a Hebrew term that is transliterated into English letters, but not translated into English words. The reason for this is straightforward: we don't know what it means.

The word – which was probably pronounced "seh-la" – appears 71 times in Psalms, scattered among 39 different psalms, and another three times in Habakkuk 3, which is written as a psalm. It may appear at the end of a stanza or section (as in 32:4, 5, and 7; at the end of a psalm; or even at the end of a quotation [Ps. 44:9]).

The term is scattered throughout the book of Psalms, suggesting that it was in use over a long period of time. Whether it was original to each psalm or added by a later hand is unclear.

Some interpreters have suggested that the term means something akin to "Amen" (another Hebrew word that we don't translate), but there are many places where an "Amen" would be appropriate that it does not appear.

The most likely suggestion is that the term has some musical significance. We must remember that the psalms are written as poetry, and many of them, if not most, would have been sung in worship at the temple. In some cases, the psalms are given a title or even the name of a tune (none of which are known).

The term appears most commonly in psalms that have titles, and most of those identify the psalm with David or one of the known temple singers such as Asaph. Three quarters of the hymns with titles in which "Selah" appears have the indication "to the choirmaster."

But if the term has musical significance, what is it? Some think it might mark the spot for an instrumental interlude, a pause for reflection, or even a clash of cymbals.

A tradition reflected among early Palestinian Jews and some Christians was that it meant "forever," although the Hebrew Bible uses other terms when it clearly intends to suggest that concept.

Sigmund Mowinkel, a notable psalms scholar, proposed that it might indicate a place where worshipers were expected to lie prostrate before God.

One possible interpretation is that *selah* could be derived from the root *sll*, which means "to raise" or "lift up" – which could imply raising the voice, singing louder, or raising the volume of any instrumental accompaniment. This, however, is not certain.

We read the Psalms today and sometimes set them to modern music without any knowledge of the original tune, but still find them profitable. That the word "Selah" remains as mysterious as the tune named "The Deer of the Dawn" (Psalm 22) should not trouble us. It probably refers to an unknown musical instruction, and unless additional insight is forthcoming, we'll have to be satisfied with that.

As Robert Alter's important work states it: "Though there is general agreement that this is a choral or musical notation, there is no way of determining the meaning or the etymology" (*The Book of Psalms: A Translation with Commentary* [W.W. Norton & Co., 2007], 8).

# First Sunday in Lent

## Third Reading
## Romans 5:12-19

# Righteous Failure

*Therefore just as one man's trespass led to condemnation for all,*
*so one man's act of righteousness leads to justification and life for all. (Rom. 5:18)*

The season of Lent comes in the spring, so it's not surprising to learn that the term derives from a word that means "spring" – the Old English *lencten*, which was related to the German *lenz* and the Dutch *lente*. Linguists think it may derive from an earlier word meaning "long," a nod to the days getting longer in springtime.

In church tradition, however, Lent has nothing to do with spring: it's about preparing for Easter, which just happens to come in the spring. Lent begins on "Ash Wednesday," a day devoted to recognizing our sins and entering a season of repentance. We would expect to mark this season with texts concerning sin and grace, and we are not disappointed. The lectionary offers a series of readings from Paul's letter to the Romans during Lent, all dealing in one way or another with the issue of human sin and divine redemption. [**Romans, the book**]

Modern readers may find some problematic interpretive issues in today's text. Paul focuses much of his argument on what appears to be a literal understanding of Genesis 2–3, while many contemporary scholars and readers consider both creation stories (Gen. 1:1-2:4a, 2:4b-25) to be metaphorical expressions of faith rather than historically or scientifically accurate records. For many, the story of "the Fall" in Genesis 3 can be appreciated as a testimony that humans have sinned from the beginning while regarding Adam and Eve as symbolic, rather than literal, characters.

Jewish teaching considered each person to be responsible for his or her own choices, whether for good or evil. The prominent rabbis of Paul's day did not accuse Adam

of dooming all persons to lives of depravity. Paul, however, saw in Genesis 3 a convenient theological rationale for his argument that humans were incapable of righteousness, lost in inherited sin that could only be redeemed by Christ. Thus, Paul not only spoke of Adam as a literal person, the founder of humankind, but also the one responsible for peoples' proclivity to sin. Readers who share that view

---

**Romans, the book:** The book of Romans was probably written from Corinth during Paul's third missionary journey, around 57–58 CE, assuming that his time in Greece was spent at Corinth (Acts 20:1-3). It is addressed to Christian believers in Rome, most of whom were Gentiles.

Paul had expressed a hope that he could travel as far as Spain in his efforts to spread the gospel, and he would need a western base of operations. Paul did not establish the church in Rome and had not visited it before. The letter, then, was not primarily to provide instruction or deal with problems, as in other letters. Rather, he seems to be concerned with a clear explication of his theology, perhaps hoping that the Romans would give him a warm reception when he arrived, and that they would assist him in his plans to preach in Spain.

Romans is widely regarded as the most mature expression of Paul's faith and theology. The book makes considerable use of ancient rhetorical methods, including frequent repetitions of thought from slightly different angles.

Much of the book deals with issues related to Paul's understanding of sin, grace, and salvation, especially the concept of justification by faith. Upcoming lectionary texts are derived from chs. 5–8, in which Paul constructed a rather cohesive section that emphasized how Christ had liberated believers from the powers of our human heritage (symbolized by Adam) and resulting issues such as sin, the law, death, and "the flesh."

**Paul, expanded:** Paul's discussion of Adam and Eve – literally interpreted – has led to the development of divergent doctrinal beliefs with broad implications. The fourth–fifth century theologian Augustine called upon Paul's arguments in supporting the doctrine of "original sin," interpreted so strictly that even infants were thought to be lost sinners who were doomed to hell if not baptized. Many denominations continue to practice infant baptism, some mainly as a sign of the baby's introduction to the Christian family, but others because of a belief that infant baptism is a sacrament that absolves original sin. This practice is difficult to defend from scripture.

James D.G. Dunn put it this way: "Paul could be said to hold a doctrine of *original sin*, in the sense that from the beginning everyone has been under the power of sin with death as the consequence, but not a doctrine of *original guilt*, since individuals are only held responsible for deliberate acts of defiance against God and his law" (*Romans 1–8*, vol. 38A, Word Biblical Commentary [Zondervan, 1988], 291).

will not be troubled by Paul's reasoning. And, those who see Adam and Eve as symbols of humankind (their names mean "human" and "life") can look beyond Paul's literalism and still appreciate his arguments.

Paul clearly understood the point of Genesis 3: humans have sinned from the beginning, and sin has negative consequences. Whether one regards Genesis 3 as a metaphorical faith story or as a historical narrative, the pervasiveness of human sin throughout history is affirmed, and few of us would question it. [**Paul, expanded**]

## The legacy of sin
### (v. 12)

The literary structure of Rom. 5:12-21 is exceedingly complex and subject to varying interpretations. Is there a logical progression, or was Paul repeating himself? Perhaps the best course of understanding is that Paul began with a statement in v. 12 but left it open-ended, then launched into a series of parenthetical statements (vv. 13-17) before returning to his main thought in v. 18.

Paul opened his case by saying that sin came into the world through one man, and death came through sin (v. 12a). Lest we think that Paul laid all the blame at Adam's feet, however, he added "and so death spread to all *because all have sinned*" (v. 12b). Paul reasoned that sin entered the world through Adam, but all humans since

have followed his lead. This suggests a bit of a paradox: humans are destined to sin, but they also sin by choice. In this part of the argument, Paul stressed the innate fate of inherited sin, but in other places, such as Romans 6, he put more stress on sin as a personal choice.

The story in Genesis 3 taught that humans have sinned from the beginning – and have sought to weasel out of responsibility from the start. The story credits both Adam and Eve with trying to "pass the buck" and blame their sin on someone else. Adam not only blamed Eve for giving him the fruit, but he also dared to indict God for putting her in his life. Eve, in turn, blamed the serpent. It's always tempting to shuffle off our wrongdoing on someone else, but we cannot avoid personal responsibility for the choices we make.

## The gift of grace
### (vv. 13-17)

As mentioned above, vv. 13-17 can be read as parenthetical statements building on Paul's comparison of Adam and Christ. He began with an excursus on sin, death, and the law in vv. 13-14, and a series of comparisons in vv. 15-17.

In v. 13, Paul stated the obvious: sin existed before the law was given to Moses. He argued, however, that sin was "not reckoned" – that is, not counted as sin – when there was no law. Perhaps Paul meant to say that sin could not be labeled until it was defined, but the effects of wrongdoing were not different: he acknowledged that "death exercised dominion from Adam to Moses" (v. 14). In a world without a written law, someone may cheat, steal, and kill without officially breaking a legal dictum – but the deathly effects of those actions are no different.

The story in Genesis 3 is set long before the introduction of Mosaic law, but the account assumes that God had identified unacceptable behavior (Gen. 2:16-17). Other stories from the primeval history indicate that humans were held responsible for their sins long before Moses and the covenant law. Adam, Eve, and Cain all suffered consequences for their errors. The flood was deemed necessary because "The LORD saw that the wickedness of humankind was great in the earth, and that every inclination of the thoughts of their hearts was only evil continually" (Gen. 6:5). While Paul seemed to argue that sin was not officially a "transgression" until there was a law to transgress, his purpose was to show that possession of the law brings an even greater responsibility for obedience.

God's gift of grace in Christ differs from our legacy of sin in Adam, Paul said, because grace brings life, not death (v. 15). Both have widespread effects. "Many died" through Adam's sin, but Christ's gift of grace "abounded for the many."

Expressing the contrast in more theological terms, Paul contended that the judgment following Adam's sin brought *condemnation*, while the gift of grace in Christ brought *justification* (v. 16). By participating in Adam's legacy, we fall under condemnation due to our misbehavior. By accepting Christ's freely offered grace, we are justified (put into a right relationship with God) despite our many sins.

In more practical terms, the legacy of Adam brings the dominion of death, but those who receive grace may exercise dominion in life through Christ (v. 17). The power of death is a fearsome thing, but it is no match for the living Christ, who offers abundant and eternal life to those who live in grace. Paul emphasized the abundance of grace and the possibility of righteousness to remind the reader that Christ alone is responsible for our redemption from sin.

## The importance of choice
### (vv. 18-19)

Verse 18 brings us to the closure of Paul's governing comparison. The first half of the verse repeats the thought of v. 12, and the second half finishes the comparison: "Therefore just as one man's trespass led to condemnation for all, so one man's act of righteousness leads to justification and life for all."

> **Grammar matters:** As evidence that Paul was not teaching universalism, despite his claim that death for all came through Adam but life for all through Christ, Dan Via has noted that when Paul speaks of human involvement with the sinful legacy of Adam, he uses the aorist tense and the indicative mood to indicate factuality (vv. 15a, 17a, 19a, 21a). When Paul speaks of the effect of Christ's freely offered grace, however, he uses the future tense or subjunctive mood to indicate possibility (vv. 17b, 19b, 21b). The one exception is v. 15b, where he uses the aorist to say that grace has already abounded ("Romans," in the *Mercer Commentary on the Bible* [Mercer University Press, 1995], 1145-46).

On first reading, this verse (along with vv. 19-21) may seem very deterministic, as if Adam made everyone sinners, and now Christ has made everyone righteous. Paul was not teaching universalism or predestination, however. He was very careful in his use of verbal tenses and moods to show that the choice of sin is inevitable but the way of righteousness is a potential path – not a forced destination. **[Grammar matters]**

As James R. Edwards has noted, "This is not necessarily to assert universal salvation, however. In v. 17 Paul spoke of 'those who *receive* God's grace and righteousness.' Salvation by grace is not salvation by fiat, much less coercion. Grace is only grace where it grants the other freedom to receive – or reject – Christ's self–sacrifice for forgiveness at the cross" (*Romans*, Understanding the Bible Commentary Series [Baker Books, 2011], 152).

Paul's message is clear. Sin came into the world as quickly as humans understood they could make choices about their behavior. Since that time, none save Christ have escaped its dominion. Whether we're as comfortable as Paul in blaming the introduction of sin to a literal Adam, we all can acknowledge that wrongdoing has always been a universal phenomenon. Though sin has persisted, God's grace has abounded. Indeed, Paul said it has "super-abounded," adding an intensive prefix to the Greek root (v. 21). Believers can be super grateful for that. Those who choose to accept God's grace need no longer fear the death that comes through sin: they may anticipate the hope of eternal life.

### The Hardest Question
#### Were a literal Adam and Eve responsible for human sin?

The creation story in Gen. 2:4b-25 does not use proper names for the two humans: they are called "a man" (*'adam*) or "the man" (*ha-ādām*) and "a woman" (*'ishshâ*) or "the woman" (*ha-'ishshâ*). The man is still unnamed in ch. 3, though 3:20 says he gave his wife the name "Eve" (*chavvâ*) "because she was the mother of all living" – *chavvâ* means "life."

Not until ch. 4 do both appear by name. Adam's name literally means "man" in a generic sense, or "humankind." The English name "Eve," as noted above, means "life." Both "human" and "life" appear to be intentionally symbolic, rather than personal names.

Readers may be surprised to know that, except for brief mentions in two genealogical lists (Gen. 5:1, 3, 4, 5 and 1 Chron. 1:1), Adam is never again mentioned in the Old Testament, except as the name of a location in Josh. 3:16 and Hos. 6:7. This indicates that the stories of Adam and Eve played little or no role in Israel's theology, which focused primarily on God's covenant with Abraham's descendants, with special and frequent attention given to the deliverance events and covenants with Israel at the heart of Exodus and Deuteronomy.

Sin abounds in the Old Testament, but neither the narrators of Israel's history nor the prophets ever blamed it on Adam and Eve. Israel's persistent rebellion was recognized as the result of personal choices made by individuals and the nation as a whole – not as a sinful nature inherited from the earliest putative ancestors.

The notion of Adam as responsible for human sin did not receive prominence until the New Testament period and beyond. It figured prominently in the apocryphal book of 2 Esdras, a largely apocalyptic work. While ascribing sin to Adam, however, the book acknowledged that all are responsible for their own sin: "O Adam, what have you done? For though it was you who sinned, the fall was not yours alone, but ours also who are your descendants" (2 Esd. 7:118[48]). Esdras, which was written in the late first and into the second century CE, is a composite work that contains elements of both Jewish and Christian

teaching. It would have been written after Paul's writings, however, so it could not have influenced him.

Jewish teaching of Paul's day had little to say about Adam, but it followed the Old Testament testimony that one could live a righteous life that pleased God through following the Torah and putting his or her faith in God. Why should God continue to send prophets calling for repentance and a return to God if such a thing was impossible? Old Testament heroes such as Noah (Gen. 6:9), Abraham (Gen. 15:6), Caleb (Num. 14:24), and King Josiah (1 Kgs. 22:2) were described as righteous. Job was memorably described as a man who "was blameless and upright, one who feared God and turned away from evil" (Job 1:1). Although the Pharisees are routinely portrayed negatively in the New Testament, they were consciously dedicated to keeping the law and living what they believed were righteous lives. Jesus charged the Pharisees with missing the mark by focusing on ritual purity rather than caring for others. He called them to repent, but he did not suggest that they could not do better.

None of Jesus' recorded teachings mention Adam or imply that humans inherit sin. If Paul did not originate the idea that Adam and Eve doomed humans to an inherited, "original" sin, he was the one who popularized it. In service to rhetoric as much as theology, Paul took an ancient story largely ignored within Judaism and turned it into a rhetorical hinge upon which his arguments about sin and salvation turned: all died through Adam, but all can live through Christ.

# First Sunday in Lent

## Fourth Reading
## Matthew 4:1-11

# Passing the Test

*One does not live by bread alone, but by every word that comes from the mouth of God. (Matt. 4:4)*

Lectionary selections for the first Sunday of Lent leave no doubt about the theme: "temptation" is writ large across the story of "the Fall" (Gen. 3:1-7), a transgressing but forgiven psalmist (Psalm 32), Paul's peroration on sin and grace (Rom. 5:12-19), and Matthew's account of Jesus' temptation in the wilderness.

We might come to the text with the idea that it is designed to help us deal with temptation, but Matthew's main concern was to continue introducing Jesus, whose birth and baptism (chs. 1–3) give way to one more step of preparation, a test of determination and dependence on God.

### Forty days
### (vv. 1-2)

The text begins with Jesus' tunic still dripping from his baptism, as Matthew reports "Then Jesus was led up by the Spirit into the wilderness to be tempted by the devil. He fasted forty days and forty nights, and afterwards he was famished" (vv. 1-2).

Matthew, like Luke, offers a gentler picture than Mark, who says the Spirit "drove him" or "threw him out" into the wilderness (Mark 1:14). We often assume that "wilderness" indicates a desert area, but it could just as well have been a swampy, scrubby, or deeply forested region. The word mainly refers to a desolate, uninhabited, or solitary place. **[Mount of Temptation]**

Modern folk may think of backcountry or wilderness areas as attractive places of retreat, but we would not venture there long without extensive preparations. We would also find them difficult and dangerous if we were lost and without food or shelter.

**Mount Temptation:** The "Mount of Temptation," located near Jericho, is traditionally associated with Jesus' temptation, since the site of his baptism in the Jordan was not many miles away. There is no evidence that this is where Jesus fasted for 40 days, but it is a suitably desolate place. The tradition was strong enough to attract a monastery that includes cave dwellings, in addition to a high-end restaurant reached by a cable car.

Jesus was not lost, but he was intentionally unprepared for physical comforts, though well equipped for spiritual testing. Only Matthew indicates the purpose of the Spirit's wilderness leading right up front: it was "to be tempted by the devil."

Matthew also suggests greater intentionality about Jesus' lengthy lack of food. While Luke says only that Jesus "ate nothing at all during those days" (Luke 4:2), Matthew explicitly says that "he fasted forty days and forty nights." Food may have been available, if nothing more than locusts and wild honey, but he chose not to eat for more than a month. **[Fasting]**

**Fasting:** Roman Catholics continue to observe Ash Wednesday, Good Friday, and all Fridays during Lent as fasting days, but it's not a complete fast: for the most part they are to eat moderately and avoid meat on those days.

Orthodox Christians put more stock in fasting as a discipline of spiritual growth. During Lent, observant followers don't eat meat, eggs, or dairy products, though fish is allowed on Annunciation Sunday and Palm Sunday.

Protestants don't generally have or follow official church positions on fasting, but many believers choose to forgo a favorite food, beverage, or entertainment such as social media during Lent as a personal practice of self-denial and penitential preparation for Easter.

Instead of subtracting, however, others opt to add a new spiritual discipline or intentional acts of service during the period of Lent.

Whether consciously or not, Jesus was following the footsteps of Hebrew heroes such as Moses and Elijah when he went 40 days in the wilderness without sustenance (Deut. 9:9, 1 Kgs. 19:8), and his successful sojourn is a sharp contrast to Israel's 40 years of wandering.

Matthew is again more emphatic than the other synoptics: while both Mark and Luke mention "forty days," Matthew is careful to say "forty days and forty nights," specifically calling to mind the accounts of Moses on Mount Sanai, where he remained for "forty days and forty nights" and "neither ate bread nor drank water" (Exod. 24:18, 34:28; Deut. 9:9, 11, 18, 25; 10:10).

Moses must have had some divine sustenance. Medical experts agree that the average person could survive for more than a month without food, but for only a matter of days without water, especially in the absence of any moisture-rich food. None of the gospels say that Jesus went without water, only that he ate nothing.

In any case, they agree that after 40 days without food, he was "famished."

## Three temptations
### (vv. 3-10)

No doubt, Jesus would also have felt weak and tired, a prime target for manipulation by someone else. This is where the tempter enters the picture. Matthew uses multiple terms for Jesus' wilderness adversary. He is intro-duced as "the devil" (*diábolos*), then called "the tempter" (*peirázōn*), and dismissed as "Satan" (*satanas*).

*Diábolos* is used most commonly (vv. 1, 5, 8, and 11). It is a combination of the preposition *dia* and the verb *ballō*: together they mean something like "to throw over," and it was used in the sense of "slanderer" – one who seeks to overthrow another's reputation through telling false-hoods about them.

Contemplating the basic meaning might be helpful: though we may hope to stand firm, temptation – especially in times of weakness – can throw us over.

Matthew, like others of his day, thought of the devil/Satan as an evil, supernatural being who opposed God's ways and God's people. Many modern believers think of the devil in more metaphorical terms, but that makes our situation no less dangerous, for we are our own best tempters.

For obvious reasons, we think of Jesus being tempted in three different ways, but the temptations were really three variations on a single theme: the appeal of power.

The tempter did not doubt that Jesus was the Son of God, as implied in most translations of v. 3: the sentence could just as easily be translated "*Since* you are the Son of God, command these stones to become loaves of bread."

The Judean desert is littered with flat stones that might have been reminiscent of the round, pita-type bread commonly baked on the sides of clay ovens, but the temptation was not sufficient.

Jesus, having shared Moses' experience of 40 days and nights of fasting, found strength in words attributed to Moses: "One does not live by bread alone, but by every word that comes from the mouth of God" (v. 4, quoting Deut. 8:3). The temptation was to escape the reality of human hunger by calling on divine power, but Jesus would not forsake his purpose on earth or step aside from the human form he had adopted. He chose to remain hungry rather than forgo his calling.

The second challenge (vv. 5-6) has the devil taking Jesus to Jerusalem and putting him on "the pinnacle of the temple" with a challenge to leap from there and trust that angels would catch him. [**A different order**]

The devil sought to make the temptation more palat-able, perhaps, by quoting from Ps. 91:11-12, though out of context, a reminder that even scripture can be twisted for harmful purposes.

> **A different order:** Matthew and Luke differ on the order of the second and third temptations. Matthew takes a more logical approach: Jesus is tempted to make bread, to be popular, then to be powerful. Luke follows a more geographic approach: Jesus is tempted to make bread in the wilderness, to become all-powerful (from a high place), and then to win popularity (in Jerusalem).
>
> While Matthew says the devil took Jesus to "a very high mountain" (Matt. 4:8), Luke says that he "took him up," presumably to a high place, though nothing tangible is mentioned. Based on the text in Luke, one could imagine the devil and Jesus flying high into the sky, using supernatural abilities to float above the earth and examine the kingdoms below. As in Matthew's version, however, we are probably to imagine a high mountain location. Both should probably be understood as visionary.

Shakespeare was aware of this. In *The Merchant of Venice*, he had the ambitious Bassanio comment on the human tendency to shape things to their own purpose, concluding "In religion, what damned error, but some sober brow will bless it and approve it with a text, hiding the grossness with fair ornament?" (Act 3, Scene 2).

Jesus resisted the twisting of scripture by returning to Deuteronomy, but quoting properly: "Again it is written, 'Do not put the Lord your God to the test'" (v. 7).

Again, the temptation was to assume a power beyond what is available to humans, a power that would betray the purpose of the incarnation. Jesus would not choose the way of the spectacular, flying from the height like a superhero and living as a selfish celebrity. If he could not resist the allure of stepping outside of human limitations to save himself there, how could he endure the temptation to avoid the pain and consequences of the cross?

With the final temptation, the devil laid his cards on the table, showing Jesus a vision of "all the kingdoms of the world and their splendor," and offering to grant him power to rule them all (vv. 8-9).

The Bible is clear in teaching that ultimate authority over the world is God's alone, but the devil claimed to have been given present authority over the earth (cp. John 12:31, 2 Cor. 4:4). He offered to trade that power to Jesus in return for service and adoration.

Surrendering to the power of world domination would make Jesus precisely the kind of Messiah that many people hoped for, a warrior who would conquer Israel's enemies and restore the nation as a world power. Jesus could have done much good by establishing some sort of righteous rule, but he understood that sometimes the greatest temptations are to do what seems good but in the wrong way.

This is a temptation all Christendom has faced. From at least the time of Constantine's institution of Christianity as an imperial religion, through the Crusades and Inquisitions, through wars between Protestants and Catholics, Christ's followers have proven themselves to be suckers for the temptation of power.

We see this no less clearly in contemporary times, especially in America, where a significant faction of the populace believes the country was founded as a "Christian" nation and should be run in accordance with that group's understanding of what "Christian" means. Even casual observers, however, can see that Christian nationalism is not about Christ, but about power.

Jesus would not have it. Again, he resisted by calling upon scripture as it should be understood: "Away with you, Satan! for it is written, 'Worship the Lord your God, and serve only him'" (Deut. 6:13).

### One victory
### (v. 11)

Jesus endured. Even at a point of enervating weakness, he chose purpose over power, remaining true to his incarnate identity and the calling that was upon him.

In going *mano-a-mano* with temptation personified, he absorbed every punch and remained standing.

But he was still weak and hungry.

The appearance of angels who "came and waited on him" may lead us to wonder if Jesus didn't end up relying on divine help after all. How is the arrival of food-bearing angels different from turning stones to bread or catching a smooth ride to the ground?

The difference is that Jesus did not command or call for divine help when tempted to do so. Whether he anticipated angelic care afterward is not reported, nor any specifics about their ministry.

Matthew, indeed, is the only one who mentions angels. Luke notes that the devil "departed from him until an opportune time" (Luke 4:13), then jumps directly to

Jesus, "filled with the power of the Spirit," returning to Galilee (Luke 4:14).

Perhaps the point is that Jesus, even in extremity, trusted in God, and at the right time, God provided for him.

As noted above, Matthew does not tell the story as a means of teaching Christ-followers how to overcome temptation: his purpose is to tell us more about Jesus, his character, and his commitment to mission.

That does not mean we cannot learn from the story. In a sense, most of our temptations can also be traced back to power, whether it is power over pain or poverty or people.

### The Hardest Question
### How can we recognize temptation?

The story of Jesus being tempted in the wilderness is an account of three blatant, in-your-face enticements. We might read the story and assume that, surely, we also would have overcome.

In our world, though, temptation does not advertise itself. The desire for power does not come knocking on our door and show its ID card. The inclination to serve self over others is likely to wear a mask that suggests higher motivations.

Maryetta Anschutz offers a helpful reminder that seduction may take many forms:

Temptation comes to us in moments when we look at others and feel insecure about not having enough. Temptation comes in judgments we make about strangers or friends who make choices we do not understand. Temptation rules us, making us able to look away from those in need and to live our lives unaffected by poverty, hunger, and disease. Temptation rages in moments when we allow our temper to define our lives or when addiction to wealth, power, influence over others, vanity, or an inordinate need for control defines who we are. Temptation wins when we engage in the justification of little lies, small sins: a racist joke, a questionable business practice for the greater good, a criticism of a spouse or partner when he or she is not around. Temptation wins when we get so caught up in the trappings of life that we lose sight of life itself. These are the faceless moments of evil that, while mundane, lurk in the recesses of our lives and our souls. (*Feasting on the Word, Year A*, ed. David L. Bartlett and Barbara Brown Taylor, vol. 2 of Accordance electronic ed. [Westminster John Knox Press, 2010], para. 6637.)

The first step in overcoming temptation is to recognize it. As Anschutz notes, that's not always easy. Perhaps our prayer should not be just "lead us not into temptation," but "help us to see and know temptation for what it is."

# Second Sunday in Lent

## First Reading
## Genesis 12:1-9*

# A New Start

*I will make of you a great nation, and I will bless you, and make your name great,*
*so that you will be a blessing. (Gen. 12:2)*

Have you ever watched an episode of a TV series that included so much conflict or violence that you couldn't wait for it to end, hoping the next episode would bring resolution or happier days?

The story of God's call to Abraham is not unlike that, appearing like a bright light at the end of a long tunnel. The first 11 chapters of Genesis (often called the "Primeval History") begin with two marvelous stories of creation, but quickly move to describe a downward spiral of human rebellion and divine cursing.

Adam and Eve followed their own wisdom, and the earth was cursed so that it would not produce as easily as before (Genesis 3). Farmer Cain killed his shepherd brother Abel and was cursed to become a homeless wanderer (Genesis 4). The world became so wicked that a grieving God sent a flood to cleanse it, but even faithful Noah's family soon fell into disharmony and cursing (Genesis 5–9). Genesis 10 claims that Noah's descendants obeyed God's command to spread throughout the earth, but Genesis 11 relates a separate story of how humans chose instead to concentrate their population and efforts in one place, building a monument to their pride. They also fell under the curse, and a scrambling of languages forced them to scatter.

So it is that Genesis 1–11 describes humanity's beginnings as a whirlpool of sin and rebellion, spiraling down the drain of history with no hope in sight – until Abraham. With God's call to the future progenitor of Israel, the cycle of cursing gave way to the possibility of blessing.

## A radical call
### (v. 1)

We are familiar with the idea that Abram – Abraham's name prior to being changed in Gen. 17:5 – grew up in "Ur of the Chaldees" before his father decided to move the family to Canaan, but stopped instead in the northern Mesopotamian city of Haran (11:31-32; see "The Hardest Question" for more on the location of "Ur of the Chaldees").

Haran was a large city by the Balik River (now in southern Turkey). Rather than going on to Canaan, the family remained there until Terah died. Afterward, according to the text, God spoke to Abram and called him to renew the trek to Canaan, promising to bless his family in remarkable ways. [**Haran**]

We may wonder how Abram recognized the voice of Yahweh (the name for God used in this text) when he would have grown up worshipping other gods. The text assumes that God had no difficulty in communicating.

Note the progressive nature of the call account. God instructed Abram to leave his *country*, with its many deities and attendant cultural practices. Then, he was to leave his *kindred*, the large tribal unit to which his family belonged. Finally, God told Abram to leave his *father's house*, his immediate family.

> **Haran:** The city of Haran was settled no later than the Late Bronze Age, and probably earlier: tablets from Ebla mention it as early as 2300 BCE. It was located on a major north-south trade route from Mesopotamia or Egypt into Anatolia. As a result, it developed into a large cosmopolitan city.

---

*\*A longer reading, Gen. 12:1-9, is used in Year A, Proper 5. The fuller text is more instructive, and will also be used here.*

Thus, God called Abram to leave behind all that was familiar to him – without telling him where he was to go: "Go from your country and your kindred and your father's house *to the land that I will show you*." Abram's immediate and apparently unquestioning response to such an ambiguous call is testimony to tremendous trust. It is no wonder that we, like the writer of Hebrews, look to Abram as a model of faith (Heb. 11:8-16).

The story leads us to wonder how we would respond in a similar situation. What would it take to convince us that the sense of calling was really from God?

## Radical promises
### (v. 2)

God offered impressive promises in response to Abram's obedience. First was the promise to show Abram a new land, which also implied continued protection and guidance along the way. Abram was assured that God would travel with him and show him where to go.

God also offered promises that were more explicit and remarkable in their scope. According to the story, God told a 75-year-old man with no children that "I will make of you a great nation, and I will bless you, and make your name great, so that you will be a blessing" (v. 2). The reader already knows that Abram's wife Sarai was barren (11:30), so this seems to be an unlikely outcome indeed. How could Abram become *a great nation* when his wife was unable to bear a single child?

God did not tell Abram *how* the promise would come to pass: that Abram trusted God while knowing so little about what God expected is a further testimony to his faith. God had promised both guidance and blessing, and that was enough.

The narrator says that Yahweh also promised to bless Abram with *a great name*. That may be a purposeful contrast to the preceding story, in which the builders of Babel set out to "make a name" for themselves (11:4). Despite their many resources, their prideful effort resulted in a scattering of the people and a loss of their name. Abram had little with which to build, but Yahweh promised to make for him a great name, and countless generations have looked up to "Father Abraham" as the progenitor of Israel and a model of faith.

## A radical blessing
### (v. 3)

God's intention was not only to bless Abram, but also to make him a blessing to others (v. 2). The thought is expanded in v. 3: "I will bless those who bless you, and the one who curses you I will curse; and in you all the families of the earth shall be blessed."

Abram would become a channel of blessing to *all the families of the earth*, not just for his descendants, but for all who might learn from or be inspired by them. The promise was not unconditional, but rife with potential. Those who recognized Abram as the servant of God and the source of blessing could experience the blessing of knowing God, too. In contrast, those who opposed Abram were also opposing the work of God, and would experience the consequences that accompany such rebellion.

Some modern versions translate the last phrase of v. 3 as "by you all the families of the earth shall bless themselves" (RSV), meaning that Abram's name would be used in blessings. This is possible because the *niphal* form of the verb can be translated either in a passive or reflexive sense as context demands. The NRSV translation (along with NET and NIV11) favors the interpretation that Abram would become a source of blessing to all persons. [**Bless themselves?**]

The promised stream of blessing would become evident in many ways. The text makes it clear that Lot, Abraham's nephew, was richly blessed through their association. Laban (a descendant of those who remained in Haran) was later blessed through his affiliation with Jacob, Abraham's

---

**Bless themselves?** While the NRSV translates God's promise to suggest that other nations would be blessed (passive tense) through Abraham, the *nifal* form of the verb can also be translated in a reflexive sense, as in "bless themselves."

As it turns out, according to a note in the NET, the *nifal* form of the verb for blessing "is only used in formulations of the Abrahamic covenant" (Gen. 12:2, 18:18, 28:14).

Though the passive interpretation seems to be more apt in 12:3, some later texts regarding God's covenant with Abraham use the *hithpael* form of the verb instead of the *nifal* (Gen. 22:18, 26:4). The *hitpael* is by definition reflexive, suggesting the idea that other nations would pronounce blessings on themselves in the name of Abraham, seeing him as a prime example of divine blessing: "May God bless us like Abraham …."

grandson. This blessing was not limited to other family members: the Egyptian official Potiphar prospered from his association with Joseph, Abraham's great-grandson. Prophetic hopes centered on a day when all nations would come to Jerusalem to seek God's wisdom and blessings (Isa. 2:2-4). The greatest blessing to the world, in time, was the birth of Jesus Christ, born as a descendant of Abraham.

Gerhard von Rad, a leading Old Testament scholar of the 20th century, described the resultant blessing in another way: "The promise given to Abraham has significance, however, far beyond Abraham and his seed. God now brings salvation and judgment into history, and man's judgment and salvation will be determined by the attitude he adopts toward the work which God intends to do in history" (*Genesis* [Westminster Press, 1961], 160). In von Rad's view, the blessing is not so much through the promises to Abraham, but through the new channel of response to the God who promises.

The Apostle Paul later interpreted the life and work of Christ as the ultimate fulfillment of God's promise to make Abraham a blessing to all people (Gal. 3:6-14).

Are there ways in which we have seen God continue to bless others through the heritage of Abraham today?

## Radical obedience
### (vv. 4-9)

"So Abram went," the text says, "as the LORD had told him; and Lot went with him" (v. 4a).

Surely Abram must have had many questions, but the text says nothing about them. It tells us only "So Abram went …." The note that his nephew Lot traveled with him (v. 5) will become significant later on, as Lot plays a role in several stories that highlight Abram's character and faith.

[A perpetual deed?]

A brief itinerary follows: in Canaan they came first to Shechem, in the central hill country. A note adds "At that time the Canaanites were in the land" (v. 6). Indeed, the Canaanites never left the land: despite a few hyperbolic claims in the book of Joshua, the Canaanites were never driven out. Israel lived among Canaanite people throughout the Old Testament period, even as modern Israelis live among Palestinians, despite continuing efforts to drive them out and take over their land. The ruins of ancient

**A perpetual deed?** Many Zionists hold that the modern state of Israel should have rights to the entire land without ceding any of it to the Palestinian residents whose families have lived there for more than a thousand years. Supporters of annexing Palestinian lands often cite these promises to Abraham as justification for the belief. Even tour guides sometimes tell their groups "God gave us this land, and no one can take it from us."

Others take note that, despite God's promise of the land, Israel's own scriptures suggest that it was conditional, and that the Hebrews lost the land through centuries of faithlessness and going after other gods, resulting in the exile. Prophetic promises of a full return anticipate an eschatological future, not a decision by the United Nations to establish a Jewish homeland.

While we can rejoice that it is possible once again for Jewish people to have a homeland, we should be cautious in ascribing it to the promises of Genesis, as if God granted to Abraham a perpetual deed to the land.

Shechem are now surrounded by the Palestinian city of Nablus, one of the largest in the West Bank.

Though the land was occupied by Canaanites, v. 7 records a divine promise that God would one day give the land to Abram's offspring, and Abram responding by building an altar to commemorate the promise, and perhaps to lay some sort of claim to the territory.

From Shechem Abram moved his family further south, where they camped for a while between Bethel and Ai. There Abram built another altar "and invoked the name of Yahweh," an indication of worship and claiming Yahweh as his family's God (v. 8).

So, the text says, "Abram journeyed on by stages toward the Negeb" (v. 9). The Negeb was the large area comprising the southern part of Canaan. Though desert-like now, it was a populous place of pastures and small cities during the Middle Bronze Age, the era of the patriarchs. It was a most suitable place to provide pasturage for Abram's considerable flocks, and so it became his home.

Abram's travel "by stages" suggests a helpful lesson for those who pay attention. He did not reach his destination immediately, or even know in advance exactly where he was going, but he made steady progress, figuring it out along the way. This is the way life works: we grow through stages of childhood, youth, young adulthood, and greater maturity before reaching our senior years. Every stage of life calls for continued learning, continued growth – and continued openness to God's leadership along the way.

What happens when we look at this text through the lens of Jesus' life and teachings? Through Christ, has God not also called us to follow him in lives of obedience and service? Our text insists that God did not tell Abraham in advance where he was going, but challenged him to go in trust "to the land that I will show you."

When Jesus called Peter and James and John, he didn't tell them where they were going, but said only "Follow me." When the spirit of Christ appeared to Saul on the road to Damascus, he gave the crusading rabbi no hint of all the places he would go. When saints through the ages have heard and responded to God's call, they did so without knowing what lay ahead.

Have any of us been given a detailed map of where our life will lead when we responded to Christ's call to repentance and faith and following? No, but we can trust that when we choose to follow Jesus, we are not alone. The Spirit goes with us, leading us to places of blessing and growth.

### The Hardest Question
### Where was "Ur of the Chaldees"?

Many readers have long assumed that Abraham's birthplace, "Ur of the Chaldees," should be identified with the great city of Ur, located in southern Mesopotamia, an area known in ancient times as Sumer. From the time of Leonard Wooley's productive excavations in Ur in the 1920s, his claims that the Sumerian Ur was a city "worthy of Abraham" led to that location becoming near orthodoxy in scholarly circles. That identification is problematic, however.

The Bible makes several references to God bringing Abraham from 'Ur-Kasdim, translated as "Ur of the Chaldees" (Gen. 11:27, 31; 15:7; Neh. 9:7). Some of the texts imply that Abraham went straight from Ur to Canaan, but the story in Gen. 11:27-32 says that he moved with his father Terah from Ur-Kasdim to Haran, but stopped there, remaining until Terah died. Genesis 12 picks up the story there, with God's call for Abraham to proceed to "the land that I will show you" (12:1).

There were no Chaldeans in southern Mesopotamia during the time associated with Abraham, though they had arrived by 1000 BCE, centuries later. Afterward, the Neo-Babylonians also became popularly known as Chaldeans. Since the stories were written long after Abraham, when the area was associated with Chaldeans, it would not be surprising for the writer to think they had always been there. It is apparent, however, that the Chaldeans' original home was in Anatolia, now a part of Turkey, before some of them migrated south.

A cuneiform tablet found at Ugarit contains a letter from a Hittite king named Hattusili III, also located in Turkey. The king of Ugarit had complained about the activities of certain merchants from a city named Ura – which would come into Hebrew as 'Ur, and the Hittite king pledged to regulate them.

This is likely the same city, in southern Turkey, that is now called Urfa. Local Islamic tradition has considered it the birthplace of Abraham for more than a thousand years. Christian literature written in Syriac spelled it Orhai.

Could this be Abraham's 'Ur-Kasdim?

Consider also that Gen. 24:4, 7, 10, and 29 describe Abraham's birthplace as being in Aram-Naharayim ("Beyond the River"), a region defined as being east of the Euphrates River. The northern Ur was in that area, but the southern city of Ur was built on the west side of the river.

Another geographical problem is this: if Abraham's father Terah had set out for Canaan from the Sumerian Ur, he would have gone north along the Euphrates, bearing west around the top of the fertile crescent, then turning south and traveling through Syria until reaching Canaan. But Terah wound up in Haran – which means he would have had to make a sharp right turn at the Balik River and travel many miles upstream to reach Haran, a significant detour. If they had departed from the northern Ur, however, Haran would have been right along the way south to Canaan.

Cyrus Gordon, who dug at the Sumerian Ur with Leonard Wooley and never accepted Wooley's identification of the southern Ur as Abraham's "Ur of the Chaldees," consistently argued for the northern location. The later discovery of inscriptions pointing to a northern city of Ur appears to have confirmed the validity of his arguments.

(For further reading, see Cyrus Gordon, "Where Is Abraham's Ur" [http://www.michaelsheiser.com/TheNakedBible/Where%20Is%20Abrahams%20Ur.pdf], and Gary Rentdorf, "Ur Kasdim: Where Is Abraham's Birthplace?" [https://www.thetorah.com/article/ur-kasdim-where-is-abrahams-birthplace]).

# *Second Sunday in Lent*

## Second Reading
## Psalm 121*

# Preservation

*I lift up my eyes to the hills – from where will my help come? (Ps. 121:1)*

We all need help now and then. The difficulties we face may be as simple as opening a stubborn jar of jelly, as complex as a leaky roof, or as deep as an emotional crisis.

A stronger grip can handle the jar and a contractor can fix the roof, but what do we do when the whole world seems dark or our heart is in shreds? To whom do we turn?

We don't know what troubles, fears, or insecurities the author of Psalm 121 faced, but he or she was also looking for help.

### The source of help
### (vv. 1-2)

Psalm 121 is called a "Song of Ascents," and may have been sung by pilgrims as they traveled to Jerusalem for one of the three annual festivals, or as they made the steep climb into the city itself. [**Going up?**] Another possibility is that such songs could have been sung by priests as they climbed steps leading into the temple.

While the text came to be included in the collection of 15 psalms labeled as "Songs of Ascents" in Psalms 120–134, its origin could have been much earlier. The mention of David in the editorial superscription doesn't necessarily mean that David wrote the psalm, only that it was associated with him by later writers.

Feeling a sense of need, the psalmist begins "I lift up my eyes to the hills: from where will my help come?" (v. 1). While a pilgrimage might have been an appropriate setting, the prayer could have been offered at any place, at any time.

> **Going up?** Psalm 121 is one of 15 psalms, collected as Psalms 120–134, that begin with the superscription "A Song of Ascents." The precise meaning of this phrase is uncertain, but scholars commonly speculate that such songs arose for use by pilgrims as they journeyed to Jerusalem for one of the annual festivals, or on a personal pilgrimage to the temple.
>
> Jerusalem is about 2,500 feet above sea level, and surrounded by deep valleys, so one has to "go up" or ascend in order to enter the city.
>
> Another possibility is that the psalms would be sung by the priests as they ascended the steps into the women's court, but the pilgrim reference has greater appeal.

The word for "hills" could also be translated as "mountains," but are these heights emblematic of inspiration or danger? Readers typically imagine the psalmist looking toward beautiful rolling hills or scenic mountains as a source of divine inspiration. Most mountains in Israel, however – especially those from Jerusalem southward – are rugged and austere, fraught with danger for travelers.

Does the traveler feel fretful of the perils of his upcoming journey on a steep and hazardous road, or does she find in mountain majesty the assurance of divine aid for daily life?

Perhaps the distinction is not as important as the direction: the psalmist was *looking up*. Whether hills or mountains are in our line of sight or not, we often look heavenward, as the psalmist did, as we groan with sorrow or voice our prayer and wonder if there will be any help for us.

Looking up and offering a prayer implies a posture of hope, and posture alone can sometimes kick-start us on

---

*Psalm 121 is also read in Year C for Proper 24.*

the path toward a better state of mind. This is especially true when we consciously look toward God, and that is precisely what the psalmist is doing, seeking help from "the LORD, who made heaven and earth."

We know, of course, that God is not directional. God is every bit as much beneath our feet as above our heads, but we seem to be hard-wired to think of God as being up, or out. When we look up to God, we get the physical benefits of an uplifting posture and the spiritual benefits of putting our trust and our hopes in God. [**Posture and positivity**]

When we worship together, singing praise in the face of troubles and trials, we feel less alone. We feel more hopeful. We feel stronger. We feel more confident that we can indeed make it another day, and another day, and another one after that.

Surprisingly, churches filled with the most oppressed or downtrodden people tend to have the most joyful worship. Perhaps it is because they have learned that, no matter how heavy and how hard their burdens, standing together with heads up and hearts out, with hands and voices raised to heaven, brings a sense of comfort in believing one's prayer has been heard.

We believe there is a God, and that God is able to help.

---

**Posture and positivity:** Social psychologist Amy Cuddy has done intriguing research on how our physical posture affects our mental outlook. (See her presentation on "Ted Talks" at http://www.ted.com/talks/amy_cuddy_your_body_language_shapes_who_you_are.html).

Cuddy observed that an inward, drawn-in, head-down posture leads to a self-defeating attitude. By simply standing or sitting straight in an upward-looking "power pose" for just two minutes, she discovered, the level of testosterone in our brains will go up, and the level of cortisol will go down.

For both men and women, an adequate level of testosterone boosts our feelings of confidence and makes us more assertive. On the other hand, cortisol is a stress hormone. The higher one's cortisol level, the more stressed one feels.

Improving our brain chemistry through a more confident posture won't answer our prayers, but it helps to put us in a receptive frame of mind.

---

## The source of security
### (vv. 3-6)

We may believe that God is able to help, but how much practical help do we attribute to divine intervention? Can this psalm be believed?

On the surface, the text seems to promise that God will provide such perfect guidance and care that those who trust will suffer no harm or hardship in life, but we know from experience that this is manifestly not true. We all live in a world where bad things happen, often to good people, and sometimes they happen to us.

Two observations can help us to appreciate the hopeful comfort of this psalm without either expecting too much of God or writing off the psalm as nothing more than wishful thinking.

The first thing is to note that the context of the psalm appears to be one of blessing or benediction. While the first two verses are written in the first person as the question and testimony of the worshiper, vv. 3-8 are written in the third person, as if someone else is responding to the question.

We might think of this psalm as a parting blessing shared by family or friends, but another likely scenario is to be found in worship, either at the beginning or the ending of a pilgrim festival. The congregation – or a representative worshiper – could chant or sing vv. 1-2, asking where one might find help while affirming that Yahweh is the creator of all things and thus the ultimate source of aid.

At that point a priest or chorus of temple singers might respond with vv. 3-8, offering words of blessing and benediction to those gathered. The verb forms in v. 3 can be read as either imperfect ("He will not let your foot be moved," NRSV) or jussive ("May he not allow your foot to slip," NET).

If we translate the verbs in v. 3 as jussives, the psalm takes on the character of a blessing or benediction, even if the remaining verbs are rendered as promises.

It seems best to recognize that the psalm has characteristics of both blessing and promise, with the power of the blessing lying in the belief that God can indeed provide the help we seek.

"May he not let your foot slip" is not only a wish for sure footing on mountain paths, though it may include that, but is also an idiom for standing firm in life. Few people relish uncertainty, feeling lost, alone, or at loose ends.

Those who trust Yahweh have a "keeper" who never sleeps but constantly stands guard (v. 4). As a result, those who trust in Yahweh are never alone or unnoticed.

Take note of how often forms of the word "keep" appear in the psalm: vv. 3, 4, and 5 contain participles referring to "the one who keeps," while vv. 7 and 8 contain three uses of the imperfect form of the verb: "The LORD will keep."

The word translated "keep" is from *shāmar*, the same word used to describe a shepherd's keeping of the sheep. It suggests watching over, guiding, protecting, and being present with the flock.

Thus, "the LORD is your keeper" suggests a picture of one who keeps watch over the personified sheep of Israel or others who trust in Yahweh, one who stands ready at the right hand, where a favored counselor might be positioned.

Yahweh's protection extends to shelter from both sun and moon. The dangers of too much sun are obvious: the ancients would not have understood the relationship between ultraviolet light and skin cancer, but they would have been familiar with the uncomfortable heat, desiccating effects, and blistering of skin that come with too much sun.

But what about the moon? Modern people think nothing of walking beneath a full moon and may delight in it (unless they're afraid of vampires and werewolves), but many ancient peoples believed that too much exposure to moonlight could lead to disease or even madness: the term "moonstruck" originally had nothing to do with love.

The presence of Yahweh, according to the psalmist, would provide protection from the moon's sinister rays, comforting pilgrims who might be camping out without a tent.

### The source of life
### (vv. 7-8)

With vv. 7-8, the benediction shifts from physical dangers to spiritual ones. "The LORD will keep you from all evil" (or "May the LORD keep you …") could be read in different ways. The word translated as "evil" could refer to personal wickedness, to the harmful results of wrongdoing, or to calamity in general.

We could use protection on all counts, hoping to avoid the temptation to choose evil in our own lives, as

---

**The power of hope:** We learn from the psalmist that there is power in hope. That's one of the reasons God is so willing to hear our prayers, even when they're focused on complaints.

Of course, looking up, looking forward, looking to God does not mean that we forget where we are entirely. It doesn't mean that we ignore our troubles and the troubled world around us and put our head in the clouds. No, we work. We strive. We do our best to make things better both for ourselves and for others, but whether we succeed or not, we live on in hope.

More than 1500 years ago, in a commentary on Psalm 64 – a psalm of deep lament in troubled times – Augustine echoed a similar thought, and challenged his readers to sing in the face of trouble and to look ahead with hope: "Now let us hear, brothers, let us hear and sing; let us pine for the city where we are citizens … By pining we are already there; we have already cast our hope like an anchor on that coast. I sing of somewhere else, not of here: for I sing with my heart, not with my flesh" ("Commentary on Ps 64," on v. 3, in Peter Brown, *Augustine of Hippo: A Biography* [Faber, 1967], 315).

---

well as to escape harm that might come from others' bad actions or from the dangerous vicissitudes of daily life.

A more positive way of affirming God's care is found in the assurance that God "will keep your life." The word *nefesh* could be translated as either "soul" or "life." One's *nefesh* was one's innermost being, one's essence, what makes a person alive. Ancient Hebrew thought did not separate body and soul, as Greek philosophers did. The belief that God would keep one's life included everything related to this life and to whatever lies beyond. **[The power of hope]**

Many readers find special comfort in v. 7. Even though we shouldn't expect God to step in or send angels to protect us from all harm, we can be confident that God is present with us in all situations, even tragic ones.

The final verse summarizes all that has come before, a benedictory hope that "the LORD will keep your going out and your coming in from this time on and forevermore" (v. 8).

"Going out and coming in" serves as an idiom for all of life, whether traveling or at home, whether coming or going. The psalmist would not have understood the New Testament concept of heaven, but still trusted God to be both present and protective for as long as time shall last.

Modern readers may share the poet's confident trust, and even more so in the light of the New Testament's similar images of Christ as the Good Shepherd who watches his sheep and doesn't allow any to become lost.

As the psalmist found strength in the multiplied assertions that God is a present "keeper" both day and night, both coming and going, so followers of Jesus may affirm with Paul that "the peace of God, which surpasses all understanding, will guard your hearts and your minds in Christ Jesus" (Phil. 4:7).

### The Hardest Question
### Is Psalm 121 a promise, or a blessing?

It's easy to misunderstand Psalm 121, because a surface reading in most translations seems to promise more than the psalm delivers: God does not provide the perfect protection the psalm appears to affirm.

One interpretive approach to this conundrum is to recognize that the psalm has characteristics of a blessing or benediction in addition to a promise: it is a wish for God to provide constant protection and also an affirmation of God's faithful presence.

One clue to this is found in v. 3, where the verbs might best be translated in a volitive sense. For most verbs in Hebrew, the imperfect and jussive forms are identical. The imperfect form typically refers to uncompleted action, and depending on context can describe past, present, or future events. The jussive form indicates a wish or command, either a precatory "May he give" or a more imperative "Let him give."

While most translations have rendered the verbs as imperfects, giving the entire psalm the character of a promise, the NET regards the verbs in v. 3 as jussives, giving the remainder of the psalm the form of a blessing or benediction.

Consider the memorable Aaronic blessing of Num. 6:24-26: "The LORD bless you and keep you; the LORD make his face to shine upon you, and be gracious to you; the LORD lift up his countenance upon you, and give you peace." The verbs in that text could also be read as either a promise or a wish: "The LORD will bless you" as opposed to "May the LORD bless you." The context clearly suggests that of blessing over promise.

While Ps. 121:3 appears to be more of a blessing, vv. 4-8 are more like a divine oracle in form, a priestly promise that all will be for good. Oracles were sometimes regarded as certain, especially in prophetic contexts. When uttered by priests, however, oracles could have the sense of a wish.

Following Hannah's vow in 1 Samuel 1, for example, the priest Eli responded "Go in peace; the God of Israel grant the petition you have made to him" (NRSV) – or "Go in peace, and may the God of Israel grant the request that you have asked of him" (NET).

Technically, the verb could easily be translated as "the God of Israel *will* grant the request …," but the context suggests that Eli's response is more of a hopeful blessing than a certain promise, though Hannah could have heard it in either sense.

We find a similar situation with Psalm 121. Typical translations give it the appearance of one long promise, but a closer reading suggests that the psalm combines elements of both promise and blessing: a beautiful benediction for believers.

## Third Reading
## Romans 4:1-17

# Trustful Faith

*For the promise that he would inherit the world did not come to Abraham or*
*to his descendants through the law but through the righteousness of faith. (Rom. 4:13)*

When the investment firm of Smith-Barney needed a spokesperson for their television commercials back in the 1970s, they chose veteran actor John Houseman. With his craggy looks, gray hair, and weathered voice, Houseman assured viewers that Smith-Barney gained their money "the old-fashioned way," insisting: "We *earn* it!"

The theme for the memorable commercials reflected American values: we respect people who earn their wealth more than those who inherit it or gain it by gaming the system. Perhaps that is one reason why it is so hard for many persons to accept God's offer of grace. We want to have a good relationship with God and the hope of eternal life, but we want to *earn* it by our own works. To think it could be freely given seems like cheating, or too good to be true.

### We *earn* it!
### (vv. 1-4)

The "old-fashioned" mindset of needing to earn things has an ancient history, including the idea of earning one's salvation. Paul often dealt with it in his missionary work and his writings. Many of his contemporaries took pride in earning a righteous standing with God through observing the laws and rituals of Judaism. Paul, however, had come to believe that God's operating premise was one of grace. In the previous chapter, Paul declared that Christ had revealed the depths of God's free grace toward humankind: "…since all have sinned and fall short of the glory of God; they are now justified by his grace as a gift, through

the redemption that is in Christ Jesus" (Rom. 3:23-24). Jesus himself had suggested that nothing brought more joy to God than the opportunity to grant grace to a repentant sinner (Luke 15:7).

Paul was concerned because some believers who had come to trust in Jesus believed that they must continue observing Jewish law. To counteract the inherent legalism in their faith, Paul challenged them to look to the past and consider the foundation of their heritage. Even Abraham, the illustrious ancestor of the Hebrews, had been saved

---

**Abraham and grace:** Paul's insistence that Abraham did not achieve righteousness through his works is fully in line with the Old Testament story. Though we often refer to God's "covenant" with Abraham, it was clearly more of a promise than a conditional covenant.

In Gen. 12:1-3 God came to Abraham, who had probably been raised to worship the moon god Sîn, and promised to make of him a great nation. Abraham followed God's command that he travel to Canaan, where the scriptures say the promise was repeated several times (Genesis 13, 15, 17, 18, and 22). The only story in which Abraham was required to respond to any ritual requirement is in Gen. 17:1-14, where God told him to circumcise himself and his servants, initiating a perpetual way of marking his descendants as having a special relationship with God. That story, unlike other accounts of the promise, comes from the Priestly source, which highlighted the importance of ritual requirements.

Abraham did not always act in what we would consider righteous ways. Twice, for example, he passed his wife Sarah off as his sister and allowed foreign kings to take her into their harems to avoid a perceived threat to his own safety. Yet, God still counted his belief as "righteousness."

by faith and not works, Paul said. Adopting a favorite style of rhetoric, Paul posed a question that his hearers might ask, and then answered it. "What about Abraham?" he asked (v. 1). Shouldn't "Father Abraham" be a prime example of one who was saved through works? After all, Gen. 26:5 claims that God had praised the patriarch, saying: "Abraham obeyed my voice and kept my charge, my commandments, my statutes, and my laws."

Even so, Paul insisted that Abraham's faithfulness was not motivated by a desire to earn God's love, but a belief that God had already shown grace to him. Paul recalled Gen. 15:6, where God renewed a promise to make of Abraham a great nation who would become a blessing to all peoples. In response, the narrator said, "Abraham believed God, and it was reckoned to him as righteousness." Thus, Paul argued, not even Abraham could boast of having earned his relationship with God (v. 2). [**Abraham and grace**]

In Paul's mind, Abraham's faithfulness in keeping the law, his good works toward others, and his unquestioning obedience to God's commands were all a reflection of his faith in God – not an attempt to earn God's favor. If Abraham had worked for his reward, he would have earned it (v. 4), but instead he put his trust in God's promise, receiving God's blessing through the medium of God's grace.

### He *saves* us!
### (vv. 5-8)

Abraham experienced God's grace, but the scriptures portray him as being faithful from the beginning. What about those who are not so righteous as the iconic Abraham? Paul called upon another ancient example of faith and trust; one whose reputation was less sterling.

David was remembered as Israel's greatest king and a man after God's own heart, but David also had a dark side. In his most glaring lapse, David had not only committed adultery with Bathsheba, but also tried to cover his crime by ordering that her faithful husband Uriah be sent to a certain death in battle (2 Samuel 11). Can God's grace also justify sinners (v. 5)?

Paul answered in the affirmative. David repented of his sin, cried out to God in repentance, and experienced God's cleansing grace (v. 6). To illustrate, Paul could have

---

> **David's prayer:** Paul apparently regarded the superscription to Psalm 32, "Of David," as an indication that the psalm was literally a prayer of repentance offered by David. More than two-thirds of the psalms have superscriptions, which are not original to the psalms, but were added by later editors. The expression *lᵉdawîd* can mean "of David," in the sense of "belonging to David," but could also mean "to David," as in "dedicated to David."
>
> Many modern scholars are skeptical of believing that David wrote every psalm bearing the superscription *lᵉdawîd*. Whether David wrote Psalm 32, which Paul cites, is not central to his argument, however. Whether it is a prayer of David or some other sinner, the psalm declares a belief that God is willing to forgive repentant sinners by grace.

described David's penitent prayer of 2 Samuel 12, but instead he quoted from the opening verse of Psalm 32, which was commonly attributed to David. The psalm expresses the joyful relief of one "whose iniquities are forgiven and whose sins are covered," the overwhelming release of "one against whom the Lord will not reckon sin" (vv. 7-8). The remainder of Psalm 32, like the more familiar Psalm 51, suggests that the psalmist experienced God's grace for one simple reason: he acknowledged his guilt and asked for forgiveness. [**David's prayer**]

### *Us* means *all*
### (vv. 9-17)

Some of Paul's readers may have brought up the issue that both Abraham and David were Jews: perhaps God's grace is more evident toward them than toward Gentiles. Shouldn't non-Jews have to do something to earn their right to relationship with God (v. 9)? Can the uncircumcised expect the same rights and privileges as those who bear the mark of God's covenant people?

Paul answered the question with another, returning to his initial appeal to Abraham: "Was God's grace shown to Abraham before or after he was circumcised?" The answer can only be *before* – that is, while he was still technically a Gentile (v. 10). Abraham had been born in Ur (candidates for the location are in southern Mesopotamia and eastern Anatolia). He lived much of his life in Haran. According to the stories in Genesis, Abraham was 75 when God called him, but was not circumcised until he had been in Canaan for 24 years. [**Counting years**]

> **Counting years:** According to the stories, Abraham was 75 when he left Haran for Canaan (Gen. 12:4), and he had been in the land 10 years when he conceived Ishmael by Hagar (Gen. 16:3). The command to circumcise in Gen. 17:1-14 took place when Abraham was 99 years old (Gen. 17:1), and Ishmael would have been about 13 years old.

God's grace toward Abraham clearly predated his circumcision, so Paul argued that circumcision was given to Abraham as a "seal" of the righteousness he had already experienced *by faith* – an outward mark of an inner relationship. Thus, Paul presented Abraham as the father of all believers, circumcised or uncircumcised, who put their trust in God (v. 11). He is the hope of the Gentiles as well as the Jews, the ancestor of all believers – Gentile or Jewish – who follow his example (v. 12).

Circumcision is not required of Christians, but we may think of something such as our baptism as a similar "seal" on the relationship we have with God.

Paul's argument was not complete. He knew that someone might ask "But what about the law?" If circumcision was irrelevant to receiving grace, Paul argued, then the law was even more so. By Paul's reckoning, Abraham was "regarded as righteous" several years before his own circumcision and hundreds of years before Moses. Paul saw the giving of the law as a guideline for living as people whom God has already redeemed, not as the means of entering a relationship with God.

If the law had set up a new means of relating to God by elevating obedience over faith, Paul argued, then the Abrahamic covenant of faith would become void and God's promises to Abraham's descendants would no longer apply (vv. 13-14). But, he claimed, the blessings of keeping the law were overshadowed by the curse of *not* keeping the law (the "wrath" of v. 15) – and it is quite evident that no one can keep the law perfectly.

Thus, Paul contended that a right relationship with God is not based on the conditional covenant of the Mosaic law, but the prior Abrahamic relationship of faith and promise (v. 16a). Otherwise, he argued, we would be hopeless. But, because God still relates to humans through grace, all people still have the option of finding forgiveness – God's grace is "not only to the adherents of the law but also to those who share the faith of Abraham" (v. 16b).

The promise to Abraham was not for the Jews only, Paul insisted, for God had said "I have made you the father of many nations" (v. 17a, citing Gen. 17:5).

Abraham's faith was such that he believed in a God "who gives life to the dead and calls into existence the things that do not exist" (v. 17b). God had promised to make Abraham the father of many nations, but he remained childless, even when he was very old, and his wife Sarah was long past menopause. Yet, Abraham believed that God could bring life from their aged bodies, which were "as good as dead" (cf. vv. 18-19). When Abraham weighed all the reasons why he *could not* have children against the promise of God that he *could*, he chose to believe in God.

The result of Abraham's faith is that he became not only the physical ancestor of the Jewish people, but also the spiritual ancestor of many peoples – of all who follow his example of trusting faith in God.

Today, believers who read this text may find Paul's theological argument to be hardly innovative, for Christianity has long accepted the principle of salvation by faith, and we don't need analogies based on Abraham to convince us. Even so, we can find in this text a powerful reminder of the influence one person can have. Nearly two millennia after Abraham's era, Paul remembered his example and pointed to him as a model of faith.

What kind of legacy are we leaving for our descendants? Will they remember us as one who trusted in wealth and achievements apart from God, or as one who trusted a promise that goes as far back as Abraham and as far forward as our future hope?

## The Hardest Question
### How did the ancient Hebrews connect "salvation" with eternal rewards?

Paul's argument for salvation by grace makes logical sense, but we should realize that he was, in a sense, "comparing apples and oranges." Ancient Hebrews such as Abraham did not think of salvation or righteousness as leading to an eternal reward: they believed that all who died had the same fate, a shadowy existence in an underground place known only as *sheol*. The Greeks held to a similar view, referring to the home of the dead as *hades*. We find a description of what one might expect in Job's painful complaint, when he wished that he were dead:

> Why did I not die at birth, come forth from the womb and expire? Why were there knees to receive me, or breasts for me to suck? Now I would be lying down and quiet; I would be asleep; then I would be at rest with kings and counselors of the earth who rebuild ruins for themselves, or with princes who have gold, who fill their houses with silver. Or why was I not buried like a stillborn child, like an infant that never sees the light? There the wicked cease from troubling, and there the weary are at rest. There the prisoners are at ease together; they do not hear the voice of the taskmaster. The small and the great are there, and the slaves are free from their masters. (Job 3:11-19)

Late in the Second Temple Period, during the centuries after some Jewish exiles had returned from Babylon to Jerusalem, various apocalyptic writings began to speak of a separation after death. Apocryphal writings such as 1 Enoch 22 and 4 Ezra 7 imagined that a person's place in the afterlife would depend on how he or she had lived during their time on earth. Similar ideas developed in Greek thought, where influential writers such as Plato and Lucian encouraged people to live justly in order to ensure a happier afterlife.

By the New Testament period, some Jews had come to believe in an afterlife featuring rewards and punishments, though it remained a matter of debate. This is reflected in gospel stories such as "the rich man and Lazarus" (Luke 16), but it remains a long way from the more detailed view of the afterlife developed by the early church.

Thus, Paul may speak of Abraham being counted as righteous and of David as being forgiven by grace, but neither Abraham nor David would have recognized God's favor as being salvation to eternal life, as Paul did.

The prevailing theology of the Old Testament is not based so much on promise, as on covenant: God and Israel entered a covenant (Exod. 19:1-6, Exodus 24, later renewed several times in Deuteronomy and Joshua). The covenant promised temporal blessings if the people of Israel remained true to Yahweh (God's personal name, as revealed to Israel), but threatened trouble if they turned away.

Prior to the Second Temple Period, faithfulness to God was defined mainly as worshiping Yahweh alone and turning away from idols. Keeping the law and various ritual requirements became more prominent after the exile, especially as the early rabbis developed a "hedge about the law" consisting of hundreds of minor rules designed to keep people from breaking the more important laws. Jewish identity was established by birth and only occasionally by proselytism, and one did not have to keep the law to remain a Jew: the point of being faithful was the hope of earthly blessings for oneself and for Israel as a whole.

For most of Israel's history, "salvation" meant deliverance from trouble in the present world. Later notions of individual rewards after death were still developing during the New Testament period.

Paul's primary concern was that many new Christians were teaching that people must not only trust in Jesus, but also keep the Jewish law if they expected to be in right relationship with God and gain eternal life. Thus, while Paul's use of Abraham and David as analogies is useful in teaching the importance of faith over works, the comparisons can only go so far.

(For more on the development of views of the afterlife in Judaism, see Meghan Henning's article on bible-odyssey.org, sponsored by the Society of Biblical Literature [http://www.bibleodyssey.org/en/people/related-articles/views-on-the-afterlife-in-the-time-of-jesus]).

# Second Sunday in Lent

## Fourth Reading
## John 3:1-21*

# Jesus, the Savior

*For God so loved the world that he gave his only Son, so that everyone who believes in him may not perish but may have eternal life. (John 3:16)*

Some scriptures are so familiar that they can become like white noise in the background. We know them, but we pay them little attention. With the possible exception of Psalm 23, no passage is more familiar than John 3:16 – but knowing the verse doesn't mean we understand it or live by it. [**Knowing, and living**]

We cherish John 3:16 as a comforting promise that God loves the whole world and offers eternal life to all people. But what else do we know about the verse and its context? Our goal for this study is to tune that white noise into gospel music.

---

**Knowing, and living:** Readers who watched televised sports during the 1970s and 80s will remember a man who often showed up at sporting events wearing a rainbow-colored Afro wig and waving a sign with "John 3:16" written on it.

His name was Rollen "Rainbow Man" Stewart, who delighted in mugging for TV cameras. After what he described as a "born again" experience, complete with apocalyptic visions of the world ending in 1992, he continued finagling his way into sporting events and managing to get on camera with his trademark John 3:16 sign.

With 1992 approaching and no widespread repentance, he began planting stink bombs outside some churches and other public sites to declare his view that God thought they stank. He later threatened to shoot at airplanes and took a hotel housekeeper hostage, hoping to garner a press conference that would allow him to preach. In 1992 he was sentenced to serve three life sentences in prison.

Just being a fan of John 3:16 doesn't necessarily make a difference.

---

## A night visitor
## (vv. 1-13)

The story begins with a man named Nicodemus, who was both a Pharisee and an admirer of Jesus. That may seem surprising, but labels can be misleading: the gospels often portray scribes, Sadducees, and Pharisees quite negatively, and that's unfortunate.

Jewish leaders such as Nicodemus had labored for centuries to ensure the survival of Judaism, which was often threatened. Those who opposed Jesus were sincere in their belief that he and his followers were a danger to Judaism. They saw many Jews deserting their tradition to follow Jesus (John 12:11). They also feared that Jesus' talk about a "kingdom," combined with popular messianic expectations, could bring the wrath of Rome upon all Jews.

Still, Nicodemus was intrigued by Jesus, impressed by his mighty works, and more willing than most to hear Jesus out.

Whether seeking secrecy or for other reasons, Nicodemus came to Jesus by night. He addressed Jesus as "Rabbi" and said, "we know that you are a teacher who has come from God; for no one can do these signs that you do apart from the presence of God" (v. 2).

That sounds like the flattering prelude to a question, but the author did not report it. Jesus' response seems to assume that Nicodemus wanted to hear his views on eternal life, a concept that was hotly debated at the time: some believed in an afterlife, and some did not.

---

*This text is also read on Trinity Sunday in Year B.*

Whether or not the question was voiced, Jesus stated both cryptically and emphatically: "Very truly, I tell you, no one can see the kingdom of God without being born from above" (v. 3). **[Verily and truly]**

The familiar King James Version renders it as "you must be born again," choosing an alternate but secondary meaning for the same word. Jesus would probably have been speaking Aramaic in his conversation with Nicodemus, but John's gospel, written in Greek, modified the verb "born" with the Greek adverb *'anōthen*. The author of the gospel delighted in words that have double meanings, and this one commonly means "from above" but can also mean "anew" or "again." The word appears five times in John (3:3, 7; 3:31; 19:11, 23). In the last three cases it clearly means "from above." The author writes as if Jesus meant "from above" in 3:3, meaning that if one wants to have a spiritual birth, one needs a spiritual parent, but Nicodemus took it the other way.

That misunderstanding led Nicodemus to ask how a grown man could possibly crawl back into his mother's womb and be born a second time (v. 4).

Jesus responded with another "Truly, truly" statement couched in cryptic terms. Those who enter the kingdom of God, he said, must be "born of water and Spirit" (v. 5).

What did he mean? Childbirth is accompanied by the "waters" of placental fluid. "What is born of the flesh is

> **Double meanings:** In both Hebrew and Aramaic (*ru'ach*), and also in Greek (*pneuma*), the same word is used for both wind and spirit. Thus, Jesus' statement that "the wind blows where it will" could also be taken to mean "the Spirit blows/goes where it will." Using the same word twice in the same sentence but with different meanings was a clever use of wordplay.

flesh, and what is born of the Spirit is spirit," Jesus said. So, it shouldn't be surprising that he had spoken of being born "from above," by the Spirit (vv. 6-7).

Those who prefer the translation "born again" argue that Jesus spoke of one's spiritual birth as a metaphorical second birth.

John's fondness for double meanings is also evident in the next verse, where Jesus spoke of the wind blowing where it will and those born of the Spirit having similar characteristics: the same Greek word is used for both "wind" and "spirit" (v. 8). **[Double meanings]**

Nicodemus appears to have grown even more confused. He asked, "How can these things be?" If he said anything else that night, it is not recorded (v. 9).

Jesus appeared frustrated with his guest's failure to understand, or with his unwillingness to accept his authority as "the Son of Man," the only person on earth to have also experienced heaven (vv. 10-13).

## Answers and questions
### (vv. 14-21)

Having introduced the concept of Jesus as the "Son of Man," the author says Jesus reminded Nicodemus of a Hebrew story found in Num. 21:5-9. After escaping from Egypt and entering a covenant with God at Sinai, the early Israelites were pressing on, but not without considerable complaint.

At one point they charged both God and Moses with bringing them into the wilderness just to die. God's gift of manna, they said, was miserable and detestable food.

Yahweh responded, according to the story, by sending poisonous serpents among them. Many Israelites were bitten, and many died. Soon, the people repented and asked Moses to pray that God would take away the snakes.

Moses prayed and God answered – but with a twist. Pointedly, Yahweh *did not* take away the snakes, but offered healing despite their presence. Yahweh instructed

> **Verily and truly:** The author of John often emphasizes Jesus' words by having him begin statements with "Verily, verily" (KJV) or "Very truly" (NRSV) or "I tell you the solemn truth" (NET). These are various translations of "*amēn, amēn*," the word from which we get the common expression "Amen." The word was commonly used to express a strong affirmation such as "truly," and repeating the word makes the expression more emphatic.
>
> Though written in Greek, the word was Hebrew, appearing in ritual texts such as Deut. 27:15-26 or in statements of affirmation such as 1 Kgs. 1:36; 1 Chron. 16:36; Neh. 5:13, 8:6; and in many psalms, including Pss. 41:13, 72:19, 89:52, and others.
>
> The word was used to express agreement or "so let it be," and the same meaning carried over into English. We may respond to a sermon or statement by saying "Amen," meaning that we agree and affirm the truth of what has been said, and we close our prayers with the same word, indicating an affirmation of what has been said in the prayer.

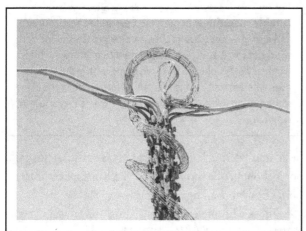

**Snakes upon snakes:** Although Num. 21:4-9 says that snake-bitten people needed only to look upon the bronze serpent, later interpreters saw the process as too much like sympathetic magic, and concluded that more must have been involved. Later Jewish writings reinterpreted the text to emphasize that the people were required not just to look upon the serpent, but to look upon it with faith that God would heal (Wis 16:5-7, Pseudo-Jonathan targum).

The healing power of the image was so impressive that the Israelites reportedly kept the bronze serpent as a holy relic. According to 2 Kgs. 18:4, at some point they began to worship it as an idol, calling it Nehushtan and burning incense to it. King Hezekiah reportedly had it destroyed during his religious reforms in the latter part of the eighth century BCE.

The sculpture pictured, by Italian artist Giovanni Fantoni, stands in the courtyard of a church built atop Mount Nebo, where Moses reportedly was allowed to gaze into the promised land. The serpent and pole together are reminiscent of a cross, a reflection of Jesus' comment in John 3:14 that "just as Moses lifted up the serpent in the wilderness, so must the Son of Man be lifted up."

Moses to fashion a serpent out of bronze and lift it up on a pole, promising that those who came and looked upon it would live. **[Snakes upon snakes]**

Nicodemus would have known the story and probably thought he understood it – but then Jesus said, "Just as Moses lifted up the serpent in the wilderness, so must the Son of Man be lifted up, that whoever believes in him may have eternal life" (vv. 14-15).

This is the prelude to the verse we remember: "For God so loved the world that he gave his only Son, so that everyone who believes in him may not perish but may have eternal life" (v. 16).

Now we have a connection between Jesus as the "Son of Man" and as the Son of God. No doubt, Nicodemus would have been even more confused.

God's purpose in Christ was not judgment, but grace, Jesus said. God had not sent him to condemn the world, but "in order that the world might be saved through him" (v. 17).

"World" translates *kosmos*, which does not refer to the earth or to evil in this context, but to the people who make up the world's population.

John's account argues that humans are prone to choosing evil over good and their own way rather than God's way, thus plotting their own course toward death (v. 18). They might choose to walk in the shadows in a vain attempt to hide the darkness within (vv. 19-20), but God loves all people and wants something better for them.

For this reason, Jesus brought God's life-giving light into the world, and "those who do what is true come to the light, so that it may be clearly seen that their deeds have been done in God" (v. 21). They don't earn their way into the light: it has been done "in God," through what God has done.

How did Nicodemus, the man who famously came to Jesus in the dark of night, respond to Jesus' claims? Did he leave in the light?

The author does not say, though he clearly remained an admirer. Nicodemus is mentioned again in John 7:50-51, where he came to Jesus' defense by reminding fellow members of the Sanhedrin that someone accused of wrongdoing should be given a hearing before they were judged. And, Nicodemus reportedly joined Joseph of Arimathea, described as a "secret disciple" of Jesus, in assisting with Jesus' burial. "Nicodemus, who had at first come to Jesus by night, also came, bringing a mixture of myrrh and aloes, weighing about a hundred pounds" (John 19:39). That would have been an extravagant gift.

An early church tradition holds that Nicodemus became a believer. He is venerated as a saint by Roman Catholics and by some Eastern Orthodox Christians.

However he may have responded that night, Nicodemus was left with much to ponder. He seems to have wanted Jesus to *show* him the way. He had not expected to hear that Jesus would *be* the way.

## An unanswered question

None of us want to waste our one and only life, but we have widely different ideas about what it means to make the most of life. Where do we find ourselves in this story?

Some of us put our faith in physical fitness, devoting endless hours to sculpting a better body or running a faster 5K. The gospel of fitness is good for our bodies indeed, but any gospel that applies to our physical lives alone is not enough.

Others follow the easier and more appealing gospel of materialism. Our culture would lead us to believe that focusing on wealth and things and pleasure is what life should be about, but this physical life is not our only life. There is something greater.

It is hard for us, in a world we think of as "enlightened," to comprehend the Spirit's work. Though we may not understand it, we may sense that our lives are not complete without it. We cannot control God's Spirit any more than we can direct the wind, but we can open the windows of our hearts to receive it.

"No one comes into the kingdom unless they are born from above," Jesus said. Those who come into the kingdom are born of the Spirit, and "the wind (Spirit) blows where it will." We had no part in engineering our conception or in bringing about our birth. We don't generate our birth from above, either – other than to turn loose of our search for physical or emotional or financial salvation, turn our hearts toward Jesus, and allow the wind of the Spirit to usher us into the kingdom.

There is a perplexing tension between grace and faith: in a mysterious way, each seems to activate the other. God offers grace freely, yet also calls for faith. We can't earn God's favor, yet we are called to believe. God's love seeks our salvation.

In this Lenten season, when we feel the March winds blow, let us remember that there is a God who loved us enough to send the beloved Son into the world so that whosoever believes in him might not perish, but have everlasting life.

Our physical life has its roots in the dust, and it returns to the dust, but there is also a spiritual element at the heart of our being. The image of God lives in us, and when the wind of the Spirit blows, that part of us resonates like wind chimes in a gentle breeze, calling us to believe, calling us to live, and not perish.

## The Hardest Question
### Why the cryptic terminology?

When Jesus spoke to Nicodemus in terms of water and birth or wind and Spirit, his purpose was not to confuse. As a leader among the Jews, Nicodemus would have been familiar with similar imagery from eschatological hopes expressed in the prophets.

Isaiah of Jerusalem, for example, predicted a coming time of exile that would serve the purpose of turning the people back to God as they longed for a return and waited for God's spirit to bring renewed blessing: "… until a spirit from on high is poured out on us, and the wilderness becomes a fruitful field…." (Isa. 32:15)

Joel, who probably preached during the hard days after the exiles had returned but faced great difficulty, also looked toward a future day when the Spirit would bring renewed life: "Then afterward, I will pour out my spirit on all flesh; your sons and your daughters shall prophesy, your old men shall dream dreams, and your young men shall see visions. Even on the male and female slaves, in those days, I will pour out my spirit" (Joel 2:28-29).

The exilic prophet Ezekiel's vision of a new age involved both Spirit and water: "I will sprinkle clean water upon you, and you shall be clean from all your uncleannesses, and from all your idols I will cleanse you. A new heart I will give you, and a new spirit I will put within you; and I will remove from your body the heart of stone and give you a heart of flesh" (Ezek. 35:25-26).

Isaiah of the exile also connected water and the spirit with renewed life as he anticipated better days to come: "For I will pour water on the thirsty land, and streams on the dry ground; I will pour my spirit upon your descendants, and my blessing on your offspring" (Isa. 44:3).

As Jesus spoke to Nicodemus about water, the Spirit, and new birth, he might have expected his Pharisee friend to remember such texts and let them inform his understanding of what Jesus was saying.

# Second Sunday in Lent

## Optional Fourth Reading
## Matthew 17:1-9*

# Keeping Secrets

*Matthew 17:1-9 is also used for Transfiguration Sunday in Year A.
A study is included in Year A, Volume 1 of this resource.*

## First Reading
## Exodus 17:1-7*

# Unbottled Water

*"I will be standing there in front of you on the rock at Horeb. Strike the rock, and water will come out of it, so that the people may drink." Moses did so, in the sight of the elders of Israel. (Exod. 17:6)*

All of us have been children, and many of us have children, and we know that childhood is fraught with insecurities. Small children like to be close to a parent and may struggle to sleep alone, fearing that if mom and dad leave the room, they won't come back.

That is a natural stage of life for children, but also something we learn to grow beyond. Children who are properly cared for soon learn that their parents will not desert them, and that their loving care is no less real in those times when they cannot be seen.

### A thirsty people
### (vv. 1-4)

Today's text pictures an emerging nation that struggled to learn that lesson from a spiritual perspective. Despite a series of mighty works that should have left the people brimming with confidence and filled with the assurance of God's powerful presence, they persistently doubted God's care. Yahweh had brought the Hebrews out of Egypt with mighty works (Exod. 7:14-10:49, 12:29-32), delivered them from Pharaoh's army at the sea (Exodus 14), and provided both water and food in times of need (Exod. 15:22-27, 16:1-36). Yet, the narrator says their doubts persisted and they insisted on putting God to the test.

The account describing Yahweh's gift of water in 17:1-7 has both similarities and differences with a story in Num. 20:1-13, which also results in a place being named Meribah ("quarreling"). [**Double trouble**]

---

**Double trouble:** The stories of Moses bringing water from a rock in Exodus 17 and Numbers 20 have both similarities and differences. In both cases, the people need water and blame Moses for their situation. In both cases, God responds, and in both cases, Moses commemorates their contentiousness by calling the place "Meribah." But, in Exodus 17, Moses is commanded to strike a rock with his staff to bring forth water (vv. 5-6), while in Numbers 20, God commands him to speak only, so that Moses is condemned for showing a lack of trust when he strikes the rock (vv. 8, 11-12). Scholars often regard these as a duplicate of the same story, but the narrator's intent is clear: he wanted to portray the people as inwardly focused and consistently unwilling to trust in God to provide for their needs.

---

The present text, like those before it, is probably a composite of several underlying sources put together by a later editor. This could be why the location was given not one, but two names: they camp at Rephidim, but Moses was told to strike a rock at Horeb, an alternate name for Sinai, which they didn't reach until ch. 19. The final editor apparently considered the two places to be close in proximity, so that the camp might be at Rephidim, but people could walk as far as Horeb to obtain water.

We note that not only are the Israelites portrayed as being at both Rephidim and Horeb, but also that Moses named the place both Massah and Meribah.

Readers may find the narrator's theme to be a bit tedious or repetitive by now: Yahweh had delivered Israel in an impressive way, but the people quickly forgot.

---

*This text is also read on Proper 21 of Year A and the First Sunday in Lent of Year B.*

As soon as times got hard, they complained to Moses and questioned God's motives. Moses took the complaint to God, who responded with yet another mighty work as a proof of the divine presence. Israel's consistent lack of trust in God remained front and center.

The recurrent theme may seem monotonous, but also bears a message: this is not just how Israel was, but how we can be. God's gifts are many and mighty, but easily overlooked and taken for granted. Many believers spend more time complaining about what God has not done than giving praise for the blessings they enjoy every day.

The location of Rephidim is no more certain than most other place names in the wilderness journey, but the author's point is to show that Israel was moving. He seeks to emphasize that the story relates a historical reality and to remind the reader that the people journeyed at God's command.

Rephidim seemed an unusual place to stop, for it had no water (v. 1). No self-respecting leader of a wilderness expedition would order an extended camp in a locale that had no water supply, no matter how level the ground might be. Moses had lived in the desert. He knew it was not feasible to camp in a waterless place. Yet, he insisted that Yahweh wanted Israel to make camp at Rephidim. From the people's perspective, the only reasonable conclusion was that Moses had lost his mind and was probably delusional when he claimed to speak for Yahweh.

Following a familiar pattern, the Hebrews sent envoys to lodge an official complaint with Moses. Can we blame them? Moses responded that their quarrel was not with him, but with Yahweh. He asked, "Why do you test the Lord?" (v. 2). In the previous chapter, the story of miraculous manna and quail, the narrator said God's purpose was to test the people (16:4). Now the people, who seem to have forgotten all that God had done for them, feel presumptuous enough to test God. Moses seemed to fear that the Lord would soon lose patience with the stubborn people.

A key word appears twice in v. 2: the verbal root *rîb* means "to dispute," "to quarrel," or even "to bring a lawsuit." In the prophetic books, Yahweh is often described as bringing a suit against the faithless people of Israel. In this case, however, the people were claiming that Moses (and hence, Yahweh) had defrauded them. Because of Israel's dispute (*rîb*) with God, Moses would later give

> **Meribah:** Many churches adopt biblical place names: "Salem United Methodist Church," "Bethlehem Baptist Church," and so forth. I can readily recall churches named for Bethel, Beulah, Cana, Capernaum, Mt. Carmel, Mt. Hermon, Mt. Tabor, and others. How many can you think of? Have you ever known a church or a denominational body that could appropriately have "Meribah"–"quarreling"–as part of its name? I've never known of a Meribah Baptist Church, but I have known both churches and denominational bodies for whom the name would be appropriate.

the place a new name: "Meribah" (notice the *rîb* in the middle), meaning "disputation" or "testing." [**Meribah**]

The people of Israel, like many persons today, were blinded by need. They could not see beyond their own hunger or thirst, holding on to distorted memories of Egypt as "the good old days." We can appreciate their concern that freedom would be of little use if they died of thirst in its pursuit, but they had lost trust that God could and would provide for them. As in the previous chapter, when food was scarce, they accused Moses of being some sort of sadistic mass murderer, leading them out of Egypt so he could watch them and their livestock die in the wilderness (v. 3).

Thirst, like hunger, is a powerful motivator that tends to grasp all our attention. The psalmist once described his spiritual thirst for God as being like a panting deer in search of a stream (Ps. 42:1). What do we thirst for most? For water? For excitement? For financial security? For God? As we seek fulfillment in life, which thirst claims the largest amount of our time, effort, and attention?

As he had done before, Moses took the people's complaint to God. He carried a complaint of his own also, insisting that the disgruntled populace was on the verge of stoning him (v. 4). We must give Moses due credit: when he didn't know the answers, at least he knew where to look. When he was powerless to deal with a given situation, he routinely turned to God.

### A benevolent God
### (vv. 5-6)

Having been challenged, Yahweh set about to answer the need while also vindicating Moses' leadership. God instructed Moses to take witnesses from among the elders

**Water from the rock:** In the southern deserts of the Middle East, mountains are often composed largely of sandstone, which soaks up the rare rains like a sponge. Inside the mountain, the water seeps down through cracks and crevices to fill an inner void or exit in a trickling stream to provide water in an otherwise desolate land. If an internal collection of water was near the surface of a rocky cliff face, it is possible that a sharp blow could result in quite an outpouring.

The sandstone mountains pictured are located in the desert lands of southern Edom where it rarely rains, but the presence of a green bush in the center betrays the presence of water leaking from inside the mountain.

An Arab tradition holds that the place where Moses struck the rock is in southern Edom, near Petra, where a spring flows into a valley called the Wadi Musa (*Musa* is the Arabic pronunciation of Moses).

of Israel and have them follow him to Horeb. He was to take his shepherd's staff, the same staff with which he had demonstrated Yahweh's power by converting it to a serpent (7:9-10), striking the Nile to call forth the first of Yahweh's mighty acts in Egypt (7:17, 20), summoning plagues of frogs and gnats (8:5-6, 16-17), and by holding it over the sea to create a dry path for Israel to cross (14:16).

According to the instructions, Moses would see Yahweh standing by a certain rock, which he was to strike with the staff in view of the elders who accompanied him, so there would be witnesses to the power of God at work in providing needed water for the people. The text gives no clue as to how Moses was to recognize Yahweh's presence, but it presumes that he could do so.

Many interpreters have posed naturalistic explanations for the miracle, proposing that there was water beneath a thin layer of shale, which Moses broke with his staff. [**Water from the rock**] Such musings are reasonable, but also beside the point, which is that Yahweh provided water where there was no water – and from the rocky face of a mountainside, an unlikely source.

### A frustrated leader
### (v. 7)

Previously, the narrator had emphasized how a time of deep need followed by a delivering miracle led the people to respond with greater faith. After the deliverance at the sea, for example, "Israel saw the great work that the LORD did against the Egyptians. So the people feared the LORD and believed in the LORD and in his servant Moses" (14:31).

In this account, however, no response is described, not so much as a "thank you." While the people showed no gratitude for Yahweh's act of deliverance, Moses responded by giving the site a name designed to memorialize their obstinate unfaithfulness.

Moses called the place by two names: Massah (testing) and Meribah (quarreling). These would serve as a perpetual reminder of the people's lack of faith that led them to put Yahweh to the test.

As we approach this text, the hardest thing to believe is not that God could bring water from a rock, but that a people who had been so recently delivered from Egypt by God's mighty acts and fed in the desert by God's caring provision could have the audacity to ask "Is the LORD among us or not?" (v. 7).

Renaming the places would serve to remind later generations of Israel's propensity for faithlessness contrasted with God's steadfast love and provision. And future generations did remember. Psalm 95:7b-9 recalls this story while warning the Hebrews against being hard-hearted: "O that today you would listen to his voice! Do not harden your hearts, as at Meribah, as on the day at Massah in the wilderness, when your ancestors tested me, and put me to the proof, though they had seen my work."

Even later, the writer of Hebrews extended the same caution to Christian believers: "As it is said, 'Today, if you hear his voice, do not harden your hearts as in the rebellion'" (Heb. 3:15).

The people's failure to trust in God foreshadowed the even more serious debacle of Exodus 32, when the people lost patience during Moses' absence and constructed a golden calf to worship – even as Moses was receiving the law from God.

"Is the Lord among us or not?" We may also be tempted to ask this question when times of trouble lead to uncertainty and doubt. We may ask "Where are you, God?" or "Are you really there, Lord?" Often, we live as if we presume the answer is "No."

Our sense of need, like Israel's thirst, is very real, but God's pervasive presence is even more real, if we are willing to recognize it and to embrace it.

When we think about our lives, can we name ways that God's presence and provision have blessed us? Will the lessons of God's faithfulness be lost on us?

## The Hardest Question
### How many Israelites were there in the wilderness?

When we read texts such as Exodus 17, we naturally wonder how many Israelites – along with their flocks – Moses had to provide for. At the beginning of the journey, according to Exod. 12:37, there were "about 600,000 men on foot, besides children." In this case, "children" may refer to young males, because obviously "men on foot" does not include women. If there were 600,000 men and most of them were married with children, one could expect the total to be more than two million people. In addition to the Israelites, 12:38 says "A mixed crowd also went up with them, and livestock in great numbers, both flocks and herds." This implies that a host of other people, impressed by the actions of Israel's God, joined them in fleeing Egypt.

A literal reading of this passage constitutes quite a problem. If there were two million people who traveled four abreast with only two feet of distance between them, they would have made a line more than 400 miles long. In the unlikely event that a mixed group could march 20 miles per day, it would take more than 20 days for people

in the back of the line to reach a point passed by those in the front. How could such a multitude – including their sheep, goats, cattle, and donkeys – cross the sea, or any other point, in a single night?

Likewise, try to imagine how much food and water would be required for a number that massive: even if there were an unending source emerging from a rock, people in the back of the line would die of thirst before reaching it.

Based on archaeology, estimates for the population Canaan supported during the period the Israelites reportedly invaded the promised land rarely exceed 100,000 for the entire area. Is it reasonable to imagine more than two million Hebrews moving in, but worried about whether they would be strong enough to conquer?

Scholars have sought to deal with the problem in a variety of ways, the most common of which is to note that the word meaning "thousand" (*'elef*) sometimes appears to be used as a reference to "clans" or military "platoons" of considerably less than 1,000. So, if there were 600 clans rather than 600,000 men, and we imagine as many as 100 persons per clan or extended family, the number would be closer to 60,000 – still an incredibly difficult number of people to lead, manage, and provide for in a wilderness area even if they had no livestock to feed and water.

Another approach is to acknowledge that these stories were probably written down long after the fact, and hyperbole (exaggeration for effect) is commonly employed by the biblical writers. Some scholars believe that multiple groups left Egypt at various times, and that their stories later coalesced around Moses. Richard Elliott Friedman, for example, has argued strongly that the Exodus narratives were based on the experience of a much smaller group of Levites only (*Exodus: How It Happened and Why It Matters* [HarperOne, 2017]).

In any case, the exact number of people is beside the point. What the narrator wants us to understand is that they could not have survived without God's miraculous intervention – and that they should have learned from God's ongoing care.

# Third Sunday in Lent

## Second Reading
## Psalm 95*

# A New Song

*For the LORD is a great God, and a great King above all gods. (Ps. 95:3)*

Preaching can take many forms. Some pastors lean toward encouraging and upbeat sermons to help people through the week. Others may focus more on comfort for the downtrodden. Some preachers gravitate toward topical sermons, promoting a series of services devoted to improving one's marriage or finances.

Some pastors prefer a more prophetic than pastoral approach. They challenge parishioners to care about social issues and be on the right side of justice. For others, the "prophetic" approach tends toward fire and brimstone as they call people to account for their sins and plea for repentance.

Some parishioners think that means the pastor has "quit preaching and gone to meddling," but others prefer the latter, thinking they haven't really been to church unless their toes have been roundly trounced.

People like that could enjoy reading Psalm 95. The psalmist begins with a big bang of praise (vv. 1-7c), then shifts to a stern sermon condemning those who fail to follow God faithfully (vv. 7d-11). [**A similar song**]

We may not like being called to account and challenged to change, but sometimes that is precisely what we need.

---

**A similar song:** Psalm 81 is similar in structure to Psalm 95. It also begins with a call to worship (vv. 1-5b), followed by a sermon-like oracle that recalls the bitterness of Meribah and the Israelites' stubborn refusal to follow God's way.

One could argue that both Psalm 81 and 95 are made of what were originally two psalms that were later combined. It is just as feasible to think of the psalms as intentionally designed in two parts for a liturgical purpose.

---

## The king of all gods
### (vv. 1-5)

Prefacing criticism with praise serves as a metaphorical counterpart to Mary Poppins' happy advice that "a spoonful of sugar helps the medicine go down." The psalm begins with three exhortations to "come" and worship (vv. 1, 2, 6). Though English translations obscure it, each call to "come" uses a different verb.

The first is an imperative of the verb *hâlak*, which can mean "to walk" (v. 1). The second is a form of *qâdam*, meaning "to come before" or "to meet" (v. 2). The third "come" is an imperative form of the word *bôʾ*, which can mean "to go," "to come," or "to enter" (v. 6).

As arranged, the verbs suggest walking toward the sanctuary, coming into God's presence, and entering sacred space.

We can envision worshipers approaching the gates of the temple as a priest, temple singer, or other worship leader shouts "O come, let us sing to the LORD; let us make a joyful noise to the rock of our salvation!" (v. 1).

The verbs suggest an exuberant, almost raucous service of singing and shouting praises to Yahweh, "the rock of our salvation." The image evokes more than a big stone. Mountains in the southern part of Israel are largely bare rock, and the word *tzur* usually refers to a large formation such as a prominent outcrop that might serve a defensive purpose. [**God as a rock**]

The connection of "rock" and "deliverance" may recall Israel's covenant with God, made by the rocky slopes of Mt. Sinai, along with God's provision of water from a rock

---

> **God as a rock:** "Rock" as a metaphor for God is common in the Hebrew Bible, and it seems to have ancient roots. For other examples, see Gen. 49:24; Deut. 32:4, 15, 18, 30, 31; Ps. 18:3, 32, 47; 19:15; 28:1; 42:10; 62:3, 8; 78:35; 86:27; 92:16; Isa. 44:8; and Hab. 1:12.

during the wilderness wandering, which will be recalled later in the psalm. Rock formations also connote thoughts of stability, security, or protection.

From a procession marked by loud and joyful singing, worshipers are called to "come into his presence with thanksgiving" and "make a joyful noise to him with songs of praise" (v. 2).

Why should one offer such ebullient praise? Because, the psalmist says, "the LORD is a great God, and a great King above all gods" (v. 3). God is large and in charge, the poet declares, the king of all other would-be gods.

It is Yahweh who's "got the whole world in his hands," in the words of a popular song from years ago. God not only holds the earth, from its deepest recesses to its loftiest heights, but also is responsible for having created it to begin with, from expansive seas to fertile lands (vv. 4-5).

Testimony that God is the creator and sustainer of the earth is a frequent theme in scripture. Note particularly how similar Ps. 24:1-2 is to Ps. 95:3-5: "The earth is the LORD'S and all that is in it, the world, and those who live in it; for he has founded it on the seas, and established it on the rivers."

## The shepherd of all people
### (vv. 6-7c)

A God who can create and sustain the nurturing earth is surely worthy of praise, but there is more to be said: God made not only the earth, but also the people who dwell on it. More pointedly, God had called out the people of Israel for a special purpose.

Thus, vv. 6-7c offer the third invitation to "come," calling participants to "worship and bow down" before God: "let us kneel before the LORD, our Maker!" (v. 6).

The word translated as "bow down" means to prostrate oneself. The setting calls for worshipers to fall face down before God, then shift to a kneeling position from which they would attend to the next stage of worship.

Modern believers who are inclined to complain about uncomfortable church pews would do well to consider what worship might be like if the sanctuary held no pews, and they were expected to line up and lie prostrate on the floor before rising to their knees for the next element of the service – a practice common in mosques, but rare in churches.

With v. 7, the imagery shifts to a more personal metaphor. Thinking of God as creator of all things should incite praise and worship, but we can also think of God as a shepherd who cares for the flock.

"We are the people of his pasture, and the sheep of his hand" brings God's care full circle: as "the depths of the earth" are in God's hand (v. 4), so are God's people, like sheep in the hands of a capable shepherd. [**God as a shepherd**]

## The trouble of all rebels
### (vv. 7d-11)

With the last line of v. 7, cozy thoughts of God as a loving shepherd disappear, and worshipers suddenly find themselves on the defensive, as if the shepherd has brought out his rod and staff.

If we imagine that this psalm was used as the liturgy for a worship service, we might visualize a prophet or priest stepping forward to shift the focus of the service. Abruptly, the threefold call to come and worship gives way to a sharp plea: "O that today you would listen to his voice!"

In Hebrew, to truly listen to God's voice is to obey. Thus, the NET translates it "Today, if only you would obey him!"

> **Gods as a shepherd:** The image of God as a shepherd is an old one, and not unique to Israel. One of the oldest writing cultures we know anything about was that of the Sumerians, who lived in southern Mesopotamia long before Abraham was born. Their writings sometimes referred to both gods and kings as "shepherds" of the people. "King of the city that flourishes like a cow, a good shepherd thou art!" says one document. A prayer of praise addressed to a minor underworld deity says: "Ningizzada, thou knowest how to lead with thy staff for all time" (cf. Claus Westermann, *The Living Psalms* [Eerdmanns, 1989], 129, citing A. Falkenstein's *Sumerische Götterlieder* [C. Winter, 1959]).

**Massah and Meribah:** Massah alone is mentioned in Deut. 6:16 and 9:22, while Meribah appears singly in Num. 20:1-13 and Ps. 81:7. Massah and Meribah appear together in Exod. 17:7 and Deut. 33:8.

The preacher contrasts his plea for proper worship and obedience with Israel's history of rebellion, giving special attention to the wilderness stories of thirst and complaint (Exod. 17:1-7, Num. 20:1-13). In both cases, a place was given the nickname "Meribah," which means "contention" or "controversy." In Exod. 17:7 the name "Massah," meaning "testing," was also added. [**Massah and Meribah**]

The notion of "testing" does not suggest a formal challenge, as with Gideon's fleece (Judg. 6:36-40), in which one sets conditions for God to prove something. Rather, when adversity arose, the people grumbled that Moses had misled them and God had not taken proper care of them. Their constant caviling tested even God's patience.

We may know what it is like to have balky children or obstreperous co-workers stretch our tolerance to the limit. If we're honest, we'll confess that we also, like Israel, have relied too much on divine indulgence and tried God's patience through the years.

We can be grateful for the grace of God we've come to know in Christ. The psalmist, living under a covenant-based understanding of God's relationship with Israel, saw only harsh judgment in store for the hard-hearted.

Recalling Israel's persistent rebellion in the wilderness, the psalmist portrayed God as declaring that "For forty years I loathed that generation" because of their straying hearts and stubborn rejection of God's teaching (v. 10a).

"Loathed" is a hard word, and one we don't like to associate with God's character. We'd rather speak of a loving God than a loathing one. The term does not suggest hatred of the people, however, but revulsion toward their actions. God did not hate the Israelites, but was clearly repulsed by their headstrong hearts and ungrateful attitudes. Thus, the NET translates "I was continually disgusted with that generation."

"They do not regard my ways" could be translated more literally as, "they do not know my ways" (v. 10b). Presumably, one who knows God's ways should follow them: the word "know" carries the connotation of personal experience. The charge that "they do not know my ways" is equivalent to "they do not obey my commands" (NET).

God's response to the people's stubborn behavior in v. 11 echoes Moses' sermon in Deut. 1:22-37, where he recalled how the people had claimed that God hated them and refused to trust God for victory in the Promised Land. As a result, Moses declared that God "was wrathful and swore: 'Not one of these – not one of this evil generation – shall see the good land that I swore to give to your ancestors'" (Deut. 11:34-35).

By the time Psalm 95 was written, the promised entry into the Promised Land had grown into an expectation of continued security and "rest" for Israel (for example, 2 Sam. 7:10b-11 and 1 Chron. 23:25). As a result, the psalmist's loose quotation declares "Therefore in my anger I swore, 'They shall not enter my rest'" (v. 11).

What does this psalm suggest to Christian readers? Few of us expect or hope to live in the territory once promised to the Israelites, but we do long for peace in

**Psalm 95 and Hebrews 3–4:** Echoes of Psalm 95 permeate Hebrews 3 and 4 in a repetitive style, as in the excerpt below, from Heb. 4:1-7:

Therefore, while the promise of entering his rest is still open, let us take care that none of you should seem to have failed to reach it. For indeed the good news came to us just as to them; but the message they heard did not benefit them, because they were not united by faith with those who listened. For we who have believed enter that rest, just as God has said,

"As in my anger I swore, 'They shall not enter my rest,'" though his works were finished at the foundation of the world. For in one place it speaks about the seventh day as follows, "And God rested on the seventh day from all his works." And again in this place it says, "They shall not enter my rest." Since therefore it remains open for some to enter it, and those who formerly received the good news failed to enter because of disobedience, again he sets a certain day – "today" – saying through David much later, in the words already quoted,

"Today, if you hear his voice, do not harden your hearts."

the present and ease in eternity – as we say in obituary language, "to enter into rest."

An anonymous New Testament writer drew heavily on this text in Hebrews 3–4, urging believers not to harden their hearts as Israel did, but to hear God's voice and follow God's way so they might enter God's "Sabbath rest" – and to do it "today" (see especially Heb. 4:1-10). **[Psalm 95 and Hebrews 3–4]**

If we are to see the world and our responsibilities as Jesus does, we also must listen for God's voice and respond with obedience. That message will preach. How will we respond?

## The Hardest Question
### Does God *need* to be worshiped?

Psalm 95's call for worshipers to sing praises, lie prostrate, and kneel before God raises the question of "why." Does God have an inner need to be worshiped, a deep insecurity that requires human worship to affirm the divine sense of self-worth?

No: when we gather for worship, we are meeting our needs, not God's. Psalm 95 is an appropriate lesson on the way that worship reminds us of our place in God's world. God is our creator, sustainer, and redeemer. God is the author of our past and the hope of our future.

Our human tendency is to think of ourselves as the center of the universe. When we adopt this posture, our ethics and morals are determined by what serves our own purposes, rather than what is best for others and for the world.

On the other hand, when we gather for worship, we are reminded that God is God, and we are not. We recall that our world, our lives, and our future hope are all grounded in God. We are challenged to love others as God loves us, to care for the poor who are so important to God, and to practice the kind of justice that makes life better for all.

We may surely affirm that God is gratified by our worship, but it is not God who needs it. Worship is not for God's benefit, but for ours.

# Third Sunday in Lent

## Third Reading
## Romans 5:1-11

# Hopeful Peace

*Therefore, since we are justified by faith, we have peace with God through our Lord Jesus Christ. (Rom. 5:1)*

The subject of pride is always a paradox for Christians. When we are young, parents or teachers encourage us to dress neatly or to work hard by taking pride in our appearance or our work. "Taking pride in yourself" is a southern euphemism for having a strong self-image and positive self-esteem.

Coaches of organized sports often preach team pride so players will try harder and support the other members of the team. Persons who have minority status often emphasize pride in their heritage or their identity as a way of claiming their place within the larger society.

There are positive aspects to the issue of pride. But there is also a flip side. A contributor to the book of Proverbs held that "pride goes before destruction" (Prov. 16:18), and the author of 1 John considered "the boastful pride of life" to be a wicked, worldly thing (1 John 2:16).

Pride, like other human attitudes, can be a mixed blessing. We need a healthy amount of pride in who we are and what we do, but we must be careful not to let personal pride overshadow our concern for others and our humility before God.

---

**Therefore…:** Paul's "therefore" in v. 1 follows from his argument toward the end of ch. 4 that God reckoned Abraham as righteous because of his faith. Paul contended that God's desire was for all people to follow Abraham's example, as the words "it was reckoned to him" could apply to us also: righteousness "will be reckoned to us who believe in him who raised Jesus our Lord from the dead, who was handed over to death for our trespasses and was raised for our justification" (4:24-25).

---

In today's text, Paul talks about three aspects of Christian faith that are proper causes for pride. He speaks of how believers can "boast" of the eternal hope they obtain through faith in Christ (vv. 1-2), in the sufferings they endure for the sake of Christ (vv. 3-5), and in the Lord who has made possible their reconciliation (vv. 6-11).

### Boasting in hope
### (vv. 1-2)

"Therefore, since we are justified by faith" (v. 1) connects ch. 5 with the previous two chapters, in which Paul had established that salvation comes through faith, not works. **[Therefore…]** Now he moves on to explain how salvation brings peace with God through Christ (v. 1). A faithful Jew could have faith in God, but Paul believed that salvation came only by faith expressed through Christ, "through whom we have obtained access to this grace in which we stand" (v. 2a).

God's grace has been ever present, and it was often evident in the Old Testament narratives. The work of Christ, however, makes God's grace more accessible to all persons. Paul taught that Jesus came into the world for our sakes, that he died for our sins, that he was raised as our example. As we trust in Christ, we can experience forgiveness of our sins, an ongoing relationship with God, and hope for eternity.

Paul reminded his readers that one's free access to God is not because of good works or high standing, but because of God's grace. God has chosen to save, and this alone is the key to our standing. Being chosen is a special thing. We take delight in being chosen for a sports team, for an honorary

> **Righteousness and peace:** Paul's combination of righteousness and peace has Old Testament roots. The prophet Isaiah urged Israel to strive for righteousness, insisting that "The effect of righteousness will be peace, and the result of righteousness, quietness and trust forever" (Isa. 32:7). Peace results when humans live in a right relationship with God.
>
> Psalm 72 is a prayer for God to grant a king who practiced justice and righteousness, recognizing that peace would result: "In his days may righteousness flourish and peace abound, until the moon is no more" (Ps. 72:7).
>
> With a memorable metaphor, the psalmist behind Psalm 85 longed for a day of divine deliverance and human faithfulness in which "Steadfast love and faithfulness will meet; righteousness and peace will kiss each other" (Ps. 85:10).

society, for a scholarship, for a job, for membership in an invitation-only club. We have access to God because God *chose* to redeem us through Jesus Christ, and because we have chosen to accept God's gracious invitation.

Because of our new standing with God, we can joyfully "boast in our hope of sharing the glory of God" (v. 2b). Paul believed that our present life of fellowship with God through the Spirit is just a foretaste of the life that lies ahead when we will share the glory of God in his fullness.

In *Surprised by God*, James W. Cox tells a story about an African-American preacher from Chicago named D.E. King. Someone asked Rev. King why Black Christians were always joyful in their worship, even when they faced many difficulties and things were not going well. The pastor explained, "We rejoice in what we are going to have."

Those of us who mourn for the loss of loved ones can rejoice in the hope of "what we are going to have" as we contemplate a joyful reunion. Those who are oppressed and downtrodden in this world may yet have hope and rejoice "in what we are going to have" in the eternal inheritance prepared for God's children. Righteousness (being justified) and peace go together. [**Righteousness and peace**]

## Boasting in suffering
### (vv. 3-5)

Lest his readers be carried away and think that Christian living is a piece of cake, Paul reminded them that suffering was not past. Believers will experience suffering just as other people do, and they have no reason to expect anything different. Paul used the word *thlipsis*, which can refer to tribulation, trouble, hardships, and suffering. The world brings suffering enough for everyone, and being Christian does not make us immune. Indeed, there are times when following Christ may even add to our suffering, especially in times of organized persecution or prejudice against people of faith.

Even so, there is a difference in the way Christians approach the issue of suffering. Paul argued that believers could take pride even in suffering, because we know that "suffering produces endurance, and endurance produces character, and character produces hope, and hope does not disappoint us, because God's love has been poured into our hearts through the Holy Spirit that has been given to us" (vv. 3-5). [**Hope and love**]

We can boast in our sufferings because we can see past the present difficulty to the future blessing. Like an athlete who endures the pain and discomfort of training for the hope of improved skills and conditioning, we can accept suffering as an essential step in the development of faithful patience and Christian character.

Through patient endurance, Paul said, we can develop character that has been proved by testing. As a structural engineer may test potential bridge components by putting

> **Hope and love:** Paul was confident that believers can have a hope that does not disappoint because they had already experienced that "God's love has been poured into our hearts through the Holy Spirit that has been given to us" (v. 5).
>
> James D.G. Dunn comments: "At all events, the point is clear: hope of completed salvation, of restoration to share in the divine glory, is not a vain or idle hope, because the process has already begun. The believer's hope for the future is based not only in a faithful and powerful God, but in what they have already experienced and received from that God—the end-time Spirit of God active in them already in end-time power. As hope of future resurrection is based in the resurrection of Christ already accomplished (1 Cor. 15:17-22), so hope of future glory is based on the experience of grace already enjoyed (v. 2), so hope of completed salvation arises out of the experience of the eschatological power of God already achieving the purposes of divine love (v. 5)" (*Romans 1–8*, vol. 38A, Word Biblical Commentary [Zondervan, 1988], 266).

them under stress, so our own character is proved and even strengthened through testing.

For Christians, the ultimate outcome of suffering is hope in the future God has prepared for us. Hope will never disappoint because it is ever-present. When all else is taken away, we still have hope. Persons who have lost loved ones to death know what it is like to be tested. In times of trauma or loss, it may be hard to have faith, but that is when we discover the incredible power of hope.

Even when we may find it hard to *believe* some things as firmly as we once did, we can *hope* them more than ever. We learn that faith, in a sense, is nothing more than hope with feet on it – hope to the point of commitment. Hope has a power all its own, a power that does not disappoint.

We should all be able to recall personal experiences in which hope has helped us through a period of suffering or trial. Have we used that experience to encourage others?

## Boasting in reconciliation
### (vv. 6-11)

Having argued that we may have hope to boast in both suffering and peace, Paul turned to Christ as the source of that hope. Four descriptive adjectives portray our former state of lostness, which has been transformed by the power of Christ: we were *weak*, we were *ungodly*, we were *sinners*, we were *enemies* of God.

"While we were still weak," Paul says – while we were still living under the world's pervasive sway — "at the right time Christ died for the ungodly" (v. 6). The word *'asthenēs* often means "sick," but can also mean "weak," or "without influence." We were weak and unable to save ourselves, Paul said. He did not distinguish between human weakness that leads to death and moral weakness that surrenders to temptation. Both can leave us far from God. Who would want to save us – especially if saving others required one's own death, and if the people to be saved are not only weak, but also living in opposition to God?

The word "ungodly" suggests lifestyles that give no thought to God. Our focus on individual desires as opposed to God's ideal is what makes us sinners who live as enemies of God. And yet, Paul said, "God proves his love for us in that while we still were sinners Christ died for us" (v. 8).

---

> **Present and future:** In thinking of salvation as both present and future, we may consider the analogy of a gift certificate or gift card. Upon receipt, what we possess may seem no more than a piece of paper or plastic, but we know it can be used to obtain a material possession or life experience that we can use and enjoy. The gift card or certificate is a present reality that points toward a future fulfillment. In a far greater way, our present relationship with Christ offers the promise of an eternal home with God.

---

We note that Paul included himself among those who needed Christ's intervention: "while *we* were still weak" (v. 6), "while *we* were sinners" (v. 8), "while *we* were enemies" (v. 10). But Paul could write as he did because he also counted himself among those who had been granted a new relationship with God: "*we* were reconciled to God through the death of his son" (v. 10), so that "*we* even boast in God through our Lord Jesus Christ, through whom we have now received reconciliation" (v. 11).

Our experience from the past gives rise to hope for the present. If Christ has truly justified us through his death on the cross, then we have confidence of a sure salvation (v. 9). According to his custom, Paul spoke of salvation in the future tense (compare Rom. 5:10; 9:27; 10:9, 13; 11:14, 26). When we trust in Christ, we are granted a right standing with God (justified), but the time of ultimate salvation lies in the future. If God loved us enough to reconcile us to himself through Christ's death "while we were enemies," then surely God will love us enough to continue that saving work through Christ's resurrection life (v. 10). [**Present and future**]

This gives us abundant cause to boast in a God who reconciles us to himself through Jesus Christ. The word translated as "reconcile" comes from a root word that means "to exchange." Here, it means "to exchange enmity for friendship." Wherever "reconcile" or "reconciliation" is used in the New Testament, it is always God who does the reconciling, and humans who are reconciled by virtue of God's work in Christ. We didn't (and don't) deserve the reconciling love of God, but we can take pride in knowing that God has chosen to extend such love to us – and pass it on to others.

### The Hardest Question
#### When is boasting acceptable?

We began this lesson be recalling how parents, teachers, or coaches want children to learn to take pride in themselves or their work. At the same time, we encourage them not to boast or to brag. Feeling a sense of accomplishment or self-worth can be admirable, but we want to avoid an overweening sense of superiority that appears to elevate us over others.

How, then, should we understand Paul's encouragement of "boasting"? Paul would have known that the Hebrew Scriptures warned against self-boasting. The psalmist had no use for those who opposed God and bragged about it: "Why do you boast, O mighty one, of mischief done against the godly?" (Ps. 52:1).

If one is to boast, he or she should boast in God. Speaking for God, Jeremiah declared: "Thus says the LORD: Do not let the wise boast in their wisdom, do not let the mighty boast in their might, do not let the wealthy boast in their wealth; but let those who boast boast in this, that they understand and know me, that I am the LORD; I act with steadfast love, justice, and righteousness in the earth, for in these things I delight, says the LORD" (Jer. 9:23-24).

Earlier in his letter to the Romans, Paul did not hesitate to criticize self-righteous Jews who claimed to boast in God but were really boasting in their adherence to the law (2:17, 23). Here, though, he encouraged his readers to boast, not in themselves, but "in God through our Lord Jesus Christ" (v. 11). Because of this, we can also boast of the hope we have in God (v. 2) and the sufferings we share as followers of Christ (v. 3). Such boasting does not elevate self, but rather serves to magnify the power and blessings of God.

Taking pride in ourselves and what we do is appropriate: excessive boasting about it is not. With Paul, if we should boast, let us boast of what God has done.

# *Third Sunday in Lent*

## Fourth Reading
## John 4:5-42

# Getting Met

*Jesus answered her, "If you knew the gift of God, and who it is that is saying to you,*
*'Give me a drink,' you would have asked him, and he would have given you living water." (John 4:10)*

Like it or not, we live in a pluralistic society, one in which people of varying ethnicities, religions, and customs share the same neighborhoods, the same water, the same grocery stores. How we respond to neighbors who are different from us is key to the quality of life for all of us.

We know how Jesus would have us relate, and today's text is a prime example.

### The well
### (vv. 5-6)

The Fourth Gospel assigns to Jesus an itinerary quite different from the other gospels. Mark, Matthew, and Luke place Jesus in Jerusalem only once during his adult life, but John has him make at least three visits, including an early Passover visit that places the "cleansing of the temple" at the beginning of his ministry, rather than the end (2:13-35).

After spending time in Jerusalem, where he encountered Nicodemus (3:1-21), Jesus went into the Judean countryside, where he reportedly preached and authorized his disciples to baptize many (3:22-36). Concerned that his popularity might lead to trouble, he determined to leave Judea and return to Galilee (4:1-3).

The text says "he had to go through Samaria" (v. 4), but there was no geographical reason that he had to go through Samaria to get to Galilee. He could have done what good Jews did, following the Jordan Valley up to the pass at Beth Shan, then turning westward into the region of Galilee through the Valley of Jezreel. If Jesus "had to go through Samaria," it was due to a sense of calling that he

> **The place:** Sychar may be an alternate name for Shechem, but was probably a small village on its outskirts. It was nestled in a beautiful valley between Mt. Ebal and Mt. Gerizim, the mountains that marked the heart of Samaritan territory. The location is now the modern city of Nablus, in today's West Bank, and the people who lived there were no more popular with the Jews in 30 CE than the Palestinians who live there are today.
>
> Jacob's well was apparently a trusted landmark, one that could bring joy to the thirsty travelers who followed the main north-south road from Judah to Galilee, the road that Jesus was traveling.

could not ignore. In doing so, he came to a city named Sychar, known in tradition as a place that Jacob had equipped with a well and given to his son Joseph. It was a lovely place for a tired and thirsty man to sit in the middle of a hot day (vv. 5-6). [**The place**]

### The woman
### (vv. 7-30)

The text implies that Jesus, apparently unequipped for water-drawing, waited patiently for someone to come along with a jug to provide for their household. It is often said that the woman who approached the well must have been ostracized by the other women, since the cool of the morning would have been a better time to draw the day's supply. That may or may not have been the case, but the woman did come alone.

She seemed surprised when Jesus asked for a drink. Not only had a Jew spoken to her, but apparently was willing to drink from a Samaritan vessel (vv. 7-9).

Jesus responded with the familiar comeback: "If you knew the gift of God, and who it is that is saying to you, 'Give me a drink,' you would have asked him, and he would have given you living water" (v. 10).

She misunderstood, wondering how Jesus, with no rope or bucket, could obtain any kind of water, much less "living water." Was it something different? Where do you get that living water?" she asked. "Are you greater than our ancestor Jacob, who gave us the well, and with his sons and his flocks drank from it?" (vv. 11-12).

Jesus stuck with his metaphor, promising that one who drank the living water would never thirst again, but "the water that I will give will become in them a spring of water gushing up to eternal life" (v. 14). Naturally, the woman was anxious for that kind of water and asked for some (v. 15).

In the following dialogue, Jesus displayed prescient knowledge of the woman's chain of previous husbands and her current partner (vv. 16-18). Perhaps uncomfortable with where the discussion was going, she sidestepped to a theological question about how he could explain why Jews worshiped in Jerusalem while her people worshiped on Mt. Gerizim (vv. 19-20).

Jesus responded that the time was coming when place would no longer matter, but it would take place "in Spirit and in truth" (vv. 21-24). When the woman expressed her own hope in a coming messiah, Jesus responded "I am he" (vv. 25-26).

And then it began to dawn on her. The veil was lifted, at least in part. She had been met ... met by the eternal "I am that I am." Her Bible, the Samaritan Pentateuch, also contained that name. Messiah had come.

Unknowing, unexpecting, walking her daily path on the outskirts of society, the woman came to Jacob's Well to find fresh water, but she found fresh truth. She came seeking a deep well, but found herself involved in something deeper still. She came looking for a simple necessity of everyday life, and she was found out by one who offered her everlasting life.

We know what happened next. Overcome with new awareness, she ignored the approaching disciples and left her water jug behind as she ran back to the city, proclaiming the good news that Messiah had come.

## The harvest
### (vv. 31-42)

While the woman was gone, according to the story, the disciples approached Jesus, more concerned about whether Jesus had eaten than with his conversation with the Samaritan woman. Jesus insisted "My food is to do the will of him who sent me and to complete his work" (vv. 31-34). He then recited an old saying about the harvest coming four months after planting. Pointing to the surrounding area – populated with Samaritans – he said, "look around you, and see how the fields are ripe for harvesting" (vv. 35-36). **[Irony]**

Citing another saying that "one sows and another reaps," he reminded the disciples that he had sent them out as reapers, building on the foundation of those who had gone before them in upholding the faith. Not said, but implied, is that the harvest would especially include those who would be drawn to faith through the work of Jesus (vv. 37-38).

As if to illustrate the impact of Jesus' work, the narrator reports that "Many Samaritans from that city believed in him because of the woman's testimony, 'He told me everything I have ever done'" (v. 39). As in other situations, people were drawn to Jesus by his works of power, or in this case, prescience. To their credit, the Samaritans wanted to learn more, and asked Jesus to stay with them for a while, a show of surprising hospitality on their part. Jesus, in response, remained there for two days (v. 40).

It's easy to overlook the significance of Jesus' agreeing to stay an additional two days: while we assume that he would have spent much of the time teaching or preaching, he also would have been eating with the Samaritans, lodging with them, perhaps joking with them. Although

---

**Irony:** The author relies on the literary device of irony in telling this story. In their initial conversation, the woman thinks only of physical water, but learns that Jesus can provide refreshment for her deep spiritual thirst. When the disciples show up, they're concerned about physical food, but Jesus spoke of a different kind of sustenance, nourishment that is found in doing the work of God. While the disciples were familiar with the planting and harvesting of grains, Jesus wanted them to catch the vision of a harvest that brought people to salvation – including the Samaritans.

**Contrast:** Note the author's intentional contrast by placing Jesus' encounter with Nicodemus and the Samaritan woman back-to-back. Nicodemus was the ultimate insider: a Jew and a Pharisee who would have known the Hebrew scriptures backward and forward. The woman was the quintessential outsider: not only Samaritan and female, but possibly ostracized by her own people. She knew that Samaritans worshiped on Mt. Gerizim rather than in Jerusalem, but not why.

With all his insider advantages and theological acumen, Nicodemus fades from the story in John 3 and does not respond to Jesus' testimony, unless it was later. Despite her position as an outsider, the woman not only accepted Jesus' message immediately, but became an effective evangelist, facilitating Jesus' stay in the village and the salvation of many others.

"thirst," and she came to know that she was dying of it. But even as she learned to name her thirst, Jesus introduced her to the source of living water, the very Spirit of God, the deep well of life itself.

We never know when we might run across a well like that, for just as surely as our faith becomes comfortable and we think we've got this religion business figured out, we get met. Someone comes along or something happens, and God gets a hold of our heart and points us toward the next stage of our spiritual journey. [**Contrast**]

### The Hardest Question
**Why did Jews and Samaritans hate each other?**

Enmity between Jews and Samaritans had been growing for hundreds of years before Jesus' day. When the Assyrians conquered Israel in 722 BCE, they forced all the leading families to leave and resettle in other lands, but they allowed poor people with little ability to rebel in place. Then, the Assyrians imported people from other nations they had conquered and displaced.

Over time, the remaining Israelites intermingled and intermarried with people from places such as Cuth and Hamath and Luash and Bit Agusi. They developed a hybrid religion based on their own version of the Pentateuch, and built their own temple on the top of lofty Mt. Gerizim. Because they lived in a geographical region known as Samaria, they became known as Samaritans.

A similar thing happened when the southern kingdom of Judah fell to Nebuchadnezzar, and waves of exiles were sent to Babylon in 597 and 587 BCE, with smaller groups being added later. Again, the poorer people were left to farm the land and pay tribute to the conquerors. Many of them also intermarried with other ethnic peoples. Some held to their Hebrew faith, while others did not.

When the Jewish exiles returned from Babylon in the late sixth and early fifth centuries BCE they considered themselves to be the only "pure" Jews remaining, because they had married among themselves. They considered the Samaritans and anyone who had intermarried with non-Jews to be unworthy of fellowship and would not allow them to assist in rebuilding either Jerusalem or the temple. Many of the returning exiles found the locals attractive and they also began to intermarry, but Ezra

he was clearly a Jew, and he had told the woman earlier that "salvation is from the Jews" (v. 22), Jesus' continued presence showed that he considered the Samaritans to be just as important to God as anyone else. Salvation may have come *from* the Jews, but it was not just *for* the Jews.

That was apparently welcome news, because "many more believed because of his word" – not just because of the foreknowledge he flashed to the first woman, but because "we have heard for ourselves, and we know that this is truly the Savior of the world" (vv. 41-42).

Eugene Lowry once observed that there are at least two ways of knowing. One way is like this: we sit down with a tough word problem in math and when we finally figure it out, we say "I got it!" The other way is different. It's like when we go to a movie, and something about the movie moves us unexpectedly and deeply. When we leave the theater, changed by the experience, we don't say "I got it," but instead we realize that "it got me" (from *Pulpit Resource*, Jan.–Mar. 1996, 42).

The woman at the well didn't set out looking for Jesus. She set out because she was thirsty, but before the day was over, she discovered a raging spiritual thirst and the one who could quench it. Surely, she did not have all her questions answered that day. She did not become an overnight theological whiz kid. But she learned what she needed to know. There was a word for that emptiness she had felt inside for so long, that yearning she had tried to fill with a string of husbands and affairs. The word was and Nehemiah vehemently forbade such marriages and demanded that they divorce non-Jewish wives and send them away. For their part, some Samaritans resented the Jews' return, and resisted their efforts at resettlement.

Many Samaritans continued to worship Yahweh in their temple on Mt. Gerizim, but they were not allowed in Jerusalem. The bitter divide between the returning Jews and the indigenous Samaritans is often called "the Samaritan schism." By the first century CE, "good" Jews would not set foot in a Samaritan town or speak to any Samaritan, certainly not to a woman.

Jesus looked past the schism and saw only people who needed his message.

## First Reading
## 1 Samuel 16:1-13

# A New King

*But the LORD said to Samuel, "Do not look on his appearance or on the height of his stature,*
*because I have rejected him; for the LORD does not see as mortals see; they look on the outward appearance,*
*but the LORD looks on the heart." (1 Sam. 16:7)*

Every four years, Americans go through a long process of choosing a president. Through a series of primaries, we narrow hopeful candidates down to one representative from each party on the ballot, all of whom claim to have the best abilities for leading the nation. Then, together, we vote.

Imagine that you alone were given the task of choosing the best president from a small field of contenders. What criteria would you use? Appearance? Experience? Ideology? Trustworthiness? Speaking ability?

In our text for today, the prophet/priest Samuel was sent by God to choose a king from among the sons of a farmer near Bethlehem whose name was Jesse. How did he do it?

### An unwelcome mission
### (vv. 1-5)

Samuel did not want the job. He hadn't been happy when the elders of Israel had asked him to designate a king (1 Samuel 8), but he believed God wanted him to do it. He had chosen Saul, a tall and promising Benjaminite (1 Samuel 9–11), but he had not been pleased with Saul's performance. Twice, Samuel told Saul that God had rejected him and would choose someone more suitable (1 Sam. 13:14, 15:26-28).

After Saul failed to completely exterminate the Midianites, as Samuel believed God had wanted him to do, the old prophet stalked away under a dark cloud of disappointment and retired to his home in Ramah. That's where God revealed his new mission: Samuel was to stop

**Samuel's fear:** Samuel's concerns about going to Bethlehem were well grounded. His home in Ramah was less than a day's walk to the north, but Bethlehem was in the tribal land of Judah, the southernmost tribe and apparently not overly supportive of Saul.

Saul had fallen victim to mental illness, exhibiting symptoms of a bipolar or manic-depressive disorder. The narrator attributed his condition to an evil spirit, the ancients' standard way of explaining emotional or mental illnesses (1 Sam. 16:14).

Samuel had recently derided Saul in public, declaring that God would give the kingdom to "a neighbor who is better than you" (1 Sam. 15:28). If word got out that he had traveled to Bethlehem to meet with local elders, Saul might think he was fomenting rebellion among the southerners.

On the other hand, the Bethlehemite elders may have thought that Samuel was on a mission from Saul, sent to spy out any disloyalty or to pronounce some doom on the town. Thus, when Samuel arrived, they came out "trembling" and asked, "Do you come peaceably?"

The small artifice of claiming he had come to offer a sacrifice provided Samuel with a rationale for his visit: God had sent him to offer a sacrifice, and he had a heifer in tow to prove it.

whining about Saul's failures and choose a new king from among the sons of Jesse (v. 1).

Samuel objected, fearing that Saul might hear of it and have him killed as a potential subversive. [**Samuel's fear**] God offered an appropriate excuse, telling Samuel to take a heifer with him and announce that God had sent him to Bethlehem to offer a sacrifice.

Even the paranoid Saul could not argue with such a sacred errand – so long as he didn't find out the true purpose beyond the sacrifice (v. 2).

Surely Samuel had more questions, but Yahweh assured him that "I will show you what you shall do; and you shall anoint for me the one whom I name to you" (v. 3).

When Samuel arrived in Bethlehem, he was met by an "unwelcome committee" of town elders who questioned his motives. Bethlehem was in the southern part of the kingdom, where Saul was less popular. The elders were suspicious of Samuel's motives. Again, he claimed that he had only come to offer a sacrifice, and invited the elders to sanctify themselves and meet him later for the ceremony. Jesse was among those invited (vv. 4-5).

## A surprising audition
### (vv. 6-10)

Whether the other elders chose not to attend or whether the narrator simply dropped them into the background, only Jesse and his sons appeared to be present for the sacral event and following meal.

Samuel wasted no time in asking Jesse to line up his sons. When Eliab, the oldest, stepped forward, he must have been an attractive man who made a strong impression on Samuel, who thought "Surely the LORD's anointed is before the LORD" (v. 6).

For once in his life, Samuel learned that he was wrong. We don't know how God spoke to Samuel, but the narrator says that Yahweh told him "Do not look on his appearance or the height of his stature, because I have rejected him; for the LORD does not see as mortals see; they look on the outward appearance, but the LORD looks on the heart" (v. 7).

---

**The eighth son:** In biblical thought, the number seven sometimes indicates completeness or something special. Beyond the Bible, superstition has sometimes led people to believe that someone who was a seventh son – or especially the seventh son of a seventh son – might have special powers.

As the *eighth* son, David may have been considered as one beyond the bounds of the seven, a visionary who could see beyond the limited horizons of ordinary people.

---

Neither looks nor age and experience were enough, Samuel learned: God had other standards. "The LORD looks on the heart."

Samuel turned to the next son, Abinadab, then to Shammah, then to the next, and the next. Each time – seven times in all – God told Samuel that this son was not the one (vv. 8-10). The number seven symbolized completeness. Surely one of them should have been chosen, Samuel thought, but all were rejected. [**The eighth son**]

## An unexpected star
### (vv. 11-13)

Samuel was confused. We can imagine him ticking off a mental list of God's instructions: "Go to Bethlehem … take a heifer for sacrifice … invite Jesse to attend … I will show you which of his sons to anoint." Samuel knew he had followed the instructions, but God had not confirmed any of the candidates before him.

Finally, like the old TV detective Columbo in his wrinkled raincoat, Samuel had an idea. He asked, "Are all of your sons here?"

Jesse admitted that there was one more. He had not brought his youngest son because he assumed he would not to be chosen – and someone had to watch the sheep while the rest of them attended the sacrifice.

Samuel was not happy. "Send for him!" he snapped. "We will not sit down until he comes here" (v. 11).

David could have been miles away with his wandering flocks, and it may have taken quite some time to fetch him. The reader suspects that David must be the chosen one, even though he was obviously young and probably unremarkable, since the narrator had gone to such lengths to say that appearances don't matter.

But when David arrived, the storyteller surprises us with unabashed adulation for the young man who would become king. He was ruddy, he tells us, which probably means that he had fairer skin than most, so one could see color in his cheeks. He had beautiful eyes, too, though a possible translation is "he was beautiful to the eyes."

More importantly, there was something special *inside* of David that only God could see, and so Yahweh poked Samuel in the heart: "This is the one: arise and anoint him!" (v. 12).

Samuel drew out his polished ram's horn filled with spiced olive oil and poured it over David's head, and as the oil brought a shine to David's face, the Spirit of God ignited a glow in his heart. "The Spirit of the Lord came mightily upon David," the narrator says, "from that day forward" (v. 13).

Why was David the one? Back in ch. 13, Samuel told Saul that God planned to replace him with a man "after God's own heart" (1 Sam. 13:14). David must have fit the bill. In the New Testament book of Acts, Paul pointed to David as a man after God's heart who would carry out God's work (Acts 13:22).

### What was it about David's heart?

We are left to ponder what made David a man after God's own heart, because the narrator doesn't say. Was it because he had a loving or compassionate heart? A loyal heart? A joyful heart? David may have had those characteristics, but surely others did, too.

What was it about David, at least during the years of his ascendancy, that set him apart as a person after God's own heart? **[God's own heart]**

We could suggest a variety of things, but two primary characteristics stood out over the next few years: a spirit of openness and an attitude of trustfulness.

---

**God's own heart:** In an academic article on the subject of David as a man after God's own heart, Mark George argued that the primary purpose of 1 Samuel 16–2 Samuel 5 – usually called the "History of David's Rise" – was not to provide a political justification for David to replace Saul as king, as typically argued, but to demonstrate in word and deed what was so special about David's heart that God was inspired to choose him.

George concluded that two primary characteristics of David's heart set him apart: First, he pointed to the many instances in which David inquired of God before making decisions, which suggests an active prayer life and an ongoing dialogue between David and God.

Second, George noted that while Saul's relationship with God seemed to focus on carrying out cultic observances, David's relationship with God was made evident not only through inquiring of God, but also through declaring his trust in Yahweh ("Yhwh's Own Heart," *The Catholic Biblical Quarterly* 64:2002, 442-459).

---

The narrator's account suggests that David's heart was wide open to adventure, to creativity, and to allowing God to work through him. He didn't have the closed heart of someone who thinks they have everything figured out.

David's heart was open to the future, open to new possibilities, open to mystery, and therefore open to the Spirit of God. A part of being open is a willingness to listen, and apparently David knew how to listen. Several stories relate that David "inquired of God," suggesting that David remained constantly open to what God might be saying in a variety of ways (see "The Hardest Question" below for more).

And, as David remained receptive to God's leadership, he also trusted that God would empower him to do whatever he was called to do. He once claimed that God had enabled him to protect the sheep by slaying lions and bears with his bare hands. Later he stepped forward to confront Goliath, apparently the only one who really believed God was alive and well and willing to help the faithful.

In David's career, at least through 2 Samuel 10, he thought of things and did things no one else would do, because he listened to God, and trusted God. People like that are still around.

I recall meeting Cheryl Allen around the turn of the millennium. Trained as a nurse, she also served as pastor of a church in one of the most crime-ridden sections of Johannesburg, South Africa. Seeing babies abandoned and often dying with AIDS, she listened to God and dared to begin an orphanage known as the "Door of Hope," a ministry that continues to care for children who might otherwise have died in a trash bin.

Most of us have known others who listened to God, trusted, and made a difference. Were we among them? Our text challenges us to look past our frailties and failures and be open to ways in which God can use us to bring light into this world, not because we are particularly strong or talented, but because we are willing. Many biblical stories reflect how God delights in surprising the world by doing great things through small people who listen and who trust.

Isn't this what it means to have a "Jesus worldview"? To live with an open spirit, taking note of the needs around us, and listening for how Jesus would have us respond?

We may never be anointed as David was, and certainly won't be made king. But we can be open and trusting and anointed by the Spirit of God. We can look to a future that is filled with unknown opportunities for life and service and joy. We can become the people God wants us to be. Are we listening?

## The Hardest Question
### How did David "inquire of God"?

The biblical narrators insist that David habitually "inquired of God" when making major decisions. In 1 Sam. 22:10, David asked the priest Ahimelech to inquire of the LORD for him regarding his next move in fleeing Saul. When Saul heard about it and accused the priest of treason for inquiring of God in David's behalf, Ahimelech described David as a faithful servant of the king, and added "Is today the first time that I have inquired of God for him? By no means!" (1 Sam. 22:15).

Saul ordered that all the priests be killed, but Ahimelech's son Abiathar escaped and joined David's band of refugees from Saul's wrath. In that capacity, he served as an intermediary to inquire of God for David. He inquired of Yahweh regarding whether to attack the Philistines who threatened the city of Keilah (1 Sam. 23:2, 4). When Amalekites burned David's adopted city of Ziklag and took the women and children hostage, David "inquired of the LORD" before pursuing them (1 Sam. 30:8).

After Saul's death, David sought God's leadership concerning whether he should go up to one of the cities of Judah, presumably to offer himself as a new king, and again to determine which city (2 Sam. 2:1).

After becoming king, David continued to seek God's guidance in military matters. Both 2 Sam. 5:19, 23-24 and 1 Chron. 14:9, 13 describe instances in which David "inquired of the LORD" regarding the advisability of engaging the Philistines in battle. In both cases, he received a positive response.

In a time of famine, David inquired of the LORD to determine the cause of the famine and what could be done about it (2 Sam. 21:1).

But how did one go about "inquiring of the LORD" in this fashion, and why were priests involved? One could simply pray and hope for an answer. People sometimes offered sacrifices and then slept nearby in hopes that God might speak in a dream, a practice scholars refer to as "dream incubation."

The most commonly attested method of "inquiring of the LORD" was to have a priest use the Urim and the Thummim as a means of determining God's will.

The Urim and Thummim were sacred lots, apparently made of stone, bone, or clay. They would have been identical in shape and size but of different colors or designs, and were kept in a pouch in the high priest's breastplate (Exod. 28:30). To use them, the priest would hold the pouch in his hand while asking God for one of two possible answers, with Urim representing one and Thummim the other. He would then put his thumb over one of the unseen objects and cast the other into his lap. Whichever lot emerged was thought to be God's answer.

Goats for ceremonies on the day of Atonement were chosen by on which "the lot fell for the LORD" (Lev. 16:9-10). The land of Canaan was to be apportioned to families based on how "the lot falls" (Num. 33:54; Josh. 18:11, 21:10; 1 Chron. 6:54; et. al.).

Examples of when the Urim and Thummim were specifically mentioned in such decision making include Samuel's choice of Saul in 1 Sam. 10:17-24 and Saul's effort to determine who had broken his oath in 1 Sam. 14:36-46.

David's frequent decisions to "inquire of the LORD," at least prior to his downfall in 2 Samuel 11, indicated his desire to follow God's will and not just his own.

# Fourth Sunday in Lent

## Second Reading
## Psalm 23*

# Lead Us, Lord

*Even though I walk through the darkest valley, I fear no evil; for you are with me;*
*your rod and your staff – they comfort me. (Ps. 23:4)*

If we find ourselves struggling and decide to look in our Bible for a comforting passage, chances are we'll end up in the Psalms, with Psalm 23 one of the most likely choices, and for good reason.

Few biblical pictures are more pleasing than the image of God as a shepherd caring for a flock of beloved sheep. **[God as shepherd]** The psalm was probably written at least 2,500 years ago, but its story of trust can also be *our* story. Whether we find ourselves at rest beside the still water, following in the paths of righteousness, or stumbling through valleys of deep shadow, this psalm has a word for us.

### In the pasture
### (vv. 1-3)

Israel's pastoral background made it only natural for a Hebrew poet to picture God as a shepherd. The metaphor identifies the worshiper with the sheep and implies a willingness to follow the shepherd's leading.

In this relationship, the psalmist says, "I shall not want." This is no promise that we will never desire more than we have, but that we will not lack God's care.

The psalmist knew that we all have work to do, for God does not rain manna from heaven when grain fields are available. But he also believed it was God who brought the sun and the rain to bear upon the grain. The Good Shepherd is concerned with our physical, emotional, and spiritual needs.

Fields of green are not always easy to find in the non-irrigated areas of Palestine. Because of the arid conditions, grass may grow only at certain times of the year, or at certain elevations. The shepherd's task includes knowing when and where the grass is growing in the territory he is allowed to use. Once in the fields, the shepherd keeps the flock moving so they will not overgraze any one spot, for the pastures will be needed again.

Sheep, like humans, need water in addition to food. When the dew is heavy, sheep don't need to drink, but as the day goes on, fresh water becomes essential. In the

---

**God as shepherd:** The biblical image of God as a shepherd is not limited to Psalm 23. Jacob's blessing of Joseph, from Gen. 49:24, speaks of God as "the Shepherd, the Stone of Israel."

Other psalms also employed the image. In a deep lament, the author of Psalm 80 cries out "Give ear, O Shepherd of Israel, you who lead Joseph like a flock!" (v. 1). On a happier note, Ps. 100:3 declares "We are his people, and the sheep of his pasture."

Isaiah of the Exile chose the image of God as a shepherd to speak words of comfort to his lost companions, assuring them of God's coming redemption and future care: "Like a shepherd he will tend his flock, in his arm he will gather the lambs, and carry them in the fold of his robe; he will gently lead the nursing ewes" (Isa. 40:11, NASB20).

The portrait of God as shepherd finds completeness in the New Testament, where Jesus took it as his own: "I am the good shepherd; the good shepherd lays down his life for the sheep" (John 10:11). Peter would later refer to Christians as those who had "returned to the Shepherd and Guardian of your souls" (1 Pet. 2:25, cf. 5:4).

---

*\*Psalm 23 is also read on the Fourth Sunday of Easter in Years A, B, and C, and on Proper 23 in Year A and Proper 11 in Year B.*

barren reaches of Palestine, water is as scarce as grass, and is typically found in fast-flowing streams. Sheep may refuse to drink from a moving stream, even if they are desperately thirsty. Because of this, the shepherd must lead the sheep "beside the still waters," literally, "beside waters of rest."

Sheep need more than food and water. Left to their own, they might eat more than is good for their health, even as humans may confuse meeting basic needs with overindulgence or acquiring luxuries. Smart shepherds periodically direct the animals to lie down to chew their cud and promote complete digestion. It would be a stretch to suggest that God brings disease or tragedy to "make us lie down" and take stock of our lives. Still, God can use difficult times to help us reflect on or "digest" what has been happening in our lives, making us stronger and better people.

God not only provides food, water, and guidance, but also "restores my soul," the psalmist said. The word for "restore" is an intensive form of the verb "to (re)turn," and it means "to bring back." The word translated as "soul" is the Hebrew *nefesh*, which speaks of one's whole life, both physical and spiritual.

Sheep are among the world's most stress-prone animals, often in need of reassurance and encouragement. When a shepherd scratches the animal or calls it by name, the sheep's sense of security and belonging increases. In such cases, the shepherd "refreshes the spirit" of the sheep.

In some cases, the shepherd must literally save the life of an animal, rescuing it from being lost, falling into danger, or rolling over and being "cast" so that it can't get up. [**"Cast-aways"**]

Christians should have little difficulty in thinking of ways in which God "restores our soul" or "brings back our

---

life." Christ, the good shepherd, saves us from those things that would "steal, and kill, and destroy" so that we "might have life, and have it to the full" (John 10:10).

Sheep left to their own devices will inevitably wander, as humans also do. Isaiah once declared: "All of us, like sheep, have gone astray, each of us has turned to his own way" (Isa. 53:6). Knowing the sheep need guidance, the shepherd leads them "in the right paths."

The word translated as "right" in v. 3 could mean either "rightness" or "righteousness." The main image is that of a shepherd leading the flock on the right or appropriate paths to get them where they need to go. The shepherd is careful to do this, not only for the sake of the sheep, but also for the sake of his own name and reputation. Who wants to be known as the shepherd who got lost?

When the application is made to persons, it is proper to think of both "right paths" and "righteous paths." As we follow his leading, the Good Shepherd will lead us in right paths – to the places we need to go, to the people we need to help, while also doing what is right.

The Good Shepherd leads us properly "for his name's sake," because that reflects God's nature. Humans cannot walk rightly in their own strength any more than sheep can always choose the correct pathway home.

### In the dark valley
### (v. 4)

A notable shift takes place in v. 4. Instead of speaking *about* God as shepherd ("He leads me," "He restores my soul"), the psalmist begins speaking *to* God: "Even though I walk through the darkest valley, I fear no evil, for *you* are with me – *your* rod and *your* staff, they comfort me."

The author appears to know what a deep, dark valley looks like. This verse may be a personal testimony of bleak times he had known, and of the Good Shepherd's comforting presence.

We must be careful not to divorce v. 4 entirely from the reference to following right paths in v. 3b, however. We may stray into a valley of deep darkness, but even the right path may involve shadowy or dangerous places. [**The dark valley**]

When Middle Eastern shepherds take their sheep to the summer grazing lands, they often go into the mountains, and there are no mountains without valleys,

---

**"Cast-aways":** Stories of sheep becoming lost or falling into dangerous places are familiar. Less familiar is the phenomenon of becoming "cast." Some sheep prefer to lie down in a shallow depression, because it is more comfortable. If a sheep is particularly fat or heavy with wool, it may accidentally roll onto its wide back, and not be able to get up. Sheep in this situation are said to be "cast," and may die unless the shepherd finds them and carefully returns them to an upright position.

**The dark valley:** Israeli tour guides often point to the deep Wadi Qelt – where St. George's Monastery perches against the wall near the bottom – as an image of "the Valley of the shadow of death."

The gorge is so deep and narrow that some parts never see direct sunlight, or do so for only a very brief period each day.

places that may be deep in shadow and frequented by wild animals or thieves. We also will walk in deep, dark valleys – all of us.

Some translations begin v. 4 with *"Even though* I walk…" (NRSV, NASB20), which seems to suggest that walking in dark valleys is only a *possibility*, to be experienced by the unfortunate. The text, however, is open to another translation, for the word *kî* can be rendered as "when" as well as "if."

*"Even when* I walk through the valley…" suggests more certainty, and is closer to our actual experience. None of us can avoid valleys altogether.

Some interpreters make a great deal of the word "through" in the translation "Even though I walk *through* the darkest valley…" (NRSV). The prepositional prefix used can indicate "through," but far more commonly means "in" or "into." There will be at least one valley we will walk *into* but not out from. The psalmist, after all, is talking about "the valley of the shadow of death."

The translation of this term has been the subject of much debate among scholars. The Hebrew expression uses the word for "valley" followed by a compound word (*tsalmawet*) that appears to be formed from the words for "shadow" and "death." A literal translation, then, is the familiar rendering of the King James Version, "valley of the shadow of death" (also NASB20, NIV).

Other translators read the word as a poetic description of deep darkness. Thus, we have versions ranging from the mild "gloomy valley" (Jerusalem Bible) to "darkest valley" (NRSV, NIV11) and "valley of deepest darkness" (*NJPS*, a modern Jewish version). Translators of the *New English Bible* found a way to include both thoughts with "a valley dark as death." None of them sound pleasant.

The important thing about this valley is not how deep or dark or dangerous it is. The significant thing is that *even in* the dark valley, God is with us. "I fear no evil, *for you are with me.*" This is a strong, intensive phrase in Hebrew, reflecting God's promises to the patriarchs. As Jacob undertook the dangerous journey to Haran, for example, Yahweh appeared to him and made this promise: "Know that *I am with you* and will keep you wherever you go…" (Gen. 28:15, see also the promise to Isaac in Gen. 26:3).

There is great power in presence. The timorous sheep can feel safe, even in a dark and dangerous place, because the shepherd is near, and will not desert the flock.

To describe his sense of security, the psalmist says "I will fear no evil." The psalm does not promise that we will face no harm in this life, only that we need not *fear* it. The Lord who is present with us has ultimate power over all that is evil.

The shepherd analogy concludes with a reference to two potent sticks that shepherds typically carried. The "rod" was a club that could be used to fend off predators or thrown to frighten them away.

The "staff" calls to mind a tall walking stick the shepherd might use to guide a sheep's direction, or to scratch its stomach in a show of affection.

God's rod and staff call to mind discipline, protection, and guidance. The beauty of nature, the love of friends, and the touch of the Spirit all speak of God's presence.

### At the table
### (vv. 5-6)

With v. 5, there is another dramatic shift. The author no longer speaks from the perspective of a sheep, but as a guest in God's house, where Yahweh is no longer the ideal shepherd, but the perfect host. Preparing a table, anointing with oil, and filling the cup are all clear images of a joyful meal in which the psalmist finds himself an honored guest at the Lord's table. [**Table, or tablelands?**]

> **Table, or tablelands?** Some interpreters ignore the shift from shepherd to host in vv. 5-6, stretching the language to retain the pastoral metaphor. Phillip Keller, for instance, speaks of the shepherd taking his sheep to the high "table-lands," where he "prepares the table" by removing poisonous weeds from the pasture. Furthermore, he explains "You anoint my head with oil" as a reference to the shepherd's provision of ointments to protect the sheep from flies and infections. This makes impressive devotional reading, but probably stretches and misses the point of the original text. (A *Shepherd Looks at Psalm 23* [Zondervan, 1970], 105-106, 114-119).

The poet paints a remarkable picture. God has not only "set in order" a table before him but has done so in the very presence of hostile opponents. While the image is different, the verse carries forward the same themes found in the previous verses: God provides not only food and rest, but also protection.

The joy of this special fellowship is indicated by the reference to anointing with scented oil. Literally, the phrase means "you make fat, with oil, my head"! Anointing oil was often scented (Exod. 25:6), and was used to set apart priests or kings (Exod. 28:41, 29:7; 1 Sam. 10:1, 16:13; Ps. 133:1-2), as well as to greet guests (Luke 7:46).

Oil is sometimes used in scripture as a symbol of joy. As Job recalled his days of blessing, he spoke of oil gushing from the rocks (Job 29:6), and when Isaiah proclaimed the Lord's coming deliverance, he spoke of how God would give the people of Israel "a garland instead of ashes, the oil of gladness instead of mourning..." (Isa. 61:3).

In praising the new king, one of the psalmists exulted: "God, your God, has anointed you with the oil of gladness beyond your companions" (Ps. 45:7, cf. Heb. 1:9). A hymn in praise of unity asserts "How very good and pleasant it is when kindred live together in unity! It is like precious oil on the head, running down upon the beard, on the beard of Aaron, running down over the collar of his robes" (Ps. 133:1-2, NRSV).

It is this image that the psalmist evokes when he speaks of sitting at God's table, being welcomed into God's extravagant hospitality with the anointing oil of gladness.

The final picture also echoes the theme: the psalmist's joy, symbolized by an overflowing cup of wine, has filled him to the point of spiritual satiation. **[A cup of joy]**

Having reflected on God's past provision and present fellowship, the psalmist turned toward the future, using an intriguing metaphor: the goodness and the steadfast love of God would "follow" him throughout his life.

This picture is comforting. Some interpreters like the impressive image of God going *before* the psalmist to the green pastures, walking *beside* him in the dark valley, and following *behind* him (in goodness and love) throughout life.

Another image is also appealing. The word translated "follow after me" derives from the verb that most commonly means "to pursue," or "to chase." God's dependable goodness and steadfast love not only *follow* us into the future but also *chase* us into closer fellowship.

Some writers interpret "house of the LORD" as a strict reference to the temple, suggesting that the psalmist intends to establish his permanent residence there. This view misses the point: the poet is not just talking about a place, but confidently expressing his hope of future fellowship with God, a fellowship based not on his own goodness but on the goodness and love of God.

This confidence in the future extends as far as the psalmist can imagine: forever.

Psalm 23 begins and ends on a note of confident joy in the presence of God. This joy is not fleeting or temporary, like a butterfly that we see and delight in for a short time. We know the joy of God's presence through the Spirit of Christ, who called himself "the Good Shepherd." God's caring pursuit of the beloved flock will last as long as time itself.

> **A cup of joy:** Wine, like oil, could signify joy (though the "cup of wrath" image is also common). Qoheleth spoke of "drinking wine with joy" (Eccl. 9:7), while both Isaiah and Jeremiah proclaimed the loss of joy in Israel by the image of vineyards that produced no wine. According to John's gospel, Jesus' first great sign was the turning of water into wine, which brought joy to the guests at the wedding feast (John 2:10-11).
>
> The joyful effects of drinking wine can also be likened to the presence of God's Spirit, if negatively: "do not get drunk with wine," Paul said, "but be filled with the Spirit" (Eph. 5:18). The author of Psalm 23 knew what it was like to touch the Spirit of God. His life was saturated with the presence, the power, and the provision of Yahweh, his heavenly host. As a result, he could celebrate: "my cup overflows."

### The Hardest Question
### What does it mean that God's "goodness and mercy shall follow me"?

God's "goodness" is here denoted by the very common word *tôv*. *Tôv* can be used in many senses, from adjectives such as "good" and "beautiful" to the comparative "better" and the noun form "goodness." *Tôv* may have either a qualitative (good vs. poor) or moral (good vs. evil) sense.

Many scriptures insist that God is good, that creation reflects the divine goodness, and that God's goodness continues to sustain the earth and humankind.

As God is good, God's people are called to be good. Throughout the "Deuteronomistic History" (Deuteronomy–2 Kings, minus Ruth), Israel's fortunes rose and fell on the basis of whether the people and their leaders chose to obey God and do good, or to reject God's way and follow evil.

Wisdom literature such as the book of Proverbs uniformly upholds the virtue of goodness, even as the prophets habitually exhort the people to do good, and not evil. At least one prophet took a stab at defining the goodness that is expected of God's people: "He has told you, O mortal, what is good; and what does the Lord require of you, but to do justice, and to love kindness, and to walk humbly with your God?" (Mic. 6:8, NRSV).

The word translated as "mercy" is *chesed*, a special word denoting a special kind of love, so rich in meaning that we have difficulty expressing it in one English word.

The basic meaning of *chesed* is "love," but there are also elements of "kindness," "mercy," "loyalty," or "steadfastness." A common translation is "lovingkindness."

God declared God's nature to Moses with this term: "Yahweh, Yahweh, a god merciful and gracious, slow to anger, and abounding in steadfast love (*chesed*) and faithfulness, keeping steadfast love (*chesed*) for the thousandth generation..." (Exod. 34:6-7a; cp. Num. 14:8-9, Neh. 9:17, Ps. 103:8, Joel 2:13, Jon. 4:2).

*Chesed*, then, refers to the love of God in all its richness, a love that is steadfast and enduring. The word is used to describe Hosea, who pursued his chosen Gomer with a love that was steadfast, despite her less-than-faithful response. "I will take you for my wife forever," he said, "I will take you for my wife in righteousness and in justice, in steadfast love (*chesed*), and in mercy (Hos. 2:19, NRSV).

Throughout the Old Testament, God pursues Israel with steadfast love, despite the people's unfaithfulness. In the New Testament, Jesus demonstrates God's faithful love on the cross. This demonstration of his love motivates us to love him in return: "We love him, because he first loved us" (1 John 4:19).

Like the psalmist, we are also pursued by the abundant goodness and the steadfast love of God. These terms are often combined in the writings of those who would offer praise to God: "Give thanks to the Lord, for he is good; for his steadfast love endures forever" (Ps. 106:1, 136:1; 1 Chron. 16:34; Jer. 33:11).

Because of love, God does not give up on us. God pursues us gently with blessings of goodness and the appeal of steadfast love. The poet recognizes that this is not a brief chase, but a life-long relationship. He believes that as long as he lives, wherever he goes, God's goodness and steadfast love will be close behind, pushing him toward God's love and care.

## Third Reading
## Ephesians 5:8-14

# Illuminated Fruit

*For once you were darkness, but now in the Lord you are light. Live as children of light … (Eph. 5:8)*

The season of Lent is a most appropriate time to focus on overcoming old, sinful behaviors, and replacing them with positive behaviors that bring goodness into the world.

What a struggle this is – try as we might, favorite sins keep popping up. Familiar ways of thinking are chemically hard-wired into our brain. Making lifestyle changes is a lifelong task.

The young Christians in Ephesus faced a similar problem, for they came from a largely pagan background, and Paul saw how they struggled toward maturity.

The city of Ephesus supported a substantial industry in making images of a goddess known to the Greeks as Artemis (Acts 19:23-41) and to the Romans as Diana. In Greek mythology, Artemis was the sister of Apollo and the daughter of Zeus. She was known as the goddess of wild nature and of huntsmen, and she was often depicted in the company of mountain and forest nymphs.

Ancient gods were not as static as one might expect. They were ascribed varying characteristics in different regions. The syncretistic version of Artemis worshiped in Ephesus also bore some of the characteristics of Semitic fertility goddesses such as Astarte and Ishtar, or the Phrygian goddess Cybele. She was worshipped as a nature goddess in control of the earth's fertility. While Greek and Roman art depicted Artemis as a beautiful and shapely young woman, Artemis of Ephesus was typically sculpted as a woman whose entire torso was covered with breasts or breast-shaped appendages. Her cult was so influential that the Ephesians celebrated a month-long festival, called the "Artemesion," in her honor. [**Artemis of Ephesus**]

**Artemis of Ephesus:** A magnificent temple to Artemis stood on the outskirts of Ephesus, so impressive that it was known as one of the Seven Wonders of the Ancient World. The temple was rebuilt several times, with the final version being about 450 feet long and 225 feet wide, with an impressive roof supported by more than 127 massive columns. The temple was damaged or destroyed by the Goths in 268 CE. Many of its columns and statues were carried away for use elsewhere, including the famed Hagia Sophia in Constantinople (now Istanbul). Today, all that remains to mark the site is one column pieced together from dissociated fragments found at the site. The image pictured, now in the Ephesus Archaeological Museum, once decorated the Temple of Artemis in Ephesus. (Wikimedia Commons)

It is no wonder that Paul worked so hard to draw his Ephesian readers away from their former religions and toward a new life directed by Christ. Artemis was only one of many gods who were worshiped in Ephesus, and none of them were associated with morality or ethics in the manner of Christianity.

Today we would be hard-pressed to find modern Christians bowing before a goddess named Artemis, but we may be just as devoted to sensuality. The image of Artemis with her many breasts could be an appropriate metaphor for our sex-obsessed society. Paul's message to the Ephesians applies to modern believers, too.

### From darkness to light
### (v. 8)

Today's text is one of several occasions in which Paul urged the Ephesians to leave their former way of life behind and to behave as mature Christians. In 4:17-24, Paul had focused on the image of the old and the new: "You were taught to put away your former way of life, your old self, corrupt and deluded by its lusts, and to be renewed in the spirit of your minds, and to clothe yourselves with the new self, created according to the likeness of God in true righteousness and holiness" (4:22-24).

Paul then challenged the believers to speak truth to one another (4:25), to control their anger (4:26-27), to do honest work instead of stealing (4:28-29), to speak positively instead of negatively (4:30), and to overcome bitter wrath with kindness and forgiveness (4:30-32) as imitators of Christ (5:1-2).

The list of behaviors to avoid continued in vv. 3-7. It includes fornication, greed, impurity of any kind, and obscene or vulgar language. Those verses set the stage for today's text, in which Paul continues to contrast the old and new way of life through the metaphor of darkness and light: "For once you were darkness, but now in the Lord you are light. Live as children of light ..." (v. 8). [**Darkness and light**]

The use of darkness and light as theological or philosophical metaphors was common in the ancient world. Paul would have been familiar with the Essenes, who made it a central tenet of their theological system. They thought of themselves as the "sons of light," while all others were the "sons of darkness."

---

**Darkness and light:** Most people have a tendency to adjust their behavior to the situation in which they find themselves. Whether we tell a dirty joke or drink to excess or participate in harmful gossip often depends entirely on whom we are with.

Whether a student succeeds or fails in college depends largely on the values of the company he or she keeps. Whether young people or even adults are able to resist the pressures related to harmful or risky behaviors depends largely on the company they keep.

Knowing the influence of others, Paul encouraged seeking out good companions and following their lead. This is not to say that we cannot work at being a good influence to those who behave badly, but we don't look for approval or support from them any more than we seek high ground in a swamp. Instead, we walk in the light that comes from Christ.

---

"Once you were in darkness," Paul says. Before coming to Christ, the Ephesians had lived the same misguided lives as their neighbors. "But now in the Lord," he says, "you are light." Those who come to Christ have come to the "light of the world" (John 8:12), and thus are called to live in his light (1 John 1:7). God has transferred them from the dominion of darkness to the kingdom of Christ (Col. 1:13).

As he often does, Paul now moves from the indicative to the imperative. Indeed, as the late New Testament scholar Malcolm Tolbert used to say, it is the indicative that makes possible the imperative. "But now in the Lord, you are light," Paul says, so "live as children of light." The word translated as "live" (*peripateō*) literally means "to walk about," implying that we are to reflect Christ's light as we go about each day. To walk in the light is to live according to the truth revealed by the light (cf. Matt. 5:16, Phil. 2:15).

If we were to mentally list our favorite behaviors, would they suggest darkness, or light?

### From bad fruit to good
### (vv. 9-13)

The evidence of walking in the light is this, Paul says: a life filled with those things that are good and right and true (v. 9). The Greek words are all nouns rather than adjectives: goodness and righteousness and truth. They mean just what they say, and they suggest that Paul was especially concerned with issues of morality and ethics.

As Paul spoke elsewhere of the "fruit of the Spirit" (Gal. 5:22), these could be called the "fruit of the light."

Walking in the light is not an automatic response for humans. It is not what comes naturally. Therefore, believers must consciously "try to find out what is pleasing to the Lord" (v. 10). "Try to find out" translates a word that means something like "to prove by testing," or "to find out from experience." It takes an effort to learn what is pleasing to God, but Paul believed it was also a Christian responsibility (cp. Rom. 12:2, 14:8; 2 Cor. 5:9; 1 Thess. 4:1; Col. 3:20).

We do not learn what pleases God by living in isolation or by contemplating abstract ideas, but by fully engaging life and responding to what it brings to us, and to do so every day. As we confront each new situation, Paul would have us to ask the question "Would this please God?" Those who make the effort of raising the right questions are much more likely to make the right responses.

While Paul points out the good fruit of the light in v. 9, he insists that the realm of darkness is inherently "unfruitful," since nothing comes of darkness but death. Those who learn to do what pleases God will avoid participating in the unfruitful works of darkness. Instead, they will seek to expose those works for the shams that they are.

How are we to do this? Preachers sometimes think to "expose the works of darkness" means to call out from the pulpit those practices they judge to be immoral. For this reason, many persons think of the word "preach" as having a negative, judgmental connotation. But do public descriptions of lurid behavior accomplish anything more than feeding our own prurient interest in what we condemn?

Paul said "it is shameful even to mention what such people do secretly" (v. 12). By publicizing the "secret sins" of others, we may add credibility to unhealthy practices, and may even plant the seed of temptation in the minds of our hearers. To the Romans, Paul suggested that even speaking against something could tempt the hearer to try it (7:7-11).

There are times when it is necessary to speak specifically about evil – after all, Paul often does – but the best way to expose wickedness is not by emphasizing the darkness, but by magnifying the light (v. 13). Those who live in the light reveal by their good example what a pitiful alternative the darkness is.

### From death to life
### (v. 14)

Paul reminded the Ephesian Christians that they had once lived in darkness, but they had been transformed by the light and brought into its realm. The light of God had the power not only to expose their former wickedness, but also to transform their lives into goodness and light.

Paul then quoted from what may have been a hymn as a reminder of his point: "Sleeper, awake! Rise from the dead, and Christ will shine on you" (v. 14b).

The quotation must have been familiar to Paul's readers. He introduces it ("Therefore it says") in the same way he normally introduced Old Testament quotations, but it is not in the Hebrew Bible. Perhaps Paul was quoting from a hymn typically used during baptismal services, since Christian baptism symbolized a dying to the old self and rising from the dead to a new way of life. **[Rise and shine]**

By using the quotation here, Paul challenges his readers to remember their baptism and to reaffirm their commitment to leaving darkness behind for a new life of walking in the light.

Paul's charge may lead us to reflect on our own baptism and the challenges it set before us. Do we consciously seek to "die to the old self" and live as a new person in Christ? When we meet someone new, what do they see in us: the darkness of self-oriented living, or the light of Christ?

---

**Rise and shine:** Paul's quotation ("Sleeper awake! Rise from the dead, and Christ will shine on you") has no exact corollary in the Old Testament, and could hardly do so, since it specifically mentions Christ.

The quote does, however, call to mind a similar charge from Isaiah 60, in which the post-exilic prophet was encouraging a downcast people to trust in God for deliverance, saying: "Arise, shine; for your light has come, and the glory of the LORD has risen upon you" (Isa. 60:1).

The prophet went on to highlight the difference between the darkness of the world and the light God can bring: "For darkness shall cover the earth, and thick darkness the peoples; but the LORD will arise upon you, and his glory will appear over you. Nations shall come to your light, and kings to the brightness of your dawn" (Isa. 60:2-3).

## The Hardest Question
### What does it mean to be fully awake?

More than 20 years ago, when I served as a pastor, one of our kindest and most supportive church members was a man named Bob Goode, who worked for many years as a Christian education consultant. Bob did not publish many things, but he was a gifted writer, and he shared some of his thoughtful pieces with me.

How can we be truly awake to the light of God? Bob once asked that question in an essay he wrote following a serious illness. In taking his departure from a popular bedtime prayer for children, Bob wrote:

I was in the hospital in the midst of a life-threatening illness when one evening I found myself saying inwardly the little prayer's most poignant line: 'If I should die before I wake.' Suddenly, I knew that what was troubling me was not so much the thought of dying – but of dying before I had fully waked from the slumber of my life. I realized that what the prayer says is: "Wake up and live, for time is flying." I promised myself passionately that never again would I take a moment of life for granted.

In that flash of illumination, I thought of what a profound word "waking" is, how close to the roots of life. The dictionary says that "to awaken" means not only to "be roused from sleep," but also "to rise to action." In short, it is to be born again into life.

The adult, like the child, should rise from sleep with spring in his heart; should, and so rarely does. Suppose we counted how many hours there were in a recent week when we moved about like children, antenna out for the winds of heaven, touching, hearing, looking, as though morning had just dawned on the earth for the first time. How many would there be? ...

... to be awake ... is the task of all of us before we die. But few people live their lives so. Instead, we drift along on the surface of things, dazed and confused like dreamers, only half alive. Then, there comes a day when the shortness of time is upon us like a dark end. What we hoped to do with our lives has not been done; the things we wanted to say have not been said; the people to whom we wanted to express our love have never received it; the wrongs we have done have not been made up for; the talents we have, have not been used.

It almost seems as though we have done it on purpose, as though drifting is what we really want. But it is not. What we really want is to live while we live. We want to wake before we die

... Inevitably we live between light and dark, life and death. Daily we come out of the thicket of darkness, live in the bright bowl of the sun and return again to the fall of night. "Now I lay me down to sleep."

When we have lived a day richly and warmly, running in the sunlight, laughing and loving, then night comes sweetly and without regret. Perhaps that other night, that longer night we call death, will come sweetly, too, if we have spent our life so that it blessed us and the others around us; come sweetly and bring, like all the nights we've known, a new and fresh awaking.

To live each day to the full, to live in the light, to make the most of every present moment while remembering we are citizens of eternity: that is what it means to be awake, to live in the light, to "redeem the time."

# Fourth Sunday in Lent

## Fourth Reading
## John 9

# Before and After

*He answered, "I do not know whether he is a sinner. One thing I do know,*
*that though I was blind, now I see." (John 9:25)*

Sight is precious to those who have it. We try to imagine living in darkness, unable to see, navigating by touch and memory, and we thank God for functioning eyes. Some people who cannot see are so well adapted that they might say they prefer it that way, but most of us find it hard to envision life without sight. We not only want to see, but to see well, so we do not hesitate to spend what is necessary for corrective lenses or surgeries that can make our vision as clear as possible.

Jesus' contemporaries likewise valued sight, and people who lacked vision often spent their lives sitting by a frequently traveled road, trusting the pity of passersby to drop sufficient alms for them to survive. If they could not find another way to be productive or earn money, they could beg.

Such was the man we meet in today's text: he was known to all as a blind beggar. Many people saw only his disability, but Jesus saw more.

### Seeing through mud
### (vv. 1-7)

The story takes place in Jerusalem, where Jesus and his disciples encountered a sightless man who became the talking point for a theological question. First-century Jews, like Hebrews of the Old Testament period, held to a covenant theology that promised prosperity to the faithful and threatened trouble for sinners, and they were not alone. Greeks and Romans of the period also held to similar ideas, thinking that persons with disabilities harbored some measure of darkness. In short, many believed that people got what they deserved: if someone

was troubled or afflicted in some way, it must have been the result of somebody's sin.

Perhaps it was not surprising, then, that the disciples asked Jesus whether the man's blindness was due to his own sin or that of his parents (vv. 1-2).

Jesus never endorsed the idea that trouble was always the result of sin. In Luke 13:1-6, for example, he countered public opinion that the murder of worshipers in the temple or deaths from a tower's collapse could be blamed on the victims' sin. In this case, Jesus responded that the man's blindness was not due to anyone's sin, but "he was born blind so that God's works might be revealed in him" (v. 3).

This statement could sound even more troubling than the idea that sin was deserved. Did God cause the man to suffer many years of blindness just so Jesus could heal him? Those who hold a firm view of providence may believe that nothing happens by chance, and that God causes everything that happens for God's own mysterious purposes.

We should not read such a fatalistic doctrine into Jesus' response. Indeed, a better understanding of the Greek manuscripts behind our text offers an obvious solution. Alicia Myers notes that the Greek manuscripts were written without punctuation, which was added later. Rather than putting a period at the end of v. 3, v. 4 should be seen as completing the thought of the previous verse. She offers the resulting translation: "Jesus answered, 'Neither this one sinned nor his parents, but so that the works of God might be revealed to him it is necessary for us to work the works of the one who sent me while it is daytime. Night is coming when no one is able to work'"

**The Pool of Siloam:** The Pool of Siloam was a large reservoir that was constantly refreshed by water from the strong Gihon Spring, which flowed underground through Hezekiah's Tunnel and emerged at the pool in the southeast area of Jerusalem, part of the original city. Half of the pool has been excavated, and visitors today can sit on the same steps that led into the pool, which was 225 ft. (69 m.) wide, with ranks of five steps on at least three sides of the pool. The unexcavated portion is beneath land owned by a Greek Orthodox Church built on the traditional site of the "King's Garden" mentioned in Neh. 3:15.

(*Reading John and 1, 2, 3 John: A Literary and Theological Commentary* [Smyth & Helwys, 2019], 193-94).

Jesus was not saying that divine purpose had caused the man's blindness, but his affliction provided an opportunity to do God's work: Jesus saw himself as one who had been sent "to bring good news to the poor ... to proclaim release to the captives and recovery of sight to the blind, to let the oppressed go free, to proclaim the year of the Lord's favor" (Luke 4:18-19).

God can bring something good even from our difficult times, but that doesn't mean that God caused the trial. Sometimes we bring trouble on ourselves. Sometimes things just happen. It happened that this man had been born blind, and came to the attention of Jesus, who was determined to "work the works of him who sent me while it is day" (v. 4). As the light of the world, Jesus was determined to live out his calling (v. 5).

Jesus often healed by word alone, but at other times, and for his own purposes, he chose to use symbolic actions or touch. Here, echoing in some ways a similar story in Mark 8:22-26, he spat on the ground, made a bit of mud, and spread it on the man's eyes, telling him to go and wash in the Pool of Siloam, which must have been nearby. The

man could not see, but he could hear. He followed Jesus' instructions, and for the first time in his life, he could see (vv. 6-7). [**The Pool of Siloam**]

Spit was a common ingredient in ancient medicinal potions, but neither the spit nor the mud effected the man's healing: his eyes were not healed until he heard and obeyed Jesus' word.

## Refusing to see
### (vv. 8-34)

After v. 7, Jesus departs from the scene and the story focuses entirely on the blind man and several rounds of questioning and testimony. The man makes known his new condition, but some people who had known him only as a blind man could not recognize him as a sighted person. Perhaps they simply couldn't believe the same man could now see, though he insisted "I am he!" and explained to them what Jesus had done (vv. 8-12).

When Jesus makes a real difference in our lives, others may have trouble believing we are the same person. Unlike the blind man, though, we know how to tell them where Jesus can be found.

Unsatisfied with the man's explanation, some of his neighbors took him to the Pharisees for further examination. Only then did we learn that this had taken place on the Sabbath, when making a bit of mud and applying to someone's eyes would have been considered "work" (vv. 13-15).

Some among the Pharisees, the author says, could not accept that Jesus could have been from God because he did not "keep the Sabbath" according to the strict rules of the oral law. Others couldn't imagine how Jesus could have done such a work unless he was somehow connected with God, so "they were divided" (vv. 16-17).

Having no unified opinion of their own, they asked the newly sighted man's opinion. The man – the only one in the room to have experienced Jesus' power – voiced his belief that Jesus was a prophet (v. 17). The following exchange did not go well.

Unsatisfied with the man's story and perhaps suspecting him of fraud, the man's questioners called his parents to testify that he had indeed been born blind. This suggests that the man may have been relatively young. Not only were his parents alive and available, but they also felt it necessary to point out that their son was "of age" and old enough to speak for himself (vv. 18-21).

Fearing retribution from the Pharisees and having no personal knowledge of their son's healing beyond his testimony, they offered no opinion as to who had healed him or whether he should be considered a prophet. The author explained, in an editorial comment, that this was because "the Jews had already agreed that anyone who confessed Jesus to be the Messiah would be put out of the synagogue" (vv. 22-23).

This led to a second round, in which the interrogators accused Jesus of being a sinner and pressed the man to agree with them. Apparently, making eye-sized patches of mud on the Sabbath was considered sufficient for the charge of being a sinner. The man responded with words that have rung through the years in both sermons and song: "I do not know whether he is a sinner. One thing I do know, that though I was blind, now I see" (vv. 24-25).

**[Once I was blind]**

The inquisition continued with a request for more details. "What did he do to you? How did he open your eyes?" (v. 26). Having explained it once already, and perhaps growing impatient, the man grew impertinent: "Why do you want to hear it again? Do you also want to become his disciples?" (v. 27).

That was more than the investigating committee could take. They "reviled him," the author said, using a sharp word that could mean "to rail at," "heap insults upon," "slander," or other indications of verbal abuse. They accused the man of being a disciple of Jesus (the accused sinner) while insisting that they were disciples of Moses, the hero of their faith. Moses they knew, believing that God had spoken to him the teachings they had followed

---

**Once I was blind:** Perhaps the most memorable hymnic recollection of today's text is in Phillip Bliss' hymn from 1875, "The Light of the World Is Jesus." The hymn speaks of the world being lost in darkness and sin, with a chorus that appeals for response:

> Come to the light, 'tis shining for thee,
> Sweetly the light has dawned upon me.
> Once I was blind, but now I can see,
> The light of the world is Jesus!

---

for more than a thousand years. As for the upstart Jesus – whose name they declined to speak – "we do not know where he comes from" (vv. 28-29).

Insulted but unwilling to surrender, the young man fired back with impunity, as if teaching the teachers. He found it "astonishing" that a man could heal his blindness, but the religious experts knew nothing about him. He then contradicted their foundational charge that Jesus was a sinner. "We know that God does not listen to sinners, but he does listen to one who worships him and obeys his will" (vv. 30-31).

The man believed that his healing had been God's will. Jesus had done the healing, so Jesus could hardly be a sinner. "Never since the world began has it been heard that anyone opened the eyes of a person born blind," he said. "If this man were not from God, he could do nothing" (vv. 32-33).

The man's argument was sound, but it fell on deaf ears. Still holding to their belief that the man's blindness had been a form of punishment, they pronounced "You were born entirely in sins, and are you trying to teach us?" That concluded the discussion: "And they drove him out" (v. 34).

While his parents played mum to preserve their standing in the synagogue, their newly sighted son was given the boot. The verb, from 'ekballō, literally means "to throw out."

## Seeing is believing
### (vv. 35-41)

Only then did Jesus re-enter the picture. Hearing what had happened, he went looking for the man and entered a much friendlier conversation, one that allowed the man to express both his questions and his emerging faith. He had first met Jesus as a man who put mud on his eyes and told him to wash in the Pool of Siloam (v. 7), then saw him as "a man called Jesus" (v. 11). Before the Pharisees, he defended him as a prophet (v. 17). He concluded that Jesus must be from God (v. 33), and ultimately, after hearing Jesus' testimony about himself, confessed "Lord, I believe" as he worshiped him (vv. 35-38).

The closing verses bring Jesus and the Pharisees together. Jesus observed to his new disciple that "I came into this world for judgment so that those who do not see may see, and those who do see may become blind" (v. 39).

The charge was not lost on the Pharisees, who responded "Surely we are not blind, are we?" (v. 40).

They apparently failed to catch the metaphor. The blindness Jesus spoke of was not related to eyesight or ignorance, but the willful refusal to see the truth in Jesus' teaching. "If you were blind," he said to them, "you would not have sin. But now that you say, 'We see,' your sin remains" (v. 41).

This story of contrasts and inversions leads us to ask, "Who is blind?" and "Who can see?" When Jesus is in view, the answer is clear.

### The Hardest Question
### Where does the story end?

While we often assume that the end of ch. 9 concludes the story, some scholars argue that it should be seen as a prelude to Jesus' discussion of himself as the Good Shepherd in the following chapter, which occurs on the same day, the last day of Tabernacles (stories about that day begin at 7:37). Karoline M. Lewis, for example, notes that Jesus does not stop talking at the end of ch. 9. She sees ch. 10 as Jesus' own comment and interpretation of the events in ch. 9, following the gospel of John's typical pattern of having Jesus perform a "sign" that is followed by dialogue and discussion of its theological significance.

In ch. 9, the blind man listens to Jesus and obeys his command to wash in the Pool of Siloam (vv. 7-8), result-ing in his healing. After the lengthy dialogue with the synagogue officials, he hears Jesus' challenge to believe in him as the Son of Man, and does so (vv. 36-38). In this sense he comes to know Jesus through personal experience and relationship.

The image of the shepherd and the sheep in the following chapter provides an interpretive framework in which the formerly blind man is an example of a sheep who knows Jesus, hears his voice, and enters the sheepfold as a disciple. Jesus, like the shepherd, found the man after he had been thrown out of the synagogue, his former spiritual home.

As Lewis puts it, Jesus "provides for him what he, as the good shepherd, gives all of his sheep: the protection of his fold (10:16; cf. also 21:15-19), the blessing of needed pasture (10:9), and the gift of abundant life (10:10). As a result, hearing and seeing are much more than ways by which one recognizes or believes in Jesus. They are, in fact, expressions of relationship with Jesus, and relationship with Jesus means also relationship with the Father (10:14-15)" (*Feasting on the Word, Year A*, ed. David L. Bartlett and Barbara Brown Taylor, vol. 2 of Accordance electronic ed. [Westminster John Knox Press, 2010], para. 7373).

Reading chs. 9 and 10 together emphasize the importance of hearing as well as seeing. Instead of being the beneficiary of an isolated miracle, the man born blind becomes an integral illustration of a sheep who follows the shepherd and knows the shepherd's care.

## First Reading
## Ezekiel 37:1-14[*]

# A New Life

*Then he said to me, "Prophesy to these bones, and say to them: O dry bones, hear the word of the LORD." (Ezek. 37:4)*

As the season of Lent grows longer and Easter nears, the familiar story of the dry bones from Ezekiel 37 recalls the spiritual desiccation we may also experience, and the hope of a rattling renewal.

The story is set in exile, among a disillusioned people who had been forced to leave their homes and march hundreds of miles before being assigned to resettlement camps in a new land.

The people in question were the most wealthy, educated, or skilled residents of Judah. When their king grew tired of paying the annual tribute demanded by King Nebuchadnezzar, the Babylonian army showed up to take both payment and people. King Jehoiachin and an initial wave of royals and other elites were taken captive in 597 BCE, though Jerusalem was spared.

Nebuchadnezzar appointed Zedekiah to replace Jehoiachin, expecting him to be more loyal, but a decade later he also withheld payment. The armies returned and destroyed Jerusalem before putting many more residents on the long march to Babylon. Only the poorest of the people were left to work the land.

It's hard to imagine how we would feel in a similar position, losing all we know and facing an uncertain future. The prophet Ezekiel knew how it felt.

### A moribund people
### (vv. 1-3)

Ezekiel's prophetic activity began during the earliest years of the exile, but he was no ordinary prophet. Most classical prophets were outsiders who spoke truth to power,

---

**Who was Ezekiel?** Ezekiel was unlike any other prophet. While most prophetic books were the work of disciples who described their teacher's prophetic activity in a biographical form, Ezekiel's words are written in the first person, as an autobiography.

More to the point, Ezekiel's words and actions undoubtedly led many of his hearers to regard him as a certified lunatic. In addition to his fantastic visions, Ezekiel seems to have adopted certain outlandish behaviors for prophetic purpose, some of which seem physically impossible. In 4:1-15, for example, Ezekiel said he was instructed to lie on the ground on his left side for 390 days without getting up, then switch to his right side for 40 more days. For the duration, he was to point his finger at a model of Jerusalem under siege and prophesy against it while also grinding assorted grains to make his own bread, to be baked over a fire fueled by cow's dung.

Prophesy was not an easy task, for Ezekiel or for others. Many years before, Isaiah reportedly went naked for three years to symbolize Israel's future fall (Isa. 20:1-5), and Jeremiah walked around wearing a wooden yoke (Jeremiah 27–28) as a sign of their coming bondage. Apparently, extreme methods were required to draw attention to their message.

---

whether people, priests, or kings. Ezekiel, however, was an insider. He had been part of the powerful priestly circle when the Babylonians deported them to southern Babylon in 597 BCE. Ezekiel and other Jews were assigned quarters in a town that came to be known as Tel-Abib, not far from the city of Nippur (3:15). The town was near the Chebar, a tributary or canal associated with the Euphrates River.

In the fifth year of his time in exile, or 593 BCE (1:2), Ezekiel was overwhelmed by a vision from God that

---

[*]*This text is also read on the Day of Pentecost in Year B.*

**Dry bones:** Ezekiel's vision of dry bones may reflect curses that were typical of ancient treaties between a conquering king and vassal nations. Any who rebelled against the ruling king were to be cursed not only by death, but also by having their bodies exposed to the elements rather than honorably buried. Assyrian kings such as Esarhaddon and Ashurbanipal often boasted of how they had defeated enemies and piled up their corpses, not allowing them to be buried. The dry bones could be seen as symbolic of Israel's punishment for breaking the covenant with God (see Margaret S. Odell, *Ezekiel*, Smyth & Helwys Bible Commentary [Smyth & Helwys, 2005], 450, citing F.C. Fensham, "The Curse of the Dry Bones in Ezekiel 37:1-14 Changed to a Blessing of Resurrection," *Journal of Northwest Semitic Languages* 13 [1987]: 59–60).

Ancient Hebrews believed that all people went to a shadowy land called Sheol after death, but still retained a tenuous contact with what remained of their bodies. Funerary inscriptions often warned potential grave robbers that they would be cursed if they disturbed the bones of the tomb's inhabitants. The thought of one's bones lying exposed to vultures and to the sun would have been exceedingly unpleasant.

changed his life and set him on a course of prophetic activity for at least the next 22 years. Prophecies in the book are often precisely dated, with the last one being in the 27th year of his exile, or 571 BCE (29:7). **[Who was Ezekiel?]**

Ezekiel's fellow exiles may have considered him to be highly eccentric, and not just because he incorporated the roles of both priest and prophet – two groups that didn't usually get along. Ezekiel's inaugural vision of God was filled with fiery wheels, strange creatures, and a rainbow aura surrounding a flying sapphire throne – so strange that some modern writers have claimed he was visited by an alien spaceship. Would we have believed Ezekiel?

Ezekiel preached more than doom. He came to believe that God had not given up on Israel, and he sought to assure the exiles that God had something good in store for them: "A new heart I will give you, and a new spirit I will put within you," he prophesied, "… and I will remove from your body the heart of stone and give you a heart of flesh. I will put my spirit within you, and make you follow my statutes and be careful to observe my ordinances" (36:26-27).

That sounded hopeful, but the people remained morose. They were allowed to live independently and

participated in the Babylonian economy, but many Hebrews still longed for their homeland, especially during the first years, before the generation of adults who had been captured had begun to die out. If v. 11 is an accurate reflection, the exiles were saying things such as "Our bones are dried up, and our hope is lost; we are cut off completely" (v. 11). **[Dry bones]**

It's no surprise, then, that God would show Ezekiel a vision of hope that began with a valley of dry bones. While Ezekiel tells the story as an actual event, phrases such as "the hand of the LORD was upon me" suggest a visionary experience taking place in a trance-like state (see also 1:3, 3:22, 8:1, 40:1). The story describes a symbolic vision, not a mass resurrection.

Ezekiel speaks of being brought to a valley filled with disarticulated skeletons. There were "very many" bones, and they were "very dry" (v. 2), indicating that their owners were also very dead. Inhabitants of the ancient Near East sought to be buried or placed in secure tombs where their bones could remain together. The thought of having one's skeleton scattered across the land would have been innately disturbing.

The image suggests the aftermath of a battlefield where thousands had been slain (vv. 9-10), perhaps suggesting both Judah's defeat by the Babylonians and the Northern Kingdom's earlier destruction by the Assyrians.

Overlooking a lifeless and apparently hopeless scene, Ezekiel was asked: "Mortal, can these bones live?" A modern scientist might envision a way to extract DNA from the bones and at least replicate the genome, but

**Lord GOD:** Attentive readers will note the unusual appearance of "Lord GOD," when "LORD God" is far more common. The difference is this: translators use uppercase letters to indicate the divine name *yhwh* (possibly pronounced as "Yahweh"). The name commonly appears in combination with the word *'elohîm*, a less personal name for God. "*Yahweh 'Elohim*," then, would be translated as "LORD God."

In a few instances, such as this one, the divine title *'Adonai Yahweh* appears. The term *'Adonai* is a generic word that means "lord." It could be used of human masters or kings, as well as for the deity. To avoid redundancy, when the title *'Adonai Yahweh* appears in the text, we typically translate "Lord GOD" rather than "Lord LORD," with the uppercase letters in GOD indicating the underlying name *Yahweh*.

Ezekiel saw only bones that were deader than dead. He had no answer beyond the obvious response: "O Lord GOD, you know" (v. 3). **[Lord GOD]**

## A lively sermon
### (vv. 4-10)

The succeeding verses tell the familiar story of how God told Ezekiel to preach to the congregation of dead bones, promising that he would reassemble the skeletons, then return to them muscle and sinew and skin before breathing once again the breath of life into their bodies (vv. 4-6).

When Ezekiel did as commanded, he felt the earth shaking with the rattling of bones as the skeletons reformed, then watched as flesh and skin reappeared like a time-lapse video of decomposition run in reverse (vv. 7-8).

At last, Ezekiel stood among a massive collection of perfectly formed bodies, but they were still dead. God then instructed him to "prophesy to the breath" that it might come from the four winds, re-enter the corpses, and return the "vast multitude" (or "vast army," NIV11, HCSB) to life (vv. 9-10).

Ezekiel is not the only biblical writer to speak of the "four winds of heaven," which also appear in Jer. 49:36 and Zech. 2:6, 6:5 as the agent of divine activity. The four winds are also mentioned in visionary sequences in Dan. 7:2, 8:8, and 11:4. The image indicates God's power to call the wind from the four points of the compass.

The Hebrew term *ruach* can be used to mean "wind," "breath," or even "spirit." The focus on breath calls to mind the creation story of Gen. 2:7, but on a far grander scale. Instead of breathing life into one man, Ezekiel envisioned God whistling up the four winds to inspirit a host of bodies and return them to life. **[Life and Breath]**

But what was the meaning of this resurrected multitude? Was Ezekiel now standing before a zombie army of the living dead, or did the scene suggest something more?

---

**Life and breath:** One of the psalmists also connected life, breath, and the presence of God: "When you hide your face, they are dismayed; when you take away their breath, they die and return to their dust. When you send forth your spirit, they are created; and you renew the face of the ground" (Ps. 104:29-30).

---

We can only imagine the questions running through the stunned prophet's mind before a word from God connected the dots for him.

## A hopeful prophecy
### (vv. 11-14)

The dried bones represented the "whole house of Israel," God said – a phrase probably intended to include the Northern Kingdom of Israel (conquered by the Assyrians in 722 BCE) along with the southern kingdom of Judah, which first fell to the Babylonians in 597 BCE and suffered several subsequent deportations.

The people had given up, thinking themselves as good as dead, "cut off completely" from home and from hope (v. 11). God, however, had not given up on Israel. In language reminiscent of the Exodus, God promised to raise the Hebrews from their metaphorical graves, restoring them to life and to the land of promise (vv. 13-14).

The new life God promised would come about through the active power of God's Spirit: "'I will put my spirit within you, and you shall live, and I will place you on your own soil; then you shall know that I, the LORD, have spoken and will act,' says the LORD" (v. 14).

As the Holy Spirit would later bring new life to the dispirited disciples on the day of Pentecost (Acts 2), the presence and power of God's Spirit promised new life to the exiles, and the hope that they might yet return to their homes in the land of promise.

Ezekiel's prophecy echoes a theological understanding of the exile as God's punishment for Israel's collective sin and rejection of the covenant. God had the power to "kill and make alive" (Deut. 32:39, 1 Sam. 2:6), to punish and forgive. The vision of 37:1-14 seems to elaborate on the promise of 36:26-27. The people of Israel had proven incapable of keeping the covenant, but God's grace would renew their lives and the promised Spirit would motivate obedience: "I will put my spirit within you, and make you follow my statutes and be careful to observe my ordinances" (36:27). What the Hebrews could not do for themselves, God would do for them.

How might this strange vision of Ezekiel speak to us?

We do not live as captives in Babylon, but we can still feel separated from God and cut off from hope. We may know very well what it is like to feel dry of bone, numb of heart, and dead of spirit. We may be exiled by grief or despair or loneliness. We may have lost hope that our family will ever be whole or that our life will ever make sense.

Like Israel, we may sometimes feel as if our emotional ribs have been picked clean by vultures and left to dry in the sun.

One might argue, however, that the people in deepest exile are those who have no worries, who think everything is fine, whose indifference to God has left them too blind to see that they are dying inside, that their spiritual bones are turning to dust.

In Ezekiel's vision, things did not begin to change until there was a great shaking and a rattling. It could be that our pathway to renewed life must also begin with a shaking of priorities that rattles the framework of a fruitless faith.

God does not want us to be exiled forever. Our own efforts may leave us feeling dry as dust, but Jesus, even more than Ezekiel, made it clear that God desires to bring us new life through the presence of the Spirit (John 14:15-16).

As we are born anew through Christ, the Spirit enables us to see the world through the lens of Jesus' love, so that we may also become life-giving agents of change to others. And there's nothing crazy about that.

### The Hardest Question
### What was it like for Israelites living in Babylon?

Abundant biblical testimony points to the sorrow experienced by those who wept by the rivers of Babylon as they remembered the glories of Jerusalem (Ps. 137:1). The book of Lamentations and sections of the book of Jeremiah speak of weeping and mourning for the loss of the land.

Yet, books such as Daniel and Ezekiel, along with encouraging advice from Jeremiah (ch. 29), indicate that the people were swiftly settled into Jewish communities and integrated into the economic and political life of the Babylonians.

Recently a cache of cuneiform documents reflecting Israelite life in Babylon has come to light. More than a hundred small clay tablets – probably looted from archaeological sites during the tumult in Iraq – suggest that the Hebrews had restricted movements but lived relatively normal lives and conducted business as usual while in Babylon.

A translation of the documents appears in a book by Laurie Pearce and Cornelia Wunsch (*Documents of Judean Exiles and West Semites in Babylonia in the Collection of David Sofer* [CUSAS 28: CDL Press, 2014]).

The tablets are written in Babylonian cuneiform, though some Hebrew letters appear in the margins, possibly for filing purposes. Since most of the tablets are legal documents, they contain dates, the earliest of which relates to the 15th year after the exile began.

The documents employ a number of Hebrew names, some of which include theophoric elements such as "Yah" or "El" (e.g., Gedalyahu, Shaltiel, and Netanyahu). The River Chebar – named by Ezekiel as the locus for some of his oracles – is cited in several of the tablets.

The tablets reflect legal transactions among Hebrew exiles living in a block of settlements between the Tigris and Euphrates Rivers. One of the towns was called *Al Jahudu*, which pays tribute (in Babylonian spelling) to the homeland of Judah, and might even be translated as something similar to "Jewtown."

The documents include lease agreements for houses and land, receipts for the trade or sale of livestock and slaves, and instructions regarding inheritances. Their mundane nature suggests that whether they liked it or not, the resettled Hebrews were very much a part of the larger social and political network in their new home. Taking Jeremiah's advice to "build houses and live in them, plant gardens and eat what they produce" (Jer. 29:5), they made the best of their situation.

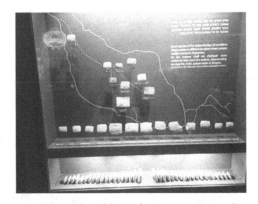

(From an exhibit at the Bible Lands Museum in Jerusalem, 2015).

# Fifth Sunday in Lent

## Second Reading
## Psalm 130*

# Hope

*If you, O LORD, should mark iniquities, Lord, who could stand? (Ps. 130:3)*

Many – perhaps most – conscientious believers have known the experience of feeling totally guilty before God, overwhelmed by a sense of sin and failure, and longing for the blessed release of forgiveness. Today's text is the story of a psalm writer who knew the feeling well.

As we approach the end of the Lenten season, the deeply stirring psalm known as *De Produndis* is a most appropriate text for study. Psalm 130 is the sixth of seven "Penitential Psalms" designated by the early church to be recited on Ash Wednesday (the others are 6, 32, 38, 51, 102, and 143) and considered most appropriate for any time of confession and repentance.

The title *De Profundis* ("out of the depths") comes from the opening two words in the Latin Vulgate translation. The psalm's penitent theme is so memorable and timeless that the title has been adopted by a variety of literary and musical works (including a ballet and a sonata), in addition to films.

### A penitent prayer
### (vv. 1-4)

The psalm's designation as a "Song of Ascent" goes back to Jewish tradition and some of our earliest manuscripts. **[Songs of Ascent]** The psalm appears to have originated as a testimony of an individual's private devotion, but it could also have found a place in worship as a corporate prayer of penitence, similar to Psalm 86.

The psalmist appears to be deeply troubled by his shortcomings, but gives no clue as to what they were. We

**Songs of Ascent:** Fifteen of the psalms, located together (Ps. 120–134), are called "Songs of Ascent." They are often thought to be sung by pilgrims coming to worship at the temple during the three annual feasts. Since Jerusalem is on a high hill, one cannot enter the city without ascending from one of the surrounding valleys.

Metaphorically, biblical language always speaks of "going up" to Jerusalem, which was the religious, political, and economic heart of the nation.

The steps in the picture, from the Second Temple period, are located below the southern wall of the Temple Mount in Jerusalem. From here, pilgrims ascended to one of several gates that led to stairways accessing the temple courts.

don't know if he was under conviction about a particularly egregious error, or if more frequent foibles had mounted up. Whatever the case, he had a sense of being in deep water, caught up in the chaos of sin and struggling to remain afloat and knowing that God was his only hope: "Out of the depths I cry to you, O LORD" (v. 1).

---

*\*This text is also read in Year B on Proper Sundays 5, 8, and 14.*

> **LORD, and Lord:** Note this psalm's characteristic pairing of two different names for God, the personal name Yahweh (or *Yah*, translated LORD), and the more generic term *'adonai*, translated as "Lord."
>
> At the end of v. 1 and the beginning of v. 2, they come together: "I cry to you, Yahweh: Adonai, hear my voice!"
>
> In v. 3, we find "If you kept records of sin, Yah – Adonai, who could stand?"
>
> The pair appears again in vv. 5-6, with "I wait for Yahweh" in v. 5 and "my soul (waits) for Adonai" in v. 6.

The word translated as "depths" could possibly refer to the abode of the dead in the depths of the earth, or to the deep waters of the ungoverned sea, which represented chaos to the ancients. Hebrew has several words that convey the sense of something deep, and the one used here often appears in negative circumstances: for those who hide the plans "deeply" from Yahweh (Isa. 29:15), or who are urged to hide from Yahweh in the "depths" of Dedan (Jer. 49:8). Hosea 5:2 appears to speak of those who are "deep" in depravity.

We may recall times of feeling overwhelmed by failure, emotionally at sea, floundering for a footing. We may have sought the ear of a friend or counselor – or we may have prayed to God, as the psalmist did (v. 2).

Fully aware of his faults – and of the pervasive nature of sin in human life – the poet sought divine mercy rather than judgment. To his plea for mercy, the psalmist added a rational appeal: "If you, O LORD, should mark iniquities, Lord, who could stand?" (v. 3). **[LORD, and Lord]**

Many believers hold to the view of a judgmental God who keeps meticulous records of wrongdoing. Some preachers take an almost perverse delight in picturing judgment day as a time when every sin would be revealed for all the world to see (1 Cor. 4:5 is sometimes cited as support for this view).

The psalmist understood, however, that God has better things to do than compile an individual encyclopedia of failures for every person on earth. He understood that God is gracious and forgiving, and that forgiveness means – well, forgiveness.

If we truly forgive someone of hurting us, there's no need to hold on to the offense or remind them of it or keep records for future reference. If God kept a daily tally and punished us for every sin, few of us would survive for very long.

Rather, the poet affirmed, "there is forgiveness with you, so that you may be revered" (v. 4).

What good would it do for God to wipe out all who sin and have no one left with whom to fellowship or for whom to have hopes and dreams? How can God be praised if there is no one left to sing hallelujahs? If anyone is to worship and pay reverence to God, it must be sinners, because there is no other type of person. And if sinners are to live and serve God, it must be because God is gracious and willing to forgive.

Many people – both believers and unbelievers – have difficulty in forgiving others, or even forgiving themselves. They keep a running tally of wrongs that amounts to a heavy load of misery. To find the joy that God wants for us, we must learn to forgive and to be forgiven, to stop keeping score and find true freedom.

### A longing hope
### (vv. 5-6)

Believing that God is gracious and experiencing forgiveness are two different things. Having confessed his sins and expressed confidence in God's forgiving nature, the psalmist waited for a sign of absolution. Verse 5 consists of three brief clauses: "I wait for the LORD, my soul waits, and in his word I hope."

A surface reading of the verse might lead some to think "in his word I hope" is a reference to trusting in the Bible, but the psalmist had no Bible. In Old Testament contexts such as this one, "his word" or "the word of God" refers to a direct word of God, usually delivered as an oracle through a prophet or priest who spoke in God's behalf.

The preposition before "his word" usually means "to" or "for" rather than "in." The psalmist is voicing a longing for a word from God to indicate that his sins have been forgiven. The poet may have hoped for something as objective as a priest ceremonially declaring that God had heard his prayer and granted clemency. Or, he may have sought a more subjective sense of inner peace and release through a divine response.

The verb for "waits" does not appear in the Hebrew text, as in many translations of v. 6. The line poetically

> **Intentional, or not?** As noted in the lesson, a literal reading of v. 6 could be "my soul (waits) for the Lord, more than the watchers of the morning, watchers of the morning."
>
> Many early commentators argued that the second "watchers of the morning" should be deleted as the error of a copyist who accidentally wrote the same words twice, a mistake known as dittography.
>
> More recent scholars, however, have argued that the repetition is intentional, used for effect to indicate the depth of the psalmist's longing for a sense of release from sin.

carries forward the sense of hope and longing from the previous verse, which ends with "I hope …" and is followed by "… my soul, more than watchers for the morning, watchers for the morning."

"Watchers for the morning" could refer to guards or others appointed to keep watch through the night, but also echoes the sense of someone who suffers deep anxiety or guilt and cannot sleep. The psalmist longs for God's forgiveness even more keenly than an insomniac or troubled person watches through the night, waiting for the light of day. [**Intentional, or not?**]

## A relieved testimony
### (vv. 7-8)

With vv. 7-8, the psalm turns from speaking *to* God (vv. 1-4) and speaking *about* God (vv. 5-6) to speaking *for* God, urging the people of Israel to seek God and find the same sense of forgiveness that he apparently received.

Some older commentaries suggest that vv. 7-8, which address Israel rather than God, were not original to the psalm, but added when it came to be used in worship. Scholars who focus on literary characteristics of the psalm are more likely to argue that the verses are theologically and structurally related to earlier parts of the psalm, and should be regarded as original.

The shift in address may suggest that vv. 7-8 were spoken by a priest or prophet who exhorted the congregation to follow the example of the petitioner from vv. 1-6 and turn to God so they may also experience forgiveness and renewed faith.

Whoever the speaker, v. 5 and v. 7 both stress the importance of hope, something more important than we often realize. We awake each morning hoping for a good day. We enter relationships hoping to find love and companionship. We hope that our lives might have some significance and that our children will appreciate us. We hope to stay healthy and to live a long time.

Furthermore, we hope for a meaningful existence that extends beyond this earthly life, though we have no human means of making that happen or any proof that it will. The basis for such a hope is found in the promises of a dependably loving and forgiving God. Just as the psalmist called on Israel to "hope in the LORD," hope is what keeps us going.

The closing verses of the psalm are addressed to Israel, but God's promise of forgiveness extends far beyond the covenant people of the Old Testament. The Hebrew Bible depicts God as gracious to all who repent, with the book of Jonah being a prime example of God's willingness to forgive, even when the preacher thought they didn't deserve it.

Viewing the text through the lens of the New Testament, we are reminded that God offers grace to "whosoever" (John 3:16), and that "If we confess our sins, he who is faithful and just will forgive us our sins and cleanse us from all unrighteousness" (1 John 1:9).

All of us know what it is like to fall short of God's expectations. Some of us have known or may now know the psalmist's feeling of drowning in failure. Even from those chaotic depths – and perhaps, especially from the depths – we can learn from the psalmist to trust in God's steadfast love and find the redemption we crave.

May it be so.

## The Hardest Question
### Does God keep score?

Many people, both in the church and without, hold to a belief that God keeps a record of our good and bad deeds, and will one day judge whether we get into heaven by weighing the good against the bad. This is not a biblical teaching. The psalms and prophets speak of the wicked being unable to stand in the judgment (Pss. 1:5, 9:16; Mic. 7:9; Hab. 1:2; Mal. 3:5), but for the Hebrews, God's judgment could take place on earth at any time rather than as a prelude to eternity: the New Testament concept of eternal life in heaven had not yet developed.

Several New Testament passages suggest that all will give an account of themselves at the judgment, with eternity in the balance (Matt. 12:36, Rom. 2:5, 2 Cor. 4:5, 1 Pet. 4:5, among others). This does not mean that God keeps a record of every wrong, however, or will replay our sins for all to see. Can you imagine how long that would take, or what a discouraging way to start eternity?

The Bible consistently holds that God is forgiving, and forgiveness is antithetical to keeping score. When we repent of our sins and seek God's forgiveness, whatever record we may have accumulated is wiped clean. That's what forgiveness means. Isaiah, looking to the future and speaking for God, wrote: "I, I am He who blots out your transgressions for my own sake, and I will not remember your sins" (Isa. 43:25).

Jeremiah spoke of a God who "will remember their iniquity and punish their sins" (speaking of Israel, Jer. 14:10), but also of a time when everyone would know the Lord, "for I will forgive their iniquity, and remember their sin no more" (Jer. 31:34).

Jesus had a lot to say about forgiveness, and about the importance of forgiving others. At the Last Supper, he said "this is the blood of the covenant, which is poured out for many for the forgiveness of sins" (Matt. 26:28). Paul spoke of how "God made you alive together with him, when he forgave us all our trespasses" (Col. 2:13). The writer of 1 John declared that "If we confess our sins, he who is faithful and just will forgive us our sins and cleanse us from all unrighteousness" (1 John 1:9).

If God kept a record of every sin and expected us to outweigh them with good, none of us could be saved. The author of Psalm 130 knew this: "If you, O LORD, should mark iniquities, Lord, who could stand?" But he also believed that God is gracious: "But there is forgiveness with you, so that you may be revered" (vv. 3-4).

To say that God forgives and does not remember our sins does not mean the acts are no longer present in the divine memory, but that God no longer holds them against us. Likewise, we are challenged to forgive others when they do us wrong. We may still recall how someone offended us, but we no longer hold it against them: it no longer holds any weight.

If God kept score as we are prone to do, we would be like a basketball team that saw every player foul out before the end of the first half, or like a baseball team that found itself 100 runs behind in the first inning. We would be hopeless and helpless.

God relates to us on the basis of steadfast love and redeeming grace that exceed our comprehension. No matter what we have done or how often we have done it, God is willing to forgive our sins and wipe the slate clean and keep us in the game.

How grateful we can be that God does not keep score.

# Fifth Sunday in Lent

## Third Reading
## Romans 8:6-11

# Mindful Spirituality

*To set the mind on the flesh is death, but to set the mind on the Spirit is life and peace. (Rom. 8:6)*

Spirituality is a crucial dimension of human life. Seminaries and divinity schools develop programs of spiritual formation. Both ministers and laypersons seek trained spiritual directors to serve as life coaches of a higher order. Ministers, rabbis, yogis, and other disciples of the inner life promote quiet retreats or daily meditation to nurture one's spiritual life.

Corporality is less talked about, perhaps because we're all familiar with the hard pull of hunger for physical gratification through food and drink, sex and play, chilling out and being entertained. We don't need special training to help us focus on desire, idolize our bodies, or obsess over financial security.

The Apostle Paul knew what it was like to be torn between the spirit and the flesh. He devoted considerable discussion in Rom. 7:14–8:5 to the inherent tension between spirit and body, good and evil, aspirations to godliness and the reality of failure.

---

**The malleable mind:** We are often reminded of how pliable the mind is. News stories abound of how terrorists have kidnapped children and used various methods to brainwash them, filling them with hatred and then sending them out as suicide bombers. Others become radicalized through exposure to Internet sites or the influence of a person skilled in mental manipulation. On the other hand, positive influences may also shape our thinking.

In most cases, though we remain subject to peer pressure, political propaganda, and subliminal influences, we retain the ability to choose our own way. Paul's concern is whether we choose the self-directed way of "the flesh," or the Christ-directed way of "the Spirit."

---

Where does one find the power to overcome temptation and move beyond? Paul celebrated a belief that "the law of the Spirit of life has set us free from the law of sin and death" (Rom. 6:2).

Still, Paul knew that spiritual liberation is not a one-time experience: we live in our bodies every day, and we are constantly subject to temptation. [**The malleable mind**]

### Spirit and flesh
### (v. 6)

Paul began Romans 8 by celebrating the redeeming work of Christ, which has "set you free from the law in and of death" (vv. 1-2). He believed that Christians find true life in voluntarily submitting our will to the Spirit of Christ, rather than leaving our thoughts to be blown about by worldly whims.

The default mode for humans is to think as our culture thinks. Paul often used the Greek word for "flesh" *(sarx)* to describe the nature of a human without Christ. In this he set "flesh" and "spirit" against each other as two poles of human experience, not as a separate body and soul. While "of the flesh" can refer in a literal sense to the physical body, Paul more commonly used it in the sense of a person's determination to trust in self rather than God.

In Paul's mind, trusting in self can lead only to death. Thus, he wrote "To set the mind on the flesh is death, but to set the mind on the Spirit is life and peace" (v. 6). Some translations avoid the uncomfortable word "flesh" and speak of those who are "carnally minded" (KJV) or have "the mind of sinful man" (NIV). Maintaining the word "flesh" reminds the reader that our minds are firmly

> **Mindsets:** Paul's phrase, "to set the mind" (NRSV), translates the noun form of a verb that means "to think," or "to set one's mind or heart on something." Thus, "it denotes the whole action of the affections and will as well as of the reason" (Fritz Rienecker, *A Linguistic Key to the Greek New Testament: Romans–Revelation*, trans. Cleon L. Rogers Jr. [Zondervan, 1980], 19). A more literal translation is: "for the mindset of the flesh (is) death, and the mind-set of the Spirit (is) life and peace."

interconnected with our bodies and in touch with our physical desires. **[Mindsets]**

For Paul, the results of following the way of the flesh or the way of the Spirit are self-evident and the proper choice between them is obvious. It involves choosing between hurtful behaviors that lead to disquiet and death, or helpful actions that promote peace and life. The character and quality of our daily experience, in addition to our eternal destiny, is determined by the direction in which we set our minds.

In Paul's commentary on the works of the flesh versus the fruits of the spirit in Gal. 5:19-23, the "works of the flesh" constitute a catalogue of negative traits: "fornication, impurity, licentiousness, idolatry, sorcery, enmities, strife, jealousy, anger, quarrels, dissensions, factions, envy, drunkenness, carousing, and things like these" (Gal. 5:19-21). In Paul's mind, the self-focused life was bound for trouble.

In contrast, the term "Spirit" (*pneuma*) speaks of the total person in relation to God. The fruits of the Spirit listed in Gal. 5:22-23 – "love, joy, peace, patience, kindness, generosity, faithfulness, gentleness, and self-control" – reflect the presence and the activity of God in the daily life of the believer.

### A mortal mind
#### (vv. 7-8)

The power of the mind is an awesome thing. We are familiar with the significant effects of positive thinking or negative thinking. We may have read articles or heard testimonies of people who credit their health or success to having positive mental attitudes. Doctors agree that hopeful and positive attitudes are important aids to healing.

We may also have observed persons who enter a downward spiral because of negative thinking. We may have experienced it ourselves. Unhealthy thinking habits can ultimately affect our emotional and physical health. These ways of thinking can become "hard-wired" into our brains, and are difficult to overcome.

Behavioral coaches sometimes teach the art of "reframing," of literally training our minds to think in more positive ways. Paul understood the need for believers to "reframe" their thinking by setting their minds on the Spirit rather than on the flesh. This, he believed, was essential for both life and peace.

Having established the basic "flesh vs. spirit" dichotomy in v. 6, Paul elaborated in vv. 7-11. The mind that is "set on the flesh" is hostile to God, Paul said: "it does not submit to God's law – indeed it cannot" (v. 7). A "fleshly" mind cannot submit to God because it has already submitted to self. As Jesus reminded us, no one can serve two masters (Matt. 6:24).

Paul saw nothing but danger in being sold out to the worldly idea that a person can be self-sufficient, that one does not need God. The acclaimed southern writer Flannery O'Conner gave voice to that idea through a crazy, obsessed character named Hazel Motes. At some point in the short story titled "Wise Blood," someone mentioned the subject of redemption. In response, Hazel sneered, "Any man who owns a good car don't need redemption."

As long as we think our own efforts can achieve all the security that matters, our mind cannot submit to God or please God (v. 8), because God is not even in the picture. By definition, the "mind of the flesh" is opposed to and closed to the mind of God.

### A spiritual mind
#### (vv. 9-11)

Having pointed squarely to the mindset that leads to death, Paul challenged his readers to steer clear of that rocky shoal and anchor their minds firmly in the safe harbor of the Spirit: "But you are not in the flesh; you are in the Spirit, since the Spirit of God dwells in you" (v. 9a). Those who belong to Christ also possess the Spirit of Christ, and the Spirit of Christ possesses them (v. 9b). Thus, having the Spirit is not a "second blessing" for super-surrendered Christians, but an essential aspect of what it means to live in relationship with Christ.

Paul spoke of the indwelling of the Spirit as both present and future. The believer's new position in the realm of the Spirit came about when he or she trusted Christ, and the Spirit of God continued to indwell the believer: "But if Christ is in you, though the body is dead because of sin, the Spirit is life because of righteousness" (v. 10).

Note that Paul made little distinction between the "Spirit of God," the "Spirit of Christ," and "Christ in you." These are equivalent expressions, all referring to the same reality, and suggesting that something approaching a Trinitarian view was present in Paul's thought.

Scholars have spilled much ink over the meaning of Paul's assertion that, while "the body is dead because of sin, the Spirit is life because of righteousness." He seems to be saying that, even for believers, our physical nature is still destined for a physical death, even as those who live in the flesh are destined for an eternal death.

Though our bodies are mortal, where the Spirit is, there is life and true righteousness. Believers who trust God's Spirit experience a new kind of life (Rom. 6:4), a fruitful life (Gal. 5:22-23), the abundant life that Christ has promised (John 10:10).

Paul believed that life in the Spirit also has a future component. The Spirit who dwells in us is the same Spirit responsible for raising Jesus from death. Thus, he said, the Spirit will also raise us, even our mortal bodies, from the dead (v. 11). The Christian belief in resurrection retains a hint of the ancient Jewish belief that the body is somehow connected to the spirit even after death. In some way beyond our understanding, our resurrection with Christ will have both a physical and spiritual component. As we often remind ourselves in funeral eulogies, "this mortal shall put on immortality" (1 Cor. 15:53).

To the Corinthians, Paul described Christ's resurrection as the "first-fruits," assuring his followers that they would participate in a full and final harvest of life (1 Cor. 15:23). Thus, the Spirit now present in us will bear fruit in our future resurrection and full participation in the kingdom of God. This assertion brings us back to where we began in v. 6: a mind set on the flesh leads to death, but a mind set on the Spirit leads to life.

Paul effectively used this promise to remind readers that their thinking should include a future component.

While it is wise to avoid the dilemma of being "so heavenly minded that we are no earthly good," Christians know there is more to the equation than what feels good in the moment.

Our human side wants to enjoy luxury, leisure, and financial security. We want to feel good, have fun, and experience pleasure. Paul would not suggest that we be fiscally irresponsible or deny every pleasure, but he clearly called upon believers to revamp their priorities. While more money in the bank and a vacation home to call our own might be nice, generosity to the poor and personal involvement in missions might be better.

Salvation involves more than the promise of "pie in the sky," but God's promise is nothing to be sneered at. Paul believed we have been promised an eternal home with Jesus, an everlasting experience of joy and peace.

To sacrifice our future hope on the altar of present pleasure is a bad deal – a deal Paul hoped his readers would be wise enough to reject.

### The Hardest Question
### I believe, but still struggle with temptation.
### Is something wrong with me?

A surface reading of the text might lead to the idea that once we trust in Christ and receive the Spirit, everything is hunky-dory and we no longer have to worry about temptation – but we all know it doesn't work that way.

Paul understood this. Though we may speak of "dying to sin" and "being raised with Christ," and though we may have prayed to receive the Spirit of Christ within us, our humanity does not cease. Temptations do not go away. As long as we live in our mortal bodies and possess a mortal mind, we face daily choices about whether we will orient our behavior toward selfish or godly goals.

James D.G. Dunn has explained it this way: in speaking to the Romans,

> Paul means neither that they have left the flesh wholly behind, nor that they are in a constant state of inspiration or permanent ecstasy. The phrases "in flesh" and "in Spirit" are much looser than that, as Paul's usage elsewhere confirms (cf, eg, 14:17 and Gal 2:20). What Paul assumes

is not that the process of salvation is complete but that it has begun, not that their total being has been completely transferred to another realm but that a decisive transfer of allegiance and lordship has already taken place, not that moral effort has been rendered unnecessary but that the inner compulsion of God's Spirit has become the most important factor at the level of primary motivation and enabling. (*Romans 1–8*, vol. 38A, Word Biblical Commentary [Zondervan, 1988], 443-444).

Are there practical ways in which we can set our minds toward a life governed more by the Spirit than the flesh? Charles Talbert has suggested a prayer-centered, three-step approach that involves a progressive "emptying" of self-orientation to make more room for the Spirit's influence.

First, he says, we should make a list of everyone we can think of who has offended us that we haven't forgiven – from childhood onward. Then, "Pray through that list until everyone has been released to Jesus," even if God is also on the list because we have harbored anger toward heaven. This is necessary, Talbert says, "... because anger and grudges take up space in the self that only God needs to fill."

Second, Talbert writes, we should make a list of everything we can remember for which we need to be forgiven, then "Pray through that list until Jesus takes every one," emptying clutter from the mind.

Third, Talbert advises, "make a list of all the areas of your life over which Jesus does not have absolute control. Pray through that list until everyone is open to him and subject to redecorating rights by him." In this way, we release our hold on the idols that take up space in our lives that ought to belong to God.

Only then, Talbert says, are we ready to ask God to come in and fill the empty space so that we may truly be led by the Spirit (*Romans*, Smyth & Helwys Bible Commentary [Smyth & Helwys, 2002], 210).

As long as we live in a mortal body, we are subject to the struggles that all humans face. Paul expressed hope that one day, even our mortal bodies will be perfected and given new life through the Spirit. In the meantime, we must consciously remember to take out the trash of our unworthy thoughts to make adequate room for the Spirit.

# Fifth Sunday in Lent

## Fourth Reading
## John 11:1-45*

# Raising the Dead

*Jesus said to her, "I am the resurrection and the life. Those who believe in me, even though they die,
will live, and everyone who lives and believes in me will never die. Do you believe this?" (John 11:25-26)*

F ew stories are more memorable than the account of Jesus raising Lazarus from the dead. Given the significance of the story, it may seem surprising that the Fourth Gospel is the only one to record it.

The resurrection of Lazarus is the last of seven "signs" (*sēmeion*, see 12:18) that the author of John portrays as especially significant in the process of Jesus revealing his identity and interpreting his work in bringing light and life to the world. **[Signs]**

Following the healing of the man born blind (9:1-41), Jesus described himself as the good shepherd who was willing to lay down his life for his sheep, leading to a mixed response from the Jews (10:1-21). A side-porch conversation on the temple grounds turned into a confrontation when Jesus affirmed his ability to grant eternal life to his sheep as well as his unity with the Father (10:22-30). Some bystanders attempted to arrest and stone Jesus for blasphemy, "but he escaped from their hands" (10:31-39) and led his disciples east from Jerusalem and across the Jordan, to a friendly place where John had been baptizing, and "many believed in him there" (10:40-42). **[Structure]**

With ch. 11, Jesus left the relative safety among believers east of the Jordan and returned to the area around Jerusalem despite the danger – and there *was* a real danger to Jesus, because Jesus was thought to pose a real danger to the Jewish people (see "The Hardest Question" for more on this).

## Jesus and the Twelve
## (vv. 1-16)

The account begins with Jesus receiving a message from Mary and Martha that their brother Lazarus was ill (vv. 1-3). We note that John identifies Mary proleptically as "the one who anointed the Lord with perfume and wiped his feet with her hair," an action that does not take place until the next chapter (12:1-8). This is a reminder that the author wrote long after the fact, and was not bound to a linear narrative, as modern readers might expect.

The message came only to Jesus at first. The sisters did not directly ask Jesus to come: the implication was that his love for Lazarus should be a sufficient motivation for him to come and heal their brother, which they clearly believed he could do.

---

**Signs:** The author of John saw several of Jesus' mighty works as more than just miraculous feats: they were "signs" of Jesus' identity and work, designed to reveal Jesus as the Son of God and call people to believe in him that they might have both abundant and eternal life. The seven works labeled as signs are:

1. Turning water into wine at the wedding in Cana (2:1-11)
2. Healing the official's son (4:46-54)
3. Healing the man who was lame for 38 years (5:1-9)
4. The feeding of the 5,000 (6:1-4)
5. Walking on the water (6:16-21)
6. Healing of the man born blind (9:1-41)
7. The Raising of Lazarus (11:1-46)

---

*A portion of this text, 11:32-45, is read on All Saints Day in Year B.*

> **Structure:** Commentators often divide the Fourth Gospel into two main parts surrounded by a prologue (1:1-18) and epilogue (21:1-25). In this view, the first part focuses on Jesus' public life, especially his performance and interpretation of signs (1:19–12:50). The second part portrays Jesus' private instructions to his present and future disciples (present and future), explaining how they should live after his departure (13:1–20:31).
>
> Alicia Myers offers an alternate structure for the gospel, seeing it in five movements, with ch. 11 marking the beginning of the fourth section (11:1–17:26). Rather than concluding the "Book of Signs," Myers argues, the story of Lazarus begins "the transition toward Jesus' departure and return to the Father" (*Reading John and 1, 2, 3 John: A Literary and Theological Commentary* [Smyth & Helwys, 2019], 33-35).

Jesus' response requires some thought: "This illness does not lead to death; rather it is for God's glory, so that the Son of God may be glorified through it" (v. 4). The text does not say that God caused the sickness, but Jesus saw that his friend's illness and demise would not be "toward death" (*pros ton thanaton*), but for the greater glory of God and of Jesus.

Despite his love for Lazarus and his sisters, Jesus did not rush to the sick man's bedside, but remained two days longer, apparently without telling the disciples about Lazarus' condition (vv. 5-6). Even when he announced plans to return to Judea – the area around Jerusalem – he did not tell them why (v. 7). The disciples, remembering the near stoning in Jerusalem, were not enthusiastic. As he had done in 9:3-5, Jesus emphasized his task of bringing light into the world (vv. 8-10).

Only then did he tell them "Our friend Lazarus has fallen asleep, but I am going there to waken him" (v. 11). As usual, the disciples did not understand, wondering why Jesus would need to endanger himself to rouse someone who was perfectly capable of waking up on his own (vv. 11-13). Finally, Jesus explained that Lazarus was dead, adding "For your sake I am glad I was not there, so that you may believe" (vv. 14-15).

Darkness and death had come in Jesus' absence: he would bring light and life back into the picture, so that others would believe – his disciples among them.

Surprisingly, it was Thomas – later to be known as "doubting Thomas" – who spoke up: "Let us also go, that we may die with him" (v. 16). This statement could be taken as ambiguous: Did he mean to die with Lazarus, or to die with Jesus? Given the disciples' fear of stoning at the hands of those who wanted to eliminate Jesus, the latter is more likely.

## Jesus and Martha
### (vv. 17-27)

The story reports separate encounters between Jesus and the two sisters. Martha, always portrayed as more practical and businesslike, left the house to meet Jesus while Mary remained at home, where "many of the Jews had come to Martha and Mary to console them about their brother" (vv. 19-20). Their home was in the village of Bethany, about two miles east of Jerusalem, on the slopes of the Mount of Olives.

We observe that John continues to offer a mixed picture of the Jews, who were often divided in their opinions about Jesus. Here many Jews are portrayed as showing compassion and care for Mary and Martha, joining in their mourning for Lazarus.

By the time Jesus arrived, Lazarus had been dead and in the tomb for four days (v. 17), so Jesus would have found them midway through the traditional week of mourning. Martha's first recorded words are reproachful: "Lord, if you had been here my brother would not have died. But even now I know that God will give you whatever you ask of him" (vv. 21-22).

Was Martha expressing faith that Jesus could raise Lazarus from the dead? This seems odd, given that she would soon protest opening the tomb lest they face the stench of a four-day-old corpse. What did Martha think Jesus might ask God for?

She did not say, but Jesus responded simply "Your brother will rise again" (v. 23).

Like the male disciples, Martha misunderstood. She expressed confidence that Lazarus would "rise again in the resurrection on the last day" (v. 24).

We are familiar with Jesus' response: "I am the resurrection and the life. Those who believe in me, even though they die, will live, and everyone who lives and believes in me will never die" (vv. 25-26). Those words of assurance could also be misunderstood as a reference to future resurrection, so we can understand her ambiguous response when Jesus added "Do you believe this?"

"I believe that you are the Messiah, the Son of God, the one coming into the world," she said (v. 27).

### Jesus and Mary
#### (vv. 28-37)

Martha still didn't understand that Jesus intended to raise Lazarus from the dead in her present world, but perhaps felt comforted as she returned home and called Mary aside, telling her that Jesus had asked to see her. Mary hurried out, meeting Jesus outside the village (vv. 30).

She did not go alone, however. Though Martha had spoken to her privately, the coterie of comforters followed Mary out, thinking she was going to mourn at the tomb (v. 31). This made them witnesses to the conversation between Mary and Jesus.

Mary showed greater obsequiousness than Martha by kneeling before Jesus, but her words were no less reproachful: "Lord, if you had been here, my brother would not have died" (v. 32).

Jesus entered no dialogue with Mary, as he had with Martha, but connected on a deep emotional level.

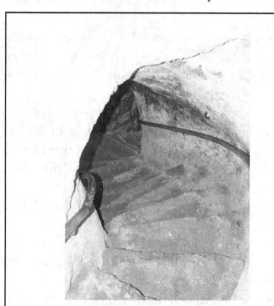

**The tomb:** The village of Bethany today is an Arab town known as 'al-Azaryah (or Al Eizariya), the Arabic name of Lazarus. The Church of Saint Lazarus is located adjacent to a rock-cut tomb with a narrow stairway leading deep below ground. With no real support other than tradition, it is known as the tomb of Lazarus.

Confronted with Mary's sorrowful sobbing and the soulful weeping of her friends, Jesus "was greatly disturbed in spirit and deeply moved." He asked only "Where have you laid him?" (vv. 33-34). **[The tomb]**

The famously shortest verse in the Bible then reports that "Jesus wept," though not in the same way as Mary and her friends. The verb used for their weeping is *klaiō*, which suggests the loud crying typical of public mourning in that culture. Jesus' weeping is described with *dakruō*, which suggests a quieter way of shedding tears without much public display.

It seems unlikely that Jesus was weeping for Lazarus, who he planned to raise from the dead. Some have suggested that his thoughts of Lazarus in the tomb caused Jesus to think of his own upcoming death, but it seems more likely that Jesus' tears were a natural response of empathy to the grief shown by Mary and her friends.

"The Jews" who had come with Mary were impressed ("See how he loved him!"), but also gave Jesus mixed reviews. His healing of the blind man had become widely known. If Jesus could open the eyes of a blind man, they wondered, couldn't he have kept Lazarus from dying? (v. 37).

### Jesus and Lazarus
#### (vv. 38-45)

When Jesus reached the tomb, it became apparent that Martha was also among those who had come with Mary. The tomb was a cave, the text says, apparently closed so tightly by a stone that the odor of decay remained inside. When Jesus told them to remove the stone, Martha objected because of the smell (vv. 38-39).

Jesus challenged her belief and reminded her of his earlier assurance, though in different words: "Did I not tell you that if you believed, you would see the glory of God?" (v. 40).

With the stone removed, Jesus prayed, clearly pitching his prayer to the ears of those standing near and to God: "I know that you always hear me, but I have said this for the sake of the crowd standing here, so that they may believe that you sent me" (v. 42).

Jesus then cried with a loud voice (*phōnē megalē*), the same expression used to describe his cry from the cross (Matt 27:46, 50; Mark 15:34, 37; Luke 23:46): "Lazarus, come out!" (v. 43).

> **Praying for others:** John's gospel reports the words of Jesus' prayers only three times: in 11:42-43, 12:27-30, and 17:1-26. In each of these prayers, Jesus indicated that his vocal prayer was for the benefit of those who were listening: the crowd in 11:42-43, and the disciples in the other two cases. For the author, Jesus' purpose in praying aloud was to inspire others to believe and thus see God's glory as reflected in Jesus.

Lazarus emerged from the tomb, still described as "the dead man." Reminiscent of modern ideas of zombies, he came out wrapped from head to toe in strips of cloth. Jesus told the others to "Unbind him and let him go" (v. 44). Surprisingly, that's the end of the scene: Lazarus did not express astonishment, ask questions, or describe what it felt like to be both dead and alive. In fact, he said nothing at all, nor did Mary or Martha. The reader is left to imagine their reactions. **[Praying for others]**

We hear only from the Jews who had witnessed Lazarus' resurrection. Many of them believed in Jesus, according to the author, while others immediately went to the Pharisees, reporting what they had seen (vv. 45-46).

The remainder of the chapter describes a developing plan to kill Jesus before he or his followers started a rebellion. "If we let him go on like this, everyone will believe in him, and the Romans will come and destroy both our holy place and our nation" (v. 48). The verdict was not reached with any joy or vendetta against Jesus, but because they believed, in the words of the high priest Caiaphas, that it was better "to have one man die for the people than to have the whole nation destroyed" (v. 50).

The resurrection of Lazarus stands as an obvious foreshadowing of the coming death and resurrection of Jesus. Caiaphas' words were both prophetic (v. 51) and ironic: he had no way of knowing just how Jesus' death would lead to the salvation of the nation, and indeed, the world.

In reflecting on this story, we are reminded of how the witnesses to Jesus' work reacted in different ways. Some believed. Some did not.

It's one thing to make that observation. The more important thing is to consider how we will respond. Will God be glorified through us?

## The Hardest Question
### Why did the Jewish officials want to arrest or silence Jesus?

While John 10:31-33 speaks of Jews who wanted to stone Jesus for blasphemy, for making himself equal with God, there were more pressing reasons for wanting to remove him from the public eye.

The Romans allowed a level of self-rule for the Jewish people, under the authority of the high priest and other officials in Jerusalem. As long as they could keep their people in line and paying their taxes, they could live in peace and observe their religious festivals as they wished.

At any hint of rebellion, however, the Romans could and would quickly step in. Luke 13 relates an account of certain men from Galilee – probably suspected of being members of the anti-Roman Zealot party – being slaughtered by soldiers while in the act of offering sacrifices in the temple. Any suspicion of revolt could bring painful consequences.

A rebellion did break out in 66 CE, when Jewish militants expelled the Romans and took control of the city. In 70 CE, Titus led a large force against Jerusalem. His army surrounded the city and put it under siege, venting their anger as the siege dragged on for five months. When heavy engines breached the walls, people who tried to escape were raped, brutalized, or crucified. The Romans suffered significant losses of their own, but ultimately retook the city and destroyed much of it, including the temple. Jews were either slaughtered outright or taken as slaves.

This was the kind of response that Jewish leaders feared when Jesus began attracting crowds, many of whom thought of him as a potential military messiah. If his followers sparked a revolt against the Romans, the price would be steep. The Jewish officials feared what would happen if a revolt broke out: they believed that silencing Jesus was a necessary step toward saving the nation.

The destruction of Jerusalem was still in the future during Jesus' lifetime, though Matthew and Luke say that he predicted it (Matt. 24:1-2, Luke 19:41-44). The horrors of the catastrophic events were still very real for both the writer of John and his readers, however. They knew what the Romans could do, and they understood why the Jewish officials were afraid.

# Sixth Sunday in Lent

## Liturgy of the Palms
## First Reading
## Psalm 118*

# Strength and Salvation

*This is the day that the LORD has made; let us rejoice and be glad in it. (Ps. 118:24)*

What is the best way to observe Palm Sunday? One option is to focus on celebrating Jesus' "Triumphal Entry" with the cheering crowds and waving of branches. Sometimes we worship by waving stems of jade or other greenery while singing joyful hymns.

In the back of our minds, though, we can't forget that it's the beginning of Holy Week and the dark shadow of Good Friday's cross looms behind the cheerful palms. How do we acknowledge Palm Sunday's split personality?

The psalmists were good at that sort of thing, often constructing poetic prayers that combined themes of suffering and salvation, or prayer and praise. It's not surprising that quotations from Psalm 118 found their way into the New Testament story of Jesus' entry into Jerusalem, and from there into the lectionary readings for Palm Sunday.

The lectionary omits vv. 3-18, but we will consider the entire psalm, which was a favorite of New Testament writers. Verse 26 is cited in conjunction with Jesus' triumphal entry in all four gospels (Matt. 19:9, Mark 11:9-10, Luke 19:38, John 12:13), and vv. 22-23 are associated with Christ's suffering and glory (Mark 12:10-11, Acts 4:11). A connection between the cornerstone of v. 22 and Jesus appears in Eph. 2:20-21 and 1 Pet. 2:4-8.

Beyond these, modern readers like to recall v. 14, "The Lord is my strength and my song, and has become my salvation"; and v. 24, "This is the day the Lord has made, let us rejoice and be glad in it!"

### A God who is good
### (vv. 1-4)

Psalm 118 is primarily an individual prayer of thanksgiving, but it also has a communal sense and the air of a processional hymn. It may have been sung liturgically as worshipers entered the temple.

This makes it an appropriate text for Palm Sunday, along with the messianic interpretation that was given to it in some circles. As the psalmist testified of divine deliverance, so Hebrews of later years saw in it hope for a coming redeemer who would lead them to the same kind of victories celebrated in the Hallel psalms. [**The last Hallel**]

The psalm appears to be the testimony of someone – probably to be imagined as a king of Israel – who was beset by enemies and in danger of death, but who believed they had been delivered by the grace of God. Thus, the psalm opens with a reminder that God is always present

---

**The last Hallel:** Psalm 118 is the last of six psalms known as "Hallels" (Pss. 113–118). "Hallel" means "praise" ("Hallelu-jah" means "let us praise the LORD!"). The Hallel psalms were all written in praise to God for deliverance in a time of trouble. Jews recite the psalms in the synagogue on various holy days, including Sukkot, Passover, and Hannukah. Psalm 136, known as "the Great Hallel," is also recited during Passover.

---

*This text is read for the Liturgy of the Palms in Years A, B, and C. Psalm 118:1-2, 14-24 is read on Easter Day in Years A, B, and C. Psalm 118:14-29 is read on the Second Sunday after Easter in Year C. This study will give some attention to the entire psalm.*

---

**An abiding love:** The words of confession in vv. 1-4 and 29 declare that God's love is not only faithful and dependable, but also lasting: it is "forever." In each statement, the word for "forever" (*'ōlam*) comes first, as if to emphasize it. In Hebrew, verbs of being that we would translate as "is" or "are" are often not written, and must be understood. That is the case here. The chorus, which is repeated four times over, could be translated as "forever – his steadfast love!"

---

and always loving. The poet emphasizes this by a careful use of both repetition and word order. The first four verses serve as a summary introduction to the larger psalm.

The psalm begins with an imperative call for praise to Yahweh because of God's inherent goodness, revealed through steadfast love: "O give thanks to the LORD, for he is good; his steadfast love endures forever!" (v. 1). The same refrain will be repeated as the last verse in the psalm, framing the entire poem with gratitude for God's dependable love.

In the next three verses, the psalmist calls on three specific groups to praise Yahweh – the personal name God revealed to Moses – and for the same reason: because "His steadfast love endures forever." **[An abiding love]**

This suggests a call-and-response element as part of worship. In sequence, Israel (v. 2), the priests ("the house of Aaron, v. 3), and all who "fear God" (v. 4) are challenged to confess "His steadfast love endures forever."

The psalmist came to know the presence and the power of God through stories from his own religious heritage. In ceremonies of worship and celebration, he had often relived the ways in which God had brought deliverance to Israel. He would have remembered Abraham, Moses, and others who played significant roles in Hebrew tradition.

Israel's spiritual path had been uneven, but God's love and grace had been constant. Those who followed the psalmist in putting their trust in God learned that they were never fully alone, never unloved, never separated from the lingering, comforting touch of the Spirit of God. That is the way God is. God's steadfast love endures forever.

As the psalmist knew the inspiring stories of Yahweh and Israel, so we recall the stories of Jesus, how he loved the poor, healed the sick, and comforted the afflicted. We remember how he died on the cross but rose again, dealing with our sin in a way that only God could do.

If we trust the word of the psalmist, the love of God is not an issue. The only issue is how we respond to God's redeeming presence in Christ, which Paul declared could never be taken away (Rom. 8:37-39) – and whether we will adopt Jesus' way of looking at and responding to the world.

## A troubled man who prays
### (vv. 5-14)

Verses 5-14 are often omitted, perhaps because they speak of distress in the midst of an otherwise celebratory psalm, and perhaps because vv. 10-14 suggest a theme of warfare. Those verses, however, are central to our understanding of the psalmist's joyful tone.

The section consists of two rounds of testimony, vv. 5-9 and vv. 10-14, in which the poet speaks of past troubles, then speaks of how, with God's help, he had overcome. The first section states that he had been in a position of unspecified distress, but he had called on "Yah" (a short form of Yahweh) for deliverance. He testified that Yah's response "set me in a broad place" (v. 5, NRSV). A literal translation would be "Yah answered me in a broad place," but the implication of deliverance from a tight spot to an open place is apparent.

As one who had experienced God's deliverance, the poet could boast that Yahweh was at his side and ready to overcome all who might threaten him (vv. 6-7). He had learned to "take refuge in the LORD" rather than mortals, even royal ones (vv. 8-9).

The second part of this section assumes that the poet is himself royal, for he speaks of distress and deliverance on a national level. "All nations surrounded me," he said, but "in the name of the LORD I cut them off!" (vv. 10). Indeed, he speaks of being surrounded "on every side" (v. 11) by enemies who stung like bees or burned like thorns on fire (v. 12). They pushed him to the edge "so that I was falling," he said, "but the LORD helped me" (v. 13).

The strong testimony of v. 14 echoes the Song of Moses after the deliverance at the sea, "The LORD is my strength and my might, and he has become my salvation" (Exod. 15:2). A similar quotation is found in Isa. 12:2: "Surely God is my salvation; I will trust, and will not be afraid, for the LORD GOD is my strength and my might; he has become my salvation." **[LORD GOD]**

**LORD GOD:** The unusual spelling of both "LORD" and "GOD" with uppercase letters in Isa. 12:2 is due to the prophet's repetition of God's revealed name in both full and abbreviated forms. Most Bible translations consistently use "LORD" when translating the name Yahweh, and occasionally use "GOD" when translating the name *'adonai Yahweh*, to avoid translating it as "Lord LORD," as in Ezek. 37:3. Here, Isaiah says "For my strength and might (is) *Yah, Yahweh*." Both versions would normally be rendered as "LORD," but the translators chose to use "LORD GOD" as a way of acknowledging the divine name on both counts while also indicating the two forms of it in Isaiah's speech.

### A God who delivers
#### (vv. 15-25)

Verses 15-18 add a new wrinkle to the psalm. While the previous portion spoke of his dire straits and Yahweh's deliverance, only here do we get the impression that the psalmist identified his sufferings as punishment for his own shortcomings. Though saved from death by "the right hand of the LORD," the psalmist expressed a belief that "The LORD has punished me severely, but he did not give me over to death" (v. 18).

While the images of national crisis and warfare suggest the experience of one of Israel's kings – and hence to have been written before the exile – the psalm could have been used in later periods by anyone who wished to commemorate God's past deliverance as well as to express hope in God's future care.

The song was probably employed in worship as a processional liturgy, sung or acted out as worshipers entered the sanctuary on certain days. Perhaps we are to imagine a victorious king returning from battle with his entourage and coming first to the temple, where he called to the priests: "Open to me the gates of righteousness, that I may enter through them and give thanks to the LORD" (v. 19).

Most commentators interpret "gates of righteousness" as the gates to the temple, but Mitchell Dahood has suggested that the martial atmosphere of the poem should lead us to think of the king calling instructions to the gatekeepers before entering the gates of Jerusalem, rather than of the temple (*Psalms III:101-150*, vol. 17A, Anchor Bible [Doubleday, 1970], 159). [**Temple Gates**]

In postexilic usage, a worship leader might have taken the role of the king in leading worshipers through the gates and into the temple.

Note the interplay between vv. 19 and 20, which probably represents an exchange between the returning king and the priest in charge of the temple. The king calls out to the gatekeeper, demanding that he open the "gates of righteousness" (v. 19), but is reminded that the gate belongs to Yahweh, and only the righteous should enter through it (v. 20).

We note a shift in number between v. 19, which refers to the "gates of righteousness" (plural) and v. 20, which uses the singular form to identify "the gate of the LORD." Some scholars speculate that the singular form refers to the door of the temple building itself rather than the outer gates leading into the temple courts.

Neither gates nor ground can be righteous or unrighteous. If the portal to the temple was a "gate of righteousness,"

**Temple gates:** We cannot know exactly how the temple mount was laid out in pre-exilic times, but during the second temple period, the temple complex had at least 13 gates leading into it. On the southern side of the temple mount, a Triple Gate and Double Gate, known together as the "Huldah Gates," led from the Southern Steps to underground ramps by which one could ascend to the temple courtyards. Most pilgrims would have entered by this way.

The photo shows the "Triple Gate." It, along with a Double Gate to the west, was blocked up during the Middle Ages. The tunnels and corridors inside are now part of the Al 'Aqsa Mosque, which was established early in the eighth century CE. It is off-limits to non-Muslims.

it would be because righteous people entered through it. The word translated as "righteousness" (*tsedek*) describes those whose behavior is just and correct, honoring God.

The psalmist's metaphor of a stone rejected by the builders being ultimately chosen as the cornerstone is so familiar from its New Testament usage in reference to Christ that many are unaware that it originally referred to the king for whom (or by whom) this psalm was written.

The psalmist thanked God for divine deliverance (v. 21). Though rejected or considered useless by others, God had made him the chief cornerstone, the most important foundation stone in a building (vv. 22-23). The same terminology was adopted by New Testament writers and applied to Christ, who was also rejected by humankind, but exalted by God as the cornerstone (cf. Luke 20:17; Acts. 4:11; 1 Pet. 2:4, 7). [**Cornerstone or keystone?**]

Verse 23 celebrates "the LORD's doing" in bringing deliverance (v. 23), and the same theme is evident in the following verse, though not in most translations. The reading of v. 24 so popular in memory and song declares "This is the day that the LORD has made; let us rejoice and be glad in it." Hebrew uses the same word for "make," "act," or "do," and the same pronominal suffix can mean "him" as well as "it." Thus, the verse could also be translated "This is the day the LORD acted, let us rejoice and be glad in him."

Careful readers may have a sense of surprise with v. 25, as the psalm turns from praise to plea as the singer prays for God's saving work to continue in every trying circumstance (v. 25): "Save us, we beseech you, O LORD! O LORD, we beseech you, give us success!"

In prayers such as this, the memory of past deliverance brings hope to present worshipers who long for salvation yet to come.

## A God who blesses
### (vv. 26-29)

"Save us!" (v. 25) comes from the Hebrew expression *hoshî'â na* (literally, "save, please"), which comes into English as "Hosanna." Though technically a request for help, the expression came to be used as a word of praise, a shout of acclamation to the one who is able to save.

It is no surprise, then, that the crowds who followed Jesus during his triumphal entry shouted "Hosanna" in conjunction with their quotation of v. 26: "Blessed is the

---

> **Cornerstone or keystone?** Verse 22 begins with the word for stone (*'eben*). While most translations see *rōsh pinnâ* at the end of v. 22 as meaning "cornerstone," as *rōsh* means "head" or "chief," while *pinnâ* can mean "corner." Thus, "the stone that the builders rejected has become the chief cornerstone."
>
> Some translators regard *pinnâ* in the more general sense of "a place of turning" (the verbal root means "to turn"), and argue that the writer has in mind the keystone or capstone that fits at the top of a stone arch, holding it firmly in place. Thus, NIV has "The stone the builders rejected has become the capstone."

---

one who comes in the name of the Lord!" (Matt. 19:9, Mark 11:9-10, Luke 19:38, John 12:13).

The spreading of branches during the Palm Sunday entry may also reflect v. 27, which speaks of leafy boughs being used in the festal procession, or to adorn the large outdoor altar that stood before the temple.

While we typically read these verses as if the people are blessing God, it is likely that v. 26 should be read as if spoken by the priests, who pronounced a blessing on the victorious king and his retinue who had entered the temple in God's name: "We bless you from the house of the LORD." Recall the poet's earlier claim that he had "cut off" his enemies "in the name of the LORD" (v. 10).

In later years, the psalm could have been used as a blessing for any worshipers who gathered in God's name to offer praise and seek God's favor.

They, like the king in the psalm's initial setting, would be moved to declare allegiance and praise to the author of their salvation: "You are my God, and I will give thanks to you; you are my God, and I will extol you" (v. 28). English readers miss the wordplay, but the psalmist's testimony in v. 28 consists of five words in Hebrew, all of them beginning with the letter *'alef*, roughly equivalent to an "a" in English.

The psalm remains meaningful, for today we continue to express our devotion to God, who has redeemed us through Jesus Christ. As the psalmist confessed, "You are my God," so Paul reminded all people "That if you confess with your mouth, 'Jesus is Lord,' and believe in your heart that God raised him from the dead, you will be saved" (Rom. 10:9).

The psalm begins and ends with praise to God, whose steadfast love endures forever. The words were written and celebrated hundreds of years before Jesus walked the earth, and thousands of years before our own pilgrimages began, but we may still echo its theme and declare our praise to the one whose steadfast love has saved us all and who sticks with us for all time.

## The Hardest Question
### Is there trouble that we missed?

The lectionary readings tend to skip over verses that we might find problematic, but serious students of the Bible have a responsibility to go beyond the easy or appealing verses and consider the hard parts, too.

For its treatment of Psalm 118, the lectionary calls for the use of vv. 1-2 and 19-29, bypassing a lengthy section about deliverance from enemies that includes some troublesome claims. I've given this section a cursory treatment in the study above, but it is worth a second look.

I included vv. 3-4 along with vv. 1-2 because they clearly form a unit. Beyond that, vv. 5-18 focus on the psalmist's testimony that he had been in a very dangerous situation, but Yahweh had delivered him from enemies all about.

The first part of that (vv. 5-9) is an impressive testimony of praise. Here's my rather literal translation:

"From a tight place, I cried out to Yah; He answered me with the spaciousness of Yah. Yahweh is for me; I will not be afraid. What can humans do to me (or, 'for me')? Yahweh is for me (as) my helper, and I, I will keep seeing those who hate me. Better (is) seeking refuge in Yahweh than trusting in humans. Better (is) seeking refuge in Yahweh than trusting (even) the noble ones."

These verses are a straightforward claim that God is more trustworthy than humans. The psalmist – who speaks as a king would – had put his trust in Yahweh, and it follows that those who are wise will do the same.

We also find little to concern us in vv. 14-18, which celebrate the victory Yahweh had given, though v. 18 brings new information. The psalmist did not think of his foes as random enemies, but he believed that Yahweh had sent them to chastise him for some fault: "The LORD has punished me severely, but he did not give me over to death."

This puts Yahweh in the position of both instigating and defeating the same enemies, using them to teach the psalmist a lesson. Such is not an uncommon theme, however: the prophets had no problem asserting that God used other nations to punish Israel before enabling Israel to defeat their oppressors.

Reading vv. 10-14 is a bit more difficult. Here, the psalmist speaks of enemy nations surrounding him on every side, swarming like bees, blazing like a fire, pushing him hard – but with the LORD's help, he testifies three times that "I cut them off" (NRSV, vv. 10, 11, 12).

A surface reading of this translation causes little concern, but if we look more closely, we discover that the verb translated as "cut them off" is the verb commonly used for "to circumcise." Michael Dahood translates the three assertions as "I cut off their foreskins" (*Psalms III*, Anchor Bible Commentary [Doubleday, 1970], 154, 157). Dahood suggests that this recalls 1 Sam. 18:25-27, in which David was sent to obtain 100 foreskins from Philistine soldiers as a bride price for Saul's daughter, Michal.

Does the author mean to imply that nations defeated by Israel were forced to convert to Yahwism, with males being required to submit to circumcision? There is some evidence of this taking place when the Jews regained temporary control of the land following the Maccabean revolt in the second century BCE, but we have no record of Israel routinely doing this during the Old Testament period.

The NRSV's translation "I cut them off" (also NIV and NASB95) apparently takes "I circumcised them" as a metaphor for the psalmist defeating his enemies (cp. HCSB, "I destroyed them"). Others take the verb as a homonym from a different stem meaning to "lean" or "incline," and render the causative form as "I warded them off" (Leslie Allen, *Psalms 101–150,* Word Biblical Commentary [Word Books, 1983], 120). The NET has "I pushed them away."

In either case, the sharp edge of the psalmist's pride in gaining victory through violence puts something of a damper on the poem's celebratory theme, apparently leading to its exclusion from the lectionary. Giving attention to the verses reminds us that the psalm is not all happiness and joy: victory in war is not without its painful and unsavory side.

## Liturgy of the Palms
## Second Reading
## Matthew 21:1-11

# The Problem with Palms

*Tell the daughter of Zion, Look, your king is coming to you, humble, and mounted on a donkey, and on a colt, the foal of a donkey. (Matt. 11:5)*

Imagine it: listen carefully, and perhaps you can hear the crowd. Off in the distance, a muffled roar, indistinguishable words, then a cheer, and a growing chant: "Hosanna! Hosanna! Hosanna!"

If you squint just a bit, you can see the bright holiday clothes of festive pilgrims gathering in Jerusalem. The Passover is not for several days yet, and the people are restless. A rumor draws them from their eating, sightseeing, or napping. "Jesus is going to be king! He's on his way to Jerusalem!"

Go into your imagination, and feel the press of people, thousands of them, packing the road from Bethany to Jerusalem. You can smell the dust, and the donkeys, and the unmistakable odor of too many unwashed people too close together.

You can sense the almost palpable excitement in the air, and soon you find yourself running into a field to tear a limb from a small tree, and then straining to see through all the other waving branches. You may even find yourself shouting "Hosanna to the Son of David! Blessed is he who comes in the name of the Lord! Hosanna in the highest!"

But who is this man on the donkey that the people are treating like a king? If he really is a new king, am I supposed to be his subject? If so, what will he expect of me?

### A king on a donkey
#### (vv. 1-5)

It was the last week of Jesus' earthly life, the crucifixion only six days away, though no one other than Jesus had a clue. The story begins in a village called Bethphage, east of Jerusalem and a little closer than Bethany, where Jesus often lodged with his friends Mary, Martha, and Lazarus. Bethany was about two miles from Jerusalem, on the southeastern slope of the Mount of Olives.

Jesus began his descent into the city from atop the Mount of Olives, which stands about 100 feet higher than the city, with the deep Kidron Valley between them. People walking the road toward Jerusalem had an unrivaled view of the impressive Temple Mount and the city's proud walls.

As reconstructed by Herod, the Second Temple was so amazing that the Talmud famously said "Whoever has not seen Herod's building has not seen a beautiful building in his life." There was more than beauty to the Temple Mount, however: the northwest corner was home to an impressive tower and fortress called the Antonia, where a contingent of Roman soldiers kept a watchful eye. The temple also had its own security detail of armed guards. For anyone who opposed the normal way of doing things, the city bristled with danger.

Jesus had come to Jerusalem despite the hazard, because there were still things he needed to say and do. One of his actions spoke more loudly than words: he rode a donkey into town. [**One story, four times**]

And why was this so significant?

The gospels never speak of Jesus riding on anything but a boat before this, but always portray him as walking with his disciples. He ate and slept and sweated in their midst.

> **One story, four times:** The story that we celebrate on Palm Sunday appears in all four gospels (Matt. 21:1-9, Mark 11:1-10, Luke 19:28-40, John 12:12-18). The accounts differ in detail and emphasis, but clearly recall the same event.

Often he drew apart from them for prayer, but he never expected any special privilege. But now Jesus had sent two of his disciples to fetch a donkey for him to ride.

Why would Jesus want to ride a donkey? Jesus knew that in Israel's heritage, royals typically rode donkeys or mules, especially during times of peace (mules are the offspring of a male donkey and a female horse). As King David neared death and named his son Solomon as his successor, he ordered his officials to "have my son Solomon ride on my own mule, and bring him down to Gihon. There let the priest Zadok and the prophet Nathan anoint him king over Israel" (1 Kgs. 1:33-34).

Thus, entering the city on a young donkey was a symbolic way for Jesus to assume a royal persona. As crowds longing for a royal messiah shouted "Hosanna," he heard their plea for deliverance and accepted their praise.

In times of war, a king might ride to or from the city in a chariot pulled by strong steeds, but Jesus chose to ride on the back of a donkey, a symbol of peace. Despite the crowd's insistence, he refused to become the military messiah that the crowds – even some of his disciples – wanted.

Jesus' choice of a young colt that had not been ridden suggests the sacred aspect of his journey to Jerusalem. Only animals that had never been used as beasts of burden could be considered suitable for sacred purposes (Num. 19:2, 1 Sam. 6:7). Jesus came not only as a king, but as the divine king. His final entrance to Jerusalem was not a political occasion, but a sacred one. [**One donkey, or two?**]

## The adoring crowd
### (vv. 6-9)

What might Jesus' disciples have been thinking as they stood on the Mount of Olives, looking across the Kidron Valley at the impressive temple complex and city of Jerusalem? As Jesus prepared to climb on the donkey's back, a string of excitement must have snapped within them and freed their pent-up hopes.

> **One donkey, or two?** Careful readers may note that Matthew's gospel appears to have Jesus riding on two donkeys at once. In v. 2, Jesus commands "Go into the village ahead of you, and immediately you will find a donkey tied, and a colt with her; untie them and bring *them* to me." We then learn that "The disciples went and did as Jesus had directed *them*; they brought the donkey and the colt, and put their cloaks *on them*, and he sat *on them*" (vv. 6-7, emphasis added). The clear implication is that there were two animals and that Jesus sat astride both donkeys – an unlikely picture.
>
> This has led commentators to a variety of solutions. One suggestion is that, since Jesus wanted to ride the unbroken colt, its mother would have been brought along to keep the colt calm. Another is that, though Jesus would have ridden only one animal, the two of them would have been seen as a unit. A grammatical argument suggests that the referent in "he sat on them" is "the cloaks," not "the donkey and the colt."
>
> The more likely solution is that Matthew appears to be trying to match the prophecy of Zechariah that he quotes in v. 5: "Tell the daughter of Zion, Look, your king is coming to you, humble, and mounted on a donkey, and on a colt, the foal of a donkey."
>
> Matthew, like most New Testament writers, quotes rather loosely from the Greek translation of the Old Testament. The Hebrew text of Zech. 9:9 is slightly different: "Rejoice greatly, O daughter Zion! Shout aloud, O daughter Jerusalem! Lo, your king comes to you; triumphant and victorious is he, humble and riding on a donkey, on a colt, the foal of a donkey."
>
> Zechariah's oracle is clearly poetic, and utilizes the common Hebrew practice of synonymous parallelism, in which two paired lines say the same thing in different words. Zechariah's prophecy did not picture two animals: "on a colt, the foal of a donkey" was merely a poetic expansion of the previous line, "humble and riding on a donkey." The colt was the foal of a donkey.
>
> Whether the author of Matthew's gospel failed to understand the basics of Hebrew poetry is unclear, but he seemed to think two animals were necessary for the prophecy to be fulfilled.
>
> The other gospels are clear in recognizing that Jesus sent for and rode just one animal (Mark 11:2, Luke 19:30, John 12:14).

They knew that Jesus was perfectly capable of walking, and not so uppity as to think he should ride. Jesus never did anything without a purpose, so he must have been saying something. Gradually it dawned on them that Jesus was agreeing to be treated like a king.

The disciples had longed for this, but they had thought it would never happen. Once they realized what was on his mind, though, the men did all they could to orchestrate a more royal procession. They draped their cloaks over the donkey's back to make Jesus' seat more comfortable and to make the donkey look more presentable. The road was already crowded with pilgrims, and many of them knew about Jesus, so it was not hard for the disciples to stir up the crowd's excitement.

Soon the road was jammed with pilgrims and locals alike. They joined the disciples in laying their cloaks across the path in homage to Jesus. They broke branches from nearby trees and waved them in the air and spread them on the road.

Readers typically assume that the crowd was using palm fronds to wave in the air and line the road. While date palms were common to southern Judea and the area around Jericho, however, they were not native to Jerusalem, which is about 2600 feet above sea level and too cool for palm trees to thrive.

Matthew's gospel says the people "cut branches from the trees" (Matt. 26:8), while Mark's version says they "spread leafy branches that they had cut in the fields" (Mark 11:8). Only John's gospel says "They took branches of palm trees and went out to meet him" (John 12:13). It is possible that some pilgrims from lower elevations could have brought palm fronds with them to use in building booths for shelter in and around the overcrowded city, but most of the branches that greeted Jesus' entrance to Jerusalem were likely from other trees and bushes.

While the cloaks and branches suggested a royal procession, the cheers of the people (v. 9) were even more significant: "Hosanna to the Son of David! Blessed is the one who comes in the name of the Lord! Hosanna in the highest heaven!"

The shout was a loose quotation of Ps. 118:25, where "Hosanna" precedes "Blessed is he who comes in the name of the LORD!" Both quotations were used in the liturgy of the Jewish feast of tabernacles, when pilgrims would commonly wave branches in the air and pray for God's help.

The kicker in the people's shout is their identification of Jesus as the "Son of David" who comes "in the name of the Lord." Based on beliefs incorporating various prophecies (Isa. 11:1, Jer. 30:9, Ezek. 34:23-24, among others), with roots going back to the God's promise to David in 2 Samuel 7, many Jews anticipated the coming of a Davidic descendant who would arise as a "new David" and lead Israel not only to independence, but also to preeminence among the nations. That would be cause for praise, indeed.

## The unfinished story
### (vv. 10-11)

As we study this scene, we must remember that the story continues. As Jesus entered Jerusalem, the people all about took notice. Matthew tells us "the whole city was stirred and asked 'Who is this?'" The crowds answered, "This is Jesus, the prophet from Nazareth in Galilee."

When we read this story, we must also ask, "Who is this?" More to the point, we must ask, "Who is Jesus to me?"

The problem with palms is that once the branches are cut from the tree, they don't last long. The problem with that first Palm Sunday is that the excitement of the crowd soon faded, and when the disappointing events of Good Friday rolled around, many of the same voices who had shouted "Hosanna!" on Sunday were likely shouting "Crucify Him!" Their love for Jesus was shallow and based entirely on their hope of what exciting things he could do for them.

Many pilgrims would happily follow Jesus on the road to the throne, but not on the road to the cross. They would wave palms before the coming king, but they could not accept the Suffering Servant.

Jesus' entry to Jerusalem was significant in many ways. Jesus knew that the end of his earthly ministry was near. It was time to do what he had come to accomplish. It was now or never. This was Jesus' opportunity to be obedient to the will of God, and to accomplish the purpose set out for him.

It was a day in history that speaks to Christians of every age. Are we also so shallow that we will wave palms on one Sunday a year, and sing occasional hymns of praise, but refuse to obey the Servant King?

There is a life ahead of us, and a purpose for us. None of us know how long our lives will be, just how much time we have.

None of us can know all that the future holds. We don't know how long we will be on this earth. But we can know that God has a purpose for us. We are called to love God and love others with the kind of love that makes a difference. Jesus has challenged us to speak out words of truth, to reach out our hands, to hold out our hearts.

We are called to do that *now*. Many people hold the ideal of one day being truly faithful to Christ, but not yet.

Serious believers recognize that day is now. We don't know how many more days there will be.

### The Hardest Question
### What does "Hosanna" mean?

We typically assume that the word "hosanna" was simply a Greek or Hebrew shout of praise, but there is much more to the story. "Hosanna" is a Greek spelling of the Hebrew expression "*hoshî'â na'*," which literally means "save please." In the Old Testament, as in Ps. 118:25, it is generally translated "Save us!" Rather than translating the expression from Hebrew to Greek, the New Testament writers simply transliterated the phrase into Greek letters, and as one word.

*Hoshî'â* is an imperative form from the causative stem of a verb that means "to save" or "to deliver." It is the root of the name Joshua (meaning "Yahweh is salvation"), on which the Greek spelling "Jesus" is based. The additional "*na'*" added to *hoshî'â* is a particle of entreaty that means "please." Together, the expression means "please save."

In the Old Testament, *hoshî'â* was used as a request for help from another person, such as the king. For example, a woman from Tekoa sought David's help in saving her son (2 Sam. 14:4), and a starving woman in Israel sought help by crying out to the king (2 Kgs. 6:26). It was also used by those seeking divine help, as in one of Jeremiah's oracles of hope: "For thus says the LORD: Sing aloud with gladness for Jacob, and raise shouts for the chief of the nations; proclaim, give praise, and say, 'Save (*hôsh'a*), O LORD, your people, the remnant of Israel.'" (Jer. 31:7)

Though technically a request for help, the expression was so commonly directed to God that it came to be used as a word of praise, mainly as a shout of acclamation to one who is able to save. It is no surprise, then, that the crowds who followed Jesus during his triumphal entry shouted "Hosanna" in conjunction with an abbreviated quotation of Ps. 118:25-26: "Blessed is the one who comes in the name of the LORD!" (Matt. 19:9, Mark 11:9-10, Luke 19:38, John 12:13).

In the psalm, *hoshî'â na'* is clearly a request for help rather than a shout of praise: "Save us, we beseech you, O LORD! O LORD, we beseech you, give us success! Blessed is the one who comes in the name of the LORD. We bless you from the house of the LORD" (Ps. 118:25-26).

Thus, when the crowds shouted "hosanna!" to Jesus, their primary intent was not just to praise him, but to plead with him to rise up as king and deliver them from the Roman occupation. They not only wanted him to be the Messiah (from the Hebrew *mashîah*, "anointed one"), but also the *môshî'a* (deliverer).

# Sixth Sunday in Lent

## Liturgy of the Passion
## First Reading
## Isaiah 50:4-9*

# Standing Firm

*The Lord GOD has given me the tongue of a teacher,*
*that I may know how to sustain the weary with a word. (Isa. 50:4a)*

Have you ever known aged saints who faced years of hardship or loss, yet maintained a steady faith in God? Rather than blaming God for the trials that come their way, they trusted in God for the strength to endure them. Instead of complaining that God has allowed them to suffer, they sought what lessons God might teach them through the painful experience.

> **Servant songs:** The "Servant Songs" are often identified as Isa. 42:1-4, 49:1-6, 50:1-11, and 52:13–53:12, but scholars disagree on their precise limits.
>
> Some, for example, consider the first song to be comprised of Isa. 42:1-4 only, while others see it as 42:1-7 and others stretch it to 42:1-9. The second song is often delimited as 49:1-6, but some scholars see it continuing through v. 13. Some identify the third song as 50:1-11, but others include only 50:4-11. There is little question about the limits of the fourth song, marked as 52:13–53:12. Some scholars interpret Isaiah 55 as a fifth servant song.
>
> Who is the servant? At times, the "servant" clearly appears to be Israel in a corporate sense, but in other instances, as here, the servant is depicted as an individual. And, while he suffers, his pain appears to be for the sake of others, rather than for his own sin (cp. the charges against Israel in Isa. 40:1-2, 42:22-25, 43:22-28, 47:6, 50:1 with descriptions of the servant in Isa. 50:5-6; 53:4-6, 9, 11-12).
>
> Early Christian believers took Isaiah's description of the "suffering servant" as prophecies of Christ, who suffered for others without complaint.

This is the picture we find in Isa. 50:4-9. The passage is commonly regarded as the third of four "Servant Songs" in Isaiah (the others are 42:2-4, 49:1-6, and 52:13–53:12), even though the word "servant" does not appear in the text. Like the second Servant Song (49:1-6) the prophet's words are written in the first person, as if *he* is the servant. **[Servant Songs]**

### A teacher who learns
### (vv. 4-5)

The words of Isa. 50:4-9 were probably penned late in the exilic period by a prophet who wrote in the tradition of Isaiah. He is often called "Second Isaiah," or "Isaiah of the Exile."

The prophet's audience consisted mainly of people who were born in Babylon and knew of life in and around Jerusalem only from stories told by their parents or grandparents. The lead-in to the third Servant Song follows the literary form of a lawsuit (50:1-3) which declares that the people's "mother" (a corporate reference to their ancestors) was guilty of iniquities and transgressions, for which the time in exile was punishment.

The prophet speaks in the voice of the servant, as one who has also suffered. Rather than complaining, he said the experience had taught him something, and he sought to encourage others by passing on what he had gained. "The Lord GOD has given me the tongue of a teacher," he

---

*This text appears for the Passion Liturgy in Years A, B, and C, and for Proper 19 in Year B.

> **Lord GOD:** Ordinarily, texts pairing these two divine names appear as LORD God, but here (50:4) they are Lord GOD. Why? The most common dual expression is *Yahweh 'elohîm*. Since the divine name *Yahweh* is always rendered in all capital letters, and *'elohîm* means "God," it translates as LORD God.
>
> Occasionally, however, some of the prophets preferred the expression *'adonai Yahweh*. "'*Adonai*," which could refer either to God or to a person in authority, also translates as "Lord." We wouldn't want to render it as "Lord LORD," so translators have conventionally chosen to spell "GOD" in all capital letters to indicate that it is a reference to Yahweh, resulting in "Lord GOD."

wrote, "that I may know how to sustain the weary with a word" (v 4a). [**Lord GOD**]

The servant had learned to make the most of his suffering, not letting his pain be wasted but transforming it into growth and greater maturity. And what the servant learned, he taught: "how to sustain the weary with a word."

What the servant was called to do in these verses, God's servants today may still do. We don't have to let trouble turn us into victims, but we may learn from suffering and turn our pain into wisdom and share it.

That kind of learning does not come easy: working through grief is a daily task. The prophet wrote that God "wakens my ear" morning by morning "to listen as those who are taught" (v. 4b) – to become a student of suffering.

Isaiah was not describing an angelic alarm clock, but a daily openness to God's Spirit. Whether suffering or not, there is much God can teach us every day if only we pay attention, thinking theologically through all the activities of daily life.

If we don't learn something about God's care every day, we're not paying attention. Our natural tendency is to be so caught up in ourselves and our needs (or wants) and our duties that we overlook the many ways in which God may be speaking.

For the servant, the key was seeking to be constantly faithful to God. The conjunction of "the Lord GOD has opened my ear" and "I was not rebellious" (v. 5) is not random: the two are intimately related. The servant "did not turn backward" from God, but faced forward, looking toward God, listening intently with open ears.

The servant, however, was talking about more than hearing. The Hebrew Bible does not have a specific word for "obey," but uses the word that also means "to hear." We understand this. When parents give children an instruction and don't get a quick response, they often ask "Did you *hear* me?" Theoretically, to hear is to obey. The implication is that if one truly hears God speak, he or she will obey, and not turn back.

Jesus would later suggest a similar thought, for many people who were within the sound of his voice did not hear his words to the point of understanding or obedience. Thus, Jesus was prone to punctuate important teachings with "He who has ears to hear, let him hear" (Mark 4:9, 23; 11:16; and parallels). While the translation "let him hear" implies permission, Jesus' intent was imperative: "Whoever has ears to hear had better listen!" (NET).

### A sufferer who perseveres
### (vv. 6-8a)

The servant of Isa. 50:4-9 said he awakened to learn from God each day. Apparently, on some of those days he awoke with a raw back and sore cheeks from being attacked by detractors. "I gave my back to those who struck me," he wrote, "and my cheeks to those who pulled out the beard; I did not hide my face from insult and spitting" (v. 6).

Apparently, the prophet's mixed message of both condemnation and consolation was not always welcome. He described physical abuse at the hands of detractors: public beatings, pulling of the beard, spitting in the face (v. 6).

All these actions suggest typical ways of shaming and humiliation in the ancient Near East. Cutting or pulling the beard, for example, was designed to call one's masculinity into question, leading to public embarrassment (2 Sam. 10:4; Isa. 7:20, 15:2; Jer. 48:37). Similarly, spitting in the face was a ritual means of insulting another person, causing public shame (Num. 12:14, Deut. 25:9). Even today, we think of it as an expression of gross contempt: "He might as well have spit in my face!"

Despite persecution experienced at the hands of those he sought to help, the servant said he persevered because "the Lord GOD helps me." The servant understood that what is shameful or disgraceful in human eyes may be honored in God's eyes. Thus, he was able to say, "I have set my face like flint" (v. 7) despite the rain of blows or spit or painful tugs at his beard. Other people may have sought to humiliate him, but it was not their opinion he valued. It was God he sought to please. "Therefore," he said, "I have not been disgraced ... and I know that I shall not be put to shame; he who vindicates me is near" (vv. 7-8a).

### A God who vindicates
### (vv. 8b-9)

The final two verses turn the assurance of vv. 6-7 into a challenge for others. Like a boxer who beckons his opponent to aim another blow at his already-bloodied face, the servant challenged those who had beaten and insulted him. In a pair of corresponding poetic lines, he cried: "Who will contend with me? Let us stand up together. Who are my adversaries? Let them confront me" (v. 8).

The servant may have been down, but not out. He was bloodied, but not beaten. Words, blows, and insulting spittle might come his way, but he was able to shake them off and feel no disgrace, because he knew something his tormentors did not understand. They did not know the God he knew. They did not comprehend true nobility.

The servant's persecutors could treat him as worthy of punishment, but he knew "It is the Lord GOD who helps me; who will declare me guilty?" (v. 9a). No man or woman can impose guilt on one who is upright in God's eyes. They may sling mud or throw stones, but the mud doesn't stick and the stones bounce away. It was the servant's accusers who were guilty and deserving of punishment (vv. 1-3): he had remained faithful to God.

The servant was confident that his perseverance would lead to God's preservation. Trials would come, but he would endure. In contrast, a more tenuous fate awaited his opponents: "All of them will wear out like a garment; the moth will eat them up" (v. 9b). His accusers might have felt right in their own eyes and powerful in their own strength, but they were no more permanent than a cloak that appears impressive today but is destined to become worn out and moth-eaten. [**Confidence**]

And what does the ancient servant have to do with us? Images from Isa. 50:4-9 are often applied to Christ as the ultimate fulfillment of what it means to be God's servant. The third Servant Song begins by describing the servant as a

> **Confidence:** Isaiah's trust in God inspired educator Page Kelley to point out years ago that the servant's "sublime affirmation of faith reminds one of the later words of the Apostle Paul, 'If God be for us, who can be against us?' (Rom 8:31, KJV)" ("Isaiah," *Broadman Bible Commentary*, vol. 5 [Broadman Press, 1971], 334]).

teacher who learns daily from God. "Teacher" was perhaps the most common title attributed to Jesus during his adult ministry. Jesus spoke of spending time in prayer and of what he had gained from the Father (Luke 10:22).

In Mark 10:34, Jesus predicted that he would be mocked, beaten, and spat upon. Accounts such as Mark 14:65 reflect the details of this prophecy in line with what the servant of 50:7-8 endured.

Although many Christians rightly see the fulfillment of Isa. 50:4-9 in the life and ministry of Christ, we must be careful not to limit the prophet's message to what happened in Jesus. Isaiah held forth an ideal for all who would find their sense of purpose and identity in the eyes of God rather than the world's view. That challenge remains: Are we listening, following, and trusting God no matter what others do?

### The Hardest Question
### What is "Second Isaiah"?

Readers commonly assume that a single author was responsible for the entire content of a biblical book attributed to Isaiah. One might argue that Isaiah of Jerusalem had God-given foresight and, during times of meditation, wrote oracles to address issues that would not arise for more than 150 years. The most likely explanation, however, is that there were at least two, if not three, prophets who contributed to the compilation of prophecies that became known by the name of its primary author.

During the latter half of the eighth century, the Israelites lived in two separate kingdoms: a northern realm called "Israel," and a southern one known as "Judah." The first Isaiah spent most of his life in Judah's capital city but spoke to the people of both nations. He lived in an age of relative peace and prosperity for the Israelites as a whole, but a time of oppression for the poor as wealthier Hebrews bought up property, often leaving the poor homeless and forced to work as indentured servants. The false security of peaceful times led many to think of religion as a system of required rituals, with no demand for personal righteousness and justice. Isaiah, who was active from roughly 742–700 BCE, joined the prophets Micah, Amos, and Hosea in decrying injustice and launching verbal barbs designed to deflate Israel's false sense of security.

Isaiah understood the political scene in addition to the economic, social, and religious aspects of life in Palestine. During Isaiah's ministry, the northern kingdom was defeated and carried into captivity. As the prophet predicted, Judah also fell under the power of Assyria, living as a vassal state. Much of Isaiah 1–39 describes this period in Israel's life.

With ch. 40, however, the scene shifts from eighth-century Judah to sixth-century Babylon. Judah fell to the Babylonian king Nebuchadnezzar in 597 BCE. Many Judahites were marched to Babylon that year, and many more were forced into captivity following the destruction of Jerusalem 10 years later.

God used Isaiah of Jerusalem to afflict the comfortable and warn them of the coming captivity. More than 150 years later, as the people languished in captivity, God raised up another prophet who spoke comfort to the afflicted. We often speak of him as "Second Isaiah." This prophet spoke words of encouragement and hope to a defeated and downhearted people. His work appears in Isaiah 40–55. As he preached in God's name, this Isaiah envisioned a coming "servant" who would suffer in behalf of his people.

Following the exile, the Hebrews who returned to Jerusalem faced different challenges, which are reflected in Isaiah 56–66. It is possible that Second Isaiah returned with the other Hebrews and continued to speak in that context. It is more likely, however, that yet a third prophet arose in Jerusalem to preach in the spirit of Isaiah. He is typically known as "Third Isaiah."

The possibility that multiple prophets contributed to the book called "Isaiah" does not take away from the book's nature as scripture, but testifies to God's interest in providing the message people need to hear at the time they need to hear it.

# Sixth Sunday in Lent

## Liturgy of the Passion
## Second Reading
## Psalm 31*

# Refuge and Redemption

*Be gracious to me, O LORD, for I am in distress;*
*my eye wastes away from grief, my soul and body also. (Ps. 31:9)*

Psalms that testify of distress and redemption gave voice to the cares and inspired the hopes of the ancient Hebrews. Embodied in the evolving Hebrew scriptures, they were also familiar to first-century Jews and early followers of Christ. Despite our very different historical and cultural settings, the same psalms remain meaningful today, as evidenced by their frequent appearance in the lectionary. Psalm 31 evokes images of the passion, including the phrase "Into your hand I commit my spirit," so it comes as no surprise that portions of the psalm would be read during Holy Week.

Four different variations on excerpts from the psalm appear in the lectionary, and those that exclude vv. 6-16 could lead one to think it is entirely a psalm of thanksgiving. When read in full, however, the psalm is primarily a lament, albeit studded with elements of both trust and praise, which is common in the psalms of lament. For study purposes, then, as opposed to a liturgical reading without comment, it's best to consider the whole. **[Structure]**

### A rock and a refuge
### (vv. 1-8)

The psalm relies heavily on formulaic language common to the poetry of lament, providing little in the way of specifics that might help us identify a particular situation of distress. The author speaks of enemies who would entrap

> **Structure:** Psalms of lament often appear unstructured, moving back and forth between cries of distress, expressions of trust, and declarations of praise, but not always in that order. That may also be characteristic of our own prayers in time of struggle: rather than bringing to God a carefully worded petition, our prayers often shift back and forth between expressions of need, appeals for help, and affirmations of trust.
>
> Peter Craigie has pointed out that Ps. 31:1-18 could be seen as having a chiastic construction leading to what may have been a liturgical break for a prophetic oracle, then concluding with a section of thanksgiving and praise. The chiastic portion can be diagrammed this way:
>
> A - Prayer (vv. 1-5)
>     B - Trust (vv. 6-8)
>         C - Lament (vv. 9-13)
>     B' - Trust (v. 14)
> A' - Prayer (vv. 15-18)
>
> That portion was followed by a shift to thanksgiving and praise (vv. 19-24). Thus, while some scholars have argued that the psalm has been stitched together from different sections, Craigie contends that "the structure (as analyzed above) suggests unity, as does the use of common terminology, repeated words and phrases extending throughout the psalm, and providing a framework of coherence" (Psalms 1–50, vol. 19 of Word Biblical Commentary [Word Books, 1983], 259).

---

*This text is used for the Passion Liturgy in Years A, B, and C. Psalm 31:1-5, 15-16 is read for the Fifth Sunday of Easter in Year A, and Ps. 31:1-5, 19-24 is read for the Ninth Sunday in Epiphany or Proper 1 in Year A. This study will cover the entire psalm, vv. 1-24.*

him (vv. 4, 7, 8), physical illness (vv. 9-10), community ostracism (vv. 11-13), and persecution from those who would lie to cause him shame (vv. 15-18). We have no way of knowing whether to read these as literal challenges or metaphorical expressions, but the distress was clearly real.

Verses 1-5 constitute a prayer for God to protect the psalmist from shame, to deliver him and become a "rock of refuge for me, a strong fortress to save me" (vv. 1-2). An editorial superscription associates the psalm with David, who fled to the "fortress of Adullam" and found refuge in the rocky cliffs and caves of southern Judea when Saul sought to kill him (1 Samuel 22–26). A psalm attributed to David in 2 Samuel 22, repeated as Psalm 18 and associated with that period begins: "The LORD is my rock, my fortress, and my deliverer, my God, my rock, in whom I take refuge, my shield and the horn of my salvation, my stronghold and my refuge, my savior; you save me from violence (2 Sam. 22:2-3).

The author of Psalm 31 likewise turns to God as a strong refuge, expressing trust that God will come through: "You are indeed my rock and my fortress; for your name's sake lead me and guide me" (v. 3). In v. 5 we find the words of trust later quoted by Jesus, "Into your hand I commit my spirit," though the context is quite different. The psalmist committed his spirit to God in hopes of being saved from whatever threatened him. Jesus committed his spirit to God without expecting deliverance, trusting God in death rather than seeking to escape it.

The poet turns to an expression of trust in vv. 6-8, suggesting a sense of assurance that God would preserve him. Compared to those who worshiped "worthless idols," he trusted in Yahweh's steadfast love, and he believed that God would save him from the unnamed enemy. In words reminiscent of Ps. 118:5, he declared "you have set my feet in a broad place."

The deliverance he asked for and trusted God for was not yet a reality, however. God had not delivered him "*into* the hand of the enemy," but had not fully delivered him *from* his predicament, either.

### A cry in distress
### (vv. 9-18)

That becomes evident with v. 9, where the poet lapses into lament, beseeching God's help in his precarious situation:

"Be gracious to me, O LORD, for I am in distress." His difficulties, whatever they were, had begun to affect his health: "my eye wastes away from grief, my soul and body also."

The troubles were nothing new, but a lengthy affliction: "For my life is spent with sorrow, and my years with sighing; my strength fails because of my misery, and my bones waste away" (v. 10). This sounds less like David in a tight spot, and more like someone facing depression. The psalmist's trials had left him feeling constant sadness.

We know that depression and stress can contribute to serious health issues, and it is widespread. According to the Centers for Disease Control and Prevention, between 2015 and 2018, more than 13 percent of Americans over the age of 18 took antidepressant medications at some point, including nearly a fourth of all women over 60 (https://www.cdc.gov/nchs/products/databriefs/db377.htm).

The psalmist had no drugs to increase the levels of dopamine or serotonin in his brain chemistry, no cognitive therapy to aid in dealing with his long-running sadness. His neighbors offered no comfort, but avoided being around him, leaving him isolated and paranoid (vv. 11-13). He felt "terror all around" as he imagined how others whispered about him and hatched plots to do him in. The author found himself surrounded by enemies, whether real or suspected.

From the depths of his misery, however, the psalmist took comfort in putting himself in God's hands: "But I trust in you, O LORD; I say, 'You are my God'" (v. 14). On the one hand, he could say "My times are in your hand," as if being resigned to whatever might happen, but he never stopped appealing for a good outcome: "deliver me from the hand of my enemies and persecutors" (v. 15).

In words that recall the Aaronic blessing of Num. 6:24-26, he prayed "Let your face shine upon your servant; save me in your steadfast love" (v. 16). [**The Aaronic Blessing**]

---

**The Aaronic blessing:** Numbers 6:23-27 relates God's instructions for Aaron to bless the Israelites. In words still quoted, often as a worship benediction, he was to say: "The LORD bless you and keep you; the LORD make his face to shine upon you, and be gracious to you; the LORD lift up his countenance upon you, and give you peace."

The petitioner appeared to fear the words of his enemies more than their knives. Perhaps they spoke evil of him, so he prayed that God would not let him "be put to shame," but instead cause "the wicked" to be shamed and sent "dumbfounded" – or perhaps "wailing" – to Sheol (v. 17). Surprisingly, the word *dāmam* can mean either "grow dumb or silent," or it could mean "to groan or wail."

Whether the psalmist wanted his opponents to die in silence or cry with pain is less certain than that he wished them an early demise. He thought it was no less than their "lying lips," insolent accusations, and contemptuous attitudes deserved.

### A testimony of trust
#### (vv. 19-24)

Even casual readers will note what appears to be a strong disconnect between vv. 18 and 19, for the cry of distress suddenly shifts to happy praise. This is not unusual in biblical laments, and we can't help but wonder why. Some commentators have suggested that the words of praise were added later, after the psalmist had experienced the deliverance he or she had requested. Others see it as a proleptic expression of trust, not unlike modern believers in certain circles who talk about "claiming the promise" as if it has already happened.

In a practical sense, when we think of how the psalm might have been used in worship, some have suggested that it could have been read on behalf of all who felt oppressed, with a break after v. 18, during which a cultic prophet or priest may have promised that God had heard and deliverance was sure.

In any case, vv. 19-24 take on a new tone of confidence and testimony. Echoing themes from his earlier appeals, the psalmist sings the praise of God's goodness toward those who find refuge in God from "human plots" and "contentious tongues" (vv. 19-20).

He prays as if deliverance has come: "Blessed be the LORD, for he has wondrously shown his steadfast love to me when I was beset as a city under siege" (v. 21). He appears to be speaking of past sorrow when he adds "I had said in my alarm, 'I am driven far from your sight,' but you heard my supplications when I cried out to you for help" (v. 22).

> **Be strong and courageous:** The psalmist's counsel to "be strong and take courage" may sound familiar, because it is a common theme in the first chapter of Joshua, a story that would have been familiar to the poet.
>
> As the book opens, with Joshua newly appointed to lead the people after Moses' death, Yahweh reportedly came to Joshua with instructions that included "Be strong and courageous; for you shall put his people in possession of the land that I swore to their ancestors to give them" (1:6) and "Only be strong and very courageous, being careful to act in accordance with all the law that my servant Moses commanded you…" (1:7), then "I hereby command you: Be strong and courageous; do not be frightened or dismayed, for the LORD your God is with you wherever you go" (1:9).
>
> Later, Joshua gave instructions to a group of commanders, who promised to obey his commands, urging him to "Only be strong and courageous." In 10:25, after a particularly bloody battle, Joshua urged his warrior chiefs to "be strong and courageous; for thus the LORD will do to all the enemies against whom you fight."

With these words of testimony, the psalmist emerges from depression to become a witness, indeed an evangelist of sorts. The final two verses no longer address God, but those gathered for worship: "Love the LORD, all you his saints," he called, testifying that "The LORD preserves the faithful, but abundantly repays the one who acts haughtily" (v. 23).

Encouragement is most meaningful when it comes from someone else who knows how we feel, who has been in our shoes, and who has lived to tell the story. Other worshipers in attendance when this psalm was read could have been facing difficulties of their own, feeling put upon or threatened by others, isolated from the community, and wondering if God still cared. To them, the happy poet offered heartening words to motivate faith: "Be strong, and let your heart take courage, all you who wait for the LORD" (v. 24). [**Be strong and courageous**]

We may have found ourselves in the psalmist's sandals – discouraged and depressed, lonely and fearful. We may have prayed for some time, with no apparent result. Yet, there is hope. We may not always get the kind of deliverance we hope for, or see others get the comeuppance we think they deserve, but we can find strength and renewed courage as we trust – and wait – for LORD. The waiting is where real trust takes place.

## The Hardest Question
### How should we hear and interpret v. 23?

We commonly read the Psalms for encouragement or comfort in times of trial. Psalms of trust such as 11, 23, or 27 can serve as a boost to our sense of hope and confidence in God. Psalms of lament can also be helpful to read as a source of both commiseration in knowing that others have struggled even as we have, and inspiration, since many of the laments also include elements of petition, trust, and thanksgiving.

In doing so, we must be careful to remember that the psalms were written by people who believed that they lived in a binding covenant with God that promised blessings to the faithful and trouble to the willful. The covenant stipulations, so clearly expressed in Deuteronomy 28, underlay much of the theology of the Old Testament.

This is reflected in the psalms of lament in two ways. One is through an awareness that the theology did not always pan out as expected: sometimes the faithful suffered and the wicked prospered. The psalms of lament often express frustration with this: the poets who wrote them may have been aware of past sins, but they were always penitent and thought of themselves as faithful and there-fore deserving of deliverance from distress, especially from those they considered to be wicked. They likewise consid-ered such wayward people to be destined for trouble.

Laments such as Psalm 31 suggest that periods of afflic-tion may have gone on for years with no sign of letting up, but the psalms generally conclude with an affirmation that God had heard their prayer and deserved due praise.

Modern readers who examine verses such as 31:23 – "The LORD preserves the faithful, but abundantly repays the one who acts haughtily" – must be careful not to assume that the verse guarantees we will be healed from sickness, saved from financial troubles, or delivered from dangerous situations. Even the Hebrews understood that it didn't always happen as expected, leading to the hard questions asked in Job and Ecclesiastes.

The psalms may still offer courage and hope, but the promissory parts shouldn't be read as assurance that all our present prayers will get a positive response. Jesus' quotation from Ps. 31:5 provides an appropriate illustra-tion of this: while the psalmist commended his spirit to God's hand while hoping to be delivered from trial, Jesus commended his spirit to God at the moment of death, not expecting deliverance, but trusting that God was present with him despite his exigency.

## Liturgy of the Passion
## Third Reading
## Philippians 2:1-13*

# Living Mindfully

*Let each of you look not to your own interests, but to the interests of others. (Phil. 2:4)*

How many left-handed people do you know? About 10 percent of the world's people are natural lefties, and I am among them. That hasn't always been popular: the English "sinister" comes from the Latin *sinistros,* for "left." *Gauche,* used to suggest unsophistication or clumsiness, is the French word for "left." The word "left" itself comes from the Anglo-Saxon *lyft,* which means "weak." During the Middle Ages, lefties were sometimes associated with the devil or accused of witchcraft.

Even so, we southpaws take some comfort in the knowledge that, since the body's motor controls for each side are generally controlled by the opposite side of the brain, we can claim to be the only ones who are in their "right minds."

In his very personal letter to the Christians in Philippi, Paul had a lot to say about being right-minded, though in a very different context. What does it mean to have the right mind for following Christ?

### Have one mind …
### (2:1-4)

Today's text, a favorite of many readers, demonstrates Paul's rhetorical and persuasive skill. In poetic, perhaps even hymnic language, the apostle pleads with the Philippians to overcome apparent divisions among them by uniting with a common mind, namely, the mind of Christ. [**Divisions**]

---

**Divisions:** What sort of divisions plagued the church at Philippi? Paul doesn't spell it out, though there are clues. We learn from 4:2 that Euodia and Syntyche, two leading women who had worked closely in the past, were having a disagreement. In 2:14, Paul warns the congregation against "murmuring and arguing." By inference, we may guess that Paul's strong efforts to promote humility and service to others suggest that issues of pride and power were at work. Philippi was a leading Roman colony, and as commentators often note, many people in Greco-Roman culture were obsessed with gaining honor or class rank. If this carried over into the church, humility may have been in short supply.

---

In vv. 1-4, Paul carefully constructs an appeal for harmony that includes three sets of thoughts, each containing four units. The first of these, v. 1, consists of four clauses that appear to be conditional, but only to make Paul's appeal more forceful.

Paul reminds believers of how they have been blessed with "encouragement in Christ," "consolation from love," "sharing in the Spirit," and "compassion and sympathy."

The Apostle challenged those who know such fourfold blessings to respond in four related ways: he calls them to "make my joy complete" by being "of the same mind, having the same love, being in full accord and of one mind" (v. 2).

The first and last responses both relate to the way we think, using the verb *phroneō,* one of Paul's favorite words. The opening "be of the same mind" could literally

---

*This text is read for the Passion Liturgy in Years A, B, and C. Philippians 2:1-13 is read for Proper 21 in Year A. This study will cover vv. 1-13.*

be translated "think the same," and the closing call to be "of one mind" means "the same thinking." Paul is not suggesting that church members become mental clones of each other and agree on every point, but that they orient their thinking toward harmonious service to Christ. It is not so much that they agree on all the same ideas, but that they share the same cooperative attitude.

Let's take a closer look at some of the words Paul uses in his fourfold appeal: "If then there is any encouragement in Christ, any consolation from love, any sharing in the Spirit, any compassion and sympathy …" (v. 1).

The word translated "encouragement" is *paraklēsis*, similar to the word we sometimes render as "paraclete," in reference to the Holy Spirit. It speaks of one being "called alongside" another to be present and offer support, a thought not unrelated to the next reality, the "consolation" or "comfort" that comes through Christ-like love (*agapē*).

"Sharing in the Spirit" would be better translated as "fellowship (*koinonia*) in/of/brought about by the Spirit," if we assume that *pneumata* here refers to the Holy Spirit, as is likely. An alternate translation could be "spiritual fellowship."

The word for "compassion" is an interesting metaphor: *splangkna* is the Greek word for intestines, which were thought to be the seat of one's affections. We use the same expression when we speak of feeling something "in our gut," but are more inclined to speak metaphorically of the heart as the seat of our emotions.

Believers can unite their thinking in common cause because they share the same love and are united in spirit: "being in full accord" translates *sumpsuchoi*, which combines "with" (*sum*) and "soul" (*psuche*) to mean something akin to "fellow-souled" or "united in spirit." A common love and a common spirit give rise to a common purpose, a common way of thinking.

Paul urges the Philippians to demonstrate their loving attitude through mutual service and humility (vv. 3-4). Again, his appeal has four components. The first and third relate what they should *not* do: they should not act from selfish ambition or conceit, nor focus on their own interests. The second and fourth challenges explain what they *should* do: they should humbly regard others as better than themselves as they look out for the interests of others.

Readers may be troubled by Paul's admonition to "regard others as better than yourselves" (v. 3b), but Paul's concern is not with a qualitative assessment of competency or maturity, but a measure of importance. The word translated "better than" is the participle of a verb formed by combining "above" or "higher" (*huper*) and the verb of being (*echo*). To regard others as "being above" us is not to make a value judgment about either their competency or our own, but to consider their needs as more important than our own.

Even that nuance does not make the advice any easier to follow. We live in a culture that believes in "looking out for number one." We've all had someone push into line ahead of us, or cut in front of us on the highway, as if assuming they are more important than us, or that their time is more valuable than ours. If we have learned what it means to live in community as followers of Christ, however, we have heard Jesus' insistence that those who would be great must learn to be servants, unselfishly loving others as he loved us.

Paul's advice challenges modern readers to consider practical ways we might see this attitude being worked out within the fellowship of our churches – and how our congregations can adopt a more charitable approach toward our larger communities.

Can we name even a single example of how we look after the interests of others at the expense of our own concerns?

## The mind of Christ …
### (2:5-11)

Having called for harmonious love and self-giving humility, Paul grounds his appeal on the example of Christ as a model for emulation. Reverting again to a form of *phronein*, Paul calls the Philippians to think as Christ thought, to have the same selfless disposition toward others that Jesus modeled and instructed his disciples to follow. [**Attitudes**]

What follows in vv. 6-11 is so artfully arranged and carefully worded that scholars typically refer to it as a hymn, though without agreement as to whether Paul quoted it or wrote it. Arranging the text into symmetrical verses requires deleting a few phrases as later additions,

**Attitudes:** The word *phronein*, which can mean "think," "have understanding," or "be concerned," is a key word in Philippians, and a favorite of Paul's: Of the 26 times it is used in the New Testament, 23 are in Paul's letters, and 10 of those are in Philippians. We often translate it with the word "mind," as in "be of the same mind," sharing a generosity of spirit toward others. Despite their diversity, Paul believed that the Philippian believers could be united in an attitude of fellowship and love.

If anything stands out as the clearest mark of a Christian person and the most evident sign of a vital church, it is the attitude expressed by its members. If anything attracts people to a church, it is a warm spirit of love and mutual affection. If anything will turn people away from a church, it is a cool attitude of distance in which the members are divided among themselves and unconcerned for the needs of others.

Unity does not mean uniformity. Our opinions may and will differ, and that is a part of what makes life fun, but if our attitudes and ultimate goals are the same, then our differences of opinion can be worked out in love.

however; even then, scholars disagree on how the text should be arranged.

The text moves in two stages: lowering and raising. In the opening section (vv. 6-8), Christ acts to empty himself, take on human form, and live on earth as a servant so obedient that he was willing to die a humiliating death on a cross. In the second part (vv. 9-11), God acts to exalt Jesus and give him the highest name of all.

Interpreters and theologians have long debated the precise meaning of these verses, but we need not worry about every nuance. In some way, we are to understand that Christ was preexistent and on equal standing with God, but he did not consider this position something to be grasped or held onto.

Rather, Christ was willing to "empty himself." Does this mean he stopped being divine? That he gave up divine attributes and powers? That he surrendered divine prerogatives? We cannot claim to understand every shade of meaning, but the result of Christ's "emptying" was the incarnation, Christ's coming to earth in human form. Jesus called himself the "son of man." He became susceptible to temptation, hunger, thirst, and every other desire known to humans. Yet, while Christ became "fully human," the church came to believe he was also "fully divine."

In vv. 7-8, Paul insists that Christ did more than simply become human: he became a slave, a servant to others, obedient to the end. Paul's picture of Christ's earthly servitude that led to heavenly glory is not unlike Jesus' own instruction to his disciples, who struggled with each other for positions of leadership: "But it is not so among you; but whoever wishes to become great among you must be your servant, and whoever wishes to be first among you must be slave of all" (Mark 10:43-44). [**Jesus vs. Adam and Eve**]

None of Christ's followers, however, could pretend to contend for Jesus' position as the one who has a "name above every name" (v. 9). On the surface, this might appear to be the name "Jesus," for v. 10 says "at the name of Jesus every knee should bend ..." It is more likely, however, that the "name above every name" is not "Jesus" – a common earthly name that he already possessed – but "Lord." Paul goes on to say that all tongues will confess "that Jesus Christ is Lord" (v. 11).

The word *kurios* was commonly used in the Septuagint (the earliest Greek translation of the Old Testament) to translate the divine name Yahweh, translated as "LORD" (all uppercase) to distinguish it from "*adonai*," which could also mean "Lord," but in a less personal sense.

Paul's declaration, whether quoting from a hymn or composing on his own, would have been encouraging, but also dangerous. "Jesus Christ is Lord" is often regarded as the earliest Christian confession – and is no doubt something the Philippian Christians already professed. That claim, however, ran squarely in opposition to Rome's political dogma that "Caesar is lord." This may have contributed to the oppression Paul hinted at in speaking of their opponents (1:28).

**Jesus vs. Adam and Eve:** Interpreters have often compared Paul's image of Christ in Phil. 2:6-11 to the story of Adam and Eve in Genesis 3. In his human life, Jesus did not see divine attributes as something to reach for. In contrast, the symbolic first humans ate from the tree precisely in an effort to become like God. Christ, through his obedience, was raised to the highest place in heaven, while the humans, because of their disobedience, were expelled from the garden and made subject to death. (For a succinct discussion of this, see Todd D. Still, Philippians and Philemon, Smyth & Helwys Bible Commentary [Smyth & Helwys, 2011], 70.)

## Obedient minds …
### (2:12-13)

In light of Christ's example, Paul shifted to a series of exhortations for the Philippians to follow Christ's example and live obedient lives.

"Therefore" connects vv. 6-11 to the following section: It is because of the Philippians' devotion to Christ, the perfect model of humble obedience, that they should also demonstrate similar fidelity.

The NRSV and some other translations add the word "me" to v. 12, as if Paul refers to them obeying him, but the addition is unnecessary. The subject at hand is obedience to God, not to Paul.

The implications are clear: believers, inspired by Christ, are called to live in obedience *to* God and reverence *before* God, as they are empowered *by* God to live out their salvation in serving others.

This is the road Jesus calls us to walk. It is a road that is guided by an attitude of love, of service, of obedience to the end. Living with a Jesus worldview doesn't put us on an easy road, but it is the good road. It is the road that leads to where we want to go, for just as Christ walked ahead of us to blaze the trail, we believe he will be there waiting at the end.

## The Hardest Question
### Must we work for our salvation?

What is meant by Paul's instruction to "work out your own salvation with fear and trembling" (v. 12)? Is not Paul the great proclaimer of salvation by faith and not works (e.g., Eph. 2:8-9)? Why, then, would he speak of working out one's salvation?

Baptists and some other evangelicals tend to assume the salvation is a once-for-all, can't-be-lost-no-matter-what-you-do experience, but Paul doesn't speak of it that way. He appears to perceive salvation as a progressive experience that begins with one's confession of Christ as Lord (Rom. 10:9, 1 Cor. 12:3) but is not fully complete until Christ's return (3:20-21, Rom. 13:11). In the meantime, believers should not adopt a proud or smug attitude about their future destiny. Rather, they should live reverently before God in such a way that the outworking of their saving experience through Christ is evident.

As Todd Still notes, however, v. 13 offers a balancing thought to v. 12. After charging believers to work out their own salvation, Paul adds "for it is God who is at work in you, enabling you both to will and to work for his good pleasure." Thus, "while the Philippians are meant to *work out* their salvation, they are not to *work for* it. Indeed, the congregation's 'outworking' of salvation is predicated upon and enabled by the divine 'in-working'" (emphasis Still's, *Philippians and Philemon*, Smyth & Helwys Bible Commentary [Smyth & Helwys, 2011], 75).

# Sixth Sunday in Lent

## Liturgy of the Passion
## Fourth Reading
## Matthew 26:14–27:66

# The Old, Old Story

*Then he came to the disciples and said to them, "Are you still sleeping and taking your rest?*
*See, the hour is at hand, and the Son of Man is betrayed into the hands of sinners." (Matt. 26:45)*

How can anyone be expected to preach or teach from a text that's a full 127 verses long? Some sermons don't typically last as long as it would take just to read the text – which might suggest that as the best approach.

Worship planners are always faced with a dilemma when choosing texts for the Sunday before Easter, as the lectionary offers a set of texts for either a celebratory Palm Sunday emphasis, or a more somber approach based on the Passion.

Palm Sunday is more celebratory, and is often the choice. Churches that hold additional services during Holy Week can logically choose the Palm Sunday texts for Sunday worship, then piece out the lengthy narrative of the passion for daily services, or read it during a doleful Tenebrae service on Maundy Thursday.

Those who attempt to deal with the entire text in a Sunday sermon – unless the congregation is willing to grant them about three hours – have little option but to present a quick overview without much exegetical background, to focus on smaller elements of the text, or perhaps to read the text dramatically with multiple speakers. One way or another, we seek to relate the "Old, Old Story" story that Katherine Hankey wrote about in her beloved hymn from 1866. For Christian believers, it is also the most important story we can tell.

Given the impractical nature of an exegetical study for the entire passage, in this resource we'll provide commentary and ideas for the lectionary's alternate fourth reading, which is still quite lengthy and challenging to deal with in a single sermon or study.

# Sixth Sunday in Lent

## Liturgy of the Passion
## Alternate Fourth Reading
## Matthew 27:11-54

# The Crux of the Matter

*Over his head they put the charge against him, which read,*
*"This is Jesus, the King of the Jews." (Matt. 27:37)*

The story of Jesus' crucifixion in Matt. 27:11-54 is familiar, but no less hard to hear because of it. Our text describes the final trial and cruel mockery of Jesus, culminating with the ugliness of execution and Christ's courageous death. It is a story of human cruelty, divine love, and unbending trust.

All four gospels contain an account of Jesus' crucifixion, and they all differ in varying respects, mostly in matters of emphasis. Matthew's gospel gives more attention to the Jews throughout, and is more emphatic in charging the Jews with responsibility for Jesus' death. In addition, the author gives greater emphasis to the public ridicule Jesus experienced.

Proof texts from the crucifixion accounts have often fueled waves of anti-Semitism leading to intense persecution against Jewish people because of the belief that "the Jews killed Jesus." The gospels do accuse the Jewish authorities of seeking to silence Jesus, but also explain that the officials were motivated by a realistic fear that Jesus could instigate a rebellion that could bring the wrath of Rome upon all Jews. The gospels are also clear that it was the Roman authorities who ordered and carried out his execution. And, though none of us can claim to know the mind of God or spell out a divine plan, the gospel accounts cite Jesus as expecting to be killed and to rise again as part of his mission. Modern believers would be far better served by befriending Jewish people as partners in our heritage of faith rather than thinking that all Jews are somehow responsible for or tainted by Jesus' death.

### Trial before Pilate
### (vv. 11-26)

According to Matthew, Jesus was arrested by a vigilante crowd who had been inspired by the chief priests and elders of the Jewish people (26:47). Matthew uses the word "crowd" (*ochlos*) as a sort of catchword to stress shared responsibility for what happened. The mob would have probably included a mix of religious and non-religious Jews along with Gentiles and passersby who were caught up in a mob mentality with little idea of what they were really doing. The unruly group delivered Jesus to a hastily called midnight meeting of the Sanhedrin, Israel's highest court. There the chief priests, scribes, and appointed elders of the people

---

**Pilate:** The Roman system of government was complicated during the first century, and more than one ruler was involved with the trial of Jesus. Pontius Pilate was appointed to serve as governor of Judea, and he did so from about 26–36 CE.

Pilate's primary responsibility was to maintain order: he ruled primarily from an administrative center and palace in Caesarea Maritima, but he would come to Jerusalem during the major festivals to oversee security operations. Because Jerusalem was within the province of Judea and Pilate alone could authorize capital punishment, Jesus was brought to him for trial.

found Jesus guilty of blasphemy. They declared the charge to be worthy of death according to the law, but had no authority to impose capital punishment. Thus, having mocked Jesus, they delivered him to the Roman governor on charges of treason (26:57-68). [**Pilate**]

Matthew's narrative suggests that Pilate never believed Jesus was guilty of fomenting insurrection against Rome. Though accused of various crimes by leaders of the Sanhedrin, Jesus declined to verbally answer the charges. The inclusion of Pilate's wife reporting to him an ominous dream underscores Jesus' innocence and Pilate's lack of enthusiasm for condemning Jesus (v. 19). Seeking a way to avoid sending Jesus to the cross, Pilate attempted a political solution by calling on a customary gesture of goodwill, the freeing of a Jewish political prisoner during the Passover season.

A notable insurrectionist was awaiting trial, a man named Barabbas, possibly "Jesus Barabbas." Though Barabbas would have been popular among anti-Roman activists, the Jewish authorities would have recognized that releasing Barabbas could be dangerous for the same reason that they feared Jesus and wanted to eliminate him. Any rebellion against Rome would be put down quickly and cruelly.

Pilate evidently hoped the people would choose Barabbas, but he was disappointed. Whatever the Jewish officials might have wanted, the crowd had taken on a life of its own, and the mob was set on seeing Jesus crucified. The rowdy multitude called for Barabbas to be released. His strategy having failed, the governor washed his hands of the matter, had Jesus flogged, and turned him over to the Roman soldiers for crucifixion. [**Herod**]

> **Herod:** The gospel of Luke describes a different trial scenario, in which Pilate tried to avoid blame by sending Jesus – a native of Galilee – for an interview with Herod Antipas, who was governor of Galilee, just as Pilate was governor of Judea. Herod was also in Jerusalem for the Passover festival, and he had indicated an interest in Jesus. According to Luke's account, Herod was disappointed when Jesus refused to work any miracles on demand, so he sent him back to Pilate (Luke 23:7-15). Matthew does not include this episode, moving directly from Pilate's surrender to the crucifixion.

> **Lithostratos:** To maintain order and keep watch over temple activities, the Romans built a large fortress called the "Antonia" at the northwest corner of the temple mount. It is possible that this is where Pilate lodged when in Jerusalem and where Jesus would have been mistreated by the soldiers before beginning his walk along the *Via Dolorosa*.
>
> The first-century street level of the fortress has been excavated, and is now well below ground, beneath a convent owned by the French Sisters of Zion. It is also known as *Ecce Homo*, named after the story that Pilate pointed to Jesus and said "Behold the man" (John 19:5). Pilgrims often take off their shoes and meditate while walking on a section of pavement where Jesus may have begun his painful trek to the cross (*lithostratos* means "pavement of stones").

## Mocking by the soldiers
### (vv. 27-31)

Roman security forces took Jesus into custody and reportedly took advantage of the charges against him for their own entertainment. According to Matthew, they stripped Jesus of whatever clothes were left after his public beating and draped one of their scarlet robes over his bleeding shoulders. They added a crown made of thorns and a scepter-like cane to the costume, playing off the charge that he had claimed to be king of the Jews. Matthew says that they abused him with mock-worship, spitting, and beatings on the head with the cane. One might argue that the practice of dehumanizing their victim would make it easier to go through with the cruel and bloody crucifixion. Throughout the entire humiliating ordeal, apparently, Jesus said nothing. [**Lithostratos**]

## Public crucifixion
### (vv. 32-54)

Archaeological and historical studies suggest that the upright part of the Roman cross was left planted in the ground at the execution site, while the condemned were sometimes forced to carry the cross-piece, which would be hoisted up. Before the actual crucifixion, the soldiers offered Jesus a drink of wine mixed with gall. Some writers see this as a humanitarian offer of a pain-killing narcotic; others contend the soldiers mocked Jesus by offering gall instead of the usual drug. Mark says the wine was mixed with myrrh, which could have had a narcotic effect (15:23). Perhaps Matthew added "gall" – which would have had a bitter taste – for greater emphasis on the cruelty Jesus faced.

The soldiers were not alone in their derision of Jesus. Matthew describes further verbal abuse from the crowd (vv. 39-40), the Jewish leaders (vv. 41-43), and even the robbers who were crucified with him (v. 44). Unlike Luke, who reports that one of the thieves repented and defended Jesus against the other (Luke 23:39-43), Matthew and Mark describe both criminals as joining in the derision of Jesus.

All who scorned Jesus used some variation of the same basic taunt: "He saved others, but he cannot save himself!" (vv. 40, 42, 44). They ridiculed his trust in God and challenged him to come down from the cross. Jesus' detractors did not understand that while Jesus could have escaped the cross, he *could not* save himself *and* save others. In the plan of God – something we cannot claim to fully understand – it was necessary for Jesus to die so the world could be saved, and the only way Jesus could accomplish that task was through his steadfast trust in God's way. The people taunted: "let God deliver him now, if he wants to" (v. 43). They had no way of understanding God's heart in that moment.

Matthew's account of Jesus' death is dominated by the cry of desolation in v. 46, a mostly Aramaic rendering of Ps. 22:1, one of several reflections of Psalm 22 in the crucifixion story. Matthew begins the quotation with the Hebrew *'Eli* ("my God"), as opposed to Mark's Aramaic *'Eloi* (16:34). *'Eli* is probably original, since it is more likely to have been confused with the name

Elijah, to whom some in the crowd thought he was appealing (vv. 47-49). Through it all Jesus had trusted the Father, but in agony he cried out *"My God, my God, why have you forsaken me?"*

Did Jesus really believe God had forsaken him? Did this mark a point at which the divine presence was somehow withdrawn? We cannot fully understand the cry of desolation, but in it we can see evidence of Jesus' humanity and his deep feeling of loneliness in that hour. We can be confident, however, that it does not mean that God had abandoned the scene. Some interpreters hold that God cannot endure sin, and that when Christ took our sin upon himself on the cross, the Father was forced to turn away. But Paul insisted that God was in Christ reconciling the world to himself (2 Cor. 5:19). One might argue that God was never closer than when Jesus trusted enough to give himself in full obedience on the cross. Christ's pain was God's pain.

Throughout the humiliating episode, Jesus endured with quiet dignity and courageous trust in God's greater plan. In Matthew's account, Jesus speaks only three times: he acknowledges to Pilate the charge brought against him (v. 11), he gives voice to his feeling of desolation (v. 46), and he cries out just before consciously giving up his spirit (v. 50). *Why was Jesus so silent?* Surely with his miraculous powers and his skills of communication, Jesus could have talked his way out of the crucifixion – but if he had done so, he could not have saved the world. Christ's silent, non-violent response in the face of persecution is a mute testimony of his love for all people and his commitment to his mission.

There were surely many occasions when Jesus was tempted to rail against his tormentors or trade insults with the cruel crowd. He must have wanted to come down from the cross, to save his own life, and to show his impudent critics that he truly was the son of God. But Jesus chose to stay. He *chose* to suffer. He intentionally adopted Isaiah's model of the suffering servant who accepts the pain that rightfully belongs to others (Isaiah 53). It was not an easy road to travel. Jesus must have struggled with its demands, even before his agonized prayer in the garden called Gethsemane (Matt. 26:36-46). Jesus was able to endure the pain and succeed in his mission only because of his commitment to God, and because of his love for God's people.

The silence of Jesus stands in stark contrast to the supernatural events that Matthew describes as washing over Jerusalem during the crucifixion. The sun was darkened, he says, the veil of the temple's holy place was torn, dead people were raised, and an earthquake split rocks apart. Jesus was silent, but the very rocks of the earth cried out in rage at the abuse Christ suffered. In the aftermath of it all, Matthew says the centurion and his soldiers added their own voices in a counterpoint of confession: "Surely he was the son of God!" (v. 54).

The example of Jesus is a constant challenge for Christ-followers who remember that Jesus told his disciples to take up their own crosses and come after him (Matt. 16:24). If we would follow Jesus, we embark on a journey that may require us to suffer in others' behalf, to experience rejection and heartache, perhaps even to face real persecution. If we would follow Jesus, we will respond to such trials with the same quiet dignity that demonstrates trust in God and love for others – even the ones who cause our suffering.

### The Hardest Question
### Why are there so many references from Psalm 22 in the crucifixion story?

All three synoptic gospels use quotations or references from Psalm 22 in their telling of the crucifixion story. Psalm 22, in its context, is a psalm of lament in which a person in distress cries out for deliverance from enemies that taunt him (vv. 1-21) before turning to an expression of trust that God would not ultimately forsake (vv. 22-31). New Testament writers came to believe the psalm was both prophetic and messianic, so their accounts of the crucifixion attempt to show ways in which elements of the psalm coincided with Christ's crucifixion.

Matthew's account reflects Psalm 22 in several ways. The soldiers' dividing of Jesus' clothes by casting dice (Matt. 27:35) reflects the psalmist's complaint: "they divide my clothes among themselves, and for my clothing they cast lots" (Ps. 22:18).

The element of mocking is present in both texts: Matthew's account that "Those who passed by derided him, shaking their heads" (27:39) recalls Ps. 22:7: "All who see me mock at me, they make mouths at me, they shake their heads."

The psalmist quoted his detractors as ridiculing him with sarcasm: "Commit your cause to the LORD; let him deliver – let him rescue the one in whom he delights!" (v. 8). Matthew echoes this in the taunts of the Jewish officials: "He trusts in God; let God deliver him now, if he wants to" (27:43).

The most memorable citation is Jesus' cry of desolation from the cross, rendered in Aramaic: "*Eli, Eli, lema sabachthani?*" (27:46). This quotes the opening line of Psalm 22 (in Hebrew, *'eli, 'eli, lama 'azabthani*): "My God, my God, why have you forsaken me?"

The presence of these and less obvious themes from Psalm 22 reveal the New Testament writers' commitment to seeing Jesus' work, and especially his crucifixion, as a fulfillment of what they believed to be Old Testament prophesies. Matthew's gospel focused especially on the Jewish people, not in an anti-Semitic way, but in hopes of leading them to trust in Christ. Portraying Jesus' work as the fulfillment of a divine plan revealed in the Hebrew Bible, however cryptically, could contribute to that effort.

## First Reading
## Acts 10:34-43*

# Who Converted Whom?

*I truly understand that God shows no partiality, but in every nation anyone who fears him and does what is right is acceptable to him. (Acts 10:34b-35)*

Have you ever changed your mind about a social custom or belief that you once held dear? Many of us who have reached our sixth decade grew up in an environment steeped in racism. Getting used to the idea that Blacks and whites could – and should! – share the same opportunities took some adjustment for many people, but now most of us think little of it: we have learned to embrace new attitudes toward people of different ethnic backgrounds. [Perspective]

Our journey to acceptance may have begun with a developing friendship with someone different. We may have been influenced by a powerful book or a prophetic sermon. Or, we may have learned from a new environment, such as a college campus or military unit, where more accepting viewpoints prevailed and friendship opportunities were greater.

Prejudice is nothing new. Peter, one of Jesus' closest disciples, had grown up in an environment of suspicion and distrust between Jews and Gentiles that went back for hundreds of years. As the Hebrew exiles returned to Judah in the fifth and sixth centuries BCE, they lived under Persian rule and had no national identity. As a means of self-preservation and an attempt to please God in hopes of future blessing, religious leaders began a campaign of ethnic uniformity that promoted purity and pedigree.

The books of Ezra and Nehemiah describe the establishment of policies that outlawed marriage to anyone outside of the Jewish community while also calling for closer adherence to purity laws and more faithful support of the temple. This conscious effort to cement a stronger ethnic identity proved successful in preserving the Jews as a people, but also drove a wedge between them and their neighbors.

This isolationist worldview prescribed by his inherited faith was all Peter knew, so God had to teach him that Christ's saving work was not restricted to the Jews. Through a vision involving a hungry disciple and a bevy of "unclean" animals, God revealed to Peter that he should not regard anyone as unclean (10:9-16).

### The Lord of all
### (vv. 34-36)

As Peter was trying to make sense of the vision, three messengers from a Roman centurion named Cornelius arrived, asking Peter to accompany them to Caesarea and meet with their commanding officer, who was described as a "God-fearer," a Gentile who worshiped the God of the Jews but had not fully converted through circumcision. The text

---

**Perspective:** While racial attitudes provide the most obvious example, traditional attitudes also have been challenged by our culture's growing acceptance of persons who have been divorced and remarried, or by changing attitudes toward gender. These issues often hit home when a family member is affected, and we begin to take a closer look at assumptions or viewpoints we had not previously examined. Even where full acceptance remains elusive, few of us could say that our perspectives on these matters have not shifted during the past 30–40 years.

---

*This text is read for Easter Day in Years A, B, and C and for Epiphany in Year A.

> **Cornelius:** A centurion was a Roman military officer who commanded 100 men. The Latin *centum*, meaning "hundred," also gave rise to our word "century" and "cent." Six units of 100 men comprised a "cohort," and 10 cohorts formed a "legion." It is not surprising that a sizable contingent of Roman soldiers would be stationed in Caesarea because that city, not Jerusalem, was the official seat of the Roman government for Palestine.

emphasizes Cornelius' piety as a man who prayed constantly and gave generous alms for the poor. **[Cornelius]**

Earlier, as Peter had knelt for Judaism's regular mid-afternoon prayer time, an angel instructed Cornelius to send messengers to bring Peter to Caesarea. Instructed by the Spirit, Peter agreed to go. When he arrived, he found not only Cornelius but also a large group of Gentile God-fearers, all eager to hear a word from God (10:17-33).

Peter knew that he was violating Jewish custom by meeting with the group and acknowledged some awkwardness about it, but when he learned that the Gentiles sought eagerly to hear a message from God, he had little choice but to preach.

Peter began by relating what he himself had only recently learned by connecting the dots between his vision of unclean but edible animals that God had declared acceptable, and a house full of "unclean" but eager Gentiles who also feared God and who wanted to know God better. "I truly understand that God shows no partiality," he said, "but in every nation anyone who fears him and does what is right is acceptable to him" (10:34b-35).

Overcoming partiality would be an ongoing challenge, not just between Jews and Gentiles, but between classes, genders, and other ethnicities. As the gospel spread and churches blossomed, Paul and others urged believers to treat all people as equal in God's sight (Rom. 2:11, Eph. 2:11-22, Col. 3:25, Jas. 2:1, 1 Pet. 1:17).

Peter, like other Hebrews, had grown up believing that while God was Lord of all nations and ethnic groups, Israel was chosen to be a special people, to live in a unique and potentially rewarding relationship with God.

Exodus 19:5-6 preserves a tradition that "all the earth" was God's, but Israel would be regarded as a special people: "Now therefore, if you obey my voice and keep my covenant, you shall be my treasured possession out of all the peoples. Indeed, the whole earth is mine, but you shall be for me a priestly kingdom and a holy nation."

Peter was now ready to declare, in preaching about Jesus, that "he is Lord of all" (v. 36b). God's love is universal, reaching out to all people, encouraging them to do what is right and pleasing to God.

### A savior for all
### (vv. 37-41)

After referring twice to God's message (literally, "word") through Christ, Peter got to the point of explaining it: that God had "anointed Jesus with the Holy Spirit and with power," which Jesus demonstrated by traveling about, doing good deeds and healing people, proving that God was with him and that he had power over evil (v. 38).

Peter spoke as a witness of what happened next, of how "they" put Jesus to death by "hanging him on a tree" (a first-century idiom for crucifixion), and how God had raised him from the dead on the third day.

Note Peter's tact in describing Jesus' death. Charges had been brought against Jesus by the Jewish authorities, but Roman soldiers had carried it out. Peter was a Jew in the home of a Roman soldier and surrounded, no doubt, by other soldiers. Instead of assigning blame in the death of Jesus, he says only that an indefinite "they" had killed Jesus.

Peter had already come to believe that Jesus' death was a necessary part of his message and work in the world. When God raised Jesus from the dead and caused him to appear before witnesses, eating and drinking in their company, the disciples became fully convinced that Jesus' message and God's message were one and the same.

Even as he spoke, Peter was learning in practical terms that the good news was intended for all people. Peter would have been present when Jesus ascended to heaven and would have heard his parting words, which Luke described as a promise to the disciples that they would be empowered by the Spirit to "be my witnesses in Jerusalem, in all Judea and Samaria, and to the ends of the earth" (Acts 1:8).

Now Peter found himself at the northwestern corner of Judea, beyond Samaria, speaking to a cosmopolitan group of people who may have come from "the ends of the earth" as far as he was concerned. Peter's status as an outsider was clear, but he plunged ahead.

## A message for all
### (vv. 42-43)

Peter recalled how Jesus had "commanded us to preach to the people and to testify that he is the one ordained by God as judge of the living and the dead" (v. 42).

What "command" did Peter have in mind? We may think of Matt. 28:19-20, commonly known as "the great commission," or of Luke's version in Acts 1:8.

Luke also had written in his gospel of a post-resurrection occasion when Jesus appeared to the disciples and "opened their minds to understand the scriptures" that both taught of him and declared "that repentance and forgiveness of sins is to be proclaimed in his name to all nations, beginning from Jerusalem" (Luke 24:45a, 47).

Peter was starting to understand in practical terms what he had previously known in theory: the gospel really was for all people, and Jesus' disciples were to proclaim it in all places.

Peter's speech suggests that he still may have been uncomfortable with the notion, for he proclaimed the gospel more as a warning than as good news. When he said the disciples were "to preach to the people and to testify," he used a word that can also describe a solemn warning. Since the context involves the prospect of judgment, a better translation might be "to preach to the people and to warn them …," as in the NET.

All will be judged, Peter said, both living and dead – and the criteria of judgment will be one's response to Jesus. [The cosmic Christ]

Peter concluded his speech with a claim that "all the prophets" had testified that "everyone who believes in him receives forgiveness through his name" (v. 43). The statement cannot be read literally: not all the prophets spoke of a coming Messiah, and none of them spoke in the specific terms that Peter described.

There was a belief, however, that the prophets had envisioned a coming age in which all peoples would come to worship God. In his speech on the day of Pentecost, Peter had quoted Joel 2:32a in saying that "everyone who calls on the name of the Lord shall be saved" (Acts 2:21).

Thoughts of Pentecost immediately arise when we read of what happened next: while Peter was still speaking (and thus, before his audience made any outward response), "the

> **The cosmic Christ:** J. Bradley Chance describes the importance of the core gospel in this way: "The proclamation of the gospel message is the means whereby the church fulfills its calling as 'witnesses' (cf. 10:41). That gospel, even in its abbreviated form as presented here by Peter, culminates in the proclamation that Jesus has been ordained by God to be judge of the living and the dead (10:42). This clear affirmation of the cosmic lordship of Christ is *the* essence of the gospel message. The miraculous deeds, the agonizing death, the triumph of resurrection, and the glory of ascension all bear witness to the central confession that 'Jesus is Lord.' Appropriately, therefore, Peter *begins* his witness with the central confession (10:36) and ends with an affirmation of that same confession as he acknowledges Jesus as the judge of both the living and the dead (10:42), which encompasses that which was, is, and will be" (*Acts*, Smyth & Helwys Bible Commentary [Smyth & Helwys, 2007], 177).

Holy Spirit fell upon all who heard the word" so that the Gentiles spoke in tongues and praised God, astounding the Jews who had come with Peter (vv. 44-46).

The evidence was clear, and the verdict was in: the gospel truly was – and is – for all people. Peter was just beginning to accept the radically inclusive nature of God's grace. Do we?

### The Hardest Question
#### Did they know?

Careful readers may note a curious thing about how Peter's speech begins. Cornelius, a Gentile, had invited Peter to come and speak because he and others wanted to learn more about the new faith that had come about through Jesus.

We learn about the invitation in the words of the messengers who came to Peter in Joppa: "Cornelius, a centurion, an upright and God-fearing man, who is well spoken of by the whole Jewish nation, was directed by a holy angel to send for you to come to his house and to hear what you have to say" (v. 22).

After Peter arrived, Cornelius was confused enough to bow at Peter's feet and had to be assured that Peter was a mortal like him (vv. 25-26). When Peter saw the large number of relatives and friends that Cornelius had gathered, he noted the awkwardness of the setting and asked why they had sent for him (vv. 27-29)

Cornelius recounted his vision from three days earlier, and indicated that he and his companions had called Peter and gathered so they could "listen to all that the Lord has commanded you to say" (v. 33).

This implies that Cornelius lacked information about Christ, but Peter began his summary of the gospel with "*You know* the message he sent to the people of Israel, preaching peace by Jesus Christ ..." (v. 36).

Did Peter assume that Cornelius and company were already acquainted with the gospel message?

In considering the question, we should remember that Luke is reporting the speech at least second-hand, and long after the actual encounter, so we can't expect it to be a verbatim account.

As Luke constructed Peter's speech for his book, the audience he had in mind was his own potential readers, not Cornelius and his friends. They would know – or should know – the heart of the gospel already. Luke's interest was to remind them that Christ's mission was for all people. Since Luke himself was a Gentile and wrote with Gentiles in mind, this message would hold special interest.

Cornelius and company may not have known the gospel message that was for all peoples when Peter arrived, but Luke's readers would have known it.

From another angle, we may want to ask deeper questions about how Peter came to break through his own prejudice and understand that the gospel was for all people. J. Bradley Chance suggests that Luke's account of Peter's growing appreciation for Gentile believers can be visualized as a play in two acts, with Act One consisting of two scenes in which Peter works miracles and evangelizes Jews as he makes his way toward Joppa, where he had been instructed to visit a man named Simon, a tanner (Acts 9:32-43). Peter's willingness to visit a tanner (whose smelly work rendered him ritually unclean) suggests a growing willingness to step outside the exclusivist box of his Jewish background.

Act Two (10:1–11:18) moves into the Gentile world and plays out in seven scenes. In Scene One (10:1-8), Luke leaves Peter in Joppa while taking the reader north to

Caesarea, where a Roman centurion named Cornelius was granted a vision from God during his afternoon prayers.

Scene Two brings us back to Joppa on the following day (10:9-16), where Peter was praying alone on the flat roof of his host's home. Peter also saw a vision, one that challenged him to recognize "What God has made clean, you must not call profane" (10:15). The vision was repeated three times, apparently to make sure Peter got the point.

Three messengers from Cornelius showed up in Scene Three (10:17-23a), and the Spirit instructed Peter to accompany them without hesitation. Employing a lesson learned from the vision, Peter invited the men to come in and rest overnight, something that strictly observant Jews would not have done.

Scene Four (10:23b-33) relates Peter's arrival and opening conversation with Cornelius and others who were gathered with him. Recognizing the odd nature of his visit in a Gentile's home, and accompanied by other Jewish Christians, Peter explained that God had taught him not to call anyone profane or unclean (10:28). Cornelius then described his own vision and asked Peter to proclaim whatever God laid on his heart (10:33).

Peter's sermon (10:34-43, the text for today) comprises Scene Five. In it, he proclaimed the basics of the gospel message, the death and resurrection of Christ, and the command to proclaim the good news to all, calling for repentance and promising the forgiveness of sins.

Peter's sermon was quickly interrupted by Scene Six (10:44-48) in which the Spirit of God was poured out on all who were gathered. The Gentile believers spoke in tongues and praised God, demonstrating the same evidence of the Spirit's blessing that Jewish believers had experienced in Acts 2.

The last scene in the lengthy story (11:1-18) finds Peter back in Jerusalem, recounting his experience to other church leaders. Some criticized him for having lodged and presumably eaten with the Gentiles, but Peter insisted that if God wanted to bless the Gentiles with the Spirit, it was hardly his place to interfere (11:17).

# Easter Day

## Optional First Reading
## Jeremiah 31:1-6

# Everlasting Love

*I have loved you with an everlasting love; therefore I have continued my faithfulness to you. (Jer. 31:3b)*

Easter Sunday, for followers of Christ, is without question the holiest day of the year. This is the day we celebrate Jesus' resurrection from the dead, a sign of victory over sin and death that brings the possibility of life to all people.

It is a day for hallelujahs and happiness, and it happens in springtime, when new beginnings are in the air and bright clothes signal the hope of good days to come.

Can you imagine celebrating Easter, though, before it happened?

The lectionary text before us today is not taken from the gospels, but from the prophesies of Jeremiah, a man who lived through the darkest days of Israel's life. He saw the city of Jerusalem burned, the holy temple lying in ashes, and the leading families of Judah marched into exile. It was a bad time; yet, Jeremiah also saw through the slaughter and smoke to another day, a day of deliverance, a day when God would call all people back from exile and establish them anew in the sacred precincts of Zion.

Jeremiah's words offered much-needed hope to the bedraggled remnant of Israel and Judah, but what is that to us? We live on the other side of Easter, in a time when God's saving work has stretched far beyond the borders and hopes of a renewed nation for the Hebrews.

Considering Jeremiah's hopeful words on Easter Sunday reminds us that God's love doesn't give up: the good news Jeremiah offered was ultimately fulfilled in the promise of life in a "new Jerusalem" to all who put their hope and trust in God.

### Hope in distress
### (v. 1)

Today's text falls within a section of Jeremiah generally known as the "Book of Consolation." After many chapters devoted to scathing predictions of Judah's coming downfall, but before Jeremiah's narration of Jerusalem's destruction (chs. 37–39), we find an unexpected but welcome collection of oracles and prose that offer words of hope.

**Compilation:** The prologue to Jeremiah says that his ministry stretched from the 13th year of King Josiah's reign (around 626 BCE) to the 11th year of King Zedekiah's rule, when Jerusalem was conquered by the Babylonians (586 BCE), and into the fifth month of the resulting exile. Further dates are few, however. When, in the course of those 40 years, would prophesies such as those found in the "Book of Consolation" be most likely?

Gerald Keown, Pamela Scalise, and Thomas Smothers have pointed to three periods that have been suggested as possibilities: (1) the reign of Josiah, between 621 and 609 BC, when hopes were high for the restoration of the Davidic-Solomonic empire and survivors in Samaria were invited to join themselves to the king and temple in Jerusalem, as in 3:22-24; (2) during the reign of Jehoiakim or Zedekiah, after Nebuchadrezzar had finally defeated Assyria and pacified the region, making the return of the Northern Kingdom exiles plausible; and (3) during the administration of Gedaliah at Mizpah in Benjamin. (*Jeremiah 26–52*, vol. 27, Word Biblical Commentary [Zondervan, 1995], 84.)

As they appear in the text, the poetic part of the "Book of Consolation" stands between hopeful letters to the exiles (ch. 29) and Jeremiah's symbolic purchase of land as a promise that the Hebrews would return from exile (ch. 32). Chapter 33 then interprets the purchase of land in the light of the promises made in chs. 30–31.

Some scholars limit the Book of Consolation to chs. 30–31, but others include chs. 32–33. While all of chs. 30–33 are built on the theme of hope, chs. 30–31 consist of poetic oracles, while chs. 32–33 narrate a symbolic action and then expound upon it in the light of chs. 30–31.

The section begins with a note that a word of the Lord came to Jeremiah, instructing him to "Write in a book all the words that I have spoken to you. For the days are surely coming, says the LORD, when I will restore the fortunes of my people, Israel and Judah, says the LORD, and I will bring them back to the land that I gave to their ancestors, and they shall take possession of it" (30:1-3).

The oracles were probably uttered after the downfall of Jerusalem, as they address an audience in distress. In the final version of the book of Jeremiah, however, they are set before the narrative description of Jerusalem's destruction. This may have been a purposeful way of indicating that, even before using the Babylonians to mediate punishment upon a sinful people, God already had plans to bring them back from exile. **[Compilation]**

The lectionary text begins with Jer. 30:1, which is actually the closing verse of a previous oracle that began at 30:18: "Thus says the LORD: I am going to restore the fortunes of the tents of Jacob, and have compassion on his dwellings; the city shall be rebuilt upon its mound, and the citadel set on its rightful site."

The hopeful oracle included a divine promise that "you shall be my people, and I will be your God" (30:22). This recalls a much older pledge to the Hebrews who lived in Egyptian captivity: "I will take you as my people, and I will be your God" (Exod. 6:7). The promise was repeated in Lev. 26:12: "And I will walk among you, and will be your God, and you will be my people." Jeremiah had echoed the same theme in 24:7.

The repeated formula evoked memories of the covenant between God and Israel, one in which God promised to bless the people with material provision and protection from enemies, and the people promised to serve only God and to be obedient. The negative side of the covenant is that God also promised curses if the people looked to other gods and became disobedient. Jeremiah was one of many who believed that the kingdoms of Israel

and Judah had been defeated and their people exiled precisely because they had not proven faithful to God.

But, Jeremiah saw past the punishment to a day of forgiveness and restoration, when once again God would say "I will be the God of all the families of Israel, and they shall be my people" (31:1). The emphasis on "all the families of Israel" pointedly includes people from the northern kingdom, called "Israel," who had fallen to the Assyrians long before, in 722 BCE. The northern tribes had become so scattered and intermingled with other people as to become nearly invisible, but God had not forgotten them.

## Grace in the wilderness
### (vv. 2-3)

With v. 2, Jeremiah begins a new oracle, marked by the messenger formula "Thus says the LORD." He begins with a declaration of God's everlasting love (vv. 2-3) and concludes with three promises that would lead to future joy.

As v. 1 called to mind God's promise to Israel in Egypt, vv. 2-3 recall God's faithfulness to Israel as the people traveled from Egypt and through the dangerous wilderness on their long trek to the land of promise.

"The people who survived the sword found grace in the wilderness," said the prophet (v. 2a). After escaping from the Egyptian army (Exod. 14:15-30), the Israelites had to fend off an attack by Amalekites (Exod. 17:13-18). Later, they were ambushed by both Amalekites and Canaanites (Num. 14:41-45) before prevailing against the Canaanite king of Arad (Num. 21:1-3).

The historical memory of Israel's deliverance in the wilderness was designed to remind the Hebrews who suffered under Assyrian or Babylonian rule that God had delivered Israel before, and God had not forgotten them. It may have seemed to them that God had become distant, but "when Israel sought for rest, the LORD appeared to him from far away" (vv. 2b-3a), declaring "I have loved you with an everlasting love; therefore I have continued my faithfulness to you" (v. 3b). **[Steadfast love]**

God's love for Israel had persevered from the call of Abraham through the wilderness wandering, the years of the monarchy, and into the exile. Jeremiah, like Hosea, believed that Yahweh loved Israel too deeply to let them go (Hos. 11:8). Jeremiah could not have known it, but

> **Steadfast love:** The word translated as "faithfulness" in v. 3 is more commonly rendered as "steadfast love." The word is *chesed* (the *ch* is pronounced in the back of the throat, as in "Loch Ness"). It was at the heart of Israel's belief about God. Yahweh's powerful self-revelation to Moses in Exod. 34:6 declared "The LORD, the LORD, a God merciful and gracious, slow to anger, and abounding in steadfast love and faithfulness." There, "faithfulness" translates a different word, *'emmet*, which can mean "firmness," "faithfulness," or "truth." Our word "Amen" is derived from the same root.
>
> The people of Israel often declared a belief in God's steadfast love, especially in the psalms, where Ps. 100:5 is one of many examples: "For the LORD is good; his steadfast love endures forever, and his faithfulness to all generations."

that same abiding love would see its crowning fulfillment on a Sunday morning just outside Jerusalem when God's manifestation on earth – Jesus – rose from the dead in victory over sin and death.

## Joy in Jerusalem
### (vv. 4-6)

The present oracle related to something more tangible for Israel: a return from exile, the rebuilding of Jerusalem, and a renewed flourishing in the land. The prophets believed that Israel's exile was due to years of unfaithfulness and worshiping other gods, so the people were hardly virginal, yet Yahweh would renew them as an innocent youth, portrayed as a virgin maiden going out to celebrate a time of victory and joy: "Again I will build you, and you shall be built, O virgin Israel! Again you shall take your tambourines, and go forth in the dance of the merrymakers" (v. 4).

The construction of buildings would be matched by a restoration of fruitful agriculture to the land: "Again you shall plant vineyards on the mountains of Samaria; the planters shall plant, and shall enjoy the fruit" (v. 5). Jeremiah's inclusion of "the mountains of Samaria" is significant: Samaria was the capital of the northern kingdom, which had been defeated more than a hundred years earlier. Jeremiah saw a day when all of Israel would be restored, including the northern tribes. The image of planting vineyards and enjoying the fruit envisions a time of peace that would allow time for planting and cultivating the vines, with adequate time for them to mature and produce fruit.

The northern kingdom again comes into play with v. 6. When Israel split from Judah after Solomon's death, the new king Jeroboam built rival temples at Dan and Bethel so the northern tribes would no longer venture to Jerusalem for worship. Jeremiah saw a day when such divisions would end, and all the families of Israel would again worship in Jerusalem. The heartland of the northern kingdom had been the hill country populated by the leading tribe of Ephraim. Jeremiah saw a coming day when the schism would be erased and the tribes reunited, "when sentinels will call in the hill country of Ephraim: 'Come, let us go up to Zion, to the LORD our God'" (v. 6).

The people of Judah did return from exile, though they were limited to a small area around Jerusalem under Persian rule. Eventually, Alexander the Great conquered the Persians but died soon thereafter, leaving Palestine and its diverse population to be torn between Egyptian (Ptolemaic) and Syrian (Seleucid) rule. A Jewish family known as the Hasmoneans led a rebellion that threw off the Seleucids and regained independence for about a century, but infighting led to internal weakness and the land came under Roman occupation.

Jeremiah's beautiful vision still awaits fulfillment – the same eschatological promise for which Christians also hope, a day when all people will be drawn to a new Jerusalem to live in harmony and service to a God whose love is everlasting and whose faithfulness will not let go.

The celebration of Easter reminds us, more clearly than any prophecy, of the extent to which God has been willing to go in our behalf. In Christ's life, death, and resurrection, God's love has reached from heaven to earth and back again, bringing hope that all people may join in singing praise to the Lord whose steadfast love never fails.

### The Hardest Question
### Is today's State of Israel the fulfillment of Jeremiah's prophecy?

Many evangelical Christians believe the modern State of Israel exists as the fulfillment of prophecy, a view that's especially popular among dispensationalist fundamentalists and a variety of charismatic believers.

Is today's State of Israel the fulfillment of Jeremiah's prophecy, or of any of the many Old Testament promises that God would restore the people of Israel to their homeland? The short answer is almost certainly "No."

But why? For most of the last two millennia, after the Roman Empire fell, Palestine has been under the control of various Muslim groups, from Arabs to Ottomans. The bloody Crusades brought portions of the land under European control for short periods between 1100 and 1300 CE, but Ottoman Turks defeated the Crusaders and ruled the land from then until their defeat in conjunction with World War I, when the League of Nations granted England control of the area through an agreement known as the British Mandate.

Meanwhile, small numbers of Zionists from Central and Eastern Europe, facing anti-Semitism at home and inspired by the Austro-Hungarian writer Theodor Herzl, began emigrating to Palestine in the late 19th and early 20th centuries. They bought property from local Arabs who owned the land and established small settlements, mostly based on agriculture.

While Zionism had the goal of re-establishing a Jewish state and welcoming Jews from their worldwide diaspora, it made little headway until after World War II and the Nazi-led Holocaust that slaughtered millions of Jews while other nations sat idle. Stricken by a guilty conscience and a desire to do something positive for the Jews, members of the United Nations voted in 1948 to offer much of Palestine as a homeland sanctuary to the persecuted Jews.

Unfortunately, that came at the cost of displacing hundreds of thousands of Palestinian Arabs – many Christians among them – who had called the land home for more than a thousand years. The land was divided between "Israel" and the "West Bank," with Jews ruling Israel and Palestinian Arabs supposedly in control of territories in the West Bank, including much of the central area south and west of the Sea of Galilee, the southern areas around Jericho and Hebron, and the Gaza Strip.

Unfortunately, the Israeli government has routinely violated international accords, allowing and then protecting the establishment of settlements large and small in Palestinian lands, appropriating large tracts of East Jerusalem, and building fenced or walled highways through Palestinian territory, sometimes cutting through farms, orchards or family settlements in a way that leaves no back-and-forth access for those who live there. The West Bank is largely under Israeli occupation. More than 70 years after the formation of the State of Israel, scores of thousands of Palestinians who were evicted from their lands still live in refugee camps. West Bank cities such as Bethlehem are surrounded by walls and tall fences; their residents are prohibited from leaving without special permission.

Modern Israel was organized to have a secular government, not a religious one. It is home to far more secular Jews than practicing ones, though its leaders (especially among the Ultra-Orthodox) often play on religion for political purposes, referring to Israel and the West Bank as "Judea and Samaria," claiming that the illegal settlement of Palestinian land is a divine mandate that goes back to Abraham.

But modern Israelis and ancient Israelites are not equivalent: the nation of Israel as we know it is not the fulfillment of Jeremiah's prophecy or any other promise foretelling an age of peace when people of every tribe would return and worship God in Jerusalem. The former Temple Mount is now home to two large mosques, each more than 1200 years old. Though many synagogues and some churches exist in Jerusalem, the number of Christians continues to dwindle as Palestinian believers find it easier to move elsewhere.

Jeremiah's hope of a joyous reunion in a renewed Jerusalem still awaits its fulfillment – one that stretches far beyond Jeremiah's vision that "all the tribes of Israel" would return to the land. Through the advent, life, death, and resurrection of Christ, *all* people can now dream of a day when everyone can experience the steadfast and everlasting love of God that will not let us go.

# Easter Day

## Second Reading
## Psalm 118:1-2, 14-24*

# Strength and Salvation

*This text is read on Easter Day in Years A, B, and C. The slightly different passage of Ps. 118:1-2, 19-29 is read for the Sixth Sunday in Lent (Palms) each year. Psalm 118:14-29 is read on the Second Sunday after Easter in Year C. A study of vv. 1-24 appears in this volume for the Sixth Sunday in Lent.*

# Easter Day

## Third Reading
## Colossians 3:1-17*

# A New Wardrobe

*So if you have been raised with Christ, seek the things that are above, where Christ is, seated at the right hand of God. (Col. 3:1)*

Have you ever lost so much weight – or gained so much – that you had to buy new clothes? It's an indication that something is different: the old clothes no longer fit, and it's time for a change.

Easter Sunday reminds us of the biggest change ever – when Christ emerged from a tomb as living, not dead. We celebrate Easter because it holds the promise that we can also find our way from death to life.

Today's text uses the metaphor of clothing, but it concerns a change from the inside rather than in outer appearance. It's the change that comes when we realize how much we've dirtied our spiritual clothes – how badly we have messed up, or how far we've gone astray, and how ready we are to make things as right as we can make them.

In those situations, we discover that the only positive way forward is to admit our failures, ask for forgiveness, and hope for the opportunity to try again.

Having that experience helps us to appreciate today's text, because it is addressed to people who had goofed up, big time. They had sinned, every one of them. They had lived at odds with God – as have we.

### Heavenly thoughts
### (vv. 1-4)

Paul was writing to members of a young church in Colossae, a highland town on the scenic south bank of the Lycus River in southwest Turkey. Members of the church, like all new Christians, had become convicted of their sin. They had repented and sought God's mercy through Christ.

They had been baptized in Jesus' name, dying to the old self and being "raised again" with Christ, experiencing their own kind of Easter.

None of the Colossian believers, however, had been perfect since their baptism. They had stumbled along the way. They needed encouragement and instruction so they could learn to develop the full potential of their new lives. They had to learn that Christian growth is not automatic but comes as the result of a conscious process.

Again, we stand on common ground.

The Apostle Paul was not perfect, either. He knew what it was like to struggle with faith and to experience failure. From his own experience, he offered advice to the Colossians that speaks just as clearly and cogently to contemporary believers.

"So if you have been raised with Christ," he said, "seek the things that are above, where Christ is, seated at the right hand of God" (v. 1).

Paul was writing to people who were already Christians, so we could also translate "Since you have been raised with Christ" (as NIV11 does). His readers knew the experience of being forgiven, buried with Christ in baptism, and raised again to a new life. [**"If," or "since"?**]

That new life is the focus of Paul's encouragement. He challenged his readers to break out of the old molds that fashioned their former way of living, and to "seek the things that are above," that is, to look toward Christ for direction.

The best way to focus our *hearts* on Christ is to focus our *minds* on Christ. How we act, how we feel, and how

---

*This week's text is Col. 3:1-4, while Col. 3:1-11 is used for Proper 13 in Year C. This study covers Col. 3:1-17.

**"If," or "Since"?** Paul begins ch. 3 by posing a situation regarding the Colossians' relationship to Christ. The NRSV translates it "So if you have been raised with Christ," while the NIV11 translates it "Since, then, you have been raised with Christ." Either translation is acceptable. The structure of the sentence, in Greek, is called a "First class conditional sentence," where the use of 'ei and a verb in the indicative assumes that a statement is true.

we respond to others depends in large measure on how we think. Thus, Paul added, "Set your minds on things that are above, not on things that are on earth, for you have died, and your life is hidden with Christ in God" (vv. 2-3).

When we talk about the "new birth," we often fail to consider that a new birth must follow an old death. Baptism symbolizes that we have died to the old self and been raised again to new life, and that new life was Paul's concern.

Paul challenges us to focus on things above because that is where our true life – our new life – is found. "Your life has been hidden with Christ in God."

To understand the treasures of wisdom and knowledge that are hidden in Christ, we must learn to focus our minds on Christ. Such focus can come through reading the scriptures, through seeking Jesus' leading in prayer or meditation, or through group Bible study and corporate worship.

We may sometimes think it is hopeless – the idea that we could understand the mysteries of God or truly come to know the mind of Christ. But there is hope for us, and not just for this life, but for the life to come.

Paul wrote: "When Christ who is your life is revealed, then you also will be revealed with him in glory" (v. 4). We like the appeal of being revealed with Christ "in glory," but should not overlook the intriguing phrase "Christ, who is your life."

In the previous verse, Paul spoke of our lives being "hidden with Christ in God." Do we ever so identify with Christ that we can resonate with Paul's insistence that Christ *is* our life? Would others agree?

### Earthly temptations
#### (vv. 5-11)

To truly live as if Christ is our life, some things must be left behind (vv. 5-11). It's not hard to think of negative behaviors that are inconsistent with a Jesus-centered lifestyle.

Paul used graphic terminology to emphasize our new way of walking, saying we must "put to death" certain characteristics of the old nature. [**Corpse-ify**]. In v. 5 he referred to a string of related vices: fornication, impurity, lust, evil desire, and greed. All of those involve some form of exploitation in which one person objectifies another and uses him or her for personal satisfaction. This giving in to selfish desires is really idolatry, Paul said. It is giving earthly things a higher claim on our hearts than Jesus, and that leads one toward judgment rather than toward Christ.

David Garland has offered a helpful explanation of how greed becomes idolatry: "Greed refers to the haughty and ruthless belief that everything, including other persons, exists for one's own personal amusement and purposes. Essentially it turns our desires into idols. It is the overweening desire to possess more and more things and to run roughshod over other persons to get them. It stands opposed to the willingness to give to others regardless of the cost to self. Greed can crave after persons and is never satiated by its conquests but always lusts for more" (*Colossians, Philemon*, NIV Application Commentary [Zondervan, 2009], 204).

That was the old way of life, Paul said (v. 7), a way also characterized by other vices that have no place on the journey into Christlikeness. Anger, rage, malice, slander, "filthy language," and lying to one another were all on Paul's not-to-do list (v. 8). Reality shows, TV dramas, and sometimes even news reports bring a parade of angry,

**Corpse-ify:** When Paul said we should keep our heaven-based life with Christ and "put to death" those characteristics that are "earthly," he used the rare verb *nekroō*, which means "turn into a corpse," rather than the more common word *thanatoō*, which means "put to death."

Nijay K. Gupta suggests that this may have been a subtle mocking of those who tried to convince the Colossians that they must become ascetics to truly please God. Through constant fasting, such persons would probably have appeared gaunt and somewhat corpse-like. Thus, Paul may have called for the right kind of deprivation, as opposed to the transcendent-ascetic philosophy that Paul considered a danger to true faith.

"Paul calls for death, but it is death to whatever is earthly – not physical things such as the body, but earthly vices" (*Colossians*, Smyth & Helwys Bible Commentary [Smyth & Helwys, 2013], 131-132).

cheating, lying characters into our living rooms. The temptation is to assume that such behavior is normal or acceptable, but we know such things are not in keeping with a Christ-like life. If we seek to be more like Jesus, we must leave self-centered behavior behind and "put on the new self, which is being renewed in knowledge according to the image of its creator" (v 10).

In that new life, the prejudices and injustices characteristic of this world will give way to a new understanding of others, Paul said, a renewed life in which "there is no longer Greek and Jew, circumcised and uncircumcised, barbarian, Scythian, slave and free; but Christ is all and in all" (v. 11).

## Helpful supplies
### (vv. 12-17)

The new life does not derive from discarding negative behaviors alone, however: Paul went on to describe positive characteristics we should pack for the journey (vv. 12-17).

The vices Paul challenged the Colossians to eliminate had in common that they exploited or minimized the needs or feelings of other people. In contrast, the positive attributes he promoted majored on caring or consideration for others. Believers should express compassion, kindness, humility, gentleness, patience, forbearance, forgiveness, and love, he wrote (vv. 12-14).

Paul's letter continues to challenge Jesus-followers to live in peace and gratitude, so centered on Christ and his teachings that we do all things, whether in word or deed, "in the name of the Lord Jesus" (vv. 15-17). Is there any question that these characteristics will make for a happier life than the negative behaviors enumerated in vv. 5 and 8?

Paul's reminder that we have died to the old self demonstrates just how new and radically different our life in Christ is to be. To find and truly understand what it means to live in Christ, we must keep seeking it, keep thinking about the things above, keep thinking about Christ and his way. We must learn, in short, to discover what Paul means by "Christ, who is your life."

When we buy a new computer, smartphone, or other electronic gizmo, we may be able to "plug and play" with its basic functions, but it takes effort to learn all the new features. There can be quite a learning curve if one seeks to become a power user – and becoming a "power Christian" is not automatic, either.

Every Christian is in a life-long search to discover all the riches of the new life we have in Christ, trusting that our path will lead us ever closer to experience the Christ-life in all its abundance.

When we pack for a trip, we leave behind things that will weigh us down or impede our ability to travel. Instead, we take clothing, equipment, or documents that we will need for the journey. Paul's encouragement to put aside negative behaviors while looking toward the heavenly Christ is reminiscent of Heb. 12:1-2 – "Therefore, since we are surrounded by so great a cloud of witnesses, let us also lay aside every weight and the sin that clings so closely, and let us run with perseverance the race that is set before us, looking to Jesus the pioneer and perfecter of our faith, who for the sake of the joy that was set before him endured the cross, disregarding its shame, and has taken his seat at the right hand of the throne of God."

To live with a true "Jesus worldview," we must leave behind those behaviors that harm relationships and alienate people, while taking with us those that build community. In doing this, we also find we are not alone: our adventure joins us with a community of others who seek to follow Jesus' pattern of living. [**Focus**]

---

**Focus:** Preachers or teachers might consider using four aspects of Paul's call for focus in our daily living.

Let us focus our *hearts* on Christ. Our relationship with Jesus is like a love affair. We do not serve Christ out of fear or duty alone, but out of love. Thus, Paul calls us to focus our hearts on Christ.

Let us focus our *minds* on Christ. All relationships involve a mental aspect. We express our love for Christ through the decisions we make, and those choices are informed by the way we think. We were born in a culture whose thought patterns are based on selfishness and greed, but our new life in Christ calls for a new way of thinking.

Let us focus our *hopes* on Christ. Our walk with Christ has a goal: exploring the full measure of the spiritual treasures that are hidden in Christ, and ultimately experiencing the presence of Christ in all its fullness.

Let us focus our *journey* toward Christ. The completion of our Christian journey will require that we leave behind all that would hinder us and focus on those things that draw us closer to Christ. As we do so, our loving behavior naturally builds positive relationships and draws others toward Christ, as we look to the day when "Christ is all and in all."

We would all do well to consider the physical, emotional, or spiritual luggage we carry around from day to day. Are there things we need to unpack? Things to add? Is it past time to get started?

## The Hardest Question
### How do we put on "the new self"?

In Col. 3:9-10, Paul calls on the Colossian believers to avoid lying because "you have stripped off the old self with its practices and have clothed yourselves with the new self, which is being renewed in knowledge according to the image of its creator" (NRSV).

What does Paul mean by this? The word translated as "self" in the NRSV is literally the word for "man," which Paul uses in a generic sense for humankind, not for males only, though he had a particular male in mind. The NASB20, ESV, and NIV11 join the NRSV in translating the word as "old self," while the KJV and NET use the more literal "old man." Something akin to "old person" and "new person" could also be used.

Who is the "old person" that must be set aside? Paul thought of Adam as the prototype of the "old man" who was sinful and chose to live in rebellion against God, while he spoke of Christ as the "new man" who came to offer forgiveness and transformation to those who would live in him.

To "put on the new self," one must first strip off the old and put on the new. Nijay K. Gupta explains it this way: "It appears to mean that the believer must be closely identified with Christ, to become like him, to conform to his image. The emphasis for Paul is on 'new vs. old.' Things

have changed; they are different than before" (*Colossians*, Smyth & Helwys Bible Commentary [Smyth & Helwys, 2013], 139).

It is helpful to give some attention to Paul's word choices. The verbs for "have stripped off" and "have clothed yourselves" are aorist middle participles, indicating an action that has already taken place. Paul is speaking to believers: in their baptism they have already exchanged the old person for the new, but their spiritual formation is still underway and needs constant attention.

When Paul spoke of putting on the new self, he described it as "being renewed in knowledge according to the image of its creator" (v. 10). The verb form behind "being renewed" is a present participle, indicating ongoing action: spiritual formation into the image of Christ is a process that lasts throughout our lives.

Peter T. O'Brien notes that this has both a corporate and an individual aspect, as Paul points out in v. 11: "Within this realm of the new man there is no inferiority of one class to another; men and women of completely diverse origins are gathered together in unity in Christ, sharing a common allegiance to their Lord. Christ is all that matters; he permeates and indwells all members of his body, regardless of race, class, or background" (*Colossians*, Word Biblical Commentary [Word Books, 1982], 194).

The most meaningful church experiences come from situations in which a church or Bible study class or other group exhibits real unity of purpose, a common devotion to Christ, and full openness to all believers. If we don't see these characteristics in our current setting, what might it take to reach that place?

# Easter Day

## Fourth Reading
## John 20:1-18*

# Best. News. Ever.

*Mary Magdalene went and announced to the disciples, "I have seen the Lord!" (John 20:18a)*

What is the most important day of the year to you? Your birthday? Your wedding anniversary? For Christians, Easter is clearly the highest and holiest of days. It marks Christ's resurrection from the dead, overcoming death and – in some way beyond our comprehension – freeing us from death, too.

Easter is a day of stories about an early-morning garden and angels robed in white and brave women who come to the tomb despite their fear, then tell the good news with breathless wonder.

The four gospels relate the discovery of the empty tomb in different ways, and each has a slightly different cast of characters. [**The greatest story ever told in four versions**]

Mark says that Mary the mother (or possibly the daughter) of James, Mary Magdalene, and Salome were first at the tomb, apparently having purchased spices the night before, as soon as the Sabbath ended (16:1).

Matthew mentions just two women, Mary Magdalene and "the other Mary," saying only that they "went to see the tomb" (28:1).

Luke implies that there were more: he first says "the women who had come with him from Galilee" followed the burial procession and saw where Jesus was laid before preparing spices and then resting through the Sabbath, as the law commanded (23:55-56). He then says that "they" came at early dawn, bringing the spices they had prepared (24:1). Only after the women reported what they found to the apostles does Luke identify them as "Mary Magdalene, Joanna, Mary the mother of James, and the other women with them" (24:10).

---

**The greatest story ever told in four versions:** Our earliest written account of the Easter story is Paul's recitation of an early church credo in 1 Cor. 15:3-8, probably written around 55 CE:

"For I handed on to you as of first importance what I in turn had received: that Christ died for our sins in accordance with the scriptures, and that he was buried, and that he was raised on the third day in accordance with the scriptures, and that he appeared to Cephas, then to the twelve. Then he appeared to more than five hundred brothers and sisters at one time, most of whom are still alive, though some have died. Then he appeared to James, then to all the apostles. Last of all, as to one untimely born, he appeared also to me" (NRSV).

The stories we remember come from the four gospels, which were almost certainly written later, and drawn from variant traditions. The number and identities of the women are different, for example, in addition to the appearance and number of angels at the tomb, and the locations and manner of Jesus' post-resurrection appearances.

In our modern, Western context, historians work diligently to reconcile conflicting accounts, get the most accurate story possible, footnote the differences, and carefully relate the story in chronological order. Modern writers would also tend to discount the role of the supernatural and seek other explanations for unexpected events. Ancient writers, however, wrote with fewer constraints, often passing on traditions they had heard with little concern for variant accounts and with less concern for an accurate chronological scheme. Their primary concern was communicating beliefs they found important.

---

*This text is used for Easter Day in Years A, B, and C.*

John's gospel says that Nicodemus had brought about 100 pounds of myrrh and aloes that were wrapped with Jesus before his burial (19:39-40). In the Fourth Gospel, only Mary Magdalene is named as coming early to the tomb on the first day of the week, where she saw that the stone sealing the tomb had been rolled away (20:1).

It is possible that other women were present, but John focused his attention on Mary Magdalene because she is the one who told Peter that Jesus' body was no longer in the tomb. When she did, however, she said "We do not know where they have laid him." Mary's use of "we" implies that she had not been alone.

Despite the inconsistencies, the gospels are agreed on several things: early on the first day of the week the tomb was discovered to be empty, and Mary Magdalene was there.

In the Fourth Gospel, Mary Magdalene does not appear until we meet her at the foot of the cross, but she becomes the first witness of Jesus' resurrection, and the first to declare the good news.

### An unlikely witness
### (vv. 1-13)

It's hard to imagine that any of the disciples, male or female, had slept very much between late Friday afternoon when Jesus had been carefully placed in the tomb and early Sunday morning when the tomb was found to be empty. As noted, Mark and Luke suggest that Mary Magdalene came to the tomb with others, laden with spices for Jesus' body, while John portrays her as coming alone, perhaps rushing ahead of the others, drawn to the tomb even as we might feel pulled to stand by the casket of a loved one. Whatever the reason, she seems to have come as soon as the law and light allowed. [**Law and light**]

We don't really know much about Mary, probably called "the Magdalene" in reference to her hometown of Magdala, which lay near the Sea of Galilee between Capernaum and Tiberius. She appears to have been the leader of a group of women who followed Jesus and provided financial support for his ministry (Mark 15:40, 47; 16:1; Matt. 27:55-56; Luke 8:2-3, 24:10). Among the stories of Jesus' ministry and last days, Mary Magdalene features more prominently than any other woman.

Many readers think of Mary Magdalene as a reformed prostitute, based on a longstanding but almost certainly

> **Law and light:** The Law of Moses forbade the Hebrews from traveling at all on the Sabbath day (Exod. 16:29), but that was clearly not very practical, so the rabbis later ruled that one could travel up to 2,000 cubits (about 1,000 yards) from home on the Sabbath, basing their reasoning on an angular interpretation of Josh. 3:4, which instructed the Israelites to follow 2,000 cubits behind the Ark of the Covenant. As time went on, some rabbis added various exceptions to the rule, allowing one to travel up to 8,000 cubits in certain instances. Thus, depending on where Mary Magdalene was staying, the tomb might have been beyond her reach until sundown on Saturday, when the Sabbath ended. Light became a problem then (remember that streetlights and flashlights did not exist), making dawn of the following day the earliest time that Mary could practically go to the tomb.

erroneous tradition. The story in Luke 8:2, where she is described as a supporter of Jesus who had been relieved of seven demons, immediately follows the story of a sinful woman who anointed Jesus' feet (Luke 7:36-50). Some patristic and medieval interpreters surmised that both stories referred to the same woman, identifying Mary as a harlot whom Jesus had healed and forgiven, giving her good cause to love him. [**Mary the Tower?**]

While the seductive image of Mary as a former harlot has provided dramatic grist for productions ranging from *Jesus Christ Superstar* to *The Last Temptation of Christ*, there is no biblical evidence to suggest that Mary Magdalene was anything other than an honorable and prosperous woman who was a leader among Jesus' followers.

Jesus' earlier predictions that he would die and rise again are not as clear in John as in the synoptic gospels, where each one includes three specific pronouncements (for example, Mark 8:31-33, 9:31-32, 10:32-34). John's gospel contains just one mysterious reference to Jesus' dying and being lifted up (12:23-34), and a cryptic prediction that the disciples should anticipate a time of grief and mourning that would be followed by joy (16:17-20).

All the gospels agree, however, that the disciples were shocked by the resurrection. Even the faithful Mary Magdalene did not expect to find Jesus alive. When she found the tomb empty, she assumed that his body had been stolen, and ran back to the disciples to report "They have taken the Lord out of the tomb, and we do not know where they have laid him" (20:2).

**Mary the Tower:** Some scholars have argued that "Mary Magdalene" was really Mary of Bethany, Martha's sister, who became such an important leader that she was given the honorific title "Mary Magdalene," meaning "Mary the Tower" or "Mary the Great." The Aramaic word *magdala* (Hebrew *migdal*) means "tower" (Mary Ann Beavis, "Reconsidering Mary of Bethany," *Catholic Biblical Quarterly* 74 [2012], 286-87).

More commonly, scholars assume that the Mary in question came from a town known as Magdala, with "Magdalene" used to distinguish her from other women named Mary.

Magdala (now called Migdal), on the northwest corner of the Sea of Galilee, was home to a large fishing industry. The town was covered by a landslide in the first century and lost to history until it was rediscovered in 2009 during mandatory excavations prior to the construction of a Catholic guest house.

The site contains pools for salting and drying small fish along with a residential section, but it is best known for the discovery of a first-century synagogue with a unique stone table that may have been used for unrolling the scrolls during synagogue services. The photo shows the synagogue with a replica of the stone table, with the residential and industrial area beyond. Jesus was active in that area, and it is likely that he would have taught there.

When Peter and John bolted for the tomb to check her story, Mary followed again, her account vindicated only when Peter and John saw the empty tomb. [**Racing to the tomb**] Despite the cocoon-like and carefully arranged grave clothes that the Fourth Evangelist describes – which should have alerted them that the body had not been stolen – the fearful followers did not yet appear to understand that Jesus had risen from the dead (v. 9).

**Racing to the tomb:** Gail O'Day, in *The New Interpreter's Bible*, notes that John's description of John outrunning Peter to the tomb has led to some interesting interpretive comments. Some commentators suggest that John's fleet feet indicate that he was younger than Peter, if not as impulsive.

Noting that Peter entered the tomb first, Rudolf Bultmann proposed that he represented Hebrew Christianity, which emerged first, with Gentile Christianity, represented by John, coming after. Others see the account as reflecting a later rivalry between churches established by Peter and John.

As O'Day observes, such elaborations get away from the point of the story, which is the significance of the empty tomb ("John," vol. 9, *The New Interpreter's Bible* [Abingdon Press, 1995], 840).

Though the men returned home, John tells us, Mary remained at the tomb. Still thinking that someone had stolen the body, she had little to do but weep over loss upon shocking loss. The Fourth Gospel is the only one to indicate that Mary was weeping, and it does so with emphasis. Mary wept outside the tomb (v. 11), the angels asked why she was weeping (v. 13), and later Jesus asked the same question (v. 15).

After a while, the story suggests, Mary crept inside the small tomb, where she saw something Peter and John had not seen. Two men were there, clad in brilliant white, sitting at the head and foot of the rock-cut shelf where Jesus had been laid. John clearly calls them "angels" (v. 12), as opposed to Mark, who speaks of a young man dressed in a white robe (Mark 16:5); Luke, who says there were two men in dazzling clothes (Luke 24:4); and Matthew, who describes a single angel whose "appearance was like lightning, and his clothing white as snow" (Matt. 28:3).

Mary was too grief-stricken to be impressed by angels, however, and when they asked why she was weeping, she answered as she would have to any person. We can still sense the hollow grief in Mary's heart as she replied: "They have taken my Lord away, and I do not know where they have put him" (v. 13).

### A tearful witness
### (vv. 14-17)

Mary's grief soon came to an abrupt and surprising end. It's not clear whether Mary had left the tomb when she "turned around and saw Jesus standing there" (v. 14), but the author of John's gospel insists that Mary did not recognize the man she had loved and followed so closely.

How could Mary be so confused as to think Jesus was a gardener? Was she too numb with grief or too blinded by tears to see clearly? Had Jesus' resurrection body taken on a different appearance? Could she simply not wrap her mind around the idea that Jesus could be standing up?

Jesus asked why she was weeping, then "Whom are you looking for?" (*tina zēteis*, v. 15). It is the same question he had asked of Andrew in 1:38 (*Ti zēteite*), the first words attributed to him in John's gospel. He spoke the same words when soldiers came to arrest him in the garden (18:4, *Tina zēteite*). All could be translated "Who do you seek?" or "What do you want?" From beginning to end, Jesus invited others to know him and follow him. When we come to church, especially on Easter, who are we looking for? What do we want?

The brief conversation between Jesus and Mary followed her interaction with the angels almost verbatim – until Jesus said one word, one magical word: "Mary" (*Mariam*). As Alicia Myers has noted, it is the first time Jesus called a woman by name in the gospel, and the first name he called following the resurrection. It is likewise a reminder of the earlier promise from 10:3 that the shepherd "calls his own sheep by name and leads them out" (*Reading John and 1, 2, 3 John* [Smyth & Helwys, 2019], 200).

In hearing the familiar way Jesus called her name, Mary's eyes and heart were opened. We can only imagine the many things she wanted to say in that moment of recognition, but all she could get out was "*Rabbouni!*"

The Fourth Evangelist describes it as a Hebrew word for his Greek audience, but "Rabbouni" is the Aramaic form of a word also known in Hebrew. While the author explains that it means "teacher" (v. 16), the word is an intensive and personal form of the word, which can also mean "master," and could be rendered here as something akin to "my dear lord." The "*i*" on the end is a suffixed first-person possessive pronoun: she did not just call Jesus teacher, but "*my* teacher."

We can fully understand why Mary must have yearned to run into Jesus' arms for a big hug filled with happy tears, and the story suggests that she must have wanted to hold onto Jesus, but he would not allow it (v. 17).

This seems troublesome to us. Surely Jesus knew how much Mary longed to touch him, perhaps to confirm what her eyes had seen as much as to express affection. Why did he respond as he did?

The language is ambiguous, because the Greek verb used in v. 17a could mean either "touch" or "hold." Jesus' first post-resurrection command could be interpreted as "Don't touch me" (NET, KJV "Touch me not"), or "Don't hold on to me" (NRSV, NIV11, CEB). The NASB20 has "Stop clinging to me." Did Jesus sense Mary's intent and wave her away before the first touch? Or had she already taken hold of an arm or his knees, so that he was indicating that she could not keep clinging to him?

Later, Jesus did not object to being touched, and even invited Thomas to inspect his wounds (v. 27), so the latter option seems more likely. In either case, Mary had to learn that Jesus' reappearance in physical form was only temporary. Both she and the others would have to let go of his physical presence and to depend on his spiritual reality after his ascension.

The Fourth Evangelist considered Christ's ascension to be particularly important, as seen in the instructions he has Jesus give Mary: "I have not yet ascended to the Father. But go to my brothers and say to them, 'I am ascending to my Father and your Father, to my God and your God'" (v. 17b).

In these astonishing words, Jesus indicated that his death, resurrection, and ascension had created the possibility of a new relationship in which human disciples can know God even as Jesus does: Jesus speaks of the disciples as his brothers. Earlier in John's gospel, Jesus had called his disciples "servants" (13:16) and "friends" (15:15). Now, significantly, he calls them "brothers" (20:17), indicating that the mysterious dynamics of the cross and resurrection event had opened the door to a new kind of relationship between God and humankind.

## A joyful witness
### (v. 18)

An earlier part of the text told us that when the apostle John had entered the tomb and saw the empty grave clothes, "he saw, and believed" (v. 8). Whether John yet believed Jesus had risen from the dead or just believed that his body was missing is not clear. There's no question, however, that Mary's newfound belief, spawned by both hearing and seeing, included Jesus' new life.

Jesus not only lived, but he also gave Mary a command to go and tell the other disciples important news. Surprisingly, she was not to report simply that Jesus had risen from the dead and would meet them again, but that "I am ascending to my Father and your Father, to my God and your God" (v. 17b).

With her abject fear transformed to giddy joy, Mary tore herself away from Jesus and obeyed his command, running to tell the other disciples: "*I have seen the Lord!*" (v. 18). Surprisingly, the author records no reaction from the disciples, only that "she told them that he had said these things to her." Were they too stupefied to speak, or still disbelieving because the witness was a woman?

In first-century Israel, a woman's word was not considered as trustworthy as a man's (cf. Luke 24:11). In addition, Mary could have appeared over-tired, over-stressed, and possibly blubbering with tearful excitement. Why should anyone believe her? A committee of humans might never have selected Mary to be the first bearer of such life-changing, world-changing news, but God did.

Mary's experience implies a profound truth for modern disciples. Although we may feel like the least of God's children, we may become harbingers of hope to a world that often feels lost in darkness. Like Mary, we may shed tears of fear, of grief, of despair — but through it all the Lord Jesus calls our name, beckons us to believe, and turns our tears to joyful faith.

### The Hardest Question
### Why does the Fourth Evangelist focus on the ascension while Jesus was still in the garden?

Readers may wonder why the Fourth Gospel has Jesus talking about the ascension in his first words to Mary, while still in the garden. This does not happen in the other gospels, where the focus is clearly on Jesus' resurrection from the dead and his appearances on earth. Matthew's gospel closes with "the Great Commission" (Matt. 28:19-20), but it does not describe Christ's ascension to heaven. In Mark, Jesus' ascension appears only in a longer ending that was added to some manuscripts many years later (Mark 16:19), not in the original gospel, which ended at 16:8.

Luke describes the ascension in his gospel (Luke 24:50-53), and again in the Book of Acts (1:6-11), but he seems to present it mainly as the conclusion of Jesus' earthly ministry, as something that happened as a matter of course and should not have been surprising.

The Fourth Evangelist, however, writing later and in a more philosophical vein, ascribes great theological significance to the ascension. He appears to connect the resurrection and ascension closely: though he relates further stories of Jesus' post-resurrection appearances, he does not include a separate story of Jesus' ascension to heaven. Some interpreters think this means that his ascension occurred almost immediately after the resurrection, that Mary interrupted him before he could ascend, and that later appearances of Jesus in the gospel are not just post-resurrection, but post-ascension experiences.

For the author of the gospel of John, the ascension of Christ rounds the circle and completes the work of Christ as the *logos* or "Word" who came into the world as God wearing skin, and who returned to the Father clothed in glory. In John 3:13, Jesus had spoken of having descended from heaven and ascending back to it. With his resurrection from the dead, the "descent" phase of Jesus' work was ending, and the time for ascending back to heaven was near. Christ's crucifixion, resurrection, and ascension were all connected parts of his glorification as Son of God and savior of the world.

Contemporary believers can rejoice today that this new relationship of faith and fellowship and family was not for Mary's friends alone, but for followers through the ages. The Fourth Evangelist declared near the beginning of his gospel that those who believe are given "power to become children of God" (John 1:18). Jesus' ascendant glorification in 20:17 opens the door to that new possibility of living as children of God and "brothers" of Christ: Hallelujah.

# Easter Day

## Optional Fourth Reading
## Matthew 28:1-10

# Who's Afraid?

*He is not here; for he has been raised, as he said. Come, see the place where he lay. (Matt. 28:6a)*

Easter: for Christian believers it is the highest and holiest day of the year. It is a day that, more than any other, reaffirms our faith and renews our hope. It is the day a crucified teacher rose from the dead and was transformed from the earthly Jesus to the cosmic Christ. It is a day made for celebration.

What are your favorite memories of Easter? Are they more likely to involve sunrise worship services and stirring hymns, or new clothes, egg hunts, and a basket of candy from the Easter bunny? Like Christmas, Easter has come to us with mixed messages, an amalgam of secular and sacred, or pagan and prophetic.

As an adult, what makes a meaningful Easter celebration for you? Do you like to attend passion plays or watch *Jesus Christ Superstar* on DVD? Do you look for a local concert of Handel's *Messiah*, or attend lunchtime Holy Week services offered by many churches?

It's hard to imagine an Easter Sunday passing without attending some sort of worship service, even for those who rarely warm a pew. A student once described his religious background by telling me he came from a family of "C&E Christians." I thought he was talking about an obscure denomination until I realized he meant "Christmas and Easter."

Whether we celebrate Easter through drama, music, or preaching, our focus is the same: we want to remember the story, the amazing Easter story of death and resurrection, of shock and awe, of sad desperation and exuberant hope.

### An earth-shaking discovery
### (vv. 1-4)

Details of the Easter narrative vary in the four gospels but are nonetheless familiar. They all begin with the aftermath of Jesus' shocking and unexpected crucifixion, leaving his followers, family, and friends at a loss for what to do next. Discrepancies in these stories are obvious, but all four gospels insist that (1) Jesus rose from the dead, (2) his followers were surprised and amazed, and (3) women were the first to discover the empty tomb and hear the news that Christ was born.

Matthew and Mark agree that a man named Joseph of Arimathea (Matt. 27:57-61) had the resources, the position, and the presence of mind to step forward and request custody of Jesus' body, offering his own tomb as a resting place. Only the very wealthy could afford to construct a rock-cut tomb in the side of a stone cliff, with a rolling stone for a door. **[Joseph of Arimathea]**

In Jerusalem, tourists can visit such tombs, including one that is just outside the walls of the old city. Called

---

**Joseph of Arimathea:** Mark describes Joseph of Arimathea as "a respected member of the council," the ruling body of the Jews known as the Sanhedrin (Mark 15:42). Despite his high position in Jewish life, Joseph appears to have followed Jesus. John's gospel says he "was a disciple of Jesus, though a secret one because of his fear of the Jews," who went directly to Pilate to ask for Jesus' body (John 19:38).

Luke describes him as "a good and righteous man named Joseph, who, though a member of the council, had not agreed to their plan of action" in seeking Jesus' death, and who went to Pilate to request custody of Jesus' body (Luke 23:50-52).

Matthew describes Joseph simply as "a rich man from Arimathea" and "a disciple of Jesus" before crediting him with personally preparing Jesus' body for burial (Matt. 27:57-61).

**Rolling stones:** Tombs covered with rolling stones could be large enough for a person to walk into, or so small that they could be entered only by crawling. A small rock-cut tomb with a rolling stone door was discovered near Megiddo during highway construction (left). The other photo is the Garden Tomb in Jerusalem, one of the traditional places for Jesus' burial site.

the "Garden Tomb," it is located near Gordon's Calvary, and revered by many as the traditional site of Jesus' burial. The tomb, which was located near a large wine press, is cut into a sheer limestone cliff. It no longer has its rolling stone, but a rock-cut groove marks a track where one could have stood. The site with the oldest tradition is inside the Church of the Holy Sepulchre, but the outer part has been whittled away and covered with a small chapel, so it no longer bears any resemblance to a tomb. [**Rolling stones**]

Jesus was buried on a Friday just before sundown, which marked the beginning of the Jewish Sabbath (from sundown Friday until sundown Saturday). Mary Magdalene and "the other Mary" had watched as Jesus' body was laid in the tomb (Matt. 27:61), but they could not return to add traditional burial spices on the next day because of rabbinic rules preventing travel on the Sabbath. As dawn of the following day approached, however, Matthew says they both hurried to the tomb.

Matthew says nothing of the women bringing spices, as do Mark and Luke, only that "Mary Magdalene and the other Mary went to see the tomb" (v. 1). Matthew alone reports that their visit was accompanied by an early morning earthquake, or that the women were witnesses to it. Likewise, only Matthew describes an angel descending

from heaven, rolling the stone aside, and then sitting on it. The angel's appearance was "like lightning," Matthew said, "and his clothing white as snow" (v. 3). The other gospels report one or two angels appearing inside the tomb, after the stone was moved.

The blazing appearance of the angel and the special effects contributed by the earthquake left the guards trembling in fear (v. 4), as we might imagine. Readers may find amusing irony in Matthew's comment that the guards "became like dead men." As the dead man in the tomb arose to new life, the living soldiers who were set to guard him acted as if they were dead. The power of God can turn things around very quickly.

### A world-changing commission
### (vv. 5-10)

The women, no doubt, were also shaking with fear, but the angel comforted them and announced simply that Jesus had risen from the dead "as he said" (vv. 5-6). Matthew does not describe the women's entrance into the empty tomb, leaving the reader to assume they accepted the angel's invitation to "see the place where he lay."

As Matthew tells the story, however, there is no pause between the invitation to see the empty tomb and the commission to go and tell the disciples. The two women were to bear this message: "He has been raised from the dead, and indeed he is going ahead of you to Galilee; there you will see him" (v. 7). Luke and John describe resurrection appearances in Jerusalem, but for Matthew (and Matthew alone) the most important manifestation of the risen Christ was to take place in Galilee.

The region of Galilee was some 80 miles north of Jerusalem, a walking journey of several days. Bordered on the south by the Jezreel Valley and reaching as far north as Lake Huleh (now a drained area of fertile farmland), the hills of Galilee and the shores of Lake Kinneret had been the location for much of Jesus' ministry.

The Galilee is a large area: How were the disciples supposed to know where to find Jesus? Perhaps we are to assume that they would choose a favorite rendezvous from earlier days. Matthew 28:16 implies that Jesus had directed them to a particular mountain, but vv. 7 and 10 do not mention it. Faith would be required for the journey, for Jesus would not be alongside to show them the way. Rather, according to the angel, Jesus was going ahead, alone.

As Matthew tells it, the women accepted the angel's commission and ran from the tomb with a stomach-churning mixture of both "fear and great joy" (v. 8). They must have been totally shocked when Jesus himself stepped into their path. His one word of greeting, apparently, was enough to convince them that it was he. As one, the women fell to their knees, took hold of Jesus' feet, and worshiped him (v. 9). In John's gospel, Jesus instructed Mary not to touch him, but Matthew speaks of no such warning. The word for "took hold" can also mean "seize." The two Marys took a firm grip on Jesus' knees, and they did not want to let him go.

Jesus would have understood their desire, but he had other work for them. Repeating the angel's instructions for the disciples to meet him in Galilee (v. 10), Jesus sent them on their way, no doubt with even greater joy.

Matthew says nothing about the women's reunion with the other disciples, either what they said or how it was received. The message must have been accepted, however. After speaking of a priestly plot to claim that Jesus' body had been stolen (vv. 11-15), Matthew has the disciples immediately hit the road to Galilee and "to the mountain to which Jesus had directed them" (v. 16).

Though Matthew makes no mention of the male disciples' skepticism (unlike Luke, who says they thought the women were telling "idle tales," Luke 24:11), the women's testimony might have been hard to accept, despite the evidence of the empty tomb. Faith would have been required to leave Jerusalem and begin the long walk to Galilee in hopes of finding Jesus there.

As Matthew tells it, though, this was not the first time Jesus had mentioned a post-resurrection meeting in Galilee. Near the end of the Last Supper, he says, Jesus had predicted that his disciples would desert him and that he would be killed. "But after I am raised up," he had said, "I will go ahead of you to Galilee" (26:32).

The disciples knew that they had abandoned Jesus following the crucifixion. Perhaps they wondered if the Lord would ever trust them again. For this reason, Jesus' invitation and his choice of words were especially significant. He said to the women, "Go and tell *my brothers* to go to Galilee." Jesus' love was unchanged by the disciples' desertion: Jesus understood their fear but saw beyond it. He believed in the men and women who had devoted their lives to him even more than they believed in themselves.

It's good to know that Jesus believes in us, too. He knows that we have many doubts and questions. Though we may sometimes live as if we have given up on him, Jesus doesn't give up on us. Our rendezvous may not be in Galilee, but we are also called to go and meet the risen Lord. As for the first disciples, our journey toward encountering and following Jesus requires faith and trust, but it is well worth the effort.

Jesus calls each of us to be Easter people – to experience our own spiritual resurrection through Christ, and to share the joy and hope we have found with others.

Our text tells us that the women who first met the risen Lord overcame their fears and did as he asked. How will *we* respond?

### The Hardest Question
#### How did Easter get its name?

This question isn't directly related to the text, but offers a response if someone should ask why we call the celebration of Christ's resurrection "Easter." Unlike the observance of Jesus' birth ("Christmas" comes from "Christ's mass," referring to a Catholic worship service), Easter does not derive from the Christian tradition at all, but from the name of an Anglo-Saxon goddess.

Evidence suggests that long ago, pagans celebrated the arrival of spring with a festival of feasting and prayer. They may have erected public representations of the nature goddess' symbol and taught their children to honor the goddess who was believed to restore life to the earth each spring.

When Christian missionaries moved into northern Europe and England, they quickly noticed that the festival to the dawn goddess occurred very close to the time they traditionally celebrated the resurrection of Christ. As new believers began to practice their faith, Christian holidays came to be clothed in the robes of local custom. Thus, their celebration of Christ's resurrection included some elements from the Saxons' worship of the dawn goddess.

In 325 CE, the Council of Nicea, by authority of the Roman Emperor Constantine, declared that Christ's resurrection should be celebrated each year on the first Sunday after the first full moon on or after the vernal equinox, which occurs on March 21. That is why the date can range from as early as March 21 to as late as April 25. By that time, the number of Christians in Britain had grown so much that the old Celtic celebration of spring was largely forgotten, though certain of its customs continued in the Christian celebration of Christ's resurrection.

The name of that celebrated dawn-goddess apparently derives from the word *aus* or *eos*, meaning "East," because that is where the sun rises. The goddess' name was variously represented as *Eostre* or *Ostara*.

Some of this is conjectural: the first clear mention of the name "Eostre" comes from the early church historian Bede in the eighth century. In a work called *De temporum ratione*, he said that pagan festivals were held to Eostre during the month of *Eosturmonap* (the spelling is approximate), but that they had died out by his time.

However fuzzy its origins, the name "Easter," like the bunny rabbits and eggs that may also represent spring and new birth, has no biblical foundation, but derives from a pagan celebration that Christian missionaries sought to supplant, even as the date of Christmas was chosen to overshadow the Roman feast of Saturnalia.

## First Reading
## Acts 2:14-36

# Making Sense of It All

*This Jesus God raised up, and all of that all of us are witnesses. (Acts 2:32)*

We've all had this happen: We hear an eruption of sirens wailing down a street near us, and we want to know what happened. We see a large crowd gathered near a store, and we want to know what's going on. We're driving on what is normally a calm road, and suddenly the traffic comes to a standstill. What could explain it?

Some questions have no easy answers. The book of Acts recounts a memorable occurrence in Jerusalem nearly two millennia ago, when a mass of people gathered in a public square. They were asking questions about something they could see, and something they could not see. Word had spread that the followers of Jesus, who had gone underground after his crucifixion, were suddenly out in public, and they were preaching strange new ideas about Jesus, and they were doing it in every language spoken in that part of the world, and some that weren't.

What was going on? Who could explain this amazing transformation of Jesus' followers?

### What you have seen…
### (vv. 14-15)

The first readings for Sundays from Easter to Pentecost in Year A bypass the Old Testament and come from the book of Acts. The second, third, and fourth Sundays offer excerpts from the post-Pentecost section of Acts 2 in highlighting the earliest days of the earliest church.

The text for today introduces Peter as the speaker in v. 14a, then skips to a latter part of his sermon (vv. 22-32), but stops short of the end. Considering all of vv. 14-36 will enhance our study. [**How likely?**]

---

**How likely?** Acts 2:14-36 is presented as an off-the-cuff sermon from Peter, though its content has the appearance of having been worked out over time. It's possible that Luke took the early church's developing understanding and ascribed it to Peter, but there had been time for the disciples to think things through.

Seven full weeks between Easter and Pentecost had passed. Whether the disciples had remained sequestered or not, they had ample time to reflect on Jesus' teachings and to consider ways in which his work could be seen as the fulfillment of Old Testament prophecy. In his gospel, Luke indicated that Jesus himself had given them a head start. As Jesus walked with two disciples toward Emmaus after his resurrection, Luke said, "beginning with Moses and all the prophets, he interpreted to them the things about himself in all the scriptures" (Luke 24:27).

Bolstered by weeks of discussion and emboldened by the Holy Spirit, Peter would have been amply prepared to offer a cogent defense of the gospel as he and the others had come to understand it. It is unlikely that anyone would have been standing by with a wax tablet or parchment pad to record Peter's sermon, but very likely that the scripture quotations and central argument would have been remembered.

---

Peter was generally the most outspoken of the disciples, so it would not have been surprising that he would become the infant church's most prominent spokesperson. On the day of his initial sermon, the streets would have been filled, not only with Jerusalem's normal inhabitants, but also with thousands of Jewish pilgrims who had come for the Festival of Pentecost.

Peter knew that onlookers were not accustomed to the sort of behavior the Spirit-infused disciples were demonstrating. He recognized that it looked strange for men and women to come out of hiding and start speaking so boldly, especially when others could not understand what some of them were saying. Some in the crowd had accused them of being full of wine.

So, Peter stood up before a large crowd of people and shouted: "Men of Judea and all who live in Jerusalem, let this be known to you, and listen to what I say. Indeed, these are not drunk, as you suppose, for it is only nine o'clock in the morning" (vv. 14-15).

Wine was generally consumed with the evening meal: the newly loquacious believers were not inebriated by distilled or fermented spirits; they were drunk on the Holy Spirit.

## What it means…
### (vv. 16-21)

Peter spoke as if his listeners should not be surprised at what they saw. He described this miraculous movement of the spirit as nothing more than the fulfillment of a prophecy from Joel, who predicted a time when God's Spirit would be poured out on all people, so that "your sons and your daughters shall prophesy, and your young men shall see visions, and your old men shall dream dreams. Even upon my slaves, both men and women, in those days I will pour out my Spirit; and they shall prophesy" (vv. 16-18, Joel 2:28-29).

Peter reminded the crowd that Joel had spoken of this happening on "the Lord's great and glorious day," when cosmic portents would darken the sun and turn the moon to blood, signs in heaven and on the earth not unlike the three hours of darkness that Mark and Matthew described in conjunction with the crucifixion (vv. 19-20, cf. Joel 2:30-31, Mark 15:33, Matt. 27:45).

The result, Peter said, again citing Joel, was that "Everyone who calls on the name of the LORD shall be saved" (v. 21, Joel 2:32). Joel anticipated a cosmic cataclysm and would not have recognized Peter's reinterpretation of his words, but the early church saw enough of a similarity to believe the prophecy had been fulfilled in ways that Joel had not expected.

## What really happened…
### (vv. 22-28)

Knowing that the crowd consisted mainly of Hebrew people, Peter attempted to explain the complex relationship between Jesus and the Jews. Addressing the "men of Israel," Peter said Jesus had been "attested to you by God with deeds of power, wonders, and signs that God did through him among you, as you yourselves know…" (v. 22). Jesus was known to them, his reputation was known, and the account of his death was known.

Peter's next words contained elements of both blame and absolution. He accused the Jews of crucifying and killing Jesus "by the hands of those outside the law," but also said that Jesus had been "handed over to you according to the definite plan and foreknowledge of God" (v. 23). It was as if he was saying they were guilty, but not at fault, because Jesus' death had been part of God's plan.

That was not all of God's plan, however: "But God raised him up, having freed him from death, because it was impossible for him to be held in its power" (v. 24). The NRSV glosses over a significant word: God did not just deliver Jesus from death, but from "the pains of death" (ōdinas tou thanatou). The Greek word translated "pains" typically refers to "birth pangs." If this was what Peter had in mind, the pain of Christ's death was like the pain associated with being born into new life through the resurrection.

Peter then shifted, not to a prophecy, but to a psalm that came to be understood as a prophecy by no one less than David. He quotes from the LXX version of Psalm 16, whose superscription associates it with David, applying to Jesus the psalmist's testimony that God's presence had saved him from death (vv. 25-28, Ps. 16:8-11):

"For David says concerning him, 'I saw the Lord always before me, for he is at my right hand so that I will not be shaken; therefore my heart was glad, and my tongue rejoiced; moreover my flesh will live in hope. For you will not abandon my soul to Hades, or let your Holy One experience corruption. You have made known to me the ways of life; you will make me full of gladness with your presence'" (vv. 25-28).

Some rabbis had also interpreted Ps. 16:9 as support for the hope of resurrection: the church took the interpretation further.

> **Christ as executor:** Careful readers may note that Joel had declared that God would pour out the Spirit upon all people (v. 17, Joel 2:28), but Peter depicted Jesus as receiving the promise of the Spirit from God and then acting on God's behalf to pour out the Spirit as a gift, at least upon those who were open to receiving it (v. 33).

## And furthermore …
### (vv. 32-36)

Peter clearly regarded David to be both a prophet and the author of psalms associated with him, even though modern scholars are much more skeptical regarding the accuracy of editorial superscriptions that were attached to the psalms. Nearly half of the psalms – 73 of them – have *lədawîd* as all or part of the superscription.

The preposition *lə* rarely means "by," though it can mean "belonging to." It more commonly means "to" or "for." Though some superscriptions connect psalms to a particular period in David's life, others may simply have been dedicated to him or associated with a "Davidic" collection. Internal evidence indicates that some of the psalms attributed to David were clearly written later.

But, Peter was a child of his own time, and not of ours. Like other Jews of the day, he assumed not only that David had written the psalms associated with him, but also that David had the gift of prophecy, giving such psalms the authority of prophetic oracles.

With regard to Ps. 16:8-11, Peter declared that since David himself was obviously dead and buried, but that God had promised to put one of his descendants on the throne (an allusion to 2 Sam. 7:12-13 and Ps. 132:11), he must have been predicting the resurrection of the Messiah when he said "you will not abandon my soul to Hades, or let your Holy One experience corruption" (vv. 27, 31), a very loose citation of Ps. 16:10.

Modern exegetes would consider such logic to be an overly large interpretive jump, but it was fully in line with rabbinic exegesis that looked for deeper meanings in a text, even if not intended by the original author. Thus, Peter felt confident in concluding that David had predicted Jesus' resurrection (v. 32).

As if that were not enough, Peter also claimed that David had predicted Christ's ascension to heaven. Jesus had been raised to the right hand of God, he said, and had poured out the promised Spirit that was manifested in what "you both see and hear" (v. 33). David himself had not "ascended to heaven," Peter said, yet he wrote "The Lord said to my Lord, 'Sit at my right hand, until I make your enemies your footstool'" (vv. 34-35), a quotation from Ps. 110:1. Such words could only apply to Jesus, Peter insisted, who had now been exalted to his heavenly throne as the Christ, the anointed one, Israel's Messiah and Lord. **[Christ as executor]**

For Peter, and for the early church, the quotation was further evidence that David had foreseen the coming of Christ as the promised descendant who would sit on a throne at God's right hand.

Like a modern student of apologetics who seeks to prove the truth of the gospel, Peter believed he had built a case for Jesus that any Jew would find convincing: "Therefore, let the entire house of Israel know with certainty that God has made him both Lord and Messiah, this Jesus whom you crucified" (v. 36).

For Peter, the texts he interpreted as prophesies were enough to affirm with certainty that Jesus was who they claimed him to be: *asphalōs* means "safely," or "assuredly." And his words must have been convincing, for Luke reports that more than 3,000 people sought baptism that day (vv. 37-42). Others were not so sure.

Peter will always be remembered as the first follower of Jesus to preach an evangelistic sermon, with results any proclaimer could envy. Today, when we express our belief that Jesus Christ was the Son of God who came to earth and died and rose again as a part of God's eternal plan, we are echoing the same basic gospel that Peter and his friends first declared so many years ago. We may not rely as heavily on rabbinic exegesis, but the essential message remains the same: Jesus is Lord.

### The Hardest Question
**Must we agree with Peter's interpretive approach?**

Many modern readers are less likely than Peter to appeal to the psalms as prophecy, or even to assume that David wrote every psalm attributed to him in the editorial superscriptions. Even fewer are likely to think of David as a prophet – especially as the *key* prophet – when building a case for Jesus as God's messiah.

Although it was popular among patristic and medieval writers, and it remains in vogue today among Christians with a more mystical bent, few scholars adopt the type of "second meaning" exegesis that Peter relied on when compiling evidence for why his Jewish audience should accept Jesus as the promised messiah.

Should we? It's important to remember that Peter was pitching his argument to Jewish people who had long harbored hopes of a coming messiah, and he was using language and interpretive methods that both he and they understood. Joel's prophecy would have been familiar as a hope for the "last days," but the specific connections Peter drew between Davidic psalms and the coming of Jesus may have been new to most of his audience. Peter hoped to use the authority of their own scriptures to convince fellow Jews that Christ was the fulfillment of all their hopes, and it was apparently a very effective argument. Luke's report says that Peter's hearers were "cut to the heart" and asked what they needed to do (vv. 37). Following Peter's instructions, "about three thousand persons were added" and began devoting themselves to the apostles' teaching (vv. 41-42).

In our day, we may find Peter's arguments to be interesting, but we also have the rest of the gospel story to consider. We have the testimony of the gospels and the epistles that came to be regarded as Christian scriptures. We have the witness of believers through the ages who have sensed the presence and the power of Christ in their lives. We have opportunities for worship surrounded by people of faith who have found strength in their relationship with Christ.

The good news comes in many forms.

# Second Sunday of Easter

## Second Reading
## Psalm 16*

# The Path of Life

*You show me the path of life. In your presence there is fullness of joy;*
*in your right hand are pleasures forevermore. (Ps. 16:11)*

Was King David a prophet, and did he predict the resurrection of Christ? This question may seem far-fetched, and yet both the Apostle Peter and the Apostle Paul cited Psalm 16 as a prophecy that God would not allow death to claim Jesus.

Before exploring that question further, we need to dig into Psalm 16 itself, which a superscription describes as "A Miktam of David." In the Bible used by Protestants, 116 of the 150 psalms have superscriptions that attribute authorship, suggest the occasion of writing, or provide liturgical instructions for the psalm's use in Israel's worship. The superscriptions were not part of the original psalms, but were added in antiquity as the psalms were collected and compiled into what is often called "The Psalter."

The Hebrew word *miktam*, like *selah*, defies certain definition. It appears in the superscriptions of six psalms, all of which are associated with David, and all but Psalm 16 occur consecutively (Psalms 56–60). Four of those five include specific descriptions of some peril the scribe imagined that David had faced. Since Psalm 16 concludes with a testimony that Yahweh had saved the psalmist from Sheol and granted life instead of death, it is likely that this psalm's original setting may have been a time of crisis. Whether the threat came from enemies or illness, the psalmist turned to God for help.

## A hopeful entreaty
## (v. 1)

The psalm begins with a plea: "Protect me, O God, for in you I take refuge" (v. 1). The prayer for protection implies the existence of a serious threat. Was the author being pursued by enemies who wanted to kill him? Was he weakened by illness or injury? We have no way of knowing the source of the problem, but it must have been beyond the psalmist's ability to overcome alone: his state of exigency has left him praying for God to protect him.

The verb translated as "seek refuge" is used mostly in poetic texts, or with a figurative sense. The psalmist does not think of God as a cave-like hideaway, but as a protective presence with the power to shield him from death.

## A loyal assertion
## (vv. 2-4)

Verses 2-4a are notoriously troublesome to translate. Hebrew poetry is a challenge to read in the best of circumstances. When it includes unexpected verbal forms, rare words, and ambiguous syntax, any translation remains tentative.

The question begins with the first word, the verb for "say," which most translations render as "I say," even though it is written as a second person verb and vocalized as feminine. As written, it would be translated "You say," as spoken by a woman.

A second issue concerns who is speaking and just what he or she means. Some translators assume that in

---

*Psalm 16 is also read on Proper 28 in Year B and Proper 8 in Year C.*

vv. 2-4a the psalmist is quoting the words of an acquaintance who dares to worship both Yahweh and other gods. Others believe the psalmist speaks for himself, setting himself apart from those who worship other gods.

Peter Craigie understands vv. 2-4a to portray the psalmist in dialogue with another person who has become a syncretist, worshiping both Yahweh and other gods. We know such persons existed, or else Israel's theological historians and prophets would not have railed against them so (1 Kgs. 11:5, 7; 2 Kgs. 17:7, 15-18; etc.).

In this scenario, the psalmist could be charging the syncretist with saying "You have said to the Lord, 'You are my master, my welfare indeed rests on you.' (You have said) to the holy ones in the land 'They are my mighty ones! All my pleasure is in them'" (vv. 2-4a, from *Psalms 1–50*, vol. 19, Word Biblical Commentary [Zondervan, 1983], 153). In this case, "the holy ones" would be a euphemism for other gods. When in danger, the syncretist would appeal both to Yahweh and to other gods for help.

The NET takes a different tack, reading v. 2 as the psalmist's claim and vv. 3-4a as a charge that "the holy ones," understood as priests or leaders the psalmist had formerly admired, had gone after other gods.

The NRSV also assumes that v. 2 is the psalmist's address to Yahweh: "You are my Lord, I have no god apart from you." The NRSV then takes v. 3 as an assertion that the unidentified "holy ones in the land" have delighted him with their nobility, perhaps in contrast to those who worship other gods.

A literal translation of v. 4 would begin: "they multiply sorrows, another, they pay the price" (or 'pay a dowry'). Though word order varies from typical narrative text and the preposition "to" is not present, it could be translated as "They multiply sorrows, they offer gifts to another (god)."

The gist is clear: others may have chosen to add other gods to their theological repertoire, but the psalmist would remain true to Yahweh alone. He would not seek the aid of other gods: "their drink offerings of blood I will not pour out, or take their names upon my lips" (v. 4).

Hebrew rituals included drink offerings, but always of wine (Exod. 29:40, Lev. 23:13, and others) or "strong drink" (probably a type of beer, Num. 28:7), never of blood. The notion of taking – literally, "lifting up" – the name of a god was often an allusion to taking oaths or

vows in that god's name, usually promising an offering or action in return for the god's aid.

Though the precise translation is obscure, the message of vv. 2-4 is clear: others might turn to pagan gods in time of need, but the psalmist would trust in Yahweh alone, declaring "I have no god apart from you."

## A confident testimony
### (vv. 5-11)

The latter part of the psalm expresses complete trust that God will provide the protection requested. Or, it may have been written after the danger had passed, as a personal testimony of God's deliverance.

Verses 5-6 call up a historical image of the apportionment of the land of promise to the tribes, each of which further subdivided their territory among clans, and then among families. The land was to be worked and passed down within the family through inheritance. Apparently, tribal officials cast lots for predetermined plots of land, and some families received more fertile or appealing acreage than others.

For the psalmist, a fortunate allotment of land and a bounteous cup of wine (from fruit of the fields) served as a figure for Yahweh's presence and provision (v. 5). [**Part of a portion?**] Under God's care, he said, "The boundary lines have fallen for me in pleasant places; I have a goodly heritage" (v. 6).

The psalmist's life had been so good that he wanted to publicly "bless the LORD who gives me counsel" (v. 7a). Both God and the psalmist's inner being contributed to wisdom: the parallel line declares "in the night also my heart instructs me" (v. 7b). The word translated "heart" (*kilyōt*) is not the typical word for heart (*lēb*), but one that meant "kidneys," sometimes thought of as the seat of one's moral character. English speakers are more

---

**Part of a portion?** Translated literally, v. 5 begins "Yahweh (is) portion of my portion." Two different words for "portion" are used. Instead of suggesting that God is only part of the psalmist's inheritance, however, the doubled expression serves to intensify the meaning: Yahweh is "my choice portion," or perhaps "the portion of portions."

likely to associate emotions and character with the heart, which is reflected in modern translations.

Trusting God for counsel and safety, the psalmist declared "I keep the LORD always before me; because he is at my right hand, I shall not be moved" (v. 8). To think of keeping God both "in front of me" and "at my right hand" is not a contradiction in terms. To keep God before one implies a commitment to following in God's way. When Hebrew kings held court, their most influential counselor would stand just to their right – hence our image of a "right hand man" as someone's most trusted assistant or advisor.

The psalmist's expression demonstrates his trust in God's counsel and his commitment to God's way: because of that, he said, "I shall not be moved," or "I shall not be shaken." **[I shall not be moved]**

### An unshakeable faith
### (vv. 9-11)

The word for "be shaken" in v. 9 and the Hebrew word for "die" are very similar: the consonants for "to shake" and for "to die" are very similar: both end in "t" sounds that are slightly different. The psalmist may have used this expression intentionally as he segued into an affirmation that God had preserved his life.

Because of his determination to remain close to Yahweh, the psalmist could declare "Therefore my heart is glad, and my soul rejoices; my body also rests secure. For you do not give me up to Sheol, or let your faithful one see the Pit" (vv. 9-10).

Ancient Hebrews believed that everyone, good or evil, went to an underground abode of the dead known as Sheol when they died. "The pit" was used in poetic contexts as a synonym. Having passed the crisis that led

him to cry out to God in v. 1, the psalmist could now praise God for having delivered him from death.

Perhaps we are to gather that Yahweh's wise counsel of vv. 7-8 has guided the psalmist through the trial and to renewed life. Thus, he could conclude "You show me the path of life. In your presence there is fullness of joy; in your right hand are pleasures forevermore" (v. 11). "The path of life" may carry a double meaning, describing both the obedient path that leads to a good life with God, and the particular path that led to the psalmist's survival of a life-threatening crisis.

But what about our initial question? Psalm 16 is clearly a personal testimony of a happy man. Though he may have hoped others would follow his example and find deliverance, nothing about the psalm indicates that his intention was to predict a coming messiah whom God would preserve from death.

Rabbinical exegesis of the Old Testament, however, did not hesitate to draw connections between ancient

**Psalms in Acts:** Peter's use of Psalm 16 is discussed in more depth in the previous lesson in this volume, a study of Acts 2:14a, 22-32. Here is a fuller account of how Paul drew on the same text while preaching in the synagogue of Antioch of Pisidia, reading the psalms as prophecy:

And we bring you the good news that what God promised to our ancestors he has fulfilled for us, their children, by raising Jesus; as also it is written in the second psalm, "You are my Son; today I have begotten you."

As to his raising him from the dead, no more to return to corruption, he has spoken in this way, "I will give you the holy promises made to David."

Therefore he has also said in another psalm, "You will not let your Holy One experience corruption."

For David, after he had served the purpose of God in his own generation, died, was laid beside his ancestors, and experienced corruption; but he whom God raised up experienced no corruption. Let it be known to you therefore, my brothers, that through this man forgiveness of sins is proclaimed to you; by this Jesus everyone who believes is set free from all those sins from which you could not be freed by the law of Moses. (Acts 13:32-39)

scriptures and what might be seen as a contemporary fulfillment. Some rabbis saw in this text evidence for a resurrection, and in Peter's Pentecost sermon, he drew on a loose quotation from the LXX version of Ps. 16:8-11 as a prophecy of Christ's resurrection, "For you will not abandon my soul to Hades, or let your Holy One experience corruption" (Acts 2:27).

Later, as the Apostle Paul preached to the Jews of Antioch of Pisidia, he called on both Psalm 2 and Psalm 16 to speak of God's son (Ps. 2:7) who God raised from death, as "he has said in another psalm, 'You will not let your Holy One experience corruption'" (Acts 13:35). [Psalms in Acts]

The psalmist was more interested in testimony and praise than in prophecy, but we can understand why early Christians found in Psalm 16 a reflection of Christ's work: while the psalmist found confidence and guidance to survive death (at least temporarily), Jesus entered full-steam through death's door, but was delivered from its clutches. And in his work, the evangelists proclaim, Jesus enabled us to claim the promise, too: God will not abandon us to death, but has shown us the path to life.

Thus we may gladly join the psalmist in praise to the God of our salvation: "In your presence there is fullness of joy."

## The Hardest Question
### What is a *miktam*?

As indicated in the lesson, the definition of the Hebrew word *miktam* is uncertain. The early Greek translation called the Septuagint (probably third century BCE) rendered it as *stelographia*, a word that described an inscription on a stele, a slab of stone used in some ancient religions to give human testimony of divine blessing. Many Phoenician and Punic inscriptions are known in which a worshiper prayed for a particular blessing from the gods and promised to erect a testimonial inscription if the prayer was answered. Since several of the "Miktam Psalms" refer to dangers from which the psalmist has been spared, this is a reasonable suggestion.

The Hebrew word for "write" is based on the consonants *ktv*, and some suggest the possibility of a related root, *ktm*, that might have meant "engrave." The addition of the letter *mem* (*m*) to the beginning of a verb could be used to form participles and nouns: thus *mktm* could mean "engraving" or "inscription."

This remains conjectural, however. Others have suggested translations such as "golden psalm," based on an uncommon word for gold, *ktm* (probably a loan word from another language) that was sometimes used in poetic texts, as in Ps. 45:9, Isa. 13:12, Lam. 4:1, and six other instances.

Less likely definitions included "humble" or "blameless" as an epithet of David, "a silent prayer," and "an atonement psalm," among others. (Drawn largely from Peter C. Craigie, *Psalms 1–50*, vol. 19, Word Biblical Commentary [Zondervan, 1983], 154.)

Six psalms (16 and 56–60) are called "A Miktam of David" in the editorial superscriptions, which were added later. Most of them imagine a particularly dangerous time in David's life.

Psalm 56: To the leader: according to The Dove on Far-off Terebinths. Of David. A Miktam, when the Philistines seized him in Gath.

Psalm 57: To the leader: Do Not Destroy. Of David. A Miktam, when he fled from Saul, in the cave.

Psalm 59: To the leader: Do Not Destroy. Of David. A Miktam, when Saul ordered his house to be watched in order to kill him.

Psalm 60: To the leader: according to the Lily of the Covenant. A Miktam of David; for instruction; when he struggled with Aram-naharaim and with Aram-zobah, and when Joab on his return killed 12,000 Edomites in the Valley of Salt.

Psalm 58 does not mention a specific crisis, but also includes the enigmatic command "Do Not Destroy," which might be the name of a tune, such as "The Dove on Far-off Terebinths," as in Psalm 56.

The superscription to Psalm 16 does not suggest a particular crisis point in David's life, but the psalm itself speaks of David being in danger, crying out to God, pledging faithfulness to God, and being delivered from death.

If we are to think of the Miktam Psalms uniformly as testimonies of deliverance from danger, it could be reasonable to assume that the psalms might have been engraved or inscribed in some way as a lasting testimony and word of praise for God's saving grace.

# *Second Sunday of Easter*

## Third Reading
## 1 Peter 1:1-9

# A New Future

*Blessed be the God and Father of our Lord Jesus Christ! By his great mercy he has given us a new birth*
*into a living hope through the resurrection of Jesus Christ from the dead … (1 Pet. 1:3)*

Easter worship, whether at sunrise or in the sanctuary, is a highlight of the year for practicing Christians. But what do we do *after* Easter, when the hallelujahs have faded and routine returns? The book of 1 Peter offers encouragement for Christ-followers who may flounder in the wake of the resurrection, and the lectionary offers a series of epistle readings from 1 Peter during the weeks after Easter in Year A.

Being Christian is not always easy: Jesus promised his followers a comforter, but also a cross. Peter's letter to Christians of the late first century addresses the difficulties faced by those who try to live the Christian life in a pluralistic culture that in some ways was not so different than our own.

No one can say with certainty whether the Apostle Peter wrote this letter, as it bears several marks of having been written long after his death. Still, it is likely that his teaching inspired it. In our studies, we will refer to the author as "Peter," but with the understanding that someone else may have written it in his name. [**Who wrote 1 Peter?**]

When Christians changed their lifestyles and no longer participated in their pagan cultures, opposition was inevitable: we recall how idol-makers in Ephesus started a riot when their business suffered because of the Christian movement (Acts 18:23-41).

The letter of 1 Peter appears to have been written during a time of oppression. Empire-wide outbreaks of persecution against Christians arose under Nero (ca. 62–64 CE), Domitian (ca. 90–97 CE), and Trajan (ca. 111 CE). Smaller, localized pogroms broke out at other times, and Peter's readers could have faced one of those.

---

**Who wrote 1 Peter?** The letter we call 1 Peter is written in an excellent, almost literary style of Greek, and it seems to address Gentile converts more so than Jews. Many modern scholars are convinced that the apostle Peter could not have written this book, since he is believed to have died before the outbreak of widespread Roman persecution, was described as an uneducated man (Acts 4:13), and was primarily known as a rustic fisherman who became an apostle mainly to the Jews (Gal. 2:7-9).

Thus, scholars usually assign the book to one of Peter's disciples, or to another early leader who used Peter's name as a pseudonym, a common practice in the ancient world. Other writers find those arguments lacking and confidently assign the book to the apostle Peter himself. Some suggest that a professional scribe in the church at Rome could have worked with Peter to compose the missive.

Several other ancient works were attributed to Peter, though they are clearly apocryphal. These include The Acts of Peter, the Gospel of Peter, the Preaching of Peter, the Apocalypse of Peter, and the Judgment of Peter.

(For a comprehensive and accessible discussion of these matters, see Richard Vinson, "1 Peter" in *1 & 2 Peter, Jude*, Smyth & Helwys Bible Commentary [Smyth & Helwys, 2010], 1-26.)

---

Those who accept Petrine authorship date the book from 60–64 CE, since an old church tradition holds that Peter was executed in Rome during the persecutions of Emperor Nero. The tradition claims that Peter insisted on being crucified upside down, saying he was unworthy to die in the same way as Jesus. Roman Catholics hold that the Clementine Chapel, beneath St. Peter's Basilica in

Rome, marks the site of his execution. A tomb said to hold his bones is also inside the basilica.

Those who believe another author who was influenced by Peter's teaching typically cite literary evidence suggesting that the letter was written late in the first century.

Whatever the specific occasion, the writer of 1 Peter sought to encourage and comfort those Christians whose changed lifestyle had made them unacceptable within their cultural world. We may experience some of the same pushback in our own society, whether from non-Christians or from fellow believers who hold to different doctrine or values.

## A living hope
### (vv. 1-5)

First Peter begins with a salutation (1:1-2) in the style made popular by Paul, replacing the typical word "greetings" with "grace and peace." The letter is addressed to the "exiles of the Dispersion" (NRSV), which usually refers to the "diaspora," or scattering of Jewish exiles throughout the known world. The writer, however, apparently considered both Jewish and Gentile Christians to be part of the diaspora. This terminology is a reminder that all Christians have connections with God's covenant people.

The address mentions the provinces of Pontus, Galatia, Cappadocia, Asia, and Bithynia, all in the northern half of what was then called Asia and is now the country of Turkey.

It is likely that the letter was designed to circulate among churches in the region so that all might learn and be encouraged (5:12). Its message did prove to be helpful, so much so that the letter traveled to other areas and eventually came to be accepted as scripture, inspired by God and instructive for churches and Christians in all places and all times.

Christian letters often included a prayer of thanksgiving after the greeting, so we are not surprised that vv. 3-12 – a single, convoluted sentence in Greek – offer a prayer of praise for what God has done in the lives of believers. The writer begins, appropriately, by offering thanks for God's great mercy. It is because God is merciful that we are freely offered a new birth (literally "re-begotten"), he says, made possible through the resurrection of Jesus Christ from the dead. This gives to believers "a living hope."

We can't overemphasize the importance of hope, and for Christians, eternal hope is firmly grounded in Christ's resurrection. If there had been no resurrection, there would have been no church. It was Christ's resurrection that convinced his disciples that Jesus truly was the Son of God, victorious over death and evil. The resurrection led them to trust in his promise of eternal life to those who are "born again" (John 3:3).

Some Old Testament prophets hoped for a resurrection in the future, at the end of the age. In contrast, the resurrection of Christ gave to Christians a *living* hope for the present, a confident assurance of life beyond the grave.

While the new birth can lead to an abundant life here on earth, the writer also speaks of "an inheritance that is imperishable, undefiled, and unfading, kept in heaven for you" (v. 4). We normally think of an inheritance as something we receive when someone else dies, but this inheritance comes when *we* die.

Three adjectives describe this eternal inheritance: it is imperishable, undefiled, and unfading. The writer adds a nice alliterative touch, for the three words all begin with the negative particle *a*: *aphtharton, amianton, amaranton.* **[Alliteration]**

The word for "imperishable" means "not subject to spoiling." The term translated "undefiled" is related to a word that can mean "to stain or dye." With the negative particle, it means "unstained." The word for "unfading" derives from the name of a flower, the *maranth*, with a negative prefix attached. It is used only here in the New Testament, but it appeared in Greek literature to describe a flower whose beauty never fades (Daniel Arichea and Eugene Nida, *A Translator's Handbook on the First Letter from Peter* [United Bible Societies, 1980], 18).

The author also thanked God for the protective promise of salvation that ensures our future (v. 5). We usually think of salvation in the context of one's initial experience of trusting Jesus and being assured of eternity (cf. Luke 19:9). Paul sometimes speaks of it as a present

---

**Alliteration:** The author's use of alliteration goes beyond the adjectives in v. 4. The word for "inheritance" and the repeated word for "and" (*kai*) both begin with the letter "k," so there is an artful repetition between words beginning with "k" or "a": *klēronomian aphtharton kai amianton kai amaranton.*

possession being worked into a finished product (Phil. 2:12). At other times, "salvation" refers to the consummation of God's redeeming work at the second coming of Christ (Rom. 13:11, Heb. 9:28), and that is probably its meaning here. Christians experience this sense of security through the living hope of committing their lives and their eternity to the power of God.

## Trial by fire
### (vv. 6-7)

Salvation calls for rejoicing, even if current troubles limit our rejoicing to future hope. "In this you rejoice, even if now for a little while you have had to suffer various trials" (v. 6). This theme recurs throughout the letter. [**Persecution**]

The writer did not spell out the "various trials" his readers had suffered. Persecution is not limited to violent or physically harmful acts. The word here translated as "suffer" was most commonly used for "grieve." It speaks of the emotional effects of suffering more than physical

---

**Persecution:** Few Christians in America suffer persecution as did the recipients of 1 Peter. We may feel slighted or disrespected for our faith, but physical or social repercussions are rare.

Sometimes the fiercest criticism we get comes from fellow believers. Persons who hold very conservative social values they identify as "Christian" or as a "biblical worldview" may feel rejected or looked down on by those who take a liberal or progressive stance and hold different values. At the same time, socially progressive believers who emphasize Jesus' teachings about showing preference to the poor may receive sharp criticism from conservative folk who preach self-sufficiency.

Some cry "persecution" when the courts do not allow them to open municipal meetings with a Christian prayer, or to erect a monument containing the Ten Commandments in front of the courthouse, or to refuse service to gay or lesbian persons. That is not persecution, but a practice of honoring the Constitution in a pluralistic society that respects all beliefs, as the founders intended.

Nevertheless, trials and tribulations are often our lot in life, whatever the cause, and hard times put our faith to the test. If we cannot remember any experiences in which our faith was tested by fire and we grew through the experience, we might ask ourselves why.

---

pain. The distress of grief may seem overwhelming, but in comparison to eternity, it is but "a little while."

Pain, whether it arises from persecution or misunderstanding or heartache, is not just to be endured: it can be tapped for self-growth and increased maturity. Like a smelting fire that burns away impurities and renders gold more valuable, the heat of public derision or opposition could serve to purify the believers' faith and prove it genuine. That kind of faith, according to the author, will result "in praise and glory and honor when Jesus Christ is revealed" (v. 7).

The metaphor of gold is helpful, but it falls short of describing true faith. Although gold is fireproof, it is not destruction-proof. In contrast, genuine faith that has been through the fire is imperishable. Counterfeit faith is inherently worthless and brings shame upon both Christ and the church. Faith that has been tested and proven to be genuine brings greater glory to the author of our faith.

## The outcome of our faith
### (vv. 8-9)

Faith involves believing in something for which one has no visible proof. [**Faith in what we do not see**] In trying times, faith may falter, or it may grow stronger. The writer of 1 Peter recognized the tested and true faith of the Christians in Asia Minor by affirming "Although you have not seen him, you love him; and even though you do not see him now, you believe in him and rejoice with an indescribable and glorious joy" (v. 8).

If the apostle Peter wrote these words, the author would have been an eyewitness to Christ's life, work, and resurrection. In contrast, the people to whom he wrote had not heard Jesus teach, seen his miraculous works, or witnessed his resurrection – yet they believed. They walked by faith and not by sight (cf. 2 Cor. 5:7, John 20:29).

The believers not only believed in Christ – they *loved* him. Through the experience of faith and love, they experienced the joy of knowing the presence of Christ's spirit and the assurance of their final salvation, the ultimate outcome of faith (v. 9). Suffering is not required for faith, but pain can strengthen us along the pathway to our ultimate salvation.

Jesus' central command was for Christians to love God, and to love each other (Matt. 7:12). He taught his followers to respond to others with love, even when

> **Faith in what we do not see:** Compare Peter's assertion about belief without seeing to a similar passage in Hebrews:
>
> "Although you have not seen him, you love him; and even though you do not see him now, you believe in him and rejoice with an indescribable and glorious joy, for you are receiving the outcome of your faith, the salvation of your souls" (1 Pet. 1:8-9).
>
> "Now faith is the assurance of things hoped for, the conviction of things not seen" (Heb. 11:1).
>
> And as the Apostle Paul put it, "We walk by faith and not by sight" (2 Cor. 5:7).

persecuted (Matt. 5:38-48). Few of us face persecution, but we may experience occasional ridicule or pushback due to our beliefs. Our response should likewise be guided by love.

Scholars have often noted that 1 Peter has many similarities to the writings of Paul. The comparison is particularly evident in this moving introduction to 1 Peter. The author begins with an affirmation of the Christian's living *hope* (v. 3), then speaks of genuine *faith* (vv. 5, 7), and finally moves to joyous *love* (v. 8). These are the three things that remain when all else fails, aspects of Christian maturity that Paul often emphasized (1 Cor. 13:13; 1 Thes. 1:3, 5:8). For Christians who face the intense pressures of an unbelieving culture, these three virtues are central.

Everyday life often leaves us with a level of tension between our daily behavior and the life to which we are called. We shouldn't give up, though: in Christ we have a hope that *lives*.

### The Hardest Question
### What does it mean to have a "living hope"?

The most powerful phrase in today's text may be Peter's prayerful claim that the resurrection of Christ can bring a new birth "into a living hope."

We like the notion of being alive, and we know something of the importance of hope that keeps the windows of the future open, but what did Peter mean in saying that we are born through Christ into "a living hope"?

I can still remember a statement from a "January Bible Study" book used when I was a young pastor. In *1 Peter: Message of Encouragement*, John McClanahan wrote: "A *living hope* is hope which refuses to give up and die" (Convention Press, 1982, 17). I can also remember times in my life when I was tempted to give up hope, but I didn't. Hope kept me going.

Still, we should acknowledge that there is a difference between just keeping on, and truly living. In a 2013 "Ted Talk," therapist Esther Perel spoke of growing up among Holocaust survivors in Belgium. Her neighbors could be divided into two groups, she said, "those who didn't die, and those who came back to life." Those who simply "didn't die" became closed in, insecure, unwilling to open themselves to risk and love and the larger world. Those who "came back to life," in contrast, had hope enough to believe there was life beyond the traumas they had faced. They learned to live again.

Richard Vinson emphasizes that "hope is 'living' because Jesus Christ was raised from the dead" (*1 & 2 Peter, Jude*, Smyth & Helwys Bible Commentary [Smyth & Helwys, 2010], 52). It is Christ's life that gives life to our hope.

Those who have a living hope don't just muddle through, continuing to breathe but with no discernible purpose or joy. When we have a living hope that is grounded in Christ's resurrection, we can learn to find growth and strength even on difficult days. We can trust in God's good future for us. We can refuse to give up or hide from risk, opening our hearts to live fully into every moment of life, even the hard ones. That is a living hope.

# Second Sunday of Easter

## Fourth Reading
## John 20:19-31*

# A Disciple We Can Like

*Jesus said to him, "Have you believed because you have seen me?*
*Blessed are those who have not seen and yet have come to believe." (John 20:29)*

In the village of Glendale Springs, North Carolina, just off the Blue Ridge Parkway, sits a tiny Episcopal church called both "Holy Trinity Church" and the "Church of the Frescoes." A marvelous fresco painting covers the entire wall behind the pulpit area, attracting thousands of visitors each year. The scene depicts Jesus and the disciples gathered around a long table for their last Passover meal. The artist used local people as models for the different disciples, and included the pastor posed in a serving role. The artist's own face is in the picture, too: Ben Long painted himself as "Doubting Thomas."

Visitors to the church note that, no matter where they are standing, Thomas seems to be looking directly at them, as if asking "What do *you* think?" [**Thomas**]

### Absent Thomas
### (vv. 19-23)

Thomas does not appear in the first scene of the story that so shaped his reputation, and he is not mentioned at all until the second scene. Unlike the disciples who cloistered themselves in secrecy following Jesus' crucifixion, Thomas was out and about. Was he out keeping watch, or obtaining provisions, or just needing some time alone? The text does not say.

It was evening of the first Easter Sunday that John says Jesus suddenly appeared to the dumbfounded disciples, who were quite certain they had locked the doors. Seeing their shock and fear, Jesus offered what their

**Thomas:** The Apostle Thomas appears at the far right of Ben Long's touching fresco painting of the Lord's Supper at the Church of the Frescoes in Glendale Springs, N.C. A short video at https://vimeo.com/560704793 (linked from Long's website) shows Long working on the portrait and talking about its significance.

*This text is also read for Pentecost Sunday in Year A.

> **A spiritual infusion:** The Hebrew words for "breath" and "spirit" are the same, but the Greek words used to describe Jesus' "breathing" on the disciples to bequeath them the Spirit are different. The word used for "breathed" (*enephúsēsen*) lies beneath our English word "infuse." This seems to be not so much a variant tradition of Pentecost as a preparatory event leading to the fuller experience with the Spirit, which would come only after Christ's ascension – when there was no longer any apparent physical means of relating. The infusion of the Spirit that began with a gentle breath would then break forth "like the rush of a violent wind" (Acts 2:2).

troubled hearts needed most: "Peace to you," he said. His followers needed peace: they must have thought they were seeing a ghost. As the angels who predicted Jesus' birth had offered comforting words to Mary and Joseph (Matt. 1:20, Luke 1:30), as angels at the tomb had told the women to fear not (Matt. 28:5, 10; Luke 1:13, 30; 2:10), so Jesus counseled peace.

Some version of "fear not" or "do not be afraid" may be the most common command in the Bible. In the KJV, where it is most common, the phrase "fear not" appears 63 times, while "do not fear" occurs 13 times.

Knowing that the disciples would be confused and questioning, Jesus voluntarily showed them the marks in his hands and feet (v. 20). It was important for them to understand that, despite the apparent differences in Jesus' appearance (after his *dis*appearance!), he was not just some spectral visitor, but the same person they had loved and followed along the dusty roads of Galilee. Still, something was also remarkably different. Jesus was helping his disciples to trust his spiritual presence by showing them a physical connection.

The faith of the early church is clearly reflected in the way this story was remembered and related, for the author immediately has Jesus turn to the church's mission, and to the empowering spirit. As John tells it, Jesus said "As the father has sent me, so send I you" (v. 21). Other early traditions preserved Christ's commission in different ways, but with the same intent (cp. Matt. 28:19-20, Acts 1:8). As Christ was related to the Father, so Christians were related to Christ. As Christ had come into the world to accomplish his unique mission, so his followers were to venture forth in pursuit of their own calling to spread the

good news of the kingdom of God. The death and resurrection of Jesus had opened wide the kingdom's doors: to his followers lay the task of leading others to find the way.

According to John, the Holy Spirit came and rested upon Jesus at the beginning of his ministry (1:32-33), and Jesus had promised to bless his followers with the Spirit (14:15-31). Now, Jesus "breathed on them" and said, "Receive the Holy Spirit" (v. 22). [**A spiritual infusion**]

The Spirit's presence and leadership would be necessary for the church to carry out its role of mediating both forgiveness and judgment to the world (v. 23, cp. Matt. 16:19, 18:18). The idea that Christians have the authority to forgive – or to withhold forgiveness – is a bit frightening. Yet, Christ clearly empowered the church to practice grace in a hard and demanding world. The same command in Matthew is followed by a rather extensive discourse on the supremacy of forgiveness over judgment (Matt. 18:21-35).

## Doubting Thomas
### (vv. 24-25)

The text says nothing about how Jesus departed from the bewildered disciples on that first Easter evening: readers often assume that he vanished as suddenly as he had appeared (cp. Luke 24:31). In any case, v. 24 moves us to a time when Jesus has left the scene and Thomas enters.

A study of Thomas' intriguing character must begin with his name. "Thomas" was not a proper name, but a Hebrew or Aramaic nickname, meaning "the twin." "Didymus" is simply a Greek version of the same name. Scholars have scratched their collective heads in wondering who Thomas' twin was, but without result.

Thomas was a devoted and occasionally outspoken disciple. When Mary and Martha sent word to Jesus that Lazarus was sick, the religious authorities were already seeking to do him harm (John 10:31). It would be dangerous for Jesus and his followers to leave the relative safety of their trans-Jordanian camp and travel to Lazarus' home in Bethany, only two miles from Jerusalem. But, when Jesus insisted on going, Thomas declared his willingness to join him, even if it meant death (John 11:6).

Thomas' desire to remain close to Jesus is also reflected in John 14. During the Passover meal, Jesus spoke of his coming death in terms of going to the Father's house to prepare a place for his followers, adding "you know the way

> **No maps:** When Jesus responded to Thomas' request for directions in John 14:5, he did not respond as Thomas might have liked. He did not give him a road map, GPS coordinates, or a AAA Triptik with the best route highlighted in yellow. Instead, he said "I am the way, and the truth, and the life. No one comes to the Father except through me. If you know me, you will know my Father also. From now on you do know him and have seen him" (vv. 6-7).
>
> The only thing Jesus told Thomas he could *know* was Jesus himself. If Thomas trusted in what he knew about Jesus, he would also know what he needed to know about the Father, and the way to the Father's house. The same remains true for us.

where I am going" (vv. 1-4). All 12 disciples must have been confused, but it was Thomas who spoke up: "Lord, we do not know where you are going; how can we know the way?" (v. 5). Jesus responded with the familiar but enigmatic "I am the Way, and the Truth, and the Life. No one comes to the Father except through me" (v. 6). **[No maps]**

Perhaps these vignettes are intended to suggest the depth of Thomas' grief when Jesus was indeed taken away from him. When he returned to join the others after Jesus' appearance, the news seemed too good to be true. Surely Thomas *wanted* to believe that Jesus had risen from the dead, but his grief was too deep for facile acceptance of someone else's word. The others claimed to have seen the Lord, including wounded hands and side. Thomas refused to believe Jesus was truly risen until he could see and touch Jesus' scars for himself.

It could be helpful to try putting ourselves in Thomas' sandals. What would it have taken to convince *us* that Jesus had truly risen from the dead?

### Believing Thomas
#### (vv. 26-31)

A week later, according to John, Jesus again appeared among his disciples without bothering to open the door that they kept firmly closed. This time Thomas was present, and Jesus sought to open the door of faith that had remained closed in Thomas' heart. We can only begin to imagine the quiver in Thomas' stomach when Jesus called his name and challenged him to touch his hands and side (vv. 26-27). When he had done so, Thomas said the only thing he could say: "My Lord, and my God!"

Thomas acknowledged that Jesus was not only alive, but also divine, and worthy of worship.

Thomas' presence in scripture is of immense value to the church, for we can identify with his struggling honesty as he sought to believe something far too good to be true. Most thoughtful Christians have periods of doubt as they travel life's journey. Sometimes, like Thomas, our questions are raised by things that seem "too good to be true." Is there really a loving God behind this great universe, and if so, does he really care about individuals like me?

On the one hand, isn't it just too incredible to think that the eternal God would choose to enter the world in human form and experience death in our behalf? On the other hand, if the gospel message were not too good to be true, it would hardly be good enough to save us. As Jesus challenged Thomas, so he challenges us to believe, even though we have not seen (John 20:29).

John concludes ch. 20 by moving beyond doubting Thomas to confront doubting readers. Jesus did and said much that was not recorded, John wrote, but the things in his gospel were written "so that you may come to believe that Jesus is the Messiah, the Son of God, and that through believing you may have life in his name" (v. 31).

Doubt comes easy to us. We may doubt God's presence when something happens that seems too bad for a real God to allow. But, if we did not question our faith in the face of tragedy, we wouldn't be thinking at all.

When we doubt God's presence because innocent people suffer, we would do well to remember the truly innocent one who endured the cross for our sakes. By the power and presence of Christ, we may also learn to accept tragedy, to absorb it, and to overcome it with grace. When we are tempted to cry that life is not fair, we can remember that the great Lord of the universe has nail prints in his hands and a wound in his side that goes all the way to the heart.

Doubt is a natural part of life, and it is the growing edge of faith. An unquestioned faith is an untested faith, and much less likely to hold up in times of trial. The strongest Christians are those who have worked through their doubts to the point of experiencing Christ's benison: "Blessed are those who do not see, and yet believe."

## The Hardest Question
### How can *we* believe?

The wonderful thing about this story is that Jesus met Thomas right where he was, amid his doubts and questions. He allowed Thomas to experience the touch of his hand and his side, and Thomas responded with faith. That's a great story. We all wish we could have been there. We wish we also had a chance to meet Jesus face-to-face and put our fingers in his hands and our fists in his side, but we can't.

Jesus knew it would hardly be practical for him to keep showing up in physical form to prove himself again and again. A day was coming when he would depart the earth and stay departed. Those who believed would have to learn to believe despite their doubts and questions. They would have to learn to live with mystery and ambiguity.

That's really at the heart of authentic faith. If we *know* everything, there's no need for faith. If we have all the answers, there's no need for trust. If we have the blueprints for heaven in hand, as some folks think they have, there's no need for hope. But Jesus does not call us to certainty as much as he calls us to *faith*, and genuine faith can only grow from the soil of uncertainty.

Frederick Buechner's memorable comment is both trenchant and appropriate: "Doubts are the ants in the pants of faith: they keep it awake and moving" (*Wishful Thinking* [Harper & Row, 1973], 20).

When I was ordained to the ministry in January 1973, I had just turned 21 years old, and I knew everything. I could tell you what heaven would look like and why the streets of gold were described as being like glass. I could tell you precisely how the atonement worked, and I could assure you that God had your life planned out in every detail ase a book just waiting to be read.

I knew all these things because I was a naïve young literalist, full of myself and full of ideals and full of something pungent that you often find in barnyards. My biggest problem was that I didn't know it yet. As I grew older, I began to suspect that life and faith and the Bible were not as simple and straightforward as I had thought them to be. For a while I stubbornly held on to the idea that I could know all the answers. The older I grew, though, the more of those answers I had to give up. I had to learn to say, "I don't know."

Old habits die hard. Even later, while working on a Ph.D. at Duke University, I once turned in an assignment to Father Roland Murphy, a Carmelite priest and gifted Old Testament scholar. The assignment was to interpret a text from Ecclesiastes and use it as the basis for a sermon. I argued that Qoheleth, the author of Ecclesiastes, was miserable because he hoped for something beyond this life, but could not know it. In contrast, I wrote, because of the New Testament witness we can *know* there is a life beyond, we can *know* how to get there, we can *know* our eternity is sure.

In every sentence, Father Murphy took a red pen and marked through the word "know," and replaced it with "believe." He forced me to confront my own arrogance, and that experience became a pivotal step in my faith development. In our human hubris, we would like to think we can know it all, but when it comes to something as important and ultimate as our faith and our eternal future, those are things that are beyond human knowing.

Like Thomas, we can't *know* everything we want to know. What we can *know* is Jesus. We can't *see* Jesus, nor can we *touch* him, as Thomas did. Even so, through the personal experience of prayer and trust, we can enter a relationship with Jesus. It is not a knowing that we can prove to anyone else, because it is not an empirical thing but an experiential one.

Out of our faith and trust in Christ, we come to hope in other things, and even to believe, but we are deluding ourselves if we think we can have certain knowledge of the spiritual world. Our soul understands that. That is why we get such a lift out of sunsets and rainbows and waterfalls. That is why it charges our spiritual batteries to stand in close communion with our family of faith and sing praises to God, who does not speak to us in the rational categories of the scientist, but in the language of experience and imagination.

All of us have dragons of doubt and uncertainty within us. It is useless for us to deny that they are there. It is helpful for us to realize that they are not the enemy, but rather a part of us.

There was a time when I said "I *know*." Then there was a time when I was comfortable saying "I *believe*." The older I grow, the more likely I am to say "I *hope*." Hope requires less knowing and more faith. Faith is "hope with feet on it." Faith is hope to the point of committing our lives to Christ, doubts and all.

# *Third Sunday of Easter*

## First Reading
## Acts 2:14a, 36-41

# Cut to the Heart

*Peter said to them, "Repent, and be baptized every one of you in the name of Jesus Christ*
*so that your sins may be forgiven; and you will receive the gift of the Holy Spirit." (Acts 2:38)*

What does it take to for you to be so convicted that you feel "cut to the heart"? Today's text speaks to an occasion when thousands of people had that experience. What caused it? Could it happen again?

The lectionary devotes three weeks to readings from post-Pentecost events in Acts 2. The first focused on Peter's sermon to those gathered in astonishment to see what was going as the newly Spirit-anointed disciples emerged and began to proclaim the gospel in a surprising manner of speaking (a study of this is found in this resource under the Second Sunday of Easter).

Peter, speaking mainly to Jews in the crowd, presented the gospel as a fulfillment of prophecies from Joel and the Psalms. Taking David as the author of several psalms, he argued that David had foreseen not only the coming of the Messiah, but he had also predicted the resurrection.

### A charge and a question
### (vv. 36-37)

Peter concluded his sermon – or came to a pause – with a stirring challenge to Jews who were present: "Therefore let the entire house of Israel know with certainty that God has made him both Lord and Messiah, this Jesus whom you crucified" (v. 36). Koine Greek didn't use much punctuation, but we can guess that an exclamation point would have been justified.

As noted in our study for the previous week, Peter charged the Jews with killing Jesus by means of the Romans, while at the same time portraying the act as part of God's plan. As also noted, we must be careful not to let this lead us into anti-Semitic attitudes, as if modern Jews are somehow responsible for the actions of a few very frightened religious leaders two millennia ago.

We remember that Peter was speaking as one Jew to another. He addressed them as "Fellow Israelites" (v. 29). He knew that he himself had denied Jesus three times. There was plenty guilt to go around – but there was forgiveness also.

Despite Peter's loose exegetical approach to prophecy, his message was sufficiently compelling to bring conviction. "They were cut to the heart," John says, and asked, "Brothers, what should we do?" (v. 37).

The expression "cut to the heart" or "pierced to the heart" was an obvious idiom referring to severe emotional distress: we could say they were stunned, dumbfounded, thunderstruck. The Greek reflects this in the address of their question, which is obscured in most translations. They didn't just say "What should we do, brothers?" The word for "brothers" (*'adelphoi*) is preceded by a word meaning "men" (*'andres*). It's as if they were testing

---

**It matters:** Sometimes we hear things and just absorb them as information, while passing over or ignoring things that do not interest us. Think of it as the difference between hearing that there has been an automobile accident on a highway nearby, and hearing that one of the cars was driven by someone you love. Suddenly, *it matters*. Peter's arguments convinced his audience that he wasn't just speaking to be heard: his message really mattered.

whether their relationship as fellow Jews still held: "What should we do, men … brothers?"

Peter's audience had come to understand that his defense was more than an explanation of why so many followers of Jesus were on the street testifying in languages they didn't know the day before. What Peter was saying mattered. **[It matters]**

The people in the crowd realized that what Peter was saying about Jesus' death and resurrection as the fulfillment of their longstanding Hebrew hopes called for a personal response. Peter's concluding challenge sounded like an accusation, but they heard it as an invitation to learn more and to take action, so they not only asked, but also asked with urgency: "What should we do?"

### An act and a promise
### (v. 38)

So, Peter told them: "Repent and be baptized, every one of you, in the name of Jesus Christ for the forgiveness of your sins. And you will receive the gift of the Holy Spirit. The promise is for you and your children and for all who are far off – for all whom the Lord our God will call."

Repent: That's where it begins, with repentance, with recognizing that we've been going in the wrong direction, and we need to change course. To repent is not to say "I'm sorry." Repenting is not apologizing. To repent is to turn around. To repent is to leave the old way of life behind and begin anew. Repenting may involve words, but it is mainly about action.

"Repent and be baptized," Peter said. To be baptized was to make a public declaration of one's faith and one's intentions. To be baptized was to mark the end of one path and the beginning of another.

We don't know by what method Peter and the others performed baptisms, but the practice of immersion offers the clearest symbol of what baptism signifies. As Paul later explained it, we go into the water and bury the old self, then rise from the water as a new person committed to a new life (Rom. 6:3-14).

Most of the crowd probably knew about John the baptizer. Some may have heard him preach and knew about his call for people to repent and be baptized. They may even have heard him declare that, while he baptized with water, another was coming who would baptize with the Holy Spirit (Mark 1:8, Matt. 3:11, Luke 3:16).

Now the crowd heard Peter declare "Repent and be baptized, every one of you, in the name of Jesus Christ for the forgiveness of your sins. And you will receive the gift of the Holy Spirit."

Forgiveness we understand: Peter promised that those who repented and were baptized would have their sins forgiven, but what did he mean by the words "and you will receive the gift of the Holy Spirit"? Was he suggesting that they would also speak in tongues, as they had witnessed among those who emerged from the upper room early that morning (vv. 5-13)? Was he promising that they would receive the "gifts of the Spirit" that Paul later talked about (1 Cor. 12:4-12, 27-31)? Or was it a more generic promise that the Spirit of Christ would be the effective agent in cleansing them of sin?

Some of us may also wonder if Peter was pointing to a needed progression of repentance leading to baptism, followed by the Spirit. But when Peter later preached to a group of Gentiles in Caesarea, they received the Spirit *before* they were baptized (Acts 10:44-48).

We needn't worry too much about such things: Peter was not laying out a precise doctrinal course of action, but relaying the good news that forgiveness, salvation, and the Spirit were available to all who repented and sought baptism as a mark of their faith.

### A sizeable response
### (vv. 39-41)

Some commentators have interpreted this statement from Peter as an endorsement of infant baptism: "For the promise is for you, for your children, and for all who are far away, everyone whom the Lord our God calls to him" (v. 39).

The early reformers, despite their break with the Catholic Church, retained the practice of infant baptism, in part due to this verse, since Peter said "the promise is for you and for your children." Again, we must note that Peter was not teaching doctrine, but preaching good news. The point of this verse is that the gospel was not just for the Jews who heard Peter that day, but also for their descendants, *and* for all who were far away. While this may include a reference to Gentiles, Peter probably had

**The diaspora:** Long before the first century, Jewish people had become scattered across the known world. When the Assyrians conquered the northern kingdom of Israel in 722 BCE, they forced leading or influential residents to leave and settled them in other Assyrian-controlled territories.

When Judah fell to the Babylonians in 587 BCE, much of the population was deported to Babylon while others escaped to Egypt. Many Jews remained in Babylon long after Cyrus opened the door for them to return to Judah. They continued to move and scatter as the Persian empire grew. These factors, along with natural migrations and opportunities for trade or other business led to a diaspora (literally, scattering of seed) across the known world.

Earlier in the story, Luke noted that people who had come to Jerusalem for the Jewish festival included "Parthians, Medes, Elamites, and residents of Mesopotamia, Judea and Cappadocia, Pontus and Asia, Phrygia and Pamphylia, Egypt and the parts of Libya belonging to Cyrene, and visitors from Rome, both Jews and proselytes, Cretans and Arabs" (vv. 9-11).

in mind the Jewish diaspora: by the first century, Jewish people were scattered across the known world. [**The diaspora**]

Peter would later come to the certain conviction that the gospel was for Gentiles when he visited Cornelius in Caesarea and declared what he had learned: "I truly understand that God shows no partiality, but in very nation anyone who fears him and does what is right is acceptable to him" (Acts 10:34-35).

We shouldn't write off the possibility that Peter (or at least Luke, who wrote the story), was including Gentiles in the promised opportunity to repent, be baptized, and receive the Holy Spirit. The promise, he said, was available to "everyone whom the Lord our God calls to him." That sounds like a promise that extends to all.

Again, we must be careful not to read too much doctrine into Peter's statement. Those who hold a firm doctrine of predestination and believe that only the "elect" can be saved have used this verse to argue that God calls certain people but not others. That does not appear to be Peter's intent. He himself still had much to learn, but he had caught the vision that the good news was for everyone.

Peter had not only gained this new understanding, but he had also become passionate about it. This was not the end of his sermon or of his appeal, for he apparently went on for some time: "And he testified with many other arguments and exhorted them, saying, 'Save yourselves from this corrupt generation'" (v. 40). [**Auto-save**]

The verb for "testified" suggests a solemn witness before God. The verb for "exhorted" (*parakaleō*) literally means "call to one's side," and could be used in the sense of comforting, but here it has the sense of urging, admonishing, or pleading. It's in the imperfect tense, indicating a continual act.

The "corrupt generation" Peter warned against was not limited to the Jewish establishment that had opposed Jesus, but to all who refused to hear and respond to the gospel.

Peter's message was ultimately effective, according to Luke. He reported that about 3,000 people "welcomed his message" and were baptized, a huge spurt of growth for the nascent movement of Jesus followers who would become the church. Many of those who believed would have been from the diaspora, and they could have returned home to spread the gospel or start new fellowships in their own lands. That was good news indeed.

**Auto-save:** The conclusion of Peter's sermon contains both promise and challenge. The promise is for all, but the response is made by individuals, and our decisions have consequences.

Back in the early days of computing, when Microsoft's first version of "Windows" had just come out, I once spent several hours working on an article for publication, only to be greeted by the sudden appearance of a message box that read: "General Protection Fault. You should save your work to another location before exiting, or you will lose it."

The problem was, the computer had already crashed and would not let me save the work. The only thing that would respond was the "Power Off" button, so all my work evaporated into the electronic ether. That inspired me, of course, to find an "Auto Save" function, which I set for five minutes, figuring that I'd never lose more than a paragraph or so.

Wouldn't it be nice if people came with an "Auto Save" button – if we could click on an icon and guarantee that our friends, and family, and neighbors would be saved from their sin to faith in Christ? But it doesn't work that way. There is a place for us, like Peter, to get involved, to inform, even to plead.

### The Hardest Question
### Where do we distinguish
### between individuals and community?

Peter's sermon offers a promise of forgiveness to all who respond through repentance and baptism, assuring them that they will receive the Holy Spirit.

We must be careful not to parse things too closely, but giving attention to the verb tense and number in v. 38 may offer some insight. Peter's command to repent is an aorist imperative, second person plural verb, indicating something that everyone needed to do at a point in time. It was a mass call to repentance.

The verb for "be baptized" is also aorist, indicating something done at a particular moment, but it is second person singular, reinforced by "each of you," indicating that the challenge was for everyone, but each person must decide individually whether to respond and be baptized.

The verb used in "you will receive the Holy Spirit" reverts to a plural form, but it's also a future middle indicative, suggesting that the receiving of the Spirit would be an ongoing matter, not just a one-time thing – and that it would be more of a community experience than an individual one. The Spirit would be present in the community of which individual believers were a part.

A clearer understanding of this could have saved Paul much heartache among the Corinthians who competed over which individuals had more of the Spirit as exhibited in spiritual gifts. It might also offer insight to contemporary Christians who have been told they must pray to receive a "second baptism" with the Holy Spirit, as if the Spirit's presence is an entirely individual matter. When the Spirit had first come upon the believers the day of Pentecost (v. 4), they were gathered in community.

# Third Sunday of Easter

## Second Reading
## Psalm 116*

# Paying Vows

*What shall I return to the LORD for all his bounty to me? I will lift up the cup of salvation and call on the name of the LORD. (Ps. 116:12-13)*

Have you ever been at death's door, or felt as if you were? Sickness is always a problem, but consider the difference between being ill in the modern world and the ancient world. Today an attack of appendicitis or gallstones, along with many other internal diseases, can be diagnosed, treated, and cured with little drama. Broken bones can be repaired, and worn-out joints can be replaced. Infections can sometimes be challenging due to the rise of drug-resistant bacteria, but they are usually curable. With the development of monoclonal antibodies, even many cancers and other diseases are responding to treatment.

Imagine living in a world where cleanliness was a constant challenge and antibiotics were unknown. A broken leg could lead to a permanent deformity, and a nasty cut could lead to a serious infection. Issues relating to internal organs were basically untreatable. Abdominal puncture wounds suffered in combat would likely lead to a lingering and painful demise. A serious case of the flu or of pneumonia could become life-threatening – or at least leave people thinking they were at death's door.

The book of Psalms contains many prayers of people who believed they were in danger of dying, whether from illness or from enemy action. Without quality medical care, an appeal to God might be someone's only hope.

### Testimony and trial
### (vv. 1-4)

The lectionary's psalm reading for the previous week, Psalm 16, was the testimony of someone who had escaped a narrow scrape with death. Now, 100 psalms later, we find another hymn that celebrates survival after someone prayed for deliverance in the face of mortal danger.

Psalm 116 has no superscription, nothing to indicate even an ancient belief about who wrote it, or what specific illness or issue threatened the writer's life. This can be a good thing: the lack of specifics allows later readers to apply the psalm's lessons to their own situations.

The psalmist writes from a post-crisis standpoint: he or she had faced a perceived life-threatening situation, probably an illness of some sort, and had cried out to God for help, promising to offer public praise and a thank-offering if he survived. With health restored, the exuberant psalmist now acts to fulfill the vow.

The psalm begins with a declaration of love: "I love the LORD, because he has heard my voice and my supplications" (v. 1). Yahweh had proven true to the psalmist's belief that faithful obedience would lead to blessing, according to the covenant made between God and Israel at Sinai, introduced in Exod. 19:6. The book of Deuteronomy expanded on the covenant theme, promising a host of blessings to the Israelites if they remained faithful, and threatening concomitant troubles if they did not (see Deuteronomy 28, for example). Stories found in the books of Joshua through 2 Kings illustrate practical ways in which both individuals and the nation found prosperity or peril in keeping with their faithfulness or rebelliousness toward God.

---

*A slightly different text, Ps. 116:1-2, 12-19 is read on Proper 29 in Year B. This study will include the entire psalm.*

Israel's part of the covenant was summarized in Deut. 6:4-5, famously called the "Shema" because the first word is *sh'ma*, an imperative verb meaning "hear" or "listen." The first requirement was that people of the covenant should love God. "Hear, O Israel: The LORD is our God, the LORD alone. You shall love the LORD your God with all your heart, and with all your soul, and with all your might."

In context, the call to love was primarily a command to be loyal. The people were challenged to love God with all of their being, period. As with humans, however, love and loyalty grow best in the context of a mutual and reciprocal relationship. Partners in a marriage grow in love as they do things for each other. God, having created and redeemed us, is worthy of our love from the beginning. Still, as we actively engage in relationship with God, as we experience God's love and blessings, our love for God and commitment to God grows more intense.

The psalmist believed that God heard and responded to his prayers ("he inclined his ear to me," v. 2a), leading him to trust that God would always be faithful: "therefore I will call on him as long as I live" (v. 2b).

In v. 3 we find a figurative description of the psalmist's former plight in three parallel statements: "The snares of death encompassed me; the pangs of Sheol laid hold on me; I suffered distress and anguish."

From the depths of that wretched state, the author looked heavenward: "Then I called on the name of the LORD: 'O LORD, I pray, save my life!'" (v. 4). The Hebrew construction of the prayer is more forceful: "*Please*, LORD, save my life!" The word translated "life" is *nefesh*, a word sometimes translated as "soul," though it basically describes the essence of oneself, what makes a person alive. [**Save my life**]

### Deliverance and praise
### (vv. 5-11)

Having told the story in short, the psalmist now embarks on an exultant celebration of God's goodness. He first recalls God's gracious and merciful nature (v. 5), then declares "The LORD protects the simple; when I was brought low, he saved me" (v. 6).

The word translated as "simple" does not mean "simple-minded," but was a term common to the wisdom literature that described someone who was immature or

---

**Save my life:** The Hebrews believed that God was the author of life, and therefore able to save life. Having the breath of God was symbolic of life. The creation story of Genesis 2 says that after God formed man from the dust of the ground, God "breathed into his nostrils the breath of life; and the man became a living being" (Gen. 2:7).

In the familiar story of the "dry bones," God instructed the prophet Ezekiel to prophesy to a valley filled with disarticulated skeletons, whereupon the bones rattled and came together and then were covered with flesh, so that they appeared as people, but not alive. God then told the prophet to call to the four winds to bring breath to corpses, and "I prophesied as he commanded me, and the breath came into them, and they lived, and stood on their feet, a vast multitude" (Ezek. 37:10).

Christians celebrate a similar belief when we sing the old hymn by Edward Hatch and Robert Jackson, "Breathe on Me, Breath of God." The fourth verse affirms a belief that God can grant, not just physical, but eternal life:

> Breathe on me, Breath of God,
> So shall I never die,
> But live with thee the perfect life
> Of thine eternity.

---

naïve, still learning to distinguish between wisdom and folly. Though he may have been lacking in maturity, God had saved him, bringing relief to the stressful anxiety that had plagued him (v. 7).

With v. 8 the psalmist again returns to the theme of deliverance from death and misery, so that he can "walk before the LORD in the land of the living" (v. 9). Interpreting vv. 9-10 seems to require the assumption that other people had downplayed God's role in saving the psalmist, or had scoffed at the notion of facing affliction with faith. That might explain the psalmist's insistence that "I kept my faith, even when I said, 'I am greatly afflicted'; I said in my consternation, 'Everyone is a liar.'"

While humans offered no comfort, and may even have added to his distress, the psalmist found both health and rest in God.

### Promises and fulfillment
### (vv. 12-19)

The content of vv. 12-19 tells us that the psalmist had done more than pray for deliverance: he or she had made a vow. While modern English uses the word "vow" in the sense of an unconditional promise, such as a wedding vow or monastic vow, the concept of vow-making for the Hebrews and their ancient neighbors was expressly conditional. Narrative vows consisted of two parts: a specific request from God, and a promise to give or do something for God if the request was fulfilled. The Old Testament's legal materials contain specific rules about vow-making (Numbers 6, 30), and the narratives include stories about people who made vows. **[Vows in the Old Testament]**

Vows can also be found in the psalms, though the form is not as obvious. In some cases, such as Psalm 116, we find references to vows that were made offstage. In others, the psalm includes the vow. In all cases, vows were considered serious business: once made, they must be paid, if their request had been granted.

Psalmists often made vows, sometimes including sacrifices, though they were more likely to promise that if God answered their prayer, they would offer public praise and testimony of God's goodness. The author of Psalm 116 appears to have promised a drink offering and a thanksgiving sacrifice in addition to public praise, all introduced by the question "What shall I return to the LORD for all his bounty to me?" (v. 12).

"I will lift up the cup of salvation and call on the name of the LORD" (v. 13) probably refers to the pouring out of wine as a drink offering to the accompaniment of praise to God. Such libations were commonly associated with thanksgiving sacrifices, as in Exod. 29:40-41; Lev. 23:18, 37; and Num. 28:7. Here, the thanksgiving sacrifice is mentioned in v. 17.

Verses 13b-14 and 17b-18 are identical: both the drink offering and the thanksgiving sacrifice take place in the context of calling on – that is, praising or glorifying – the name of Yahweh, and "in the presence of all his people." The closing verse clarifies the location: the vows are to be paid, not only in public, but in the courts of the temple in Jerusalem, the only place sacrifices could be acceptably made (v. 19).

With his life having been preserved, the psalmist declared that God cared about both life and death for those who are faithful (v. 15): "O LORD, I am your servant; I am your servant, the child of your serving girl" (v. 16). The expression "serving girl" translates a word used

---

**Vows in the Old Testament:** Vows to God were a serious matter: if one made a votive promise and the request was fulfilled, the petitioner was obligated to fulfill the vow. A desperate woman named Hannah vowed that if God would give her a son, she would give the child back to God (1 Sam. 1:11). When he was weaned, she did (1 Sam. 1:24-28).

A warrior named Jephthah, seeking to become Israel's leader, vowed that if God would grant him victory in war over the Ammonites, he would sacrifice whatever came out the door of his house upon his return. He probably hoped it would be a sheep or goat (animals were kept on the first floor of many homes), but it was his daughter, and he kept his vow (Judg. 11:30-40).

While making their way through the wilderness, the people of Israel vowed that if God would give them victory against the Canaanite king of Arad, they would destroy all the plunder as a way of giving it to God rather than keeping it for themselves, and they did (Num. 21:1-3).

Votive promises did not have to be so severe. Jacob vowed that if God would protect and provide for him, he would worship and pay tithes to Yahweh (Gen. 28:10-22). Absalom claimed to have vowed that if God would allow him to return to Jerusalem from his exile in Geshur, he would go to Hebron and worship (2 Sam. 15:1-8). Later, people often made vows that if God did something for them, they would live as Nazirites for a specified period (Numbers 6).

---

for female slaves who belonged to a master: her children would belong to the master, too. Such language is discomfiting in our current culture, but was a natural analogy for the psalmist, who lived in a society in which slavery was an accepted way of life. **[Faithful ones]**

Have you ever prayed to God when in trouble, promising some gift, service, or change in lifestyle if God would only provide healing or release from a sticky situation? If such a prayer met with a positive answer, did you keep your promises? "Testimony meetings" aren't as common as they used to be. Perhaps we should consider bringing them back, and offering a natural opportunity for us to offer public thanks and praise to God for the blessings we have received.

---

**Faithful ones:** The word for "faithful ones" in v. 15 is *hasidi* – the same word used to describe "Hasidic Jews," the Ultra-Orthodox who consider themselves most faithful to the rabbinic law.

## The Hardest Question
### Why did the psalmists vow praise more often than sacrifice?

As noted in today's study, psalmists who offered vows were more likely to promise public praise to God rather than specific deeds, gifts, or sacrifices. For example, in Ps. 22:21-22 (my translation) we read: "Save my life from the sword, My only one from the claws of the dog; Save me from the mouth of the lion, and from the horns of the wild ox, answer me! (Then) I will tell of your name to my brethren, in the midst of the assembly I will praise you."

Psalm 69:29-30 has a similar theme to that of Psalm 116: "But I am afflicted and in great pain, Let your salvation, O God, set me on high! (Then) I will praise the name of God with song, and I will magnify him with thanksgiving" (my translation).

Similar examples can be found in Pss. 61:7-8, 69:29-30, 109:29-30, and others. Sacrifices are sometimes still associated with the payment of vows, as in Psalms 66 and 116, but increasingly, the psalmists came to believe that God valued praise over sacrifice or other deeds. Why?

The answer may well lie in context. During the Exile, the Hebrews had no temple or ability to offer sacrifices, but they could still offer praise to God. The psalmists were convinced that public praise was pleasing to God. In a practical sense, if God did not deliver petitioners from life-threatening situations, they would not be alive and available to fulfill the promise, for "the dead do not praise Yahweh" (Ps. 115:17a). If human praise is truly valued, then it would be to God's advantage to save those stricken ones who promise to praise God if they live.

(For more, see my book, *Vows in the Hebrew Bible and the Ancient Near East* [Sheffield Academic Press, 1992], 150-161, or an earlier article, "Conditional Vows in the Psalms of Lament: A New Approach to an Old Problem," in *The Listening Heart: Essays in Psalms and Wisdom in Honor of Roland E. Murphy, O. Carm.*, ed. Ken Hoglund, et. al. [Sheffield, JSOT Press, 1987], 77-94.)

# Third Sunday of Easter

## Third Reading
## 1 Peter 1:13-23

# A New Birth

*You have been born anew, not of perishable but of imperishable seed,*
*through the living and enduring word of God. (1 Pet. 1:23)*

Have you ever messed something up and wished for a do-over? We can do that with an essay or a painting or even a casserole if we have adequate time and supplies. Relationships are another story: it's hard to start over and pretend past offenses haven't occurred.

In the most important arena, however, we do have a chance to begin anew. When our spiritual life has gone awry, Jesus offers the hope of salvation. What's more, the experience of living a redeemed life leads us to share and receive mutual love.

Do you like the thought of living with confidence, of loving and being loved? Then read on.

The lectionary text from the epistles for the third Sunday after Easter is 1 Pet. 1:17-22, which speaks of the redemption we have in Christ through the power of the resurrection. Those verses, however, are integrally related to a larger unit of the text, vv. 13-25. Since we are more concerned with understanding the scripture than with exact adherence to the lectionary, we will consider the larger text.

### Of hope and holiness
### (vv. 13-16)

The letter of 1 Peter begins with a prayer that praises God for the good news of salvation through Jesus Christ, and for the readers' acceptance of it (vv. 3-12). The writer was not satisfied to celebrate salvation as if that's all that matters, however. The prayer is a call to action for believers, a mandate for a new and different kind of life.

"Therefore," the author writes, "prepare your minds for action" (v. 13a). Right behavior begins with right thinking.

"Prepare your minds" translates the ancient idiom "gird up your loins," a reference to someone gathering up the skirt of his or her robe and tucking it into the belt in preparation for running or some other physical action.

Peter applies the idiom to mental rather than physical activity, adding a second modifier to suggest the need for a sober or disciplined mind.

To "gird up the loins of your mind" is to get mentally prepared for the challenge ahead. It means to tuck in the loose ends of things that would distract us and to focus on what is most important. Christians of every generation must wrestle with their faith, interpret the scriptures, and apply the gospel message to the culture in which they live.

With disciplined minds ready for action, believers learn to think for themselves. They don't blindly accept everything they hear or read, whether it comes from a televised prosperity preacher, a popular book, or their own pastor. They think it through and reach their own understanding of what it means to follow Jesus.

In doing so, believers recognize that their ultimate hope lies in Christ alone. "Set all your hope on the grace that Jesus Christ will bring you when he is revealed," Peter said (v. 13b). The word "hope" is used five times in 1 Peter, beginning in 1:3 — "he has given us a new birth into a living hope …." Believers are to "set all your hope on the grace that Jesus Christ will bring you when he is revealed" (1:13), so that their "faith and hope are set on God" (1:21). In ch. 3, the author speaks of "the holy women who hoped in God" (3:5) and "the hope that is in you" (3:15). **[Past or future?]**

**Past or future?** A closer look at the author's word choices near the end of v. 13 raises a question. The NRSV translates it as "set all your hope on the grace that Jesus Christ will bring you when he is revealed." The NET has "set your hope completely on the grace that will be brought to you when Jesus Christ is revealed." Most modern translations follow the same pattern.

The passive participle translated as "will bring you," "will be brought to you," or "to be given you" (NIV), however, is in the present, not in the future tense. In his life, work, death, and resurrection, Christ has already brought grace to the world. "When he is revealed" probably refers to Christ's future return, however, so translators tend to give the participle a future sense.

Richard Vinson comments: "Either orientation makes sense: Christ's appearance brought God's grace to the world and would serve as grounds for the readers' hope, while Christ's second coming will complete God's work of grace and may also be the resting place for their hope. If the author meant the second coming, then one can either fudge the translation of the participle (the NRSV translates it 'will bring' as if it were future), or infer that he was looking at the future with such confidence that the readers could count the delivery as already made" ("1 Peter," in *1 & 2 Peter, Jude*, Smyth & Helwys Bible Commentary [Smyth & Helwys, 2010], 66).

Christ-centered hope and disciplined thinking lead us to become more like Jesus and less like those who are shaped by selfish interests and cultural pressures (vv. 14-15). As we become more like Christ, we fulfill the covenant command that "You shall be holy, for I am holy" (v. 16, quoting from Lev. 19:2).

Peter's call for believers to consciously follow Christ rather than being conformed to the world calls to mind Paul's similar challenge in Rom. 12:1-2: "I appeal to you therefore, brothers and sisters, by the mercies of God, to present your bodies as a living sacrifice, holy and acceptable to God, which is your spiritual worship. Do not be conformed to this world, but be transformed by the renewing of your minds, so that you may discern what is the will of God—what is good and acceptable and perfect."

Can we honestly say that we are shaped more by Christ than by our culture? What is the evidence for either?

## Reverence and redemption
### (vv. 17-21)

Having called on believers to get their thinking right and their living straight, Peter moves to the subject of healthy associations: a right relationship with God (vv. 17-21) that relates to others in helpful and healthy ways (vv. 22-25).

Relating rightly to God begins with the understanding that God judges all people impartially "according to their deeds" – a statement that would leave all of us falling short, for none live without fault. But the judgment we all deserve – the fear of which should keep us living in humble reverence before God (v. 17) – is tempered and held in tension by the grace that God has offered through Christ.

The author speaks of this atoning grace through the metaphor of paying a ransom, one of several images used in scripture and developed by the church to try and explain the mystery of how Christ's earthly life, death, and resurrection reconciled us to God.

No attempt at explaining the atonement fully captures a truth that only God can truly comprehend. The metaphor of Christ's death serving as a ransom payment (v. 18) or sacrifice (v. 19) for our sins is an incomplete image, but a powerful one. It is a reminder that Christ died for us, and that in some way beyond our understanding, Christ's death and resurrection opened the door for us to be reconciled and brought into a positive relationship with the Lord of all.

Peter's purpose is not to elucidate the atonement, but to remind his readers that it is through Christ that we can come trustfully to God, "who raised him from the dead and gave him glory, so that your faith and hope are set on God" (v. 21).

## Love and loving
### (vv. 22-25)

The author of 1 Peter believed that loving God would naturally lead to loving others: "Now that you have purified yourselves by obeying the truth so that you have genuine mutual love, love one another deeply, from the heart" (v. 22).

God created us to live in community. From the creation stories of Genesis 1–2 to the Ten Commandments to the preaching of the prophets, the scriptures challenge

> **Strong love:** Peter's call for real and reciprocal love is emphatic. The Greek word behind "mutual love" is the root of our word "Philadelphia" – famously known as the "city of brotherly love." The modifier is *anupokriton*: "not hypocritical," thus, sincere or genuine.

God's people to love and care for others, especially widows, orphans, and strangers. Jesus reflected the same ethic of caring for all, even "the least of these."

Christ-followers, especially, are called to "have genuine mutual love," to "love one another deeply from the heart" (v. 22). **[Strong love]**

Love is to be not only reciprocal and real, but also fervent and heartfelt. "Love deeply" translates a verb that describes unconditional love with an adverb that means "earnestly," "eagerly," "intently," or "constantly."

Talking about love and demonstrating it are quite different things. A spiritual relationship grounded in God's love inspires a community characterized by love in action, something more than high ideals or empty talk. It is a love that walks.

If we are to get our thinking straight, get our living straight, and get our relationships straight, we need each other. We need mutual support and unconditional love. We need someone to care, even when we are not acting very lovable.

This is why we need the church as a family of faith to encourage us, to inspire us, to hold us accountable, to love us in good times and bad times. We all need others who believe in us and love us deeply, from the heart.

Such love should come naturally to those who truly "have been born anew" through their response to the gospel message, Peter suggests (v. 23).

The author's mention of "the living and enduring word of God" that brings us into relationship with God led him to a tangential quotation from Isa. 40:6-8. Humankind and human glory are no more permanent than grass or flowers that grow and then fade, but "the word of the Lord endures forever" (vv. 24-25a).

This verse is often taken out of context and used as a reference to the Bible or in defense of an interpretation of scripture that someone claims to be unchanging. The verse is not about the Bible, however, or even the Old Testament.

When used in scripture, "word of God" commonly refers to a special revelation from God, a clear word that comes through a prophetic oracle or other means.

Lest we misunderstand – as many have done – Peter explained his meaning in the conclusion of the verse, a part that is rarely quoted: "*That word* is the good news that was announced to you" (v. 25b). While Peter made it clear that his use of "God's word" was in reference to the good news about Jesus, we are reminded that the Fourth Gospel connects God's word with Jesus himself: "In the beginning was the Word, and the Word was with God, and the Word was God" (John 1:1).

"Good news" translates a form of the Greek word *euangelizō*, "to proclaim good news." It is the word from which we derive "evangelize." It refers to the gospel message of Jesus, the good news of salvation for those who put their faith and hope in God through Christ.

That good news – that word from God – endures forever.

The love of those who live in relationship with God should likewise be as sure as it is sincere, both ardent and lasting. It is this kind of life that both experiences and lives out what it means to participate in the kingdom of God.

From the perspective of the last verse in ch. 1, we should look back to the first, where Peter addressed his readers as "exiles of the dispersion." The terminology would suggest an audience of immigrant Jews living in the northern reaches of Asia Minor. Some, no doubt, would have been members of the churches addressed in this letter.

The author's use of the term "exiles" (vv. 1, 17) is not limited to Jews no longer living in Palestine, however. The churches would also have included Gentile believers, who may well have been in the majority. **[Exiles]**

The "exile" that Peter had in mind is a lifestyle so devoted to Christ that it puts believers at odds with the materialistic and pagan culture in which they live. As they love God and love each other with the kind of fervency that Peter described, they become, not "strangers in a strange land," but strangers in their own land, people who live apart from the norms of polytheistic worship and self-focused living.

**Exiles:** Whether prompted by forced exile under the Assyrians and Babylonians, famine, discrimination, or economic opportunity, Jewish emigrants had spread to every corner of the known world by the first century, a scattering commonly known as the "diaspora."

The language of exile should set all of us to thinking. Do we feel a bit like outsiders in the overtly materialistic and morally misguided society that surrounds us, or do we feel perfectly at home in our culture?

As far as Peter is concerned, feeling too comfortable could be to our peril.

## The Hardest Question
### How can we understand the Atonement?

Several theories for understanding the atonement have developed through the years, all of them based in one way or another on varying interpretations of scripture.

The "ransom theory," a view held by some early church fathers, holds that Christ offered himself as a ransom for human sin. The "Christus Victor" theory is a modified view of this theory, arguing that humankind was held hostage by a hostile power and that Christ died to win our freedom. Both views imply that the debt of our sin was paid to Satan, but Satan could not keep his prize, and Christ arose victorious, setting sinners free.

The "recapitulation theory," argued in the second century by Irenaus, sees Jesus as a new Adam, as one who undoes the damage and rights the wrongs caused by the first man.

The "satisfaction theory," developed by Anselm of Canterbury in the 11th century and reflecting medieval views of defending one's honor, holds that God's honor was so affronted by human sin that only the death of Christ could provide satisfaction to the besmirching of God's honor. In this view, God in Christ pays humanity's debt to God's self.

The "penal substitution theory" became popular among the reformers in the 16th century. They began with Anselm's view but argued that it wasn't God's honor that human sin offended, but the moral law centered in God's

justice and holiness. Humanity's sin had to be punished, according to this view, but the sin was so great that no human could pay the penalty for it, so Christ took our punishment upon himself, paying our debt to God.

The "moral influence" or "moral example" theory, attributed to Peter Abelard in the 12th century, sees no reason to insist that Christ had to die for God's sense of honor or justice to be appeased. Rather, this view holds that Christ's death was an open declaration of God's deep love for humankind, a sacrifice so amazing that people would be drawn to repent, follow Christ's example, and live for God. In this view, Christ's death doesn't pay a necessary debt to either Satan or to God, but displays sacrificial and exemplary love for the people of God's creation.

A "governmental theory" of the atonement was developed by Hugo Grotius in the 17th century. It argues that God is free to forgive whomever God wishes to forgive, and that no payment or penalty is required. Jesus' death, then, was to uphold divine standards and demonstrate how seriously humans had violated God's moral governance of the world, thus moving them to accept God's offer of forgiveness.

These are not the only theories of the atonement, but they are the most prominent. What should we conclude? Should we study each view far more deeply than this brief review, with an eye toward determining which one is correct, or should we acknowledge that the mystery of the atonement is much too complex and close to God for any human to fully understand?

The late Australian scholar Leon Morris saw profit in trying to learn something from each of the differing views, while leaving the full answer to God: "So we need all the vivid concepts: redemption, propitiation, justification, and all the rest. And we need all the theories. Each draws attention to an important aspect of our salvation and we dare not surrender any. But we are small-minded sinners and the atonement is great and vast. We should not expect that our theories will ever explain it fully. Even when we put them all together, we will no more than begin to comprehend a little of the vastness of God's saving deed" ("Theories of the Atonement," in the *Evangelical Dictionary of Theology*, 2nd ed., ed. Walter Elwell [Baker Books, 2001], 116-19).

## Fourth Reading
## Luke 24:13-35*

# The Road to Hope

*They said to each other, "Were not our hearts burning within us while he was talking to us on the road,*
*while he was opening the scriptures to us?" (Luke 24:32)*

Have you ever run into someone who seemed very familiar to you, but you just couldn't put a name to the face or a finger on the connection? Imagine how you would feel to discover that the person was Jesus! The text for today tells just such a story. The Emmaus encounter is unique to Luke, and it beautifully displays his literary ability.

### Two confused disciples
#### (vv. 13-16)

The account begins late in the afternoon of the first Easter day. Two disciples were walking away from Jerusalem and toward Emmaus, their apparent home. They had been present with the others when the women came to report that the tomb was empty and that angels had proclaimed Jesus alive. Peter and John had gone to confirm their story. They found the empty tomb, but not Jesus. Perhaps this was the last straw for these two disciples. With the loss of Jesus' body, their hopes were vanquished. They decided to go home.

One of the disciples was named Cleopas (v. 18). Some writers have suggested that Cleopas is a variant spelling of "Clopas," the husband of another Mary who stood with Jesus' mother at the foot of the cross (John 19:25). We can't be more specific about their identity, and it really doesn't matter if they were the two who walked the dusty road to Emmaus. [**Emmaus**]

Whatever their identity, the two disciples were engaged in a heavy conversation about the devastating

> **Emmaus:** "Emmaus" is the Greek spelling of the Hebrew word *hammat*, which means "hot springs." The exact location of Emmaus has been lost, though many candidates have been proposed. Luke says it was 60 stadia from Jerusalem. A Greek stadion was about 600 feet, so the distance would have been about seven miles. A few Greek manuscripts have either seven stadia or 160 stadia as the distance, but 60 is by far the best attested.

events of the previous week (v. 14). They had placed their hope in Jesus, and their hope had been crushed by his betrayal and crucifixion. The curious story of the empty tomb seemed to confuse them more than to encourage them. Luke portrays the two as being so engrossed in their conversation that they did not notice when Jesus began walking along with them (v. 15).

When they became aware of Jesus, they did not recognize him. This is in keeping with other post-resurrection appearances, in which Jesus remained incognito until he chose to reveal himself. Luke does not suggest that the travelers were not paying attention, but that "their eyes were kept from recognizing him" (v. 16). Perhaps Jesus wanted them to think through their theology without being distracted by the knowledge of his identity. Like Thomas, he wanted them to believe in his word, even when they couldn't see his face.

That aspect of the encounter calls to mind other texts suggesting that Christ is fully known to us only by revelation (Luke 10:22, Matt. 16:17, 1 Cor. 2:6-16). How can

---

*\*A longer version of this text, Luke 24:13-49, is read for the Third Sunday of Easter in Year B.*

we prepare our hearts and minds to receive what the Spirit of Christ might reveal to us? What obstacles might interfere with our being open to the message?

## Two surprised reactions
### (vv. 17-27)

Jesus' question "What are you discussing with each other?" means literally, "What are you throwing back and forth to each other?" (v. 17), an expression that could imply a heated discussion, even an argument. They stopped, Luke says, "looking sad." The drama – and trauma – of the past week had taken its toll on them.

The two disciples expressed surprise that their unknown companion seemed unfamiliar with the subject of their discussion, for he had also come from Jerusalem. Incredulously, Cleopas replied: "Are you the only stranger in Jerusalem who does not know the things that have taken place there in these days?" (v. 18). Jesus first asked the disciples to express their understanding of what had happened. Only then could he help them to grow in their discernment of his purpose.

The travelers responded with a quick review. The events concerned Jesus of Nazareth: since "Jesus" was a common name, "of Nazareth" helped to identify him. They had understood Jesus to be a prophet who had demonstrated himself to be powerful in word and deed before God and all the people (v. 19). Only with God's approval, they reasoned, could Jesus have done the mighty works that characterized his life and made such an impression on the people.

Others had not been so pleased with Jesus. The chief priests and rulers had perceived him as a threat, and had instigated his death by Roman hands (v. 20). The following contrast is emphatic: "But *we had hoped* that he was the one to redeem Israel" (v. 21a). Faithful Jews expected a messiah, but they commonly expected him to be a military messiah, one who would deliver Israel from the power of Rome. The death of Jesus had put an end to their hope that he was the promised one.

Even the evidence of the empty tomb had done little to encourage them. The travelers knew of the women's report, but they spoke with amazement rather than conviction (vv. 22-24). They were not yet convinced that

> **Scriptures:** The Hebrew Scriptures are divided into three parts: the *Torah* or Law (often known to Protestants as the Pentateuch); the *Nevi'im*, or Prophets, including both the narratives of Joshua–2 Kings and the more classical prophetic books; and the *Kethuvim*, or Writings, which include the Psalms, Wisdom literature, 1 Chronicles–Nehemiah, and the "Five Scrolls" (Ruth, Esther, Song of Songs, Lamentations, and Ecclesiastes).

Jesus had been raised from the dead, or that he could be the Messiah.

Jesus responded with amazement, as Luke describes it, astonished that they had misunderstood both the scriptures and his own teaching. His response may have seemed shockingly bold for one who appeared to be a new acquaintance: "Oh, how foolish you are, and how slow of heart to believe all that the prophets have declared! Was it not necessary that the Messiah should suffer these things and then enter into his glory?" (vv. 25-26).

Like many contemporaries, the two disciples would have been selective in their study of the Hebrew scriptures, preferring to ignore texts that suggested the Messiah would suffer. Shifting into a "rabbi mode," Jesus offered his own interpretation of the scriptures that spoke of a suffering Messiah. **[Scriptures]**

Jesus began with the Law, Luke says, and moved through "all the prophets," interpreting ways in which the scriptures could be seen to predict his life and work. And, in a later conversation, he mentioned "the Psalms" (v. 44).

The gospel record does not name the passages Jesus used, though we can imagine some that would be appropriate. From the law, he might have used the *protoevangelicum* of Gen. 3:15, or the scapegoat ceremony of Lev. 16:1-34. In Deut. 18:15, Moses (who suffered greatly) predicted the coming of another prophet like himself, which Acts 3:22-23 and 7:37 identify as Christ.

Several texts from the prophets could have been appropriate. Jesus may have quoted from the last two "Servant Songs" of Isaiah, for these predicted a coming servant of God who would suffer willingly, and vicariously, for his people. Though cut off from the land of the living, he would rise to see life again (Isa. 50:4-9, 52:13–53:12). Those texts, more than any other, were quoted elsewhere in the New Testament to show why it was necessary for

Christ to suffer. Jesus may also have referred to Zechariah, who spoke of a king who rides a donkey (9:9), a pierced victim (12:10), a wounded friend (13:6), and a smitten shepherd (13:7).

The book of Psalms belongs to the writings. Jesus may have referred to Ps. 69:21 ("for my thirst they gave me vinegar to drink"), or Psalm 22, which speaks of one forsaken by God (v. 1), who is mocked by the crowd and taunted to pray for deliverance (vv. 7-8) as others cast lots for his clothing (v. 18). Jesus' own cry of dereliction from the cross recalled Ps. 22:1. "My God, my God, why have you forsaken me?"

Perhaps he would have mentioned Psalms 16 and 110, which Peter cited as prophecies of Christ's resurrection in his Pentecost sermon (Acts 2:25-36).

### Two amazing events
### (vv. 28-35)

As the travelers drew near to Emmaus, the author suggests, Jesus continued walking as if he planned to go on, but his companions insisted that he stop for the night and lodge with them (vv. 28-29). Jesus agreed, and they were soon reclining around the dinner table. At the table, the guest became the host. In traditional Jewish fashion, Jesus took a small loaf of bread, broke it, and passed it to the others while reciting a blessing. An ancient blessing still used today goes like this: "Blessed art thou, O Lord our God, King of the Universe, who bringeth forth bread from the earth."

In that moment, Luke says, "their eyes were opened, and they recognized him" (v. 31a). Was it the sound of those familiar words, or did they see nail prints in his hands when he passed the bread? It matters not. Their eyes had been veiled, but now were uncovered. No doubt, it was significant for Luke and the early church that Jesus became known through word and what came to be thought of as sacrament, as Jesus expounded the scriptures and broke the bread.

Luke's story takes on a sudden and unexpected twist. In the very moment that the amazed disciples recognized Jesus, he disappeared: literally, "he became unseen" (v. 31b). In retrospect, the two were amazed that they did not recognize him earlier. "Were not our hearts burning within us while he was talking to us on the road, while he was opening the scriptures to us?" (v. 32). Memory plays

> **Seeing Jesus:** If we want to see and understand more about Jesus, how can we go about it? Cleopas and his companion came to see Jesus through a process that involved listening to Jesus on the road, inviting him into their home, and sharing a meal. Though they didn't understand what they were doing at the time, can we learn from their actions? What are ways in which we can listen to Jesus, invite him into our homes, and even share a meal?

an important role in understanding, and now the two disciples were beginning to understand. **[Seeing Jesus]**

Faithful disciples know the importance of sharing what they have learned. Thus, the two friends, as tired as they must have been, immediately got up and hurried back across the seven miles to Jerusalem and shared the good news with the other disciples. There they discovered that Jesus had also appeared to Peter, and he had convinced them that it was true: the Lord was risen (vv. 33-34). Cleopas and his companion then shared with them all they could remember of their conversation with Jesus on the road to Emmaus.

Today's text is a charming story, but it is more than charming. We cannot underestimate the importance of this report: much of the early church's understanding of Christ, and thus, much of our own theology, may have had its roots in what the gathered disciples learned on that first Easter night.

### The Hardest Question
### Why does Luke so often speak of "breaking bread"?

Luke's version of Jesus' life and mission often plays on the importance of meals, which Jesus used to demonstrate the inclusive spirit of his work. He developed a reputation for eating with tax collectors and sinners (5:30), for example, and he notably invited himself to a meal with Zacchaeus, known as a "chief tax collector." Others grumbled, but Zacchaeus met Jesus, and his life was changed.

But Jesus also ate with more socially acceptable people. Luke relates several teachings of Jesus that involve meals, including three within the context of a single Sabbath meal at the home of a Pharisee (14:1). Noting how people jostled for places of honor, he taught them about the importance of both humility (14:7-11) and generosity (14:12-14). In the same setting, he told the parable of the great dinner that some refused to attend by offering excuses, leading to an invitation for the poor, the blind, the lame, and people from the highways and byways to enjoy the meal (14:15-24).

The familiar story of the lost son circles around the significance of eating: the prodigal became so poor that he ate with the pigs, but his father welcomed him home with a banquet, much to the consternation of his brother (15:25-32). Jesus' memorable story contrasting a selfish rich man and poor but faithful Lazarus begins with a meal from which Lazarus was not offered the smallest crumb, and ends with the rich man pleading for Lazarus to offer him even a drop of water (16:19-31).

More to the point, Luke relates that Jesus became known to the disciples in Emmaus when he broke bread, blessed it, and shared it with them (vv. 30-31). This naturally recalls the story of how Jesus taught crowds of people about the kingdom of God, and then fed them with five loaves and two fish: "And taking the five loaves and the two fish, he looked up to heaven, and blessed and broke them, and gave them to the disciples to set before the crowd" (9:16).

The "Lord's Supper" offers an even more obvious connection, as Jesus shared a final Passover meal with his disciples. There "he took a loaf of bread, and when he had given thanks, he broke it and gave it to them, saying, 'This is my body, which is given for you. Do this in remembrance of me'" (22:19).

Perhaps all of these may have impacted the early church's emphasis on breaking bread together. Luke was also the author of Acts, in which he noted that those who were converted on the day of Pentecost "devoted themselves to the apostles' teaching and fellowship, to the breaking of bread and the prayers" (Acts 2:42), and the members of the early church "spent much time together in the temple, they broke bread at home and ate their food with glad and generous hearts" (Acts 2:46). Accounts of Paul's journeys include references to "breaking bread" (20:7, 11). As a prisoner enroute to Rome, on a storm-tossed ship, Paul encouraged the sailors and other passengers to eat and strengthen themselves against the coming days, promising that they would survive. "After he had said this, he took bread; and giving thanks to God in the presence of all, he broke it and began to eat" (Acts 27:35).

Fellowship meals, whether or not they included an official observance of the Lord's Supper, became significant as occasions for both physical and spiritual sustenance – and as opportunities for revelation.

# Fourth Sunday of Easter

## First Reading
## Acts 2:42-47

# Signs and Wonders

*They devoted themselves to the apostles' teaching and fellowship, to the breaking of bread and the prayers. (Acts 2:42)*

Perhaps you have heard someone comment on another person's appearance or misbehavior by saying "That's so common." Wealthy or famous people generally avoid having to associate very much with "common" people other than those they have hired to work for them, or others providing a service to them. Most of us, though, don't like to think of ourselves as "common."

In contrast, New Testament writers admired the first Christians as common folk who lived in an uncommon relationship with each other: they chose to share a common fate, eat at a common table, and to "have all things in common," selling their possessions to support one another.

Would this surprising movement last? In some ways, yes. In other ways, no. Throughout much of the world, believers still gather to worship and fellowship as the church of Christ. Having "all things in common," one of the trademarks of the movement's first glow, is another matter.

Acts 2:42-47 is often described as a portrait of the early church, but we should keep in mind that no real organization had yet been formed. Luke's intent was to portray the distinctive behavior of new believers in the early days following Pentecost: it was not to portray that behavior as a model for all churches to follow. **[Bridging]**

It would be a mistake for us to think we must pattern churches of our era after the halcyon days following Pentecost, but we can also err by ignoring the characteristics that made the early Christian movement so distinct and powerful that it has persisted – in a wide variety of forms – for two millennia.

Luke mentioned four notable characteristics of the first Christians in v. 42, adding details in vv. 43-47. He noted

> **Bridging:** From a literary perspective, Acts 2:42-47 serves as a bridge between Peter's sermon at Pentecost (2:14-41), which resulted in 3,000 people seeking baptism, and his sermon at the temple (3:1–4:4), after which Luke claims there were 5,000 believers.

that the early Christians devoted themselves to: (1) listening to the apostles' teaching, (2) experiencing fellowship with one another, (3) breaking bread together, and (4) devoting themselves to prayer. The word we translate as "devoted" carries a sense of close personal involvement that is both intense and persists over time, even in the face of difficulty.

### Devoted to teaching
### (v. 43)

The early believers, Luke says, were "devoted to the apostles' teaching." Where else could they turn? Jesus was no longer with them, so they had to rely on the disciples' memory of Jesus' teaching in addition to their Spirit-empowered preaching. There is little distinction between "teaching" and "preaching" at this point: both were designed to proclaim the gospel in ways designed to convict and instruct new believers.

The samples of their teaching and preaching that we find in Luke were firmly grounded in the Old Testament. The earliest believers are portrayed as coming entirely from the Jewish community: the people who heard the Spirit-empowered believers speaking their own languages may have been "from every nation under heaven," but were also "devout Jews" (2:5). Paul would later declare that the gospel was "the power of God for salvation to

**Peter's preaching:** What were the apostles teaching? We remember initially that the first congregation of Christians consisted almost entirely of Jews. In his opening sermon, Peter addressed them as "Men of Judea and all who live in Jerusalem" (2:14), as "You that are Israelites" (2:22), as "fellow Israelites" (2:29), and "the entire house of Israel" (2:35).

When people in the crowd addressed the apostles as "brothers" and asked what they should do, Peter instructed them to repent and be baptized to receive forgiveness and the Holy Spirit (2:38), "For the promise is for you, for your children, and for all who are far away, everyone whom the Lord our God calls to him" (2:39). While this implies an openness to Gentiles, the early core of believers consisted of Jews. They did not desert their Jewish background, but they believed firmly that Jesus' coming had fulfilled messianic hopes that grew from the Hebrew scriptures.

The excerpts that Luke records may be instructive. Peter's preaching consisted mainly of loose quotations from the Old Testament. In his Pentecost sermon, he began by citing Joel's prophecy that the Spirit would be poured out on all people, adding interpretive comments to the text (2:17-21, from Joel 2:28-32). He then turned to Psalm 16, interpreting it as a prophecy of David that God would not let the Messiah remain in the grave (2:25-31, from Ps. 16:8-11). Finally, he quoted from Psalm 110, which celebrated a king's accession to the throne, claiming that Jesus was the Messiah (anointed one) who would sit at God's right hand with enemies as his footstool (2:34-35, from Ps. 110:1).

In his sermon at the temple, after the healing of a lame man, Peter insisted that "the God of Abraham, the God of Isaac, and the God of Jacob, the God of our ancestors has glorified his servant Jesus" (3:13). He cited a belief that Moses had predicted the appearance of another prophet like himself (3:22), and he insisted that prophets from Samuel onward had "predicted these days" (3:24). Addressing Jews, he reminded them of God's covenant with Abraham and his descendants, that God would bless them and bless other nations through them. Jesus came first to the Jews, Peter, said, declaring that "When God raised up his servant, he sent him first to you, to bless you by turning each of you from your wicked ways" (3:26).

Early Christian preaching was grounded firmly in the Old Testament.

everyone who has faith, to the Jew first and also to the Greek" (Rom. 1:16).

In the days following Pentecost, many people must have been searching the scriptures and listening to the disciples recount Jesus' core teachings. Luke focused mainly on Peter's evangelistic preaching, but we may assume the apostles also recounted ways in which Jesus had reframed the Jewish law and called for an ethic focused on love for God and for one another.

Ongoing instruction was necessary, not only to orient new believers to Jesus' teachings, but also to keep them on track through continued reminders of what it means to follow Jesus.

For the new Christian community, it was important to understand how Jesus had come as a Jew to fulfill the messianic hopes of the Jews. Modern believers should likewise recognize that the Old Testament is part of our Bibles. Our genealogy may not be Jewish, and we don't live under the covenant instituted at Sinai, but the roots of our faith also grow from Israel's story. Just as knowing the story of our own family background contributes to our self-identity, being in touch with our spiritual ancestors promotes a more well-rounded image of who God has called us to be. [Peter's preaching]

## Devoted to fellowship
### (vv. 43-45)

Luke noted that "Awe came upon everyone, because many wonders and signs were being done by the apostles" (v. 43). This implies miraculous healings or other surprising acts, but perhaps the biggest miracle to emerge from Pentecost was a new sense of fellowship that bound together Jews "from every nation under heaven" in common cause and common concern.

The Greek word for it is *koinonía*, a term that came to be used as a prime description for people who lived in a close fellowship of mutual appreciation and generous sharing. "All who believed were together and had all things in common," Luke said, "they would sell their possessions and goods and distribute the proceeds to all as any had need" (vv. 44-45).

This is the point at which modern readers breathe a sigh of relief that today's church members are not generally expected to follow their example. The spirit of sharing in the days following Pentecost may have been less ideal than we often imagine, but it still represented a sea change in values for many, as the new believers demonstrated a care for others that went beyond what the law required. It's likely that the apostles' teaching had included Jesus' condensed version of what it means to live rightly: "I give you a new commandment, that you love one another. Just as I have loved you, you also should love one another. By this everyone will know that you are my disciples, if you have love for one another" (John 13:34-35).

Luke's account of the Christian movement's early days was written many years later and based on stories told by others. It is likely an idealized picture that contains some exaggeration. Luke's story clearly indicates a new Spirit-inspired level of generosity, and many believers were in fact willing to share their resources with others, even when they had to sell property to do it. But were all the thousands of new believers committed to selling all they had to support the poor among them?

Such a system would have required an extensive system of collection and distribution that we would not expect to find within a brand-new movement. The story of the prototype "deacons" in Acts 6 – just seven men to oversee the distribution of food – shows that the need for a system emerged. Apparently, the loving spirit that looked beyond ethnic lines soon waned. As the number of Christians mushroomed (more than 5,000 by Acts 4:4, according to Luke), the bloom was off the rose. Jewish widows who spoke Greek complained that they were being passed over while widows who spoke Hebrew (or more likely, Aramaic) got the lion's share of assistance.

And, whether communal generosity declined, or whether the community went bankrupt trying to keep up with poorer members, just two decades later the Apostle Paul felt a need to raise money from Gentile churches in Asia to aid the poor saints in Jerusalem (1 Cor. 16:1-4, 2 Cor. 8:1–9:15, Rom. 15:14-32).

To what extent do we consider the physical or financial needs of others, including those in our own church fellowship? Luke may not have been prescribing a common treasury for all, but he clearly stressed the importance of generosity. Should any community member go without food or medical attention or housing when there are Christ-followers who could help?

As we continue to follow the first believers in learning from the apostles' teaching, we also do so in community, with an awareness of the very real people all around us, and their very real needs. If the Spirit of God is in us, the call to community will be there, too.

## Devoted to breaking bread
### (v. 46)

A sign of the early believers' newfound sense of community was their notable interest in eating together. Indeed, the focus on time spent together over food recalls the many scenes in which Jesus enjoyed table fellowship with others, particularly with people who were considered too "common" to eat with upright folk.

Luke's characterization of this as "the breaking of the bread" (literally) has led many interpreters to suppose that this is a reference to the Eucharist, and that may have been part of it, though Will Willimon suggests that early believers may not have recognized the difference: "In good Jewish fashion, when the blessing is said at the table, the table becomes a holy place and eating together a sacred activity" (*Acts*, Interpretation [John Knox Press, 1988], 41).

If the Lord's Supper is implied, it must have been observed daily, for v. 46 says that "Day by day, as they spent much time together in the temple, they broke bread at home and ate their food with glad and generous hearts."

The Greek expression rendered "at home" (NRSV) or "in their homes" (NIV11) could also be translated as "from house to house" (KJV, NET, HCSB, NAS95). Literally, it reads something akin to "breaking – according to house – bread," "or breaking bread house-wise." One would think this referred to people eating in their own homes, but the context speaks of breaking bread together. Thus, it's likely that we are to think of the early believers as sharing meals in each other's homes on a regular basis, much as many churches today emphasize small group fellowship over meals in group members' homes.

Whether or not the Lord's Supper was included in each meal, eating together was clearly seen as an outward sign of the inner sense of love and sharing within the community.

## Devoted to prayer
### (v. 47)

Luke's reference to prayer in v. 42 includes the direct article: they devoted themselves to "the prayers." This may indicate a continued observance of the assigned Jewish hours of prayer. The new believers had not stopped being Jewish, but celebrated Jesus as the ultimate fulfillment of their Hebrew hopes. Thus, "they spent much time together in the temple"

**Temple prayers:** We know little about how much individual worshipers could participate in organized worship at the temple. Sketches from the New Testament suggest a large open compound where worshipers could gather for formal events, but also where vendors could sell temple-related merchandise, money changers could exchange special coins for the temple tax, and rabbis could sit with their pupils. It's likely that the new believers gathered in the temple grounds not only to pray new prayers at the appointed times (morning, afternoon, and evening), but also to hear the apostles teaching and preaching about the new covenant in Christ.

Acts 3:1 may be illustrative: it describes a day when Peter and John went up to the temple at 3:00 p.m. for the afternoon prayer. They facilitated the healing of a lame man who had been parked near one of the temple gates (the gate called "Beautiful"), and this attracted a crowd who listened to Peter preach from an open-air part of the temple known as "Solomon's Portico." Solomon's Portico was located on the east side of the temple complex, a covered walkway consisting of two rows of columns and a roof. In the picture, from a large-scale model of the temple at the Israel Museum in Jerusalem, Solomon's portico would have been on the near side, facing the front entrance of the temple.

(v. 46), "praising God and having the goodwill of all the people" (v. 47). [**Temple prayers**]

Prayer is important for private devotion, but also meaningful within the worshiping community. Prayer leaders should recognize the sacred character of the moment, and not trivialize prayer with trite phrases nor offer polarizing sentiments that may please some parishioners but alienate others. Prayer is crucial to the development of a strong faith community. Early believers were wise to spend much time in prayer, which continues to be a vital force, especially among people who are oppressed or living closer to the margins of society or the edge of survival. The more successful and self-sufficient we feel, however, the less emphasis we are likely to put on prayer.

We need not assume that Acts 2:42-47 portrays the ideal model of church life. We rarely consider the first version of something to be the best, or prototypes to be better than the later models.

Striving to be just like the first-century church is not what the 21st-century world needs, but that doesn't mean we can't learn important lessons from those early believers. They focused on growing in community through learning together, sharing together, eating together, and praying together. If those elements aren't present in our churches, perhaps a reevaluation of our priorities is in order.

### The Hardest Question
### Why do we call the Last Supper "Communion"?

This question might not naturally arise from a reading of Acts 2:42-47, but both the question and answer are related to the text, which speaks of *koinonia* and of the breaking of bread.

Jesus' final meal with his disciples is variously called "the Last Supper," "the Lord's Supper," or "the Eucharist." Why do we also refer to it as "Communion"? We noted above that the early church's commitment to *koinonia* and "the breaking of the bread" together might indicate the frequent celebration of the Lord's Supper. The word *koinonia*, translated in Acts 2:42 as "fellowship," also appears in Paul's discussion of the Last Supper in 1 Cor. 10:16: "The cup of blessing that we bless, is it not a sharing in the blood of Christ? The bread that we break, is it not a sharing in the body of Christ?" (NRSV).

Modern translations usually translate *koinonia* as "sharing" in this context (NRSV, NET, NASB 95). The NIV11 translates it as "participation." The KJV, though, renders it as "communion": "The cup of blessing which we bless, is it not the communion of the blood of Christ? The bread which we break, is it not the communion of the body of Christ?"

The widespread influence of the KJV – the predominant English translation for nearly 400 years – was such that the connection between the bread, the cup, and communion with Christ became embedded in our vocabulary, and the Lord's Supper came to be known as "Communion."

It is a celebration of our oneness, our participation in the life of Christ.

# Fourth Sunday of Easter

## Second Reading
## Psalm 23*

# Lead Us, Lord

*Psalm 23 is also used for the Fourth Sunday in Lent for Year A; for the Fourth Sunday of Easter in Years A, B, and C; and for Proper 23 in Year A and Proper 11 in Year B. A study appears in this volume under the Fourth Sunday in Lent.*

# Fourth Sunday of Easter

## Third Reading
## 1 Peter 2:11-25

# A New Example

*For to this you have been called, because Christ also suffered for you, leaving you an example,*
*so that you should follow in his steps. (1 Pet. 2:21)*

As the social gospel movement was gaining ground in the late 19ᵗʰ century, a Congregational minister named Charles M. Sheldon sought to encourage his congregation to get serious about following Jesus. He approached this goal by writing fictional stories about a church in which the pastor challenged parishioners to go a full year in which they would preface every decision with the question, "What would Jesus do?"

Sheldon used the inspirational stories as Sunday night sermons, attracting full houses. Later, the stories were published serially in a weekly Congregational newspaper called *The Advance*, then published as a ten-cent paperback novel called *In His Steps: What Would Jesus Do?*

More than 100,000 copies were sold in a few weeks. *The Advance* failed to secure a proper copyright, however, and other publishers picked up the book, spreading its popularity. Eventually, the book sold more than 50 million copies, among the best-selling books of all time. A movement to wear "WWJD" bracelets in the 1990s promoted the same theme.

In the *Nurturing Faith Commentary, Nurturing Faith Journal*, through podcasts and other online resources at Good Faith Media, we often encourage people to live with a "Jesus worldview."

The call to such faithful following is biblically rooted: in our text for today, the author of 1 Peter calls on believers to learn from Christ's example and to "follow in his steps." Our world is much different than first-century Rome, but the challenge still applies.

## Called to virtue
## (vv. 11-12)

In 1 Peter 2:1-10, the author calls for his readers to discard sinful ways and seek spiritual sustenance as they grow toward maturity and ultimate salvation (vv. 1-3). He appeals for them to join together as living stones in a spiritual house that will honor Christ (vv. 4-8), regarding themselves as God's chosen, holy people (vv. 9-10). [**The first shall be last**]

But what is involved in upright, honorable, and God-pleasing living? By choosing to follow Christ, believers inevitably find themselves at odds with a culture that worships other gods, whether they are called Apollo or Dianna, Luxury or Pleasure. That makes Christ-followers "aliens and exiles" in their own land, surrounded by the temptation to behave in ways that "wage war against the soul" (v. 11).

"Aliens and exiles" are technical terms describing levels of citizenship or status in the Roman world. The first speaks of people who were citizens of one city or territory, but permanent residents of another – roughly equivalent to a foreign citizen living in America with a green card. "Exiles" could also be translated as "sojourners," describing someone living temporarily in another country.

> **The first shall be last:** The lectionary's series of texts from 1 Peter calls for 2:19-25 to be studied the week before the preceding verses of 2:1-10, and it skips a troublesome section. For the sake of better context, we will expand our consideration to begin with v. 11. Thus, this week's text is 1 Pet. 2:11-25.

> **Non-Christians:** The NRSV translates v. 12a as "Conduct yourselves honorably among the Gentiles ...," which is accurate so far as it goes, but context suggests a better translation. The church members to whom Peter was writing were certainly not all Jews: many of them were ethnically "Gentiles" and had come into the church from other faiths or from no faith.
>
> The writer of 1 Peter seems to consider such believers to have left their "Gentile" status behind, though their ethnicity had not changed. If not technically Jews, they had become part of God's chosen people, a holy nation (*ethnos*) who were called to a new life. Christians, in Peter's mind, seem to be neither Jew nor Gentile, but a new category of persons.
>
> In this text, 1 Peter uses the word translated as "Gentiles" (also from *ethnos*, the root of our word "ethnic") in reference to anyone who is neither Jewish nor Christian. In v. 12, the plural dative form of the word *ethnesis* could be translated as "nations" or "Gentiles," but the point is that they are distinct from members of the church. Thus, the NET translates it appropriately as "non-Christians."

Unlike gospel music that sings of being pilgrims on earth while our citizenship is in heaven, Peter does not tell his readers to hang tough because their true home is in glory land. His emphasis, rather, is that those who trust in Christ should forsake the gods and some cultural aspects of their former life, even if it made them feel like aliens in their own land.

Sinful behavior obstructs spiritual growth, so believers who seek maturity must work to overcome it. We don't do it for eternal rewards alone, though. Living ethical and honorable lives also helps us to be effective witnesses to others.

Supporters of Roman and local cultures in first-century Asia Minor might incorrectly accuse Christians of doing wrong, but the writer insisted that the believers' good behavior would vindicate them and lead their neighbors to "Conduct yourselves honorably among the Gentiles," so they might "glorify God on the day he visits us" (v. 12, probably a reference to the day of judgment). Whether he hoped former critics would glorify God because they had been converted or because they would confront their errors at the judgment is unclear. **[Non-Christians]**

American Christians are rarely ridiculed for their beliefs, though some claim persecution when their Christian nationalist views or desire to discriminate runs aground of the law. Sometimes the most faithful and loving Christians may find people within their neighborhoods or work environments to be skeptical of their behavior. Have you ever felt put down because of behaviors growing out of your faith? If so, how did you respond?

### Called to submission
### (vv. 13-17)

Christians owe their ultimate loyalty to Christ, but we also live under the authority of earthly institutions. The author of 1 Peter insisted that believers acknowledge governmental authorities and submit to them, even when such leaders were self-serving. Model behavior on the part of Christians could promote the faith and show they were not a threat to the government.

"Accept the authority of every human institution" (NRSV) could be translated "be subject to every human creation." Since the writer went on to talk about relationships involving governing authorities (2:13-17), masters with slaves (2:18-21), and family members (3:1-7), he probably had the institutional sense of the word in mind (v. 17).

Readers were addressed as "aliens and sojourners," suggesting that most of them were low on the social or economic totem pole. They had little choice but to live in submission to the authorities of the city-state in which they resided.

The author offers a rationale for respecting governmental authorities: "It is God's will that by doing right you should silence the ignorance of the foolish" (v. 15). In other words, respect for authority has its roots in God's will, not the leaders' worthiness. Governmental systems and their leaders are inevitably imperfect, but well-intended authority is still preferable to anarchy. **[Government]**

> **Government:** Some form of government and law is necessary for a stable society. A collection of rabbinic teachings known as the *Mishnah* includes advice to "Pray for the welfare of the government, for were it not for the fear of it, a person would swallow his friend alive" (*m. Avot* 3.2, cited in Amy-Jill Levine and Marc Zvi Brettler, eds., *The Jewish Annotated New Testament*, 2nd ed. [Oxford University Press, 2017], 505).

Though free in Christ, believers are to live as responsible citizens who do good rather than evil. In this way, no one would have grounds to condemn them.

The gospel of Jesus Christ is liberating. It assures women and men of all stations in life that they are people of dignity and worth. The writer knew, however, that freedom has a dangerous side. Those who have been liberated by the gospel may be tempted to live without restraint, and to use the promise of forgiveness as an excuse to sin. So, he cautions against using Christian freedom as a pretext for evil (v. 16).

The author fleshes out what it means to live as servants of God with a string of four imperative instructions (v. 17). First, Christians are to show respect to all people, reflecting God's love for everyone.

Second, believers are to have a special love for their Christian family. The word "church" does not appear in this letter, but the author urges believers to love the "brotherhood," which NRSV renders as "the family of believers."

The word for "love" comes from *agapē*, a term that was given a distinctively Christian meaning. It is used in the New Testament to describe the unconditional love of Jesus, which he calls us to share with others.

While loving others, Christians are to reverence God (the third imperative). The phrase could be translated as "fear God," but the author is not suggesting that we live in terror before the Almighty. Thoughtful believers live in awe of God's majesty as creator, sustainer, and ultimate judge. Our greatest reverence belongs to the one who has the final word.

The fourth imperative again references the emperor, who is to be honored – though not revered. At times the Roman Empire treated its potentates like gods, instructing all subjects to worship the emperor by offering incense and saying "Caesar is Lord!"

There are limits to governmental submission: reverence and worship are reserved for God alone. One's proper attitude to governing authorities is described with the same word of respect used at the beginning of the verse: believers can honor people in high office without worshiping them. [**Honor the emperor**]

## Called to endurance
### (vv. 18-25)

The next few verses are difficult for modern readers. In the first-century world, slavery was pervasive and imperial Roman society depended on it at every level. Slavery was not related to race or ethnicity: the greatest number of slaves were captured in wars and forced to serve the victors. A thriving slave trade bought and sold persons. One could become a slave through kidnapping, being abandoned by parents, being born to a slave mother, or even as a criminal punishment. Slavery was ubiquitous and regarded as a reality of life.

The pervasiveness of slavery and the ethnic diversity of the slave population in the Roman Empire can be illustrated with an anecdote recorded by Seneca. Since most slaves were physically indistinguishable from free people in Rome's diverse population, the Roman Senate once debated a measure that would require slaves to wear distinctive dress. The bill was soundly defeated, however, when someone pointed out that if all slaves dressed alike, they would realize how many of them there were and potentially rebel (Seneca, *On Mercy* 1.24.1; cited in J. Albert Harrell's article "Slavery," *The New Interpreter's Dictionary of the Bible, S–Z*, vol. 5 [Abingdon Press, 2009], 304).

In a slave-based society, any discussion of relationships and authority would include slaves. In contemporary society, most people consider slavery to be abhorrent, but it still exists. By some estimates, many thousands of people still live in involuntary servitude, forced into sex work or thankless labor. [**Slavery still exists**]

Peter knew that many of his readers were literally in bondage to others: the Christian message of freedom

---

**Honor the emperor:** The author of 1 Peter instructed readers to submit to governing authorities and honor the emperor, even though both governors and emperors occasionally turned against Christians and made them convenient scapegoats, persecuting them for political purposes.

Even in such circumstances, he advised believers to honor the authorities, including the emperor. Whether this would include participating in rituals through which the emperor was symbolically worshiped, he did not say.

Today we live in a polarized society in which everyone seems to distrust a large percentage of elected officials. How can we express either support or disagreement with government officials in a respectful manner that honors Christ?

**Slavery still exists:** A 2018 United Nations report states that human trafficking has taken on "horrific" dimensions. In both 2015 and 2016, nearly 25,000 persons were reportedly known to have been forced into slavery, with the primary targets being women and girls. In 2016, 21 percent of people enslaved were men, 49 percent were women, 23 percent were girls, and 7 percent were boys. About 65 percent of women and girls were forced to work in the sex industry. Increasingly, slavery has become a tool of war in which armed groups capture women and force them to become "wives" of the soldiers or distributed to others. Slavery is less obvious in today's world, but still exists in the shadows. (The full report can be found at http://www.unodc.org/documents/data-and-analysis/glotip/2018/GLOTiP_2018_BOOK_web_small.pdf.)

in Christ was popular among slaves. The author did not express either acceptance or condemnation of the practice, but he encouraged Christian slaves to be patient and respectful to their masters, including those who were harsh (2:18-20). Even when mistreated, believers should remain faithful to God and not give in to the temptation of retribution, he wrote. Peter did not give instructions to slave-owners, though Paul did, encouraging them to treat slaves well (Eph. 5:5-9).

The thought of Christian slaves suffering unjustly led Peter to call upon Christ's example as a model for believers to follow (v. 21). When suffering comes our way – including undeserved suffering – we are to bear it with grace, trusting that our perseverance will find favor with God and sow seeds of grace in the lives of those who harm us.

To reinforce his position, in vv. 22-25 the author quoted loosely from Isa. 53:7-9, understood by the early church as a prophecy of Christ's patient endurance in the face of unjust suffering. Interspersed within the citation, the author added his own commentary. As Christ's suffering was redemptive, he said, believers should also live righteous lives and inspire their persecutors to have faith.

In other words, the text still calls for a Jesus-centered approach as we live and work under the authority of others, whether it is our parents or teachers, our supervisors at work, or governmental authorities. The author believed that the way believers comport themselves as cooperative people could have a positive effect on every level.

What kind of influence are we having?

## The Hardest Question
### Why doesn't the Bible condemn slavery?

For most of us, thoughts of slavery are completely abhorrent, especially since we know that slavery played such a large, divisive, and shameful role in American history. It is painful – though necessary – for us to think about it, if for no other reason than to oppose it ever being legalized again.

If it is so obvious to us that slavery is wrong in every way, why doesn't the Bible condemn it? Why did the Old Testament law allow it? Why did Jesus, Paul, and other New Testament writers not speak against it? How can we claim the Bible as the basis of our moral values if it fails to condemn something as despicable as slavery?

To begin with, we should note that every culture known in the ancient Near East practiced slavery of some sort, though the level of personhood and rights granted to slaves varied from place to place.

The Old Testament law allowed for slavery, but also put sharp limits on how slaves should be treated. Slaves were to observe a day of rest on the Sabbath (Exod. 20:10). Rules calling for limits in the treatment of slaves were included in Exod. 21:20-21, 26-27. If a slaveowner should put out an eye or break a tooth while beating a slave, for example, the slave should be set free as compensation.

Slaves who escaped their owners, according to Deut. 23:15-16, should be allowed to live as free persons. In many cases, those called slaves were technically indentured servants who were to be set free after six years of service (Deut. 15:18).

Other texts could be cited, though many readers will find cold comfort in the relatively more humane treatment of slaves called for in the Hebrew Bible.

And again, why did Jesus, arguably the greatest moral teacher of all time, not openly condemn slavery? Why did Paul, who argued so eloquently for human dignity and freedom, give it a pass?

One possibility is that confronting slavery could have sidetracked the gospel. The immediate concern of Jesus was the work of redemption, and the focus of the apostles was on proclaiming the good news of what Jesus had done. If either Jesus or the apostles had changed their focus to a campaign against social ills such as slavery – on which the Roman economy depended – the entire

Christian movement could have fizzled: the Romans would have done their best to squelch it completely. Thus, New Testament writers chose to live within the status quo.

Something to recognize is this: though early Christians did not confront slavery directly, the spread of the gospel and the promotion of Christian values did much to bring an end to slavery as an acceptable practice. Though 19th-century apologists for slaveowners called on the Bible in their defense of slavery, a better understanding ultimately triumphed.

The seeds of slavery's demise are present in the Old Testament's insistence that all people are made in God's image and therefore worthy of respect (Gen. 1:26-27). The seeds are present in Jesus' insistence that he came to redeem all people and that his followers should love everyone and be kind even to "the least of these." The seeds of slavery's demise were present in Paul's insistence that "There is no longer Jew or Greek, there is no longer slave or free, there is no longer male and female; for all of you are one in Christ Jesus" (Gal. 3:23, see also Col. 3:11).

So, while the Bible does not explicitly condone slavery, neither does it regard the practice as ideal. Biblical teachings, though the years, provided the spiritual, ethical, and moral impetus for humankind to recognize that slavery has no place in a just society.

A Jesus worldview recognizes that all people should be free to live as God leads them, and that all Christians are called to love and respect their fellow human beings.

## Fourth Reading
## John 10:1-10

# A Sheep's Life

*The thief comes only to steal and kill and destroy. I came that they may have life,*
*and have it abundantly. (John 10:10)*

Today's text is about relationships, specifically, the relationship between Jesus and those who trust in him. Declaring that relationships are important is no great revelation: we know they are essential.

Indeed, Walter Wangerin once defined both life and death by the presence or absence of living in relationship. "For this is what death is," he wrote, "Death is always suffered as separation … Because this is what life is: Life is always experienced in relationship" (*Mourning into Dancing* [Zondervan, 1992], 23).

Every broken relationship brings a kind of death. Moving to a new town, losing a needed job, ending a friendship, encountering an illness, or watching a loved one stop breathing all bear aspects of death and the dark shadow of separation.

As death comes through the severing of relationships, so life comes through the blossoming of a sense of connectedness, through knowing what it means to belong in this world. We have choices to make about life.

Wangerin's insight may help us to appreciate what Jesus said about life in John 10:10. "The thief comes only to steal, and kill, and destroy. I am come that they might have life, and have it more abundantly."

### The shepherd
### (vv. 1-6)

Jesus prefaced that remarkable promise of life with two careful comments about sheep, or more specifically, about the role of shepherds and sheep. The pastures of ancient Palestine had few fences, but simple paddocks bounded by walls of piled stone were sometimes used to round up the sheep for shearing or for safe keeping at night. The pen, even if topped with briers or brambles to discourage thieves, did not guarantee safety. If not for the shepherd's watchful eye, thieves could easily open the gate or climb over the low wall and make off with some of the sheep (v. 1).

Scholars often regard John 9–10 as a unit, beginning with the healing of a man who was born blind and followed by a controversy with certain Pharisees. As ch. 10 opens – remembering that chapter divisions are artificial and were added long after the original writing – Jesus was still speaking with the Pharisees, whose unwillingness to see Jesus as messiah matched the blindness of the man who had been healed. This is not to say that Jesus' story of the shepherd and sheep was directed at the religious authorities alone: it concerned anyone who failed to lead the sheep properly, allowing them to be scattered.

Every sheepfold would of necessity have a gate through which the sheep could come in and go out. The shepherd uses the gate for its intended purpose. With this in mind, Jesus described two different scenarios: In the first, a paid gatekeeper guards the sheep for the shepherd (v. 3). In the second image, the shepherd himself (or herself) acts as the gate (v. 7). Some simple paddocks may have had only a narrow opening rather than a physical gate: the shepherd would lie inside the gate for rest or sleep. In both scenarios, the shepherd controls access to the sheep.

The shepherd not only provides security for the sheep, but also leads them day by day (vv. 2-4). Jesus described a situation in which shepherds and sheep develop close bonds over time. They spend most of each day in each other's company. The shepherd knows each sheep by

**Who are the thieves?** Modern readers should be careful to avoid falling into a blame game when interpreting Jesus' statement that "All who came before me are thieves and bandits" (v. 8). Many through the years, based on a supersessionist approach, have identified the "thieves and bandits" as Jews in general, or Jewish teachers and authorities in particular. The earlier context in John portrayed Jesus participating in several verbal jousting matches with scribes and Pharisees, but we should not assume that Jesus was condemning them as "thieves and bandits."

It is possible that Jesus had in mind those who came claiming to be a messiah, but who were mainly revolutionaries. It is wise to note that Jesus did not spell out who the wrongful sheep stealers were: the point is that Jesus is the true and faithful shepherd, and to follow any other brings danger.

name, he said. Sheep have poor vision, but they learn to recognize the shepherd's voice, and to associate it with safety. Sheep do not willingly follow a stranger's voice (v. 5), even as the blind man Jesus cured in the previous chapter refused to heed the Pharisees' admonitions. Jesus categorized anyone who led the sheep astray as a thief. **[Who are the thieves?]**

Jesus' reference to sheep knowing and following the shepherd's voice is a Johannine reminder of the importance of following Jesus' words and example. Jesus was using what the author calls a "figure of speech" (*paroimia*) rather than "speaking boldly" or "plainly" (*parrēsia*), as he did in chs. 7–8, and returns to in 10:24. Still, his listeners did not understand the inference (v. 6).

## The gate
### vv. 7-10)

Jesus repeated the illustration in more personalized fashion, so they could not fail to miss the point. "*I* am the gate for the sheep," Jesus said (v. 7), as opposed to thieves and bandits (or rebels) who would lead them astray. "I am the gate," he repeated in v. 9: "Whoever enters by me will be saved, and will come in and go out and find pasture."

Jesus is the valid gate to salvation – another way of saying "the way, the truth, and the life" (14:6). A similar image appears in Rev. 3:7-8, where Jesus holds "the key of David, who opens and no one will shut, who shuts and no one opens."

Only by entering through the gate and listening to his voice do we hear the words that lead to salvation. Only by following his leadership do we find the road to life and growth. Those who heard Jesus teach may have been familiar with Psalm 23 or Psalm 100. They knew what it meant to say, "the Lord is my Shepherd" or "we are the sheep of his pasture." In essence, Jesus claimed to be the savior and shepherd of the sheep. **[Sheep without a shepherd]**

Jesus' claims reflect the prophet Ezekiel's discourse about God as the one shepherd who would one day reunite the people of Israel through the medium of "David," who came to be identified with the descendant of David who others spoke of as a coming messiah (Ezekiel 34–37, Isaiah 11).

In v. 10, Jesus again compared his role with that of a thief. "The thief comes only to steal and kill and destroy," he said (v. 10a). In this case, the thief may be a figure for Satan as conceived in first-century Judaism. Elsewhere, Jesus described the devil as a murderer (John 8:44), the thief who comes to steal and kill and destroy.

In contrast, Jesus insisted that he came so that everyone who believed in him would not be destroyed ("perish" and "destroy" come from the same verb), but would have eternal life (John 3:16; see also 6:39).

Jesus knew what it was like to be isolated, to be separated, to experience the death of relationships. During the most popular phase of his ministry, he was misunderstood by his own mother and brothers. At the climax of

**Sheep without a shepherd:** People, like sheep, need good leaders if they are to live healthy spiritual lives. Stories in the Pentateuch portray Moses as leading Israel like a shepherd for many years, but when God told him that he could not enter the land of promise, Moses reportedly responded: "Let the LORD, the God of the spirits of all flesh, appoint someone over the congregation who shall go out before them and come in before them, who shall lead them out and bring them in, so that the congregation of the LORD may not be like sheep without a shepherd" (Num. 27:16-17).

Many years later the prophet Micaiah, according to 2 Chron. 18:16, had a vision in which he said "I saw all Israel scattered on the mountains, like sheep without a shepherd."

Matthew 9:36 and Mark 6:34 both describe instances in which Jesus had compassion on the multitudes because "they were like sheep without a shepherd."

**Sheep with a shepherd:** In the image, a shepherd in the Valley of Elah keeps watch over a mixed flock of sheep and goats.

his ministry, he was betrayed by one of his best friends. Jesus knew what death is. He had seen others die. He had the power to bring others back from death. He knew that he, too, would die – yet he also expected to live again.

We can be confident that the care Jesus showed to his disciples has not ceased with believers who came after them. Jesus knows the pain we suffer, the separations we endure, the rupturing of relationships, the loss of love, the fear of one day not breathing any more. The good news is that in Jesus, we need not fear death: we have life.

Jesus not only offers life, but life to the fullest: "I came that they may have life, and have it abundantly." Jesus taught that we can experience such life through Christ himself, who is the gateway to abundant and eternal living. Through his death on the cross Jesus paved the way for our forgiveness: "While we were yet sinners, Christ died for us" (Rom. 5:8). We learn to love him, because he first loved us. **[Sheep with a shepherd]** Such life includes both present and eternal elements.

Years ago, in the comic strip *Kudzu*, the Rev. Will B. Dunn was holding forth an analogy of life as a video cassette recorder with variable speeds. "Childhood is like 'Slow-Motion,'" he said. "Adulthood is like 'Play,' and old-age is like 'Fast-Forward.'" Young Kudzu nodded and said, "I'll buy that – but what is death?" Will B. Dunn responded, "Well, that depends on whether you choose 'Stop' or 'Pause.'"

Those who have no relationship with Christ choose "Stop." When death comes to claim them, there is none to rescue. Life is over. Life is done. There is only the cold isolation of death. In contrast, those who live in relationship with Christ have the promise of eternal life. They might anticipate a momentary "Pause," perhaps, as breathing ceases, and then a whole new vista of life opening toward eternity.

But there is also a present aspect of life, the one we experience now. Jesus wants us to have abundant life, a full life. In *his* life, he taught us how. In both deed and word, Jesus demonstrated the importance of living in loving relationships with others. "I give you a new commandment, that you love one another. Just as I have loved you, you also should love one another" (John 13:34).

Abundant living involves finding our place in God's world and doing our part, leading a life with purpose. Jesus knew what it was like to work for a living, and his disciples worked. His parables were filled with stories of farmers and bankers and housewives and fishermen, all living in relationship with the world God had given us.

Living the full life also means learning to love ourselves. Jesus taught us to love God first, with our whole heart, and to love our neighbors as ourselves. Jesus made it clear that God loves every one of us. The hairs of our head are numbered. We are precious to him. We are forgivable. We are acceptable. We are loveable.

In the context of Jesus' love, we can learn to love him, to love others, to love our world, and even to love ourselves. In this love is abundant life. In this love is the strength and the courage we need to deal with death in all its many forms and faces.

Jesus came to be the shepherd who was willing to lay down his life for the sheep, and in so doing, to see that the sheep have a meaningful life, secure in their relationship with the shepherd. How that works out depends on whether we choose to be sheep who follow the shepherd and remain in community, or sheep who stray.

### The Hardest Question
### Must we think of ourselves as sheep?

While we may like the image of Christ as shepherd – and many churches feature stained glass images of Jesus holding a lamb – we may be less comfortable thinking of ourselves as sheep. Sermons on Psalm 23 routinely suggest that sheep are rather stupid creatures who don't know how to find water, stop eating when full, or find their way back home at the end of the day.

No one wants to think of themselves as stupid, but that doesn't mean we don't need a shepherd. We know that the most successful companies, schools, or sports teams are the ones that have good leadership.

While leadership also plays a role in whether Christian congregations thrive, the church's ultimate leader is Jesus, and churches (or believers) who do well are those who listen to his voice. Molly Marshall has emphasized the need for the church to "recover the theological meaning of the shepherding imagery." In the early church's symbolic iconography, she notes, the image of Jesus as shepherd was common, but by the fourth century, when Constantine declared the Roman Empire to be a "Christian" state, the shepherd imagery was replaced by Jesus as the glorious and powerful Pantocrator, more of a distant ruler than a present shepherd.

In our passage, and in vv. 11-18 that follow, Jesus portrays himself as the one shepherd who keeps the sheep together in community, calling, leading, and protecting the flock. To be faithful, the church must focus on keeping Jesus at the center, hearing his voice and following his teachings. As Marshall put it, "When christological awareness ebbs in congregational life, that is, when the story of Jesus is neglected, the church becomes unmoored and rudderless" (*Feasting on the Word, Year A*, ed. David L. Bartlett and Barbara Brown Taylor, vol. 2 of Accordance electronic ed. [Westminster John Knox Press, 2010], para. 11110).

For the church to experience true community to fulfill its calling in the world, to have a true "Jesus worldview," we must not only hear the stories of Jesus, but also follow him as the true shepherd of the flock.

# Fifth Sunday of Easter

## First Reading
## Acts 6:1–7:60

# Faithful Unto Death

*While they were stoning Stephen, he prayed, "Lord Jesus, receive my spirit." Then he knelt down and cried out in a loud voice, "Lord, do not hold this sin against them." When he had said this, he died. (Acts 7:59-60)*

Have you ever gotten off to a good start with a new job or project, only to face an early obstacle that threatened to derail your efforts? Imagine taking a sales job in a competitive environment where monthly bonuses are based on the amount of business you bring in. You start strong, but then come down with a nasty bug that keeps you out of work for days. Will you ever catch up? Or imagine that you've begun a weight-loss program that's going quite well until a family holiday surrounds you with food you can't resist. Can you get back on track?

Our text is set in the early days of the Christian movement, which got off to such an amazing start that thousands of Jews decided to follow Jesus and were baptized in a matter of days. A Holy Spirit-empowered revival broke out that saw people devoting their lives to learning about Jesus and enjoying such close communion that they shared their resources with one another as they ate, worshiped, and prayed together. What could go wrong?

### Trouble brewing
### (6:1–7:1)

The first hint of trouble within the emerging church is found in Acts 5:1-11, a dark and disturbing story of how two believers named Ananias and Sapphira sold some property and turned over part of the proceeds to the common treasury – but claimed to have given it all. Peter confronted them separately over the lie and both fell dead, one after the other, an apparent warning against attempting to deceive God.

> **The text:** The Revised Common Lectionary text incorporates only Acts 7:55-60, the stoning of Stephen, which makes for a very dark if somewhat inspirational selection. Why was Stephen being stoned? What else was going on? We need to know these things if we are to understand what comes after.
>
> Stephen's sermon and the lead-up to it are not included in other lectionary texts, so we will include a review of the events in Acts 6–7 in today's lesson, none of which appear for other Sundays in the lectionary.

Disquiet surfaced through ethnic prejudice in Acts 6:1-6, where Jewish Christians who spoke Greek complained that their widows were being shortchanged in the distribution of food to the needy, while Hebrew or Aramaic-speaking widows were getting the lion's share of the resources. The 12 apostles, who were doubtless stretched thin trying to orient so many new believers to the faith, called for the appointment of seven good people to oversee the food distribution while they focused on prayer and preaching. First chosen among the seven was Stephen, described as "a man full of faith and the Holy Spirit." [The text]

The move seemed to quell the incipient rumblings, and Luke recounts that "the word of God continued to spread; the number of the disciples increased greatly in Jerusalem, and a great many of the priests became obedient to the faith" (6:7). But there was more trouble to come, especially from the priests and their followers who did not convert, but who saw the Christian movement as a heretical threat to Judaism.

We soon learn that Stephen's work extended beyond the soup kitchen: "full of grace and power," he "did great wonders and signs among the people" (6:7). A contingent of outspoken Jews from various synagogues confronted Stephen over his new beliefs, "But they could not withstand the wisdom and the Spirit with which he spoke" (6:11). Unable to defeat Stephen in a debate, they conspired to have someone falsely accuse him of blasphemy against both God and Moses, causing such a stir that Stephen was called before the Sanhedrin. There, false witnesses accused him of constantly "saying things against this holy place and the law" (6:13).

Despite the charges, Luke reports that Stephen's countenance "was like the face of an angel" (6:14) when the high priest offered him a chance to refute the charges. Stephen happily complied, launching into a sermon designed to demonstrate both his firm grounding in Judaism and his belief that Jesus had come as the fulfillment of Hebrew prophecy, superseding the old covenant by offering himself as the ultimate sacrifice and introducing a new means of relating to God through grace.

## Trial by sermon
### (7:2-53)

Stephen began his sermon with a review of Israel's history that seemed calm enough, though his first words bristled: "Brothers and fathers, listen to me!" Like some modern preachers, he began in a low-key fashion, gradually warming up and setting the stage for the close, where he answered their heated accusations with fiery words that were bound to cause offense.

Stephen began by reflecting on God's call to Abraham and the promise that one day his descendants would inherit the land where Abraham lived as an alien before becoming enslaved in another country for 400 years and then returning to the land of promise (7:2-7). Stephen's rhetoric was powerful, though his recall of the traditions did not always match up with the texts he was quoting.

Stephen's claim that God called Abram while still in Ur differs from the account in Genesis 11, which says that Abram's father Terah decided to move the family from Ur, but stopped in Haran and remained there until he died (Gen. 11:27-31). Abram was in Haran, then, when God called him to leave his country and go "to the land that

> **Not exactly:** Stephen may have been a powerful preacher, but he sometimes got confused when citing the Hebrew Bible. He says in 7:16 that Jacob died in Egypt but was brought back to Shechem, where he was "laid in the tomb that Abraham had bought for a sum of silver from the sons of Hamor in Shechem." This is a problem on two counts.
>
> First, Gen. 50:31 is specific in saying that Jacob was buried in the Cave of Macpeleh near Hebron, which Abraham had bought from Ephron the Hittite (a story told in Genesis 23 and reinforced by Gen. 49:29-30 and 50:31).
>
> Second, it was not Jacob, but Joseph who was said to have been buried in Shechem (Josh. 24:32), and on property that was not purchased from the sons of Hamor by Abraham, but by Jacob (Gen. 33:19).

I will show you" (Gen. 12:1-3). Perhaps Stephen was aware of a different tradition, or he may have believed that Abraham had prompted his father Terah to move the family from Ur, though that would not jive with God's command for Abraham to leave his kindred and his father's house.

Afterward, God "gave him the covenant of circumcision," so that Abraham circumcised Isaac, who became the father of Jacob, the father of the 12 "patriarchs," who sold Joseph into Egyptian slavery, but were later saved from famine when Joseph gained Pharaoh's favor and brought them to Egypt (7:8-16). [**Not exactly**]

Stephen then recounted the story of the Exodus, beginning with the birth and call of the Hebrew hero Moses and moving to Israel's deliverance from Egypt and the wilderness wandering, where the people rebelled by making and worshiping a golden calf (7:17-41). This led to the worship of other gods including the "host of heaven," which Stephen supported with a loose quotation from the Greek translation of Amos 5:25-27.

Knowing how important the temple was to his audience – and believing it had become *too* important – Stephen recounted how Israel first worshiped at "the tent of testimony in the wilderness" before Solomon built the first temple in Jerusalem. He then insisted that God did not dwell in a house made by human hands, citing Isaiah's critique of people who focused on the temple while God had said "Heaven is my throne and the earth is my footstool. What kind of house will you build for me, says

> **Stiff-necked people:** Stephen's criticism of the Jewish leaders as stiff-necked people who were uncircumcised in mind and heart involved some name-calling, but it wasn't original to him. God had described Israel as stiff-necked and rebellious, according to Exod. 33:3, 5 and 34:9. Divinely inspired messages challenged the Israelites, who were described as having an "uncircumcised heart" or needing to "circumcise the foreskin" of their hearts in Lev. 26:41, Deut. 10:16, and Jer. 4:4.
>
> Likewise, Stephen's additional charges that the people rebelled against the Holy Spirit echoed Isa. 63:10, and his accusation that they had persecuted the prophets finds support in 1 Kgs. 19:10, 14; Neh. 9:26; and others. Stephen's words stung in part because he was quoting scriptural accusations against the ancestors.

the Lord, or what is the place of my rest?" (7:42-50, citing Isa. 66:1-2a).

With his critique of the temple as a foundation, Stephen "quit preachin' and went to meddlin'," as we sometimes say, addressing Judaism's highest officials as "stiff-necked people, uncircumcised in heart and ears," who were "forever opposing the Holy Spirit" as their ancestors had (7:51). Just as their ancestors had persecuted "the prophets who foretold the coming of the Righteous One," so he said they had become "his betrayers and murderers," people who had received the law but had not kept it (7:52-53). [**Stiff-necked people**]

Is there any wonder why Stephen's audience of staunch Jewish leaders were infuriated? "When they heard these things, they became enraged and ground their teeth at Stephen" (7:54). Of course they did.

## Visions and stones
## (7:55-60)

As Luke tells the story, Stephen appeared immune to the tempers flaring around him. Caught up in the Spirit, he declared "Look! I see the heavens opened and the Son of Man standing at the right hand of God!" (7:55-56).

Why would this be so objectionable that people in the crowd covered their ears and rushed to drag Stephen from the temple grounds (7:57)? Recall that Stephen had just quoted Isaiah's oracle when speaking for God: "Heaven is my throne and earth is my footstool." Stephen now claimed that he could see into heaven, where Jesus

("the Son of Man") was standing at God's right hand. This would have further inflamed those who had seen Jesus as a danger to Judaism. The burgeoning Christian movement appeared to be an even greater threat, and having people such as Stephen claiming to see Jesus working together with God could not help their cause. [**The Son of Man**]

Convinced that Stephen was a self-professed heretic, the authorities dragged him out of the city without bothering to pass an official sentence, as Luke tells the story, and began the process of stoning him to death. The physical effort involved in this is evidenced by the note that the executioners removed their outer cloaks and left them in the care of Saul, a young but rabid supporter of traditional Judaism prior to his conversion (7:58).

In his dying moments, Stephen exhibited the same spirit as the Christ he worshiped. Luke says that he prayed "Lord Jesus, receive my spirit" before crying aloud "Lord, do not hold this sin against them" (7:59-60).

What do we do with a text like this? Should we feel badly because we don't see visions of heaven as Stephen did? Should we preach sermons or make Facebook posts that are designed to offend unbelievers?

We may have difficulty identifying with either Stephen or his angry accusers. Nevertheless, Stephen's challengers remind us of the danger inherent in allowing our loyalty to tradition or an institution make us deaf to the voice of the Spirit. How many of us have known people (perhaps even ourselves) who seem to care more about keeping things the way they've always been rather than being open to new possibilities?

> **The Son of Man:** Stephen's reference to Jesus as the "Son of Man" is the only place in the gospels that anyone other than Jesus used that title for him. Elsewhere, the title "Son of Man" has apocalyptic connotations (Dan. 7:13, Rev. 1:13).
>
> While Stephen said he saw Jesus standing at the right hand of God, other texts speak of Jesus *sitting* at God's right hand (Mark 16:19; Luke 22:69; Acts 2:34; Heb. 1:3, 13). Perhaps we are to think of Jesus rising to greet his servant Stephen's entrance to heaven, as Stephen prayed "Lord Jesus, receive my spirit" (7:59).

On the other hand, Stephen's example stands as the kind of sold-out commitment that may seem alien to us. We live in a different day and a different context. Rarely do we even think of facing a challenge to be faithful unto death – but are we even willing to be faithful unto embarrassment, or faithful unto behaving ourselves when tempted?

We're not called to be Stephen, but we are called to be the best version of ourselves that we can be. How is that going?

### The Hardest Question
### How (and why) were people stoned in ancient times?

According to the Hebrew Bible, stoning was the penalty for various offenses, including the worship of Molech by child sacrifice (Lev. 20:2), blasphemy (Lev. 24:14-16), cursing parents (Lev. 20:9), or other offenses by which the authorities ordered capital punishment. Stephen was accused of blasphemy, of speaking against the traditional Jewish understanding of God.

Instructions in Leviticus directed that stoning must take place "outside the camp," so Stephen's accusers made sure to hustle their victim outside of the city walls. An old church tradition identifies the area as just outside what is now called "St. Stephen's Gate" (also called "the Lion's Gate"), a busy gate on the east side of the Old City, close to the Temple Mount.

Ordinarily, the Sanhedrin lacked authority to carry out an execution during the period of Roman occupation. After determining someone worthy of death, Jewish authorities were required to seek permission from the Roman governor to carry out the sentence: witness the need for Jesus to be tried before Pilate and Herod. In Stephen's case, the authorities acted more as a lynch mob than a governing body, apparently overcome by anger at Stephen's hard words. Luke thus portrays the Sanhedrin as being not only unable to control the mob but also complicit with it. For Luke, this would suggest that the apostles, rather than the Sanhedrin, should be recognized as the true leaders of Israel.

The Old Testament says little about how stoning should be carried out, and it may have been done in different ways. Later writings in the Mishnah, particularly section six of a tractate called "Sanhedrin," portrays an organized ritual in which the accused were stripped and forced to stand on the edge of a low cliff at least twice the height of a man. Both men and women could be stoned: women were allowed a small amount of clothing for modesty.

The condemned was to stand with their back to the cliff, and one of the accusers would then push the person's thighs so that they fell backward, landing on their head or back. Victims who landed face down were to be turned over. If the fall did not prove fatal, witnesses would drop a large boulder onto the person's chest, repeating with other stones, if needed, until the person was dead. Some rabbis argued that male offenders should also be hanged after having been stoned to death.

Recall that when Jesus confronted accusers who wanted to stone a woman caught in adultery, he challenged those who were without sin to cast the first stone (John 8:7). Although the practice of stoning seems barbaric to us, the various rules that developed were designed to preserve a measure of dignity to the person being executed and assure that the death occurred as cleanly as possible. Those who made the accusation were required to participate in the execution, reminding all concerned that false accusations were serious business.

The stoning depicted in Acts 7 does not appear to follow any careful procedure: no official verdict was issued, the Roman government wasn't notified, and there's no indication that Stephen was stripped or pushed from a height. We have the impression that multiple people were casting smaller stones at Stephen as he stood before kneeling and ultimately succumbing. The stoning is described more as the result of mob violence, rather than a legitimate execution.

(An online version of the Mishnah's Tractate Sanhedrin, chapter 6 can be found at http://www.jewishvirtuallibrary.org/jsource/Talmud/sanhedrin6.html.)

# *Fifth Sunday of Easter*

## Second Reading
## Psalm 31 (RCL 31:1-5, 15-16)*

# Refuge and Redemption

*A similar text, Ps. 31:1-5, 19-24 is read for the Ninth Sunday in Epiphany or Proper 1 in Year A.*
*Psalm 31:9-16 is used on the Sixth Sunday in Lent (Passion Liturgy) in Years A, B, and C.*
*A study of vv. 1-24 appears in this volume under the Sixth Sunday in Lent, the Liturgy of the Passion.*

# Fifth Sunday of Easter

## Third Reading
### 1 Peter 2:1-10

# A New Hope

*Like living stones, let yourselves be built into a spiritual house, to be a holy priesthood,*
*to offer spiritual sacrifices acceptable to God through Jesus Christ. (2 Pet. 1:5)*

Sylvester Stallone's star turn in the movie *Rocky* (1976) quickly became iconic, spawning five sequels. Tourists still visit Philadelphia's Museum of Art to run up the long stairway and raise their hands in his classic pose.

Stallone's character was not the first to have such a stony connotation. The apostle Peter was born as Simon, but the Fourth Gospel suggests that Jesus gave him a new name when they first met: "You are Simon son of John," Jesus said. "You are to be called Cephas" (John 1:42). Cephas is the Aramaic word for "rock," equivalent to the Greek word *petros*, which comes into English as Peter. One could argue that Peter was the original "Rocky."

It's no surprise, then, that the person who wrote 1 Peter and attributed it to the apostle should use the metaphor of rocks or stones, encouraging Christians to think of themselves as living stones built into the body of Christ. That promotes a Jesus-centered worldview from the inside out.

### Drink your milk
### (vv. 1-3)

The opening verses of ch. 2 build on earlier exhortations calling Christians to live as new and different people (1:13-25). The author had no qualms about mixing metaphors: he addressed believers as infants who need milk, as living blocks of stone built into a temple, as priests within the same temple, and as a specially chosen nation. Along the way, he cited various Old Testament texts to support his views.

> **Stripping down:** The verb translated as "rid yourselves" is a participle, rather than an imperative. Literally, it would be "Therefore, ridding yourselves of all malice ..." In context, however, the imperative translation seems justified.
>
> The verb is a metaphor drawn from the notion of removing one's clothing: believers should rid themselves of harmful habits in the same way that they strip off soiled garments.
>
> There is evidence that in the third and fourth centuries, some churches made full use of this symbolism, expecting baptismal candidates to take off their old garments and enter the water to be immersed *au naturel*. Emerging from the water, they would be anointed with oil and don a new, white robe.

Becoming a new person in Christ involves transformation of the old self. Thus, he calls believers to change their ways. "Rid yourselves" (NRSV) or "get rid of" (NET) suggests a turning away from one's pre-Christian behaviors: the same word introduces similar lists in Rom. 13:12; Eph. 4:22, 25; Col. 3:8; and Jas. 1:21. It suggests the image of taking off an old garment to put on a new one. [**Stripping down**]

The writer's litany of negative attire to be discarded includes "malice, and all guile, insincerity, envy, and all slander" (v. 1). The word for "malice" is a general term for wickedness, while "guile" begins a list of negative behaviors that disrupt community and hurt others.

In Greek, the last three vices are written in the plural form. "Insincerity" is the Greek word from which we derive "hypocrisy" (*hupocrisis*). Envy is at the root of selfish behavior that seeks to advance oneself above others.

Slander involves language that intentionally defames or harms others.

The author probably did not know many people in his audience personally. Perhaps that is why he chose rather generic terms for harmful habits to be put away. Can we name specific habits or ways of thinking that we consciously set aside when we became Christian? Are there other changes that remain to be made? If we were writing a similar letter of advice today, what negative attitudes or practices would we encourage new believers to discard?

Followers of Jesus should not only put away what hinders spiritual growth, but also hunger for what enhances it. Thus, Peter called on the repentant and newly innocent Christians to think of themselves as mere babes in the faith, seeking to grow through imbibing "pure, spiritual milk" (v. 2a).

This implies that many of the readers were recent converts. "Long for" is a strong verb that suggests a hungry yearning, no less essential to survival than a newborn's instinctive appetite.

The substance of the metaphorical milk is not identified, though it is described as "pure" (free from deceit) and as "spiritual" or "genuine." The latter word translates *logikos*, which the KJV inaccurately renders as "of the word." Despite its similarity to *logos*, the term's primary meaning is "rational" or "genuine." The translation "spiritual" is figurative.

This admonition is not about studying the Bible, then, as many KJV readers have inferred and many preachers have declared. The Bible as we know it did not yet exist when this letter was written, and few people had direct access to Old Testament scrolls. They would need to learn about their faith from the teaching of pastors, itinerant evangelists, or letters such as this from church leaders. This is not to suggest that we should not encourage new believers to read the Bible, in which we find much spiritual sustenance, but that was not the author's intent.

The sustaining "milk" that believers need includes fellowship with other Christians, worship as part of the community, communion with God through prayer, and a conscious effort to follow Jesus in loving ways. All these activities, along with studying scripture, can strengthen believers. [**Milk and honey**]

> **Milk and honey:** The metaphor of milk as a symbol for sound teaching is also found among the Essenes at Qumran, in the writings of the Jewish philosopher Philo, and in other scriptures (1 Cor. 3:2, Heb. 5:12). In some early church traditions, newly baptized persons were offered a drink made of milk and honey, symbolizing their status as infants who had entered a spiritual promised land.

How would this help believers "grow into salvation" (v. 2b)? The writer is not suggesting that new believers had no experience of saving grace, but is emphasizing both present and future dimensions of salvation. In 1:4, he speaks of an inheritance being "kept in heaven for you," followed by the reference to "a salvation ready to be revealed in the last time" (1:5). Salvation appears more present in 1:9, however: "for you are receiving the outcome of your faith, the salvation of your souls."

The phrase speaks to the importance of growing in one's appreciation and experience of salvation for those who "have tasted that the Lord is good" (v. 3). That expression is a loose quotation from Ps. 34:8, "O taste and see that the LORD is good; happy are those who take refuge in him." The Greek word translated as "good" is *chrēstos*, which was pronounced much like *Christos*, and so serves as a play on words, a reminder that Christ is the source of what is truly good.

Salvation has both present and future dimensions: those who trust in Christ live in a state of grace, but have yet to know the final, full, and eternal extent of salvation.

### Be a rock
### (vv. 4-8)

With v. 4, the writer shifts metaphors. Instead of newborn babes, he now asks believers to think of themselves as stones, citing Christ as "a living stone, rejected by mortals yet chosen and precious in God's sight." [**Stones and rocks**]

Christ-followers should likewise think of themselves as living stones that make up the greater temple of Christ's body (v. 5a), he wrote. Such stones are not static and unchanging, like the carefully shaped limestone used in many ancient temples. Rather, as we grow in maturity and faith, we continue to be formed and shaped both as individuals and as a church.

> **Stones and rocks:** The name "Peter" (*petros*) means "stone" or "rock," but the author shied away from using it in conjunction with his metaphor of living stones. In most cases he uses *lithos*, another word for "stone," from which we derive words such as "monolith" (a large, upright stone) and "Paleolithic" (the Stone Age).
>
> The one time the author does use *petros* is in the quotation of v. 8, where he speaks of a "stone (*lithos*) that makes them stumble and a rock (*petra*) that makes them fall (*skandalon*)." Richard Vinson notes that this might remind readers that Peter had been called "Rock" after declaring Christ as the Messiah of God, but was later called an offense (*skandalon*) when he rebuked Jesus for speaking of the cross" (*1 & 2 Peter, Jude*, Smyth & Helwys Bible Commentary [Smyth & Helwys, 2010], 91-92).

The writer then shifts the image from stones to priests, calling on believers who have been "built into a spiritual house" to live holy lives as priests who offer "spiritual sacrifices" appropriate to the worship of Christ (v. 5b). The work of Christ rendered animal sacrifices obsolete. Instead, we offer the sacrifices of faithful and worshipful living.

The new believers in Asia Minor would face many trials, being "rejected by mortals" just as Christ was spurned by many. Yet, they could find comfort in knowing that they were "chosen and precious in God's sight."

The author reinforces this image in vv. 6-8 by recalling several Old Testament texts. The laying of the chosen cornerstone reflects Isa. 28:16, while its rejection calls to mind Ps. 118:22, and its role as a stumbling block for unbelievers derives from Isa. 8:14.

Early believers interpreted these texts as prophetic references to Jesus, who was rejected by mortals but chosen by God and destined to become the cornerstone by which all others would be judged. As Christ stood firm in trials, the new believers were called to do the same. **[Living stones]**

> **Living stones:** I once sought to approach this text creatively through writing a short story that imagines a poor village in which a charismatic priest led church members to build an open-air cathedral from their own bodies, which were then turned to stone—with a surprise ending. It's available as "Growing Stones Gather No Moss" in *Telling Stories: Tall Tales and Deep Truths* (Smyth & Helwys, 2008), 73-80.

## Live in the light
### (vv. 9-10)

Those who cherish the doctrine of "the priesthood of the believer" have long loved v. 9, which picks up on the metaphor of believers as priests from v. 5. Quoting from God's commission to Israel in Exod. 19:5-6 (and possibly Isa. 43:20-21), the author affirms a new status for the new believers: "you are a chosen race, a royal priesthood, a holy nation, God's own people."

These labels speak not only to our privilege as God's chosen people, but also to our responsibility to live as priests who serve God in the world. In ancient Israel, priests were called to intercede with God on behalf of others, and to teach others about God so they could worship in their own words.

Therefore, the work of a priest is to represent fellow humans before God, and to represent God to their fellow humans. The author of 1 Peter believed that God has chosen all believers to live as priests, not just ordained clergy or other professional ministers. As such, every believer is called to a holy life that shows reverence to God and points others to God.

We are not called as God's chosen people and royal priesthood for our benefit alone, but that we might serve as witnesses in the world. As God has called us out of this world's darkness and into divine light, so God commissions us to lead others from spiritual darkness into light (v. 9b).

The reference to believers as God's special people led the writer to recall another Old Testament text, this one from the prophet Hosea. With his own broken marriage serving as a metaphor for Israel's desertion of God, Hosea gave his daughter the name Lo-ruhammah ("Not Pitied") and his youngest son the name Lo-ammi ("not my people"). Hosea did not give up on his children or on Israel, however, but looked to a day when God would have pity on "Not Pitied" and would say to "Not My People" that "You are my people." He, representing Israel, would respond "You are my God" (Hos. 1:9, 2:23).

The author of 1 Peter believed that very prophecy was being fulfilled as new believers responded positively to God in Christ: "Once you were not a people, but now you are God's people," he said. "Once you had not

> **A favorite quote:** The Apostle Paul used the same metaphor and also quoted from Hosea in his letter to the Romans: ... "Those who were not my people I will call 'my people,' and her who was not beloved I will call 'beloved.' And in the very place where it was said to them, 'You are not my people,' there they shall be called children of the living God" (Rom. 9:25-26).

received mercy, but now you have received mercy" (2:10).

**[A favorite quote]**

The text challenges us to ask if we have experienced both sides of the relationship described here. Can we recall a feeling of guilt before God, knowing how far we had fallen short of God's ideal? And do we recall the sense of relief that comes with repentance and the joy of knowing that God has forgiven our sins?

The author of 1 Peter wanted the Christians who read his letter to remember their former lives apart from God, and to adopt a new way of living as people who are forgiven, beloved, and focused on Jesus.

### The Hardest Question
### What are "spiritual sacrifices"?

What does the writer mean in saying we are to live as priests who offer "spiritual sacrifices" to God (v. 5)? He does not define the term. We are familiar with animal sacrifices offered by Hebrew priests while the temple still stood, but the author specifically referred to "spiritual" (*pneumatikos*), not animal, sacrifices.

Most readers of 1 Peter would never have seen a sacrifice in the Jewish temple in Jerusalem. It was not only far distant, but had been destroyed by the Romans in 71 CE. They likely would have seen sacrifices made to pagan gods, however, for temples to various Roman and Greek gods were abundant, and local persons could volunteer to serve as priests within the temple cults and offer sacrifices in hopes of gaining favor with the gods.

The writer, whether Peter or not, appears to have come from a Jewish background, so it is likely that his reference to "spiritual sacrifices" has roots in Hebrew metaphor as found in the Old Testament. Even in the Hebrew Bible, however, both prophets and poets recognized that the sacrifices God most desired were not burned on the altar but demonstrated in human lives. It is likely that he had in mind things such as prayer and praise to God, which could also be thought of in sacrificial terms.

"The sacrifice acceptable to God is a broken spirit," the psalmist said, suggesting a prayer of repentance (Ps. 51:17). Prayer as sacrifice could also be suggested by Ps. 141:2: "Let my prayer be counted as incense before you, and the lifting up of my hands as an evening sacrifice."

Overt praise could also be described as a sacrifice: Psalm 50 instructs worshipers to "Offer to God a sacrifice of thanksgiving and pay your vows to the most high" (v. 14), declaring that "Those who bring thanksgiving as their sacrifice honor me ..." (v. 23).

The book of Jonah echoes a similar thought: "I with the voice of thanksgiving will sacrifice to you; what I have vowed I will pay" (2:9).

Tangible gifts could also be considered as sacrifices. "With a freewill offering I will sacrifice to you," said the psalmist (54:6a).

The Old Testament is clear that God desires obedience and ethical living far more than physical sacrifices (1 Sam. 15:22, Hos. 6:6, Amos 5:21-24, Mic. 6:1-8).

We might think of spiritual sacrifices, then, as any act of worship, service, or compassion that honors God.

# Fifth Sunday of Easter

## Fourth Reading
## John 14:1-14

# An Eternal Advocate

*Very truly, I tell you, the one who believes in me will also do the works that I do and, in fact,
will do greater works than these, because I am going to the Father. (John 14:12)*

Some promises seem too good to be true, such as this one: "If in my name you ask me for anything," Jesus said, "I will do it" (v. 14). Could it possibly mean what it sounds like? Did Jesus offer his followers an upgrade on finding a genie in a lamp, with unlimited wishes?

A quick, surface reading might suggest that Jesus' promise was akin to winning a billion-dollar lottery, but there has to be more to the story, right? Right.

Context is everything, and these words of Jesus come from a particular setting that governs our understanding of the promise. The story is in the gospel of John, an account of Jesus' life that differs significantly from what we find in the more similar gospels of Matthew, Mark, and Luke. The Fourth Gospel was written later than the others. It has a distinct literary style and a decidedly more theological bent, focusing on the central theme of Christ as the incarnate Word of God, one with the Father, who makes access to God available in a radically new way.

The theological centerpiece of the Fourth Gospel is a lengthy farewell discourse and prayer (chs. 14–17) that the author says Jesus shared with his disciples in the hours before they departed for Gethsemane, where he was arrested. The Fourth Gospel does not include a version of the "Lord's Supper," but the author appears to have set the discourse following their last meal.

### Jesus and the way
### (vv. 1-7)

Understanding today's text requires some context. When Judas had left the room to tell the authorities where Jesus could be found, the final act had been set in motion. Though it may seem premature to readers, Jesus turned to the remaining 11 disciples and declared "Now the Son of Man has been glorified, and God has been glorified in him" (13:31).

Jesus went on to say that he would not be with them much longer, and "Where I am going, you cannot come" (13:33). That observation led to Jesus' compact instructions for how they should live in his absence – by loving one another just as Jesus had loved them (13:34-35). These verses set the mood for the remainder of the discourse: Jesus demands a love that is not only willing to die for others, but also to live in unity with them.

The conversation was heavy, and emotions were high. We can only imagine the depth of feeling and the enormity of uncertainty growing in the disciples' hearts. Not surprisingly, Jesus sought to comfort his friends. "Do not let your hearts be troubled. Believe in God, believe also in me. In my father's house there are many dwelling places. If it were not so, would I have told you that I go to prepare a place for you?" (vv. 1-2).

The natural sentiment of the promise makes this a popular text for funeral services, and a poor translation from the KJV has led generations to anticipate living in one of "many mansions" in heaven, but that was not Jesus' purpose: he wanted his disciples to know that, though they would part, it would not be forever (v. 3). He then made a curious statement: "And you know the way to the place where I am going" (v. 4).

Any of us would likely have echoed Thomas' quizzical response to Jesus' cryptic claim: "Lord we do not know

> **The heart of the matter:** Rudolf Schnackenburg described John 14:6-7 as "the high point of Johannine theology" (*The Gospel According to St. John*, vol. 3 [Seabury, 1982], 65). Gail O'Day cites this position in her commentary, noting "These verses announce in clear language the theological conviction that drives the Fourth Evangelist's work, 'No one comes to the Father except through me.' These words express the Fourth Evangelist's unshakable belief that the coming of Jesus, the Word made flesh, decisively altered the relationship between God and humanity" ("John," vol. 9, *The New Interpreter's Bible* [Abingdon Press, 1995], 743).

*where* you are going. How can we know the *way*?" (v. 5, emphasis added).

Jesus responded with what some commentators consider to be the pinnacle statement of John's theology: "I am the way, and the truth, and the life. No one comes to the Father except through me. If you know me, you will know my Father also. From now on you do know him and have seen him" (vv. 6-7). [**The heart of the matter**]

To know Jesus was to know the Father. That was a radical statement, one we may still have trouble wrapping our heads around. For the Fourth Evangelist, that was the heart of the matter, from the opening "In the beginning was the Word, and the Word was with God, and the Word was God" (1:1). Jesus was – and is – God incarnate, one with the Father.

## Jesus and the Father
### (vv. 8-11)

It was Philip, John says, who openly struggled to understand, and who asked for a clearer picture: "Lord, show us the Father, and we will be satisfied" (v. 8). Jesus' reproachful response reflects both patience and exasperation: "Have I been with you all this time, Philip, and you still do not know me? Whoever has seen me has seen the Father" (v. 9).

Theologian Bill Hull once suggested a reason why the disciples might have been confused about Jesus' assertion: "He had claimed to be 'the way,' yet his path led straight to a cross; to be 'the truth,' yet he could convince none of the religious leaders to embrace his cause; to be 'the life,' yet he would be dead in less than twenty-four hours!" (*John*, vol. 9, Broadman Bible Commentary [Broadman Press, 1970], 334).

It's no wonder that Philip asked for clearer evidence of Jesus' oneness with the Father, or why we still wrestle with the idea. What Philip and the others didn't understand is that Jesus was the ultimate self-revelation of God, the closest any human could come to seeing God. And so, Jesus asked them: "Do you not believe that I am in the Father and the Father is in me?" (v. 10a). [**Jesus and the father**]

As John put it, Jesus' identity was so enmeshed with the Father that their works were indistinguishable (v. 10b). He had done what he could do to reveal God's presence through both word and works; now it was up to the disciples to believe: "Believe me that I am in the Father and the Father is in me; but if you do not, then believe because of the works themselves" (v. 11).

John's gospel makes much of various "signs" that demonstrated Jesus' divinity and called for belief. It concludes with a word to readers that "these are written so that you may come to believe that Jesus is the Messiah, the Son of God, and that through believing you may have life in his name" (20:31).

Jesus wanted his followers to believe due to his word alone. Failing that, he called them to believe in response to the mighty works they had seen. Even skeptical observers, according to Nicodemus, had recognized that "no one can do these signs that you do apart from the presence of God" (3:2).

It's not surprising that Jesus' critics rejected his claim, but the disciples seemed to have had just as much trouble believing it. This, however, is the central thrust of the Fourth Gospel's message: that Jesus, through his life and works, death and resurrection, revealed the love of God to humankind as plainly as it could be done. This opened the door to a new way of relating to God: as Jesus could speak of a mutual indwelling relationship with the Father, so his followers could speak of being in Jesus and Jesus being in them. Later in the same conversation, Jesus insisted that he would not leave the disciples as orphans, but would

> **Jesus and the Father:** Jesus' claim that "I am in the Father and the Father is in me" calls to mind an earlier conversation with a group of Jewish leaders, to whom he had insisted that he was doing the works of the Father, urging them to believe on the evidence of his works that "the Father is in me and I am in the Father" (10:37-38).

> **Jesus in us:** When talking to children about God, it's not uncommon for us to encourage them to "ask Jesus into your heart" or to believe that "Jesus lives in your heart." That's probably not the best way to communicate this truth to children, who are still literal thinkers and might imagine a tiny image of Jesus residing inside their chests. Even for adults, the metaphysical concept of Jesus dwelling in us – and us in him – is mind-boggling. Can you think of alternate ways to express the same thought?

be reunited with them. "On that day," he said, "you will know that I am in my Father, and you in me, and I in you" (v. 20). **[Jesus in us]**

## Jesus and his disciples
### (vv. 12-14)

To think of Christ dwelling in us is astonishing; what Jesus went on to say in vv. 12-14 could be even harder to grasp. After challenging his followers to believe in him – in part because of the works he had done – Jesus solemnly declared "Very truly, I tell you, the one who believes in me will also do the works that I do and, in fact, will do greater works than these, because I am going to the Father" (v. 12).

Does this mean believers will have power to work even greater miracles than Jesus, and whenever they like? The next two verses, on the surface, seem to suggest that: "I will do whatever you ask in my name, so that the Father may be glorified in the Son. If in my name you ask me for anything, I will do it" (vv. 13-14).

The New Testament testifies to a few mighty works being done by the disciples, but we don't see widespread miracles today, do we? Does that mean we're lacking in belief, as some would contend, or lacking in our understanding of what Jesus meant? When Jesus spoke of "the works that I do," it seems clear that he had more than miracles in mind: his primary work was to reveal the depths of the Father's love, and it was about to culminate in Jesus' conclusive "hour," the climactic events of crucifixion, resurrection, and ascension.

When Jesus spoke of the works his disciples were to do in vv. 12-14, he did so in the future tense: they would do these works after his time on earth was finished and he had returned to the Father. While on earth, in his incarnate ministry, Jesus could reveal God's power through miraculous signs and speak of dying and rising again, but his hearers could easily remain skeptical. Once Jesus had finished his course, however – after he had been crucified and buried, after he had risen from the dead and revealed himself to many, after he had ascended to the Father – then the disciples would have the full story to tell.

Empowered by the Spirit, the disciples' works could be greater than those of Jesus because they could declare the complete story of God's saving revelation in Christ. Through their witness, far more people would come to follow Christ than Jesus had won over during his time on earth.

But what about vv. 13-14 and the apparent promise that Jesus would do whatever the disciples asked of him? We note first that in both verses, Jesus qualified such requests by the condition that they should be asked "in my name." Asking in Jesus' name is to ask what Jesus would ask. It rules out any selfish request, any desire to build one's reputation as a miracle-worker, or any petition outside of what God desires. To ask in Jesus' name is to ask in accordance with Jesus' desire, and what Jesus wants is revealed in the next few verses: that his Spirit-empowered and emboldened followers would live in unity and carry on his work through loving others as he had loved them.

### The Hardest Question
### What did Jesus mean in saying the disciples would do "greater works" than he had done?

In her commentary on John, Gail O'Day argues that the works of Jesus were limited during his incarnation, because the full story had not yet been revealed. After the fulfillment of Jesus' "hour" in his crucifixion, resurrection, post-Easter appearances, and ascension, the disciples would have access to the complete story and thus could proclaim the life-changing significance of Jesus' work in a more convincing manner: "Their works thus are not greater than Jesus' works because of anything intrinsic to the disciples themselves, but because they belong to the new eschatological age ushered in by Jesus' hour. As such, they continue the glorification of God through Jesus that was the purpose of Jesus' own works (v. 13b; cf. 5:44; ll:4; 17:4)." (For more, see "The Gospel of John," *The New Interpreter's Bible* [Abingdon, 1995], 746-749.)

William Hull takes a similar tack in his commentary. "Since works were intended to produce faith," Hull wrote, "this promise was abundantly fulfilled by the early Christian mission to the Gentiles that resulted in far more believers than Jesus ever won on earth" ("John," *The Broadman Bible Commentary* [Broadman Press, 1970], 335).

George R. Beasley-Murray takes a broader view but arrives in essentially the same place, arguing that the "greater works" Jesus had in mind are neither miracles nor church growth through greater evangelistic success, but the actualizing of Jesus' work to introduce the eternal kingdom of God:

> The main reality to which they point, and which makes their testimony a set of variations on a single theme, is the life eternal of the kingdom of God through Jesus its mediator. This is confirmed by the striking parallel to v. 12 in 5:20 and its following exposition: the Father shows the Son all (sc, the works) that he himself does, "and greater works than these he will show him, that you may be amazed." The context reveals that the "greater works" that the Father is to "show" the Son, greater than those given him to do thus far, are manifestations of resurrection and judgment, but with emphasis on the former (as 5:24-26 in relation to v. 17 shows). Thus the "greater works" that the disciples are to do after Easter are the actualization of the realities to which the works of Jesus point, the bestowal of the blessings and powers of the kingdom of God upon men and women which the death and resurrection of Jesus are to let loose in the world.

After noting that the "greater works" would not be initiated until after Jesus' departure, Beasley-Murray goes on to add:

> The contrast accordingly is not between Jesus and his disciples in their respective ministries, but between Jesus with his disciples in the limited circumstances of his earthly ministry and the risen Christ with his disciples in the post-Easter situation. Then the limitations of the Incarnation will no longer apply, redemption will have been won for the world, the kingdom of God opened for humanity, and the disciples equipped for a ministry in power to the nations. (*John*, vol. 36, Word Biblical Commentary. [Zondervan, 1987], 255)

In a similar vein, Alicia Myers has argued that Jesus' commands in the Farewell Discourse "can only be followed *after* Jesus' death, resurrection, return to the Father, and giving of 'another Paraclete,' the 'Spirit of truth'" (14:17, 26). This is why, she says, Peter's claim that he was willing to die for Jesus before his crucifixion was an inadvertent attempt to usurp Jesus' role (13:36-38). "He cannot show complete love *until* Jesus first models it, which requires his death and resurrection as part of his return to the Father" (*Reading John and 1, 2, 3 John* [Smyth & Helwys, 2019], 159-160).

# Sixth Sunday of Easter

## First Reading
## Acts 17:1-31

# A God Unknown

*For as I went through the city and looked carefully at the objects of your worship, I found among them an altar with the inscription, "To an unknown god." What therefore you worship as unknown, this I proclaim to you. (Acts 17:23)*

I was in Athens, studying philosophy. This was Athens, *Georgia*, where the University of Georgia campus was no less impressive to me than its Grecian namesake would have been to any ancient country boy who had come to town. My primary interest was science, but a course in philosophy was required.

On the first day of class, the professor asked me: "Mr. Cartledge, what is that you are sitting in?"

Trying not to appear too smug, I replied: "I'm sitting in a desk."

She responded: "Mr. Cartledge, how do you *know* that is a desk?"

"Because I know what a desk is," I said, with some confidence.

"Consider, Mr. Cartledge," she said. "How do you know whether that is *really* a desk, or could it be just your *idea* of a desk?"

Was she serious? It took a while for me to realize that she was introducing Plato's ideas about the difference between the ideal and the real. For someone who had always taken the reality I perceived for granted, that was a new way of thinking.

All of us want an understanding of reality that makes sense of life, though some think about it more intentionally or deeply than others. In the ancient world, the Greek philosophers and their students were most articulate in expressing their views, but an itinerant preacher named Paul had no qualms about going toe-to-toe (or head-to-head) with the intelligentsia of Athens.

## Familiar philosophies
### (vv. 1-21)

Our text derives from Paul's second missionary journey, and requires some background not included in the lectionary reading, so we'll offer a brief review. Having visited several cities in Asia Minor, Paul and his companions crossed the Aegean Sea to the region of Macedonia, where they spent a tumultuous period in Philippi before moving on to Thessalonica and Berea, winning converts along the way. When certain Jewish leaders mounted a campaign against Paul, he took ship and sailed along the coast to the city of Athens, leaving Timothy and Silas to continue the work in Macedonia for a short time, presumably in a more low-key fashion (17:1-15).

Upon his arrival, Paul made his way through the city and was distressed by the many images of gods, which he saw as idolatrous. Paul went first to the synagogues to debate with the Jews and Grecian God-fearers, as was his usual practice, but he also preached in the agora, Athens' famous marketplace (vv. 16-17). The agora was the heart of Athens: it featured several altars and temples, and was also a gathering place for those who wanted to catch the latest gossip, socialize with friends, or debate with the various philosophers and teachers who frequented the place. The primary marketplace in Athens occupied a flat area below the soaring Acropolis, where magnificent temples stood watch over the city. [The Aeropagus]

Some listeners accused Paul of teaching about foreign gods (note the plural), since he spoke of "Jesus and the resurrection" (v. 18). Ancient peoples often expected male gods to have female consorts, so Paul's hearers may have misun-

**The Areopagus:** The officials who made up the Areopagus reportedly had some judicial responsibility, and apparently were involved in public education, having authority to determine what could be taught in the marketplace.

Scholars are divided over whether Paul was courteously led to the Areopagus for further conversation, or forcefully hauled there for a more hostile interrogation. The Greek word *epilambanō* literally means "take hold of," suggesting that the latter might be the case.

The outcrop of rock pictured was known as Mars Hill, the traditional home of the Areopagus. It is just west of the Acropolis, from where the photo was taken. The agora was downhill to the right.

**Dueling philosophies:** The Epicureans were named for their founder, Epicurus, who opened a school in Athens in 310 BCE and taught there for 40 years. Epicurus based his teaching in part on the atomic theory of Democritus, believing that all matter was composed of atoms whose movements were solely responsible for the origin of all things. Epicurus taught that gods existed, but had nothing to do with humans, and were thus unnecessary. The goal of life was to achieve happiness, which was possible when one no longer feared the gods. Epicureans did not promote an "eat, drink and be merry" bohemianism, as is often thought. Rather, they sought to live simple and moral lives, finding happiness in communal friendships with each other. Epicureans scorned the possibility of an afterlife, believing that the body simply returned to atoms after death. Thus, happiness could only be achieved in this life.

While Epicureanism was especially popular with the upper classes who could more easily enjoy life, Stoicism became the dominant ethical philosophy of the Hellenistic and Roman world. Stoics took their name from the Stoa, an open colonnade in the marketplace at Athens, where Zeno had begun teaching his Cynic-inspired philosophy around 300 BCE. Stoics believed the gods existed, and in some cases identified their concept of divine "Reason" with Zeus. Stoicism taught that virtue was the ultimate good, and defined virtue as living in harmony with the *logos* (reason) or with the true rational nature of human beings. To achieve such harmony, Stoics sought to detach themselves from human desires and external circumstances. They believed that the circumstances of life were determined by fate, and that freedom came through accepting the dictates of destiny without complaint.

(Drawn mainly from Robert M. Shurden, "Epicureanism" and "Stoicism," in the *Mercer Dictionary of the Bible* [Mercer University Press, 1990]: 257-58, 857-58; and J. Bradley Chance, *Acts*, Smyth & Helwys Bible Commentary [Smyth & Helwys: 2007], 306-309.)

derstood his meaning, interpreting *anastasis* (the word for "resurrection," which has feminine gender in Greek) as the name of a goddess, hence, "Jesus and Anastasis."

The phrase translated as "foreign divinities" (v. 18) is an unusual expression. The word translated as "foreign" is *xenōn*, which typically refers to someone of a different ethnic or social background (the root of the English word "xenophobia," a fear or dislike of other ethnic groups). The word for "divinities" is *daimoniōn*, which referred to supernatural beings who were among the lesser gods.

Some of Paul's conversation partners showed little respect: they called him a "babbler," literally a "seed-picker," an expression to describe birds who pick up and eat seeds in one place, then excrete them in others. The charge indicated a belief that he was just scattering useless ideas.

Ever eager to hear new ideas, though, some of Paul's listeners took him to the Areopagus, a council of elder officials who had some ruling responsibilities. They had originally met on Mars Hill, a rocky outcrop between the agora and the acropolis, but in Paul's day they met in the Royal Stoa, an open-air building near the edge of the agora (v. 19).

Luke notes that Paul entered a debate with the adherents of two competing schools of philosophy, the Epicureans and the Stoics. Both philosophies provided belief systems to explain how life should be understood. Loquacious locals enjoyed the bantering of ideas: Luke wrote that "all the Athenians and the foreigners living there would spend their time in nothing but telling or hearing something new" (v. 20). [**Dueling philosophies**]

## An unknown God
### (vv. 22-31)

The gospel Paul preached was clearly at odds with the teachings of the philosophers, in which deities played only distant roles. Paul proclaimed the existence of a supreme God who sought an active relationship with humans.

As Paul began his defense of the gospel, he demonstrated a quick wit and a masterful use of oratory. He used gentle flattery to warm his audience and seek common ground: "I see how extremely religious you are in every way," he said (v. 22). Paul described walking through the city, so festooned with images of various gods, and said "I found among them an altar with the inscription, 'To an unknown god.' What therefore you worship as unknown, this I proclaim to you" (v. 23).

Paul probably knew that the philosophers generally regarded the Greek gods as either irrelevant or unconcerned with humans, but in a brilliant rhetorical move, he used the presence of an altar to an "unknown god" as the basis for a sermon on the God they had yet to meet.

The unknown god, Paul said, is "The God who made the world and everything in it." Furthermore, "He who is Lord of heaven and earth does not live in shrines made by human hands, nor is he served by human hands, as though he needed anything, since he himself gives to all mortals life and breath and all things" (vv. 24-25).

The philosophers would have agreed that the gods did not need human temples. Still, Paul's statement stood in sharp contrast to the Epicurean argument that life is solely the result of random atomic movements, and the Stoic belief that the gods determine the fates without concern for humans. It also challenged the worship practices of other Athenians who may have thought it needful to leave food offerings or other gifts at the altars of their patron gods.

Athenians popularly claimed to have sprung from the earth as a separate race from other peoples, but Paul called that belief into question, arguing that all people are descended "from one ancestor" who had been made by God (v. 26a).

Paul's hearers would not have caught his reference to Adam, but they were familiar with the argument that all humans are related. Paul went on to insist that, for all peoples, God had intentionally "allotted the times of their existence and the boundaries of the places where they would

> **A sense of eternity:** Paul's reference to those who had an innate sense of divinity and sought to know more is similar to an argument based on "natural theology" – the idea that one who seriously ponders the magnitude of creation may be led to think there must be some greater power behind it.
>
> The author of Ecclesiastes, sometimes thought to have been influenced by Greek philosophy, believed God had created humans with an inborn sense of something beyond earthly life, but complained that they could not fathom its meaning: "He has made everything suitable for its time; moreover he has put a sense of past and future into their minds, yet they cannot find out what God has done from the beginning to the end" (Eccl. 3:11).

live" (v. 26b). Epicureans considered the gods irrelevant and the Stoics saw them as impersonal, but Paul proclaimed a God who wished to be known and was always near to earnest seekers (v. 27). Paul believed the people of Athens held mistaken beliefs, but he gave them credit for seeking deeper understanding. [**A sense of eternity**]

Philosophical systems search for the meaning of life, but Paul argued that people cannot find it apart from God: "For in him we live and move and have our being" (v. 28a). This would not have sounded strange to the philosophers, who were familiar with the idea that divinity is immanent in creation. Seneca, a Stoic philosopher known during that period, wrote "God is near you, He is with you, He is within you" (Epistle 41.1-2, available at https://en.wikisource.org/wiki/Moral_letters_to_Lucilius/Letter_41).

Having explored areas in which there might be some common ground, Paul moved toward a sharper critique of religions that value images of the gods. He began by quoting one of the Greek poets, who had spoken of humans as offspring of the gods (v. 28b). If the deity is powerful enough to create humankind, Paul argued, then surely any human attempt to portray a god in gold, silver, or stone was doomed to failure (v. 29).

Paul's implication was clear: those who thought one could represent a god through human craftsmanship were living in ignorance. God might have overlooked that in the past, but those who knew better needed to change their ways of thinking and acting. Paul used a form of the verb *metanoeō*, which means to change one's way of life as the result of changing one's thoughts and attitudes: it is commonly translated as "repent" (v. 30).

**For further thought:** Paul insisted that God is near to us: he spoke of those who search for God, "though indeed he is not far from each one of us" (v. 27). If this is true, what things, experiences, or ideas keep us from seeing God more clearly and knowing God better?

Recall that the text begins with Paul being distressed over the evidence of idolatry in Athens. Few of us bow before any sort of image, but we would do well to ask if there are other idols in our lives: anything that takes precedence over our allegiance to God could be considered an idol. How much attention do we devote to the pursuit of money, sex, leisure, physical fitness, and so forth? All of these have their place and all can be positive, but must be kept in perspective lest they become modern-day idols.

Paul's call for his hearers to move from honoring images to putting faith in the true God was not just an exercise in right thinking: he argued that there were eternal consequences. All would face a day of judgment before Christ, Paul said, "the man whom he has appointed," who had come to reveal true righteousness and who had demonstrated his authority by being raised from the dead (v. 31).

The belief in resurrection, in judgment, and in a god who truly cared about humans would contravene both Stoic and Epicurean teachings. One might have expected the council to throw Paul out of town, and some sneered at his teaching, but others asked to hear him again. Luke records that a few people believed, including a member of the Areopagus named Dyonisius and a woman named Damaris, who must have been a woman of some reputation in the community.

What might a modern believer learn from this text? Paul's strategy shows that effective evangelism begins with finding common ground. If we hope to bring others into relationship with Christ, we need to meet them where they are, seek to understand their current beliefs, and look for points of connection before explaining why we believe Christ is the true way.

Paul's words are also an encouragement to all who live in a pluralistic world: Christian believers may be in a minority, but we can always trust that God is near to us, and that we are never alone, for "In him we live and move and have our being." [**For further thought**]

## The Hardest Question
### What poet did Paul quote, and why?

In v. 28, Paul says he is quoting from Greek poets, but it is unclear whether he is citing one poet or two. "For 'In him we live and move and have our being,'" he said, "as even some of your own poets have said, 'For we too are his offspring.'"

The NRSV takes both "In him we live and move and have our being" and "For we too are his offspring" as references to what Greek poets had said. The NIV11 takes a similar approach.

Some other translations assume the first part of the verse is Paul's statement, with only the latter part intended as the words of a Greek poet. The NET2 has "For in him we live and move about and exist, as even some of your own poets have said, 'For we too are his offspring.'" The HCSB follows the same pattern.

A central problem is that the Greek manuscripts were written without punctuation or even spaces between words. Added punctuation such as quotation marks are decisions of the translator, and all translations, to a degree, are interpretations.

Did either of these phrases occur in the work of Greek poets known to us? Commentators often note that Epimenides, a sixth-century BCE poet from Crete, had said something similar to "In him we live and move and have our being." More likely, as noted in the lesson, Paul may have been referencing Seneca, who had written "God is near you, He is with you, He is within you" (Epistle 41.1-2).

The second reference, "For we too are his offspring," is generally attributed to Aratus, who lived in Macedonia during the third century BCE. His only surviving work, titled "Phaenomena," is a paean to Zeus that praises the God for works on land and in the sea. G.R. Mair translated line 5 as "For we are also his offspring." (A.W. and G.R. Mair, *Callimachus, Hymns and Epigrams. Lycophron. Aratus*, Loeb Classical Library, vol. 129 [William Heinemann, 1921]). Whether Paul intended to quote one poet or two is unclear, but it appears that he carefully chose language that would be familiar to his audience, using it as a bridge to his own teachings about Christ.

# Sixth Sunday of Easter

## Second Reading
## Psalm 66

# Testimony

*Come and hear, all you who fear God, and I will tell what he has done for me. (Ps. 66:5)*

It was common, at one time, for churches to hold occasional "testimony meetings." Often held on a Sunday night, they offered an opportunity for church members to stand up or come to the pulpit and speak of ways they believed God had blessed them.

While there are always risks to giving a microphone to anyone who wants to speak, some churches still offer periodic opportunities for such sharing, recognizing that public testimony can be important both to the one who speaks of their experience with God, and to those who listen.

Today's text is a psalm of praise that focuses on testimony, both communal and individual. The lectionary text begins at v. 8, but we will examine the entire psalm.

### Praise for God who blesses Israel
### (vv. 1-12)

The psalm is found within the "Elohistic Psalter" (Psalms 42–72), a collection in which the preferred name for God is Elohim rather than Yahweh. Most psalms address and speak mainly of "the LORD" (*Yahweh*), but these speak to and of "God" (*'elohîm*). The first part of the psalm, vv. 1-12, is written as a communal hymn for liturgical use, while vv. 13-20 shift to an individual's testimony. The psalm is likely a composite, originating as two psalms, but later combined to show the importance of both communal and individual testimony.

Given that the psalm speaks of bringing animal sacrifices as an offering of praise, the psalm would have derived from a period when the temple existed. The psalm's upbeat tone may point to a setting in the first temple period,

though the reference to testing and survival in vv. 9-12 may suggest a post-exilic experience.

The communal part of the psalm consists of three stanzas, each of which begins with an imperative call to praise and then recites reasons why praise is appropriate.

The first stanza begins with a universal invitation: "Make a joyful noise to God, all the earth; sing the glory of his name; give to him glorious praise" (vv. 1-2). An alternate translation could be "Give a shout to God," or even "Raise a cheer for God!" The NRSV's "Make a joyful noise" assumes that cheers for God would be exuberant, as there is no word for "joyful" in the text: the same verb could be used for a war whoop, as a rallying signal, or as a cry of distress. The same phrase, where the context implies joy, is found in Ps. 98:4, 6 and 100:1, where praise is addressed to Yahweh.

The call to praise is not limited to Israel in vv. 1-4, for it recognizes God as the ruler over all. It is an idealistic portrayal that imagines all the peoples of the earth worshiping and singing praise to God – that even enemies would recognize God's awesome deeds and cringe in fear, powerless to do anything other than worship (vv. 3-4).

With v. 5, the psalm shifts to a call for other nations to "Come and see what God has done" on Israel's behalf, amazing deeds that should impress all peoples. Traditions of the Exodus were the quintessential story of deliverance for Israel, and v. 6 looks back to it. It appears to recall two miraculous accounts: how the Israelites crossed the sea on dry land in departing from Egypt (Exodus 14), and then crossed the Jordan river on foot as they entered the land of promise (Joshua 4). It is also possible that the psalmist had only the crossing of the sea in mind, using "river" as a poetic parallel to "sea." Elsewhere in the Hebrew Bible, "the river" is not used for the Jordan: in most cases it refers to the Euphrates.

In either case, the Exodus event was remembered as the prime evidence for God's delivering power and God's care for Israel. "There we rejoiced in him," the psalmist said, alluding to the triumphant songs of Miriam and Moses in Exod. 15:1-21. The point was that the display of God's power in the past should serve as a challenge for Israel to remain faithful in the present, and for their enemies to stay in their place, for God's "eyes keep watch on the nations" (v. 7).

The third stanza begins with a third imperative: "Bless our God, O peoples, let the sound of his praise be heard" (v. 8). Here the ebullience of earlier verses is tempered by memories of testing and danger as well as rescue. Why should the people bless God? Because God "has kept us among the living, and has not let our feet slip" (v. 9).

Did the psalmist have in mind battles fought and won, or the period of exile when the nation's existence seemed threatened, and yet it had survived? In either case, the poet attributed both testing and deliverance to God: "For you, O God, have tested us; you have tried us as silver is tried. You brought us into the net; you laid burdens on our backs; you let people ride over our heads; we went through fire and through water; yet you have brought us out to a spacious place" (vv. 10-12).

The imagery of being caught in a net or trampled by the enemy's horses suggests a time of severe testing, as when silver goes through the refiner's fire. "We went through fire and water" may also be related to the analogy of metallurgy when iron is formed in fire and then doused in water to temper it. It could also be understood as a literary merism, where two diverse things are named as representative of everything in between. In this case, "fire and water" could represent the whole range of trials the people had experienced.

What did the psalmist mean by the claim "yet you have brought us out to a spacious place" (v. 12)? One might picture a reference to Israel's entry into Canaan, the land of promise, as a spacious place. If we think in terms of the physical landscape, that would be more likely than a postexilic setting, in which the returning exiles were granted rights to a very small area surrounding Jerusalem. [Spacious, or saturated?]

---

**Spacious, or saturated?** The conclusion of v. 12 affirms that God had brought Israel to "a spacious place," according to the NRSV. The NET speaks of it as "an open place." But, the NIV11 and NASB20 call it "a place of abundance," following the lead of the KJV, which reads "a wealthy place."

Why the differences? The Masoretic text has the word r'vayah, which means "saturation." Most translators emend the text to r'vachah, which suggests a "wide open place," or metaphorically, a place of relief. This reading goes back as far as the early Greek translation, the Septuagint, which was based on Hebrew manuscripts preserved in Egypt. Other Greek manuscripts have ra'shēnu, which could indicate "our first" or "our head" place.

Translations implying a place of abundance or wealth apparently read "saturation" metaphorically as a well-watered place, or rely on the idea of a first-class place.

---

It is possible to read the text metaphorically, as a place of peace and well-being, but the physical image remains. The poet was clearly speaking of present experience, and images from the past were often recalled in expressing ideals of the present.

## Praise for God who blesses me
### (vv. 13-20)

Verse 13 brings us to an individual's testimony of deliverance and praise. It appears to reflect the words of a single person, but in later worship it may have been spoken in worship by a priest or other leader in remembrance of the earlier testimony. Some scholars argue, in contrast, that what follows was not really the prayer of an individual, but a model for how members of the congregation could and should respond to God in times of trial.

Whether we are to read it as a representative model or an individual testimony, the psalmist speaks of finding himself in a place of serious distress (v. 14), at which time he had made a vow to offer sacrifice and praise to God, which he now intends to fulfill: "I will come into your house with burnt offerings; I will pay you my vows, those that my lips uttered and my mouth promised when I was in trouble" (vv. 13-14).

The depth of the person's difficulties may be reflected in the magnitude of sacrifices offered: "burnt offerings of fatlings, with the smoke of the sacrifice of rams; I will make an offering of bulls and goats" (v. 15). The sacrifices

**Sacrifices:** Most sacrifices in Israel's worship, whether offered at the temple or in earlier settings, were not completely burned. With sacrifices of "peace" or "well-being" (sh°lamîm), only a tiny portion of the animals were actually burned on the altar, mainly the visceral fat. After slaughter in the temple precincts and removal of the fat to be burned, the priests were given a portion for their own use, but most of the animal would be cooked and consumed by the worshiper and his family. Only in the case of whole burnt offerings ('ôlôth) were the animals totally devoted to God and completely burned on the altar—and that is precisely the type of offering the psalmist professes to be making.

(For more, see my article "Sacrifice" in the *Mercer Dictionary of the Bible* [Mercer University Press, 1990], 783-784, or consult any good Bible dictionary.)

are not only great in quantity (rams, bulls, and goats), but also in quality (fatlings) and in extent (burnt offerings). Most animal sacrifices were eaten rather than burned, but the psalmist claims that his offerings were to be wholly devoted to God. **[Sacrifices]**

The promised sacrifices would have been very expensive, but that was not the extent of the worshiper's response to God for answered prayer. He also wants to testify of what God has done for the benefit of others: "Come and hear, all you who fear God, and I will tell what he has done for me" (v. 16). The psalmist had cried out when in trouble, but now shouted with gratitude for his deliverance (v. 17).

**He heard his voice:** Votive inscriptions from other Semitic peoples reflect similar sentiments of gratitude for answered prayer following a vow. A *stele* written in Old Aramaic commissioned by Bar-Hadad (known in the Bible as Ben-Hadad), the king of Aram, was devoted "to his lord, to Melqart, which he vowed to him, and he heard his voice" (A. Lemaire, "La stele araméene de Barhadad," *Orientalia* 53 [1984], 337-49, lines 3-5).

Phoenician and Punic votive inscriptions also typically described a request that had been made of the gods (most commonly Baal Hammon or Baal-Shemaim, often in conjunction with his consort Tannit). The inscriptions typically concluded with the phrase "because he heard his voice" and a reference to blessing (H. Donner and W. Röllig, *Kanaanäishe und aramäische Inschriften* [Otto Harrassowitz, 1964-66], inscriptions 63, 64, 68, 72A, 72B, 78, 79, 82, 84–88, 94, 97–99, 103–111, and 113–116). (See also my article "Hannah asked, and God heard," *Review and Expositor*, Spring 2002, 143-144.)

The psalmist's testimony declares his faithfulness to God as a motivating reason for God's response. "If I had cherished iniquity in my heart, the Lord would not have listened," he said. "But truly God *has* listened; he has given heed to the words of my prayer" (vv. 18-19, emphasis added). **[He heard his voice]**

The psalmist prayed from an earnest heart, believed God had responded positively, and testified of what God had done. "Blessed be God," the worshiper concluded, "because he has not rejected my prayer or removed his steadfast love from me" (v. 20).

This psalm could raise anxiety for readers who wonder why they have prayed and God did not respond in the way they wished. The text describes one case in which a worshiper did get the answer he sought, but it should not be read as a promise that all prayers – however earnest and innocent the petitioner – will be answered in positive fashion. The book of Psalms also contains many laments, some of which conclude in praise, but some still mired in distress.

The psalm challenges us to consider our own record when it comes to making good on our promises. We don't call them vows, but many of us have also prayed, in a time of trouble, something such as "Oh Lord, if you will get me out of this situation, I will turn my life around / never do it again / attend church every Sunday" or any number of other promises. How faithful have we been in upholding our end of the prayer?

The psalm does not promise that our prayers will always be answered, even if reinforced with a vow, nor does it necessarily hold up vow-making as the ideal form of prayer. It does, however, point to the importance of gratitude for blessings we have received, and of testimony, the willingness to go on record with stories of what God has done for us.

### The Hardest Question
#### Why were vows so important?

In the ancient Near Eastern context, vows were conditional promises, generally made in a time of distress, that asked something of God and promised something in return. It was hoped that the promise to do something for God would motivate the deity to respond positively. For example, when threatened by the Canaanite king of Arad, the Israelites reportedly made a vow that if God would give victory, they would destroy all of the plunder as devoted to God (Num. 21:1-3). When childless Hannah was desperate for a change of fortune, she begged God for a son and promised to return the child to God (1 Sam. 1:1-11). Narrative accounts of other vows can be found in Gen. 28:18-22 (Jacob), Judg. 11:29-40 (Jephthah), and 2 Sam. 15:7-9 (Absalom, who was probably lying).

But how would one make a vow if he or she had nothing to give? One option was Hannah's choice, but in other cases that was impractical. This was a particular problem for women, because family property officially belonged to the males. In such cases, people sometimes offered a particular type of service, such as becoming a Nazirite for a certain period of time. Nazirites displayed their devotion to God by not cutting their hair or beard, abstaining from alcohol, and refraining from touching anything dead (Numbers 6).

Other types of service or behavior are not spelled out in scripture, but might have involved abstinence from sex, caring for the poor, or other pledges. Regulations found in Numbers 30 indicate that, if a woman made a vow, her husband or father could annul the vow on first hearing, but not afterward. If a son made a vow, however, it had to be honored – which is why David had little choice in allowing Absalom to travel to Hebron, even though he may have suspected that Absalom's claim was a ruse.

Texts such as Psalm 66 show that one might also offer animal sacrifices in payment of a vow, and the psalms also give evidence that one could promise to praise God publicly in return for requests that were granted. (For more on this, see "The Hardest Question" for Ps. 116:1-4, 12-19, the second reading for the third Sunday of Easter.)

Vows were serious business. Whatever was promised must be paid: "When a man makes a vow to the LORD, or swears an oath to bind himself by a pledge, he shall not break his word; he shall do according to all that proceeds out of his mouth" (Num. 30:2). The same rules applied to women who made vows. That is why Hannah brought Samuel to live at the temple, though it must have been very hard, and why Jephthah reportedly followed through on his rashly worded vow that led to the sacrifice of his daughter.

A negative lesson comes from the Ugaritic story of Kirta (or Keret), which speaks of a king who vowed to pay the goddess Athirat much gold and silver if he could marry a princess named Huriya. He married Huriya, but failed to make good on his vow, and the goddess struck him with an illness that brought him near death before the god El intervened and saved his life (available in many publications, including J.C.L. Gibson, *Canaanite Myths and Legends*, 2nd ed. [T.&T. Clark, 1978]).

(For more on vows, see my book, *Vows in the Hebrew Bible and the Ancient Near East*, Journal for the Study of the Old Testament Supplement Series 147 [Sheffield Academic Press, 1992], 150-161; an earlier article, "Conditional Vows in the Psalms of Lament: A New Approach to an Old Problem," in *The Listening Heart: Essays in Psalms and Wisdom in Honor of Roland E. Murphy, O. Carm.*, ed. Ken Hoglund, et. al. [Sheffield, JSOT Press, 1987], 77-94; also "Were Nazirite Vows Unconditional?" *Catholic Biblical Quarterly*, vol. 51 [July 1989]: 409422; and "Women Making Vows," in Carol Meyers, ed., *Women in Scripture: A Dictionary of Named and Unnamed Women in the Hebrew Bible, the Apocryphal/Deuterocanonical Books and the New Testament* [Eerdmans, 2001]; and the generic article "Vow," *International Standard Bible Encyclopedia* [Eerdmans, 1988] 4:998-999.)

# Sixth Sunday of Easter

## Third Reading
## 1 Peter 3:13-22*

# A New Approach

*...in your hearts sanctify Christ as Lord. Always be ready to make your defense to anyone who demands from you an accounting for the hope that is in you. (1 Pet. 3:15)*

Who wants to talk about suffering? It's not a popular subject of conversation. Then again, talking about adversity is less painful than experiencing it.

Some readers might think that simply reading 1 Peter brings on a bit of suffering, for the first few verses of ch. 3 reflect the ancient author's male bias: he instructed women to live under the authority of their husbands, adorning themselves with piety rather than jewels and braided hair (vv. 1-6). Husbands, meanwhile, were to honor their wives as "the weaker sex" (v. 7)

Some modern Christians continue to celebrate the writer's endorsement of male dominance as a biblical principle, while others see it as an artifact of his societal context that did not appreciate gender equality. In either case, we need to look past the author's cultural coloring and focus on his admonishment for *all* believers to "have unity of spirit, sympathy, love for one another, a tender heart, and a humble mind" (v. 8).

### Make pain count
### (vv. 13-17)

In vv. 13-14 the writer turns to the subject of suffering, but not for the first time. In ch. 1, the author addressed his readers as exiles who suffered various trials on the road to a purified faith (1:6-7). In 2:18-21, he encouraged slaves to be patient and respond with goodness even when they suffered under harsh masters. In 3:9, he called for believers to respond to abuse with blessings rather than returning evil for evil.

The author understood that suffering is a part of life, and God does not make Christians exempt from it. Indeed, some may suffer precisely because they are Christian.

When Jesus talked about unjust suffering in Luke 13:1-5 and John 9:1-9, he did not explain why bad things happen to good people, though he did refute the popular idea that suffering is divine payback for personal or family sin. Sometimes adversity has no apparent connection with personal failure on anyone's part: everyone is responsible for his or her own behavior, and often innocent people are harmed.

The writer chose to speak about suffering because his readers faced regular ostracism and needed encouragement to help them deal with it in a positive way. In 3:10-12 he had cited a psalm that promised blessing to the righteous, and now in 3:13-17 (along with 4:12-19), he offers counsel to Christians who suffer unjustly.

Common sense suggests that helpful people would seem less likely to get hurt: "Who will harm you if you are eager to do good?" (v. 13). Yet, we know that suffering is a reality, and sometimes good people face severe trials.

How could the author say that "even if you do suffer for doing right, you are blessed" (v. 14a)? Can blessing come from suffering? Perhaps he had in mind Jesus' beatitudes about those who are insulted or persecuted for the

---

*A similar text, 1 Pet. 3:18-22, is used on the First Sunday in Lent in Year B.

> **What fear?** The reading found in the NRSV, NIV, and HCSB, "Do not fear what they fear" is a legitimate translation, but not the only one. A literal reading would be "the fear of them do not fear." The above translations take "the fear of them" to mean "what they fear" (a subjective genitive), but the context favors the objective genitive sense of "don't fear the fear of them," or "Don't let the fear of them make you afraid." Thus, NAS95 has "Do not fear their intimidation," and the KJV has "Do not be afraid of their terror," while the NET reads "Do not be terrified by them."

sake of righteousness (Matt. 5:10-11). Matthew used the same word: *makarios*, "blessed."

One of the worst aspects of suffering is the uncertainty of how long it will last or whether it will get worse. We shouldn't be afraid, the author says (v. 14b). "Do not fear what they fear" is a quotation from Isa. 8:12, where Isaiah called on King Ahaz to trust God and not fear the Assyrians, as the kings of Israel and Syria did. **[What fear?]**

Readers of 1 Peter were not troubled by Assyrian conquerors, but by neighbors or people in power who rejected or discriminated against them because of their faith. The same words can be translated as "Don't let the fear of them make you afraid."

We know that other people can be mean or hurtful, but that should not intimidate us: the fear of being harmed can be worse than the hurt itself.

When struggles come, we can cope because we have the hope that comes with knowing Christ. Rather than living in service to fear, Peter says, we are to "sanctify Christ as Lord" in our hearts, showing reverence and obedience to Christ. Confident of our relationship with Christ, we can be ready to explain what makes us hopeful and positive despite hardship or rejection by others (v. 15).

As we defend our faith, 1 Peter insists that we do so with kindness (v. 16). Christians are not immune to arrogance and the temptation to speak in harsh or self-righteous ways, but the potential benefit of our witness is more important than any satisfaction we might gain from a verbal retaliation. Others may bring shame on themselves in mistreating us, but we should not bring shame upon ourselves or the cause of Christ with a hurtful response.

Unfortunately, some who call themselves Christians have done that, for example, a hate group known as Westboro Baptist Church, not affiliated with any denomination. For years the largely family-centered church picketed both events and funerals with grotesque and offensive signs accusing the deceased of various sins and predicting eternal torment. While claiming to defend the faith, they served only to make Christians look foolish and intemperate.

Others may act more quietly, leaving strident and cartoonish gospel tracts in waiting rooms or bathroom stalls that depict sinners burning in hell. These do not serve the gospel well: a positive and hope-filled witness is far more effective than a judgmental screed, and is more likely to foster renewed courage and healing for our own hearts, too.

The power of one's witness can be proportional to the circumstances under which it is given. When life is going well, it can be easy to have faith and easy to talk about it. When times are hard, the ability to maintain our hope in Christ and speak of it may be particularly impressive. Many people have been inspired, for example, by believers such as Corrie Ten Boom and others who sheltered Jews during the Holocaust at great risk to themselves.

If we are going to suffer, Peter says, it should be for doing good and not evil. Facing suffering in this way is a part of God's will for us – not in the sense that God causes our affliction, but because faithful suffering can test and strengthen our faith. As the pain of strenuous exercise makes our bodies stronger and more fit, the testing of our faith contributes to spiritual health and confidence.

### Remember Jesus' example
### (vv. 18-22)

The author consistently pointed to Jesus as the prime example of one who faced unjust suffering with courage and conviction (1:6-7, 2:18-25, 3:18-22, 4:12-19). In vv. 18-22 he reminded readers under duress that Jesus willingly "suffered for sins once for all, the righteous for the unrighteous, in order to bring you to God" (v. 18). **[Once for all]**

But what do we make of the author's following claim that Jesus, dead in the flesh but alive in the spirit, "made a proclamation to the spirits in prison" (v. 19a)? The spirits in question lived in former times, he wrote, during the period when Noah was building the ark, and were disobedient, presumably to God (v. 20).

**Once for all:** As Richard Vinson points out, Peter's declaration that Jesus suffered for sins "once for all" is a reminder that Christians should also be done with sin and move on:

Christ suffered for sins *once*: the force of that word does not become apparent until 4:1-3, when 1 Peter argues that the time is long past for Gentile shenanigans. He is not making a supersessionist point; in other words, the idea is not "he died once, so animal sacrifice is no longer necessary," as Hebrews argues. It is not even "he died once, so that you never have to die" – the Johannine move. First Peter's point is that Jesus dealt with sin, and then started a new chapter; in the same way, you readers should be finished with sin and not still fooling around with it. ... Be done with sin; be done with the temptations your neighbors dangle. in front of you; that time is past – turn the page. (*1 & 2 Peter, Jude,* Smyth & Helwys Bible Commentary [Smyth & Helwys, 2010], 173)

Just what was the writer talking about? Ancient Hebrews believed that all people who died went to a place called Sheol, thought to be located somewhere beneath the roots of the mountains or the bottom of the sea. In Sheol, both the righteous and the unrighteous continued to maintain a shadowy existence tenuously connected to their physical remains. They were not subject to either judgment or reward; all were considered to be at rest (see Job 3:13, for example). Many readers assume this is where Peter thought of Jesus going after the crucifixion, but he says Jesus preached "to the spirits in prison." Sheol was not thought of as a prison.

The text appears to reflect an early belief that Jesus went to the land of the dead between the time of his death and resurrection, but the extent of his preaching there is unclear. It is likely that the author had in mind a tradition from the book of 1 Enoch, an apocalyptic text written late in the postexilic period and attributed to Enoch. The book was popular in the first century, known to both Jews and Christians, and cited elsewhere in the New Testament (Jude 1:14-15, 2 Pet. 2:4-5).

The book of Enoch expands on the stories of the flood, including the account of certain "sons of God" who consorted with human women in the years prior to the flood (Gen. 6:1-4). According to 1 Enoch 18, the fallen spirits were condemned to a special prison. (For more on this, see "The Hardest Question" below).

This is likely the audience the author of 1 Peter had in mind when he said that Jesus "preached to the spirits in prison." The tradition of Jesus' preaching to the dead persists in the Apostles' Creed, which asserts that Jesus "Was crucified, dead, and buried: He descended into hell; the third day he rose again from the dead ..."

While in the land of the dead, according to this view, Jesus preached the good news of repentance and grace to those who came before him – or at least to the disobedient contemporaries of Noah who died in the flood.

Perhaps the writer's intent is to suggest that Christ will go to any length to reach out to the fallen – even to disobedient angels – and offer them hope.

In any case, the reference to Noah and his family being saved "through water" led the writer to thoughts of baptism, the central symbol of public faith. Indeed, for the writer of 1 Peter, Noah's salvation "through water" was the model for "baptism, which this prefigured" (v. 21a).

We are not saved by the act of baptism, as a literal reading of v. 21b might suggest, but through repentance and trust in Christ that leads to the waters of baptism. As the public profession of our faith, baptism sets us on the road to faithful living and ultimate salvation through the resurrected Christ, portrayed as sitting at the right hand of God and exalted over all other powers (v. 22).

Suffering is a part of life, and faithfully following the road of a Jesus-centered lifestyle will not deliver us from it. Such is life, but believers are not called to an ordinary life. As followers of Jesus, our life is bound up with Christ's life. Guided by Jesus' example of confident endurance in the face of difficult days, 1 Peter claims, we may suffer, but we will be blessed, and our witness will become a powerful blessing to others. That's good news all around.

### The Hardest Question
#### Where – and to whom – did Jesus preach in 1 Pet. 3:18-20?

Jesus' preaching "to the spirits in prison" is most commonly understood to mean that Jesus went to the land of the dead between his death and resurrection and preached to those who died before his incarnation, so they might also have a chance to respond to the gospel. This belief, in Catholic tradition, is celebrated on Holy Saturday (the day between Good Friday and Easter). It is commonly known as the "Harrowing of Hell." Support for that belief draws mainly on nonbiblical writings such as "The Acts of Peter and Paul" and "The Acts of Pilate" (a subsection within "The Gospel of Nicodemus"). The tradition gets little support from 1 Pet. 3:18-22, though 1 Pet. 4:6 could be interpreted that way: "For this is the reason the gospel was proclaimed even to the dead, so that, though they had been judged in the flesh as everyone is judged, they might live in the spirit as God does."

Some scholars argue that "made alive in the spirit" is itself a reference to the resurrection. In either case, whatever preaching activity Peter had in mind would not be limited to the period between Good Friday evening and Easter Sunday morning.

The question of Jesus' destination is more important than the timing. First Peter 3:18-22 does not say Jesus went to hell (a New Testament concept) or to Sheol (the Old Testament land of the dead), but to spirits who were "in prison." The Bible does not elsewhere speak of the dead as being in prison, so it is likely that the author had in mind something other than the generic realm of the dead.

Of even more importance is the intended audience, which is related to the destination. Peter says that Jesus "made a proclamation to the spirits in prison." The word for "spirits" (a neuter dative plural of *pneúma*) is not typically used for deceased humans, who the New Testament refers to as "the dead" (*nekroi*) or as "souls" (*psychoi*). The plural form of *pneúma* commonly referred to supernatural beings such as "unclean spirits" (Matt. 8:16, 10:1, 12:45, and many others) or to angelic beings created by God (Heb. 1:14, 12:9; Rev. 1:4, 3:1, 4:5, 5:6). This fits with Peter's identification of "the spirits in prison" as those "who in former times did not obey, when God waited patiently in the days of Noah, during the building of the ark, in which a few, that is, eight persons, were saved through water" (v. 20). "Persons" translates *psuchoi*, or "souls," in contrast to "spirits."

The story of the flood, beginning in Genesis 6, preserves a tradition that certain "sons of God" saw that the daughters of men were lovely and forsook their responsibilities in heaven to live on earth and marry human women, presumably giving rise to a race of giants. In the Hebrew Bible, "sons of God" were thought of as super-

natural beings who served God, sat on the heavenly council, and did God's bidding (Job 1:6, 2:1). We would call them angels. In other contexts, heavenly beings were described with the word *mal'ach*, literally, "messenger."

So, Peter's comment in 3:18-22 seems to be limited to the "sons of God" who disobeyed and came to earth during the time of Noah, not to deceased persons who inhabited the realm of the dead.

Peter and his readers would have been familiar with the book of 1 Enoch, a nonbiblical Jewish writing we still possess, but thath most Protestants do not know. Probably written in the second or third century before Christ, the apocalypse was attributed to the ancient Enoch, portrayed in the genealogies of Genesis as the great-grandfather of Noah (Gen. 5:18-29). Enoch reportedly walked so closely with God that he did not die, but "he was no more, because God took him" (Gen. 5:24).

The book of 1 Enoch elaborates imaginatively on stories of the flood, including the fate of the spirits who intermarried with humans in Genesis 6. According to 1 Enoch 15, the angels and human women begat a race of giants, who oppressed other people, filled the earth with wickedness, and spawned demons. As a result, the fallen angels were imprisoned within a pit inside a mountain near the edge of the earth (1 Enoch 18).

Similar stories are told in the apocryphal book of Jubilees (5:2-11 and 10:1-14) and the Testament of Reuben (5:6).

These pre-Christian traditions, popular in some Jewish circles, are the most likely background of Peter's remarks. The book of Jude (vv. 14-15) specifically quotes from 1 Enoch, speaking in v. 6 of angels who left their proper dwelling and were being "kept in eternal chains in deepest darkness for the judgment of the great Day" (a verse that is quoted in 2 Pet. 2:4).

Peter does not describe either location or the content of Jesus' preaching to the "spirits." In the 1 Enoch traditions, Enoch declared God's judgment on the fallen angels. Since it is likely that Peter knew this tradition, it is unlikely that he would think Jesus needed to repeat a message of judgment alone. Thus, though 1 Peter's use of "made a proclamation" or "preached" is ambiguous, we may hope the writer had in mind a redemptive message.

# Sixth Sunday of Easter

## Fourth Reading
## John 14:15-21

# Love Shows

*They who have my commandments and keep them are those who love me; and those who love me*
*will be loved by my Father, and I will love them and reveal myself to them. (John 14:21)*

Many years ago, I spent a year teaching junior high math and science in a school that was part of an orphanage. Very few of the children were orphans in the traditional sense of the word: they had parents, but the parents were either unable or unwilling to care for them.

Never have I been surrounded by so many people who were so desperately in need of love. Some of the children openly craved attention and affection, while others hid their hurt behind a wall of anger and were hard to reach.

Today's text brings good news for those who trust in Jesus and yearn for relationship with the Father. In their last hours together, Jesus looked his closest followers in the eyes and promised: "I will not leave you orphaned." That affirmation alone makes this text worth careful study, but there is more. Read on.

### From there to here

Today's text comes midway in Jesus' "Farewell Discourse," a collection of traditions the author has put together, sometimes awkwardly, in chs. 13–17. The section purports to describe the last hours Jesus spent with the disciples before his arrest. It was a time of deep uncertainty and confusion for the disciples.

The dramatic discourse begins with a note that "Jesus knew that his hour had come to depart from this world and go to the Father" (13:1), followed by an observation that "the devil" had inspired Judas Iscariot to betray Jesus (13:2).

John's gospel does not include typical elements of the Lord's Supper, and indeed, portrays the evening's events as taking place on the night before the Passover rather than it being a Passover meal: the author wanted to depict Jesus' crucifixion as taking place on the day of preparation for the Passover, when the Passover lambs were being slaughtered (19:14, 31).

The focus at the supper is on Jesus' act of leaving the table to wash his disciples' feet, a moment of high emotion preceding his prediction that one of them would betray him (13:21-30), that he would soon depart (13:33), and that Peter would deny him (13:36-38).

The disciples were dismayed, and Jesus offered comfort, promising that though he was going to the Father, their relationship would continue, and they would do even greater works than he (14:1-14).

As we might guess, confusion reigned. The disciples struggled to understand how Jesus could be one with the Father and yet returning to the Father, how Jesus could be departing and also remain available to them.

This brings us to today's text, in which Jesus offered further consolation, if not explanation, of what was to come.

### Jesus, love, and the Spirit
### (vv. 15-17)

Jesus declared that those who truly followed him – those who would do even greater works than he – would be those who not only loved him, but who also demonstrated their love by keeping his commandments (v. 15). Earlier, Jesus had summarized his teaching in a "new commandment," namely, "that you love one another. Just as I have loved you, you also should love one another" (13:34).

> **The Paraclete:** In the Fourth Gospel, Jesus speaks of God's indwelling presence as the Paraclete or "Spirit of truth" a total of five times, all in his farewell discourse. They are found in John 14:16, 26; 15:26; and 16:8-11, 12-15.

Jesus then assured his disciples that they would not be alone: "And I will ask the Father, and he will give you another Advocate, to be with you forever" (v. 16). John's favorite term for the Holy Spirit is *paraklētos*, or "Paraclete," a word derived from someone who is called alongside another. It could also be translated as "counselor," "helper," "encourager," "comforter," or used in the sense of an "advocate" who works on behalf of another. [**The Paraclete**]

Jesus promised to send "another Advocate," the Spirit, to continue the work he had begun in them. Jesus had been a Paraclete to the disciples as he had taught and exhorted and counseled them during his earthly ministry. "This is the Spirit of Truth," he said, "whom the world cannot receive, because it neither sees him nor knows him" (v. 17a).

Earlier, Jesus had identified himself as the Way, the Truth, and the Life (v. 6). After Jesus had completed his mission on earth, the Spirit would continue his revelatory work, keeping the truth of Jesus present through the lives of believers. "The world" had rejected Jesus and would also reject the Spirit, but believers would know the Spirit "because he abides with you, and he will be in you"

> **The world:** In the Fourth Gospel, "the world" (*kosmos*) is often used, not just as a reference to the physical world ("in the world"), but as a designation for the world's population, in particular those who reject the message of Jesus.
>
> The natural state of people is to be part of the world, but those who trust in Jesus are called out of the world and into fellowship with him as children of God (1:10-13). God loved the world enough to send Jesus to save rather than condemn the world (3:16-18), but not all accept him. This leads to inevitable differences between those who remain in the world of opposition to Jesus, and those who follow him: "If the world hates you, be aware that it hated me before it hated you. If you belonged to the world, the world would love you as its own. Because you do not belong to the world, but I have chosen you out of the world—therefore the world hates you" (15:18-19, cp. 17:13-25).
>
> We continue that distinction when we refer to "worldly" desires or actions that are in opposition to Jesus' teachings.

(v. 17). Although Jesus-in-the-flesh, the first Advocate, would be departing soon, he had promised that the second Advocate "will be with you forever" (v. 16). [**The world**]

While Jesus' promise offered great comfort, the author presents it in a conditional way: "*If you love me, you will keep my commandments. And (then?)* I will ask the Father, and he will give you another Advocate …" (vv. 15-16, emphasis added). The Paraclete would come to those who loved Jesus and demonstrated their love by keeping his commandment to love others.

Later, Jesus would aver that the greatest display of love was one's willingness to die for one's friends (15:13), and in his crucifixion, he demonstrated just that kind of love. We are often so quick to seek the comfort in this passage that we fail to ponder its implications: the coming of the Spirit would be a gift, but it came with a demand. The presence of the Paraclete is not a given, even for those who claim to be believers.

### Jesus, the Father, and those who love them
#### (vv. 18-21)

Jesus expected his disciples to live out his challenge to love, and he offered further words of assurance. "I will not leave you orphaned; I am coming to you" (v. 18). This promise is the hinge around which the preceding and following verses turn. Those who love Jesus and obey his commands would not be bereft. Though people of "the world" would no longer see Jesus, he would still be present in the lives of his followers: "you will see me; because I live, you also will live" (v. 19).

Jesus' promise of presence and life in this context did not point to a future "Second Coming" or to anticipated life in heaven, but applied fully to the present: because Jesus lives, we live. When the Paraclete arrived, Jesus said, "you will know that I am in my Father, and you in me, and I in you" (v. 20). This is how we "see" Jesus, through the inner knowledge that not only is Jesus related to the Father, but he dwells among us.

Some interpreters major on the mystical in interpreting this passage, but the focus is not on an individual sort of spiritual union with Christ: it is the assurance that Christ through the Spirit remains present with those who love him and obey his commands. The pronoun "you" in this verse is plural, and the preposition for "in" (*'en*) can also be translated as "among." We experience the

Advocate/Spirit's presence most clearly in a community of faith and love where no one feels like an orphan.

There is a switch in v. 21, however, though we wouldn't know it from reading the NRSV: "They who have my commandments and keep them are those who love me; and those who love me will be loved by my Father, and I will love them and reveal myself to them."

While the NRSV translates the entire verse in the plural, the author has carefully switched to singular pronouns and verbs. It is as if he has turned from the disciples to address the reader directly, challenging each of us to know that "The person who has my commandments and obeys them is the one who loves me. The one who loves me will be loved by my father, and I will love him and will reveal myself to him" (NET).

The NIV11 takes a similar approach, using "them" in the modern sense of a singular, non-gendered pronoun: "The one who loves me will be loved by my Father, and I too will love them and show myself to them."

This does not detract from the community aspect of the promise, but serves as an individual challenge to the reader, for that is the author's purpose. He would later declare, "But these are written so that you may come to believe that Jesus is the Messiah, the Son of God, and that through believing you may have life in his name" (20:31).

There it is, then. We are never apart from Jesus' care, from the Advocate's presence – so long as we love Jesus and keep his commands. That is not the only option: we can live as selfishly as the world and be just as blind to Jesus' presence. If we would know Jesus, however, and know that he lives with us as surely as with the father, we will be people who love.

Showing our love for Jesus involves far more than singing praise songs or humming "Oh, How I Love Jesus." It involves more than wearing a cross around our necks or planting one in our front yard. We show our love for Jesus by loving each other, and by loving the people Jesus loves, even when it is hard, even when we are not loved in return.

The gospel challenges us to follow Jesus by living as he lived, loving others unselfishly and trusting in the presence of his Spirit to lead us in the right way. We may often feel lost in this world, separated from others and useless as instruments of the kingdom. But we are never so lost that Jesus cannot find us, never so far away that he cannot hear us when we call, never so incompetent that God cannot show saving love to others through us. The promises of Jesus and the presence of the Spirit remind us that we are valued and useful participants in God's ongoing kingdom because we know Jesus – and more importantly, Jesus knows us.

Jesus promised that he would not leave us adrift, those who love him, and one of the ways we show that love is to live so that no one among us feels orphaned, but accepted and drawn into relationship with the same Lord we have come to love.

### The Hardest Question
### How conditional is the promise of the Paraclete?

The author presents the promise of the Paraclete as conditioned on whether our love for Jesus is shown in love toward others. Is this a simple "this for that"? Verse 22 suggests the possibility of exclusion: "Judas (not Iscariot) said to him, 'Lord, how is it that you will reveal yourself to us, and not to the world?'"

Jesus answered, "Those who love me will keep my word, and my Father will love them, and we will come to them and make our home with them" (v. 23).

The author longs for a universal response to the gospel. He believes Jesus came "so that everyone who believes in him may not perish but have eternal life" (3:16). He writes so that readers "may come to believe that Jesus is the Messiah, the Son of God, and that through believing you may have life in his name" (20:31).

John hopes that more will be saved, citing Jesus' saying "I have other sheep that do not belong to this fold. I must bring them also, and they will listen to my voice. So there will be one flock, one shepherd" (10:16). He credits Jesus with affirming "And I, when I am lifted up from the earth, will draw all people to myself" (12:32).

There is no limit to God's love in John's gospel, but people remain free to choose whether to join Jesus' flock and know the Spirit as Comforter/Advocate.

Jesus demonstrated true love and called his followers to love as he did. The Spirit is at home within believers who are open-hearted people of love. If our hearts remain self-focused, we have chosen to follow the world rather than Jesus. The presence of the Spirit is not a matter of divine availability, but of human welcome.

# Seventh Sunday of Easter

## First Reading
## Acts 1:1-14

# An Awesome Assignment

*But you will receive power when the Holy Spirit has come upon you; and you will be my witnesses in Jerusalem, in all Judea and Samaria, and to the ends of the earth. (Acts 1:8)*

Pentecost is coming, a reminder of how Jesus' promise to send "another Advocate" (John 14:16) was fulfilled with an outpouring of the Spirit. In today's text, though, that time is not yet. The disciples are caught up in a web of uncertainty following Christ's resurrection as he appears to them, then disappears, only to show up again. Both emotions and questions overflowed as they wondered what would come next, what were Jesus' plans, and what was expected of them. [**Ascension Sunday**]

Sometimes we find ourselves in a similar position. Many people struggle to find themselves, to settle on a career, to adapt to life as a decision-making adult. Some have trouble making commitments or determining what they're willing to commit to. While these questions relate to our life as humans, our life at work, our life in relationship, we also face spiritual questions. Is there a place for spirituality in our lives? If so, what shape will it take? Who are we willing to follow – and how far?

### A promise of power
### (vv. 1-8)

Today's text comes from Acts 1, the second part of a two-volume work that Luke composed and dedicated to his friend – or possibly his patron – Theophilus.

"Theophilus" means "friend of God" (from *theos*, "God," and *philos*, "friend"). Some commentators have suggested that we understand the name as a generic term, meaning that Luke addressed his work to every "friend of God," but the address in v. 1 seems to imply a specific person.

---

> **Ascension Sunday:** Acts 1:1-11 appears to relate that Jesus' ascension took place 40 days after his resurrection. Some church traditions celebrate "Ascension Thursday," 40 days after Easter Sunday, but a more common tradition observes "Ascension Sunday" on the following Sunday, six weeks after Easter. The next Sunday, 50 days after Easter, is celebrated as Pentecost Sunday.

The lection for the day comprises vv. 6-14 only, but it can be helpful to consider a bit of background to Luke's account of the ascension.

Luke's purpose in writing was to explain the life and work of Jesus, both before and after his ascension from the earth. In his first volume (the gospel), Luke "wrote about all that Jesus did and taught from the beginning until the day when he was taken up to heaven, after giving instructions through the Holy Spirit to the apostles whom he had chosen" (vv. 1-2).

Luke began his second volume (Acts) with Jesus' final post-resurrection appearance. He wanted to emphasize that Christ remained the guiding force of the church, even after his resurrection and ascension. Thomas was not the only one who needed to be convinced that Jesus was still alive and in charge. So, Luke contends, "After his suffering he presented himself alive to them by many convincing proofs, appearing to them during forty days and speaking about the kingdom of God" (v. 3). Other gospels describe resurrection appearances, but only Luke says that 40 days passed between the resurrection and the ascension.

During that time, according to Luke, Jesus' teaching focused on the kingdom of God, declaring its nature as the eternal reign of God. Many of Jesus' followers, such as dispensational premillennialists of our own era, still expected the kingdom of God to be expressed through the Jewish nation. They had much to learn.

Jesus knew that his followers would need more than knowledge to carry out his purpose. The task ahead would require more than their current capabilities, but Jesus promised to provide what they would need: "he ordered them not to leave Jerusalem, but to wait there for the promise of the Father" (v. 4).

The promise would be fulfilled by the coming of the Spirit: "This," he said, "is what you have heard from me; for John baptized with water, but you will be baptized with the Holy Spirit not many days from now" (v. 5, cp. Luke 3:16-17).

The gospel writers were painfully honest in showing how hard it was for the disciples to grasp the true meaning of the master's teaching, and this is no exception. When they heard Jesus speak of power, the disciples imagined that Jesus was about to forcefully assert his authority and establish the messianic kingdom many people had longed for. "Lord," they asked, "is this the time when you will restore the kingdom to Israel?" (v. 6).

Again, Jesus had to correct their misconceptions. He was not talking about the eschatological future, which was entirely in the Father's hands (v. 7), but about the present. The disciples' task was an assignment for their own time, and for a different kind of kingdom than they had long imagined.

God would provide what they needed to carry out their mission: "But you will receive power when the Holy Spirit has come upon you, and you will be my witnesses in Jerusalem, in all Judea and Samaria, and to the ends of the earth" (v. 8).

The power of which Jesus spoke would become evident on the day of Pentecost, when the Spirit came like a mighty rushing wind and filled the gathered followers with a life-changing sense of God's presence and power (2:4). [The last days and the Spirit]

It's hard to imagine how the disciples would have responded to both the promise of power and the challenge to carry the gospel from Jerusalem to Samaria to the ends of the earth. They were still in hiding during the first weeks after Jesus' crucifixion, keeping a watch by the door. Now

---

**The last days, and the Spirit:** In Hebrew thought, the belief that God would restore Israel in the last days was closely associated with an expected outpouring of God's Spirit. The rabbis commonly taught that God's Spirit – understood primarily as a spirit of prophecy – had been withdrawn from the world after the death of the last prophets (Joel, Haggai, Zechariah, Malachi). The return of the Spirit, not just upon prophets but upon all, would be sure evidence that the "last days" had arrived: "Then afterward I will pour out my spirit on all flesh; your sons and your daughters shall prophesy, your old men shall dream dreams, and your young men shall see visions" (Joel 2:28, NRSV).

---

Jesus expected them to go out into the streets of Jerusalem and draw attention to themselves by preaching the gospel. That would be dangerous business, so perilous that the Greek word for "witness" (*martus*) gave rise to the English word "martyr."

Jesus not only expected his followers to witness in Jerusalem, but also throughout Judea, the homeland of Jewish power and influence. There would be opposition, antagonism, and danger every step of the way. Yet, Christ expected them to be faithful and honest in their testimony.

As if the homeland of Judaism were not threatening enough, Jesus' challenge extended beyond its borders. Samaria was only a short distance away geographically, but in a cultural sense, it might as well have been the other side of the world. Jesus' first followers were all Jewish. They would have grown up in an atmosphere of prejudice against Samaritans. Nothing less than a command from Jesus and the power of the Spirit could impel them to carry the gospel into Samaritan territory.

Jesus concluded his mandate with a phrase that has rung in the ears of mission-minded Christians throughout history: "…and to the ends of the earth." The disciples had no idea just how far the earth extended, but Jesus insisted that his message was intended for every part of it.

This is where Pentecost finds its significance. The disciples were confronted with many obstacles as they contemplated this mission. They would face the external barriers of open conflict and physical danger in confronting the Jewish authorities. They would have to navigate the hurdles of their own prejudice as they traveled on to Samaria and to the ends of the earth.

Nothing less than the power of God could lead the first believers out of their hiding places and into the light. Nothing less than the Spirit of Christ could set them free from narrow provincialism and send them forth to proclaim grace to people they had been taught to despise.

## Absence and presence
### (vv. 9-11)

This is why it was so important that Jesus impress upon his followers that, though he was leaving them physically, he would always be present through the Spirit. And then, "as they were watching, he was lifted up, and a cloud took him out of their sight" (v. 9).

The disciples had seen Jesus crucified, had seen him buried, and had seen him resurrected. Now, Luke says, they saw him ascend into heaven. Modern readers are less likely to imagine a three-story universe in which Christ must ascend upward to heaven, but we understand Luke's symbolism. The disciples could no longer see Jesus in the flesh, but they could be sure that he was still alive and active and at work in them. He was out of sight, but not out of mind.

"Two men in white robes" suddenly stood by them, Luke said, asking a question that bordered on humorous: "Why are you looking up toward heaven?" (vv. 10-11).

What else would they be doing?

What was implied in the angel's question was that Jesus no longer wanted them to be gazing skyward, but looking outward to the mission field he had given them.

The advent of the Holy Spirit at Pentecost fulfilled Jesus' promise to empower his disciples to do his will. Modern disciples need not expect to see a repetition of Pentecost, for the Spirit of Christ has not left the earth and does not need to be "prayed down" again. Those who know the power of the Spirit are not those who happen to be in the right place at the right time, but those who are humble enough to surrender their own power to the present Lord, whose power is greater than our own.

Like the disciples, we need the power of Christ's Spirit to overcome our timidity, our apathy, our prejudice, and to become faithful witnesses. Jesus' challenge has yet to be fulfilled: as long as there are people in the world who have not experienced the love of Jesus, his followers will never be out of a job.

## Next steps
### (vv. 12-14)

Tagging vv. 12-14 to the ascension story may appear awkward, but it serves to show the first steps Jesus' closest followers took in responding to his last commands. Only here do we learn that Jesus' last instructions and the story of his ascension were set on the Mount of Olives, which Luke calls "Olivet," just across the Kidron Valley from Jerusalem. [**Where did the ascension occur?**]

The disciples returned to Jerusalem, and to the upstairs room where they had been staying. Luke makes a point of naming the 11 remaining male disciples: Peter, John, James, Andrew, Philip, Thomas, Bartholomew, Matthew, James the son of Alphaeus, Simon the Zealot, and Judas son of James (vv. 12-13).

The 11 men, Luke says, "were constantly devoting themselves to prayer" (v. 14a) – but they were not alone. Women disciples often get short shrift in the gospels, though we are told they were at the cross and the first to witness the resurrection. It is likely that they were also present as Jesus spoke prior to his ascension.

Afterward, Luke says, women were also part of the community devoted to constant prayer in the upper room, for the 11 disciples prayed "together with certain women, including Mary the mother of Jesus, as well as his brothers" (v. 14b). Modern readers may find it disheartening that, after carefully naming the disciples who remained faithful, Luke says only that "certain women," including Jesus' mother, were part of the faithful praying community.

We may understand the male-centered world in which first-century authors wrote, but we could still wish they had been more attentive to crediting the many devoted women who followed Jesus along with the 12 disciples, often the ones who provided finances and provisions for the journey (Luke 8:1-3).

Luke's mention of both Jesus' mother "and his brothers" seems intended to show that they also had recognized that Jesus was more than an ordinary son, more than a sibling. They, too, wanted to be a part of carrying on his work.

The text challenges us to question whether we, too, want to participate in Christ's ongoing mission.

**Where did the ascension occur?** Acts 1:4-14 appears to be a lengthier retelling of an account found in Luke 24:50-53, which says that Jesus gathered his disciples and "led them out as far as Bethany, and, lifting up his hands, he blessed them. While he was blessing them, he withdrew from them and was carried up into heaven. And they worshiped him, and returned to Jerusalem with great joy; and they were continually in the temple blessing God."

Bethany is on the eastern slopes of the Mount of Olives about two miles from Jerusalem.

### The Hardest Question
### What about the 40 days?

The gospels speak of several specific resurrection appearances, but they all imply that the appearances occurred over a short period of time. Luke 24, in fact, seems to telescope Christ's post-resurrection appearances and ascension into a single day. This is surprising, since Luke was also the author of Acts, which asserts that Jesus appeared to the disciples over a period lasting 40 days. It is more likely that Luke cited a tradition rather than choosing a number to serve his purpose, but the motif of a 40-day period does have special significance in the Bible.

The flood lasted 40 days, according to the Yahwist's version of the flood story in Gen. 7:17. Twice, Moses was said to have spent 40 days on Mount Sinai (Exod. 24:18, 34:28). The Israelite spies took 40 days to investigate the land of promise (Num. 13:25). Goliath reportedly taunted Israel's army for 40 days before David challenged him (1 Sam. 17:16). Elijah spent 40 days traveling through the wilderness on the way to Mount Sinai/Horeb after being threatened by Jezebel (1 Kgs. 19:8). Ezekiel claimed to have lain on his right side for 40 days as a prophecy of Israel's punishment (Ezek. 4:6). Jonah's prophecy warned that God would destroy Nineveh in 40 days (Jon. 3:4).

The apocryphal books of Tobit, 2 and 3 Maccabees, and 2 Esdras contain other stories involving 40-day periods. In the gospels, Jesus fasted and was tempted for 40 days following his baptism (Mark 1:13, Matt. 4:2, Luke 4:2).

It's no surprise, then, that Luke would say the resurrected Jesus spent 40 days on earth prior to his ascension. It marks a significant and memorable period of time.

## Second Reading
## Psalm 68

# Sky Rider

*Sing to God, sing praises to his name; lift up a song to him who rides upon the clouds – his name is the LORD – be exultant before him. (Ps. 68:4)*

Superhero movies have been all the rage for some years now. Teens and younger adults, especially, revel in tales of people who can fly, run, jump, or swing higher than any normal human, heroes with superhuman strength or vision, champions who do battle with evil to defend the weak and work for justice.

Psalm 68, with its multiple references to God as a cloud rider who defends widows and orphans while overpowering wickedness, could have appealed to the same longing for a superhero to come to the rescue.

The text, apparently, was chosen for reading on Ascension Sunday because it accompanies the story in Acts 1 that portrays Jesus being taken up into the heavens, as if also riding on the clouds, soaring through the sky.

Some texts are easy to preach or teach, but this is not one of them. Aside from the superhero similarities – which don't match up well with the gospel – much of the psalm speaks of God as one who revels in the blood of divine foes, "shattering the heads of his enemies" so the victors could bathe their feet in blood and give their dogs a share of it (vv. 22-23).

It comes as no surprise that the lectionary omits those bloody bits, along with other imperial imagery from vv. 11-31, but the message of the psalm is not complete without them. What should we do with such a text?

### The God who rises up
### (vv. 1-3)

While some interpreters consider the psalm to be a collection of ancient poetic fragments, others see it as a liturgical hymn celebrating God's power, perhaps during a periodic

> **God:** Psalm 68 falls within the "Elohistic Psalter" (Psalms 42–72), which predominantly refers to the deity with the term *'elohîm* (translated as "God") rather than the more common appellative *yhwh*, the divine name revealed in Exod. 3:13-15, generally pronounced "Yahweh," and translated as "LORD." Psalm 68 is filled with "God talk." It uses *'elohim* 28 times, *'adonai* (Lord) 5 times, *yhwh* (LORD or GOD) 4 times, and *Shaddai* (Almighty) once.

observance in which the Ark of the Covenant was taken from the temple and carried before worshippers in a ritual procession used to proclaim God's past deeds of power and to pray for God's intervention in present events. **[God]**

"Let God rise up, let his enemies be scattered; let those who hate him flee before him" (v. 1). So the psalm begins, a close echo of Num. 10:35 and Israel's sojourn in the wilderness: "Whenever the ark set out, Moses would say, 'Arise, O LORD, let your enemies be scattered, and your foes flee before you.'"

A poetic triplet calls for the wicked to be driven away, to melt as wax before the fire, and to perish before God, while a second exhorts the righteous to "be joyful," to "exult before God," and to "be jubilant with joy" (vv. 2-3).

### The God who brings abundance
### vv. 4-10)

Verse 4 brings a second potential reference to the Ark as symbolic of Yahweh's divine chariot: "Sing to God, sing praises to his name; lift up a song to him who rides upon the clouds – his name is the LORD – be exultant before him."

Portraying God as a cloud rider or sky rider appears again in v. 33, which addresses God as "O rider in the heavens, the ancient heavens." Similar imagery appears multiple times in the psalms. Psalm 18:9-10 speaks of God coming in a thunderstorm with dark clouds beneath the divine feet, riding on a cherub. Psalm 104:3 addresses God, saying, "you make the clouds your chariot, you ride on the wings of the wind."

Similar imagery is found in Deut. 33:26: "There is none like God, O Jeshurun, who rides through the heavens to your help, majestic through the skies." Similarly, in an oracle against Egypt, Isaiah spoke of Yahweh as "riding on a swift cloud" as the idols of Egypt quaked at God's presence (Isa. 19:1).

The sky-riding imagery also echoes a common appellative for the Canaanite god Baal, the storm god, who was called "rider on the clouds" in texts found at Ugarit.

The imagery of God traversing the heavens with clouds as his chariot may have been reflected on earth in the design of the Ark, which was topped by two winged cherubs, imagined as both God's seat of mercy (Exod. 25:17-22, 26:34, 30:6, et. al.) and as God's footstool (1 Chron. 28:2; Ps. 99:5, 132:7). Leviticus speaks of the mercy seat upon the Ark being covered with a divine cloud (Lev. 16:2), symbolized on earth by a cloud of incense (Lev. 16:13). [**More clouds**]

---

**More clouds:** Cloud imagery not only related to God's control of the heavens, but also as a cover that both marked God's presence and made God invisible to human eyes. Wilderness traditions say that when the tabernacle was completed, it was covered by a thick cloud indicating God's presence (Exod. 40:34-38). When Solomon ordered that the Ark of the Covenant be brought up from the tent David had provided and installed in the holiest inner place of the first temple, a similar thing happened:

> And when the priests came out of the holy place, a cloud filled the house of the LORD, so that the priests could not stand to minister because of the cloud; for the glory of the LORD filled the house of the LORD. Then Solomon said, "The LORD has said that he would dwell in thick darkness. I have built you an exalted house, a place for you to dwell in forever." (1 Kgs. 8:10-13)

---

The psalmist saw God as more than a storm-bringer, though. God is "father of orphans and protector of widows" (v. 5), and one who "gives the desolate a home to live in" (v. 6a). As defender of the helpless, God "leads out the prisoners to prosperity," while "the rebellious live in a parched land (v. 6b). The "prisoners," in this case, are presumably righteous or innocent people on whom God has compassion.

The expectation of divinely wrought prosperity for the righteous and hardship for the wicked is in line with Israel's traditional theology, whether based on covenant (Deuteronomy 28) or wisdom (Psalm 1) traditions. God's identity as advocate for the needy is associated with "his holy habitation," a phrase used to describe both God's heavenly dwelling (Deut. 26:15, 2 Chron. 30:27, Jer. 25:30, Zech. 2:13) and the temple.

Imagery of God's authority over storms and rain, also echoed in Ps. 29:1-9, is again evident in vv. 7-10, which begins an imaginative and over-positive review of how God led Israel through the wilderness and into the land of promise, culminating with God's majestic enthronement in Jerusalem (v. 18), symbolized by the presence of the Ark of the Covenant in the temple.

Wilderness traditions reflected in the book of Numbers hold that, whenever the people would move from one encampment to the next, the Levites would carry the Ark at the head of the procession as the cloud of God's presence overshadowed it (Num. 10:33-35). Psalm 68:7 recalls that tradition while addressing God in praise: "O God, when you went out before your people, when you marched through the wilderness."

From there it diverges from tradition with poetic license to describe Israel's entry into the land of promise: "the earth quaked, the heavens poured down rain at the presence of God, the God of Sinai, at the presence of God, the God of Israel. Rain in abundance, O God, you showered abroad; you restored your heritage when it languished; your flock found a dwelling in it; in your goodness, O God, you provided for the needy" (vv. 8-10).

### The God who crushes enemies
### (vv. 11-31)

In one sense, the psalm is appealing as a psalm for the lowly, as James Luther Mays called it (*Psalms*, Interpretation [Westminster John Knox, 1994], 229). That would be easier to adopt if it did not proceed from gratitude to vengeance, praising God for "shattering the heads" of enemies (v. 21) so the victors' feet might be bathed in blood (v. 23). The martial imagery, as distasteful as it is, was designed to bolster the image of God's power.

Further evidence that the psalm was used liturgically, perhaps to accompany a ritual procession of the Ark into the temple, appears in vv. 24-27, which describe the order of those who follow in procession: "Your solemn processions are seen, O God, the processions of my God, my King, into the sanctuary" (v. 24).

The psalmist believed that God, once enthroned in the temple, should be worshiped. He calls on God to "Summon your might" as kings come to bear gifts (vv. 28-29), and to "rebuke the wild animals that live among the reeds" (a metaphor for enemies along the Nile), to "Trample under foot" those who sought tribute from Israel, and to "scatter the peoples who delight in war" (v. 30). In response, he believed, tribute would come from Egypt and appeals from as far as Ethiopia.

## The God who is above all
### (vv. 32-35)

Psalm 68 concludes with a closing call to praise, inviting all "kingdoms of the earth" to "sing praises to the Lord" (v. 32), and returning to the cloud rider imagery. "O rider in the heavens, the ancient heavens; listen, he sends out his voice, his mighty voice" (v. 33).

The psalmist seems overcome that the God who rules the heavens could also care for Israel. He turns to address the people: "Ascribe power to God, whose majesty is over Israel; and whose power is in the skies" (v. 34). God's power reached from heaven to earth, where God was also thought to reside in the holy place above the ark: "Awesome is God in his sanctuary, the God of Israel; he gives power and strength to his people" (v. 35).

What can modern Christians make of this ancient paean to the "rider of the clouds" who rules the heavens but also cares for the needy on earth, for widows and orphans and the people of Israel?

We are less likely to portray God in physical ways, or to equate earth's atmosphere with God's heavenly dwelling place, but we also may find comfort in the belief that there is a God who is both caring for the needy and capable of doing awesome things.

While we may celebrate with the psalmist the image of a God whose "power is in the skies," we also know that God's people are called to be at work on earth, not seeking vengeance against enemies, but showing compassionate intervention for the poor and lonely and needy. Divine care is best shown through the hearts and the hands – and the pocketbooks – of those who have found in God a model for the way we are called to live and serve.

Testimony requires more than words.

## The Hardest Question
### What about the Baal imagery?

The Canaanite storm god Ba'al was also called "Cloud Rider" more than a dozen times in the Ugaritic cuneiform texts found at Ras Shamra, near the Mediterranean coast and now part of northwestern Syria.

In an epic depicting a battle between Baal and the sea god Yam, the divine armorer Kothar-wa-Khasis creates two war clubs that allow Baal to defeat Yam, addressing Baal as "prince Ba'lu, and I repeat, Cloud Rider" (KTU 1.2:IV:8, trans. by Dennis Pardee, "Ugaritic Myths" in eds. William Hallo and K. Lawson Younger, *The Context of Scripture: Canonical Compositions from the Biblical World* [Brill, 1997], 248).

In part of the same epic, the warrior goddess Anat charges Baal to scatter Yam's remains quickly, crying "Scatter (him), O Mighty [Ba'lu],//scatter (him), O Cloud-Rider" (KTU 1.2:IV:29, Pardee, 249).

Another story describes Anat's glee in having slain so many people that she is covered in blood and gore, then "She gathers water and washes,//dew of heavens, oil of earth,//the showers of the Cloud Rider" (KTU 1.3:II:40, Pardee, 251).

In both biblical and Canaanite texts, the context of the name "Cloud Rider" most often relates to the god's role as king, as warrior, or in bringing fertility to the earth.

The intriguing parallel does not necessarily indicate that the Hebrews consciously applied them to Yahweh. When competing religions sharing similar cultural backgrounds described deities they believed to have comparative qualities, it is not surprising that they would use similar poetic motifs.

# Seventh Sunday of Easter

## Third Reading
### 1 Peter 4:12–5:6-11

# A New Strength

*And after you have suffered for a little while, the God of all grace, who has called you to his eternal glory in Christ, will himself restore, support, strengthen, and establish you. (1 Pet. 5:10)*

How long has it been since you put pen to paper and wrote an actual letter? Email, texting, and social media have virtually replaced letter writing except in the most formal of circumstances, but there was a time when the only way to communicate with friends or family at a distance was through messages written by hand.

When I was in college during the early 1970s, cell phones did not exist and long-distance calls were expensive. Though only 60 miles from home, I wrote letters to my parents to assure them I was doing well, or to request $20 for books or food.

As we study 1 Peter, it's helpful to remember that we are reading a letter. The letter was not addressed to a single person or family, but was designed to be circulated among a group of churches in what was then called "Asia" and is now part of western Turkey.

Letters found in the New Testament follow a basic form in which greetings are followed by matters of interest between the parties. Writers then brought the letter to an end with a conclusion designed to convey final words and to say goodbye.

Biblical epistles typically end with words of encouragement and advice, and 1 Peter is no exception. The author closed with a sincere wish that his readers would practice cordial humility toward each other and live in love.

## Right behavior
### (4:12-19)

Having spoken to the issue of family and community relationships (3:1-7, 4:7-11), the author returned to the subject of the believer's relationship to the world, which sometimes led to persecution or suffering. He had previously discussed this subject in 2:18-25, encouraging readers to follow Christ's example by responding patiently to suffering, without seeking vengeance.

Believers should not think of "fiery ordeals" as unexpected, "as though something strange were happening to you" (4:12). Rather, they should rejoice to the extent that they were sharing in Christ's sufferings. Those who were "reviled for the name of Christ" should consider themselves blessed, he said, "because the spirit of glory, which is the Spirit of God, is resting on you" (4:13-14).

But suffering can have other causes. Christians should have no cause to suffer as murderers, thieves, criminals, or mischief-makers (4:15). The time of judgment was coming, he said, a time for Christ's followers to avoid evil and endure any suffering for Christ's sake by entrusting themselves "to a faithful Creator, while continuing to do good" (4:16-19).

## Humble trust
### (5:1-7)

The writer concluded his epistle by turning to relations within the church, with advice about how members of the church should treat each other (5:1-5). He described himself as an "elder," and spoke to the "elders among you" (5:1) along with "those who are younger" (5:5).

Whether we are to think of "elder" as a designation of age or of office, the writer appealed to the experience and wisdom of church leaders, urging them to "tend the flock of God that is in your charge" with willing eagerness. **[Tending the flock]**

**Tending the flock:** The image of God's people as a flock is common in the Old Testament (Psalm 23, Isa. 40:11, Jer. 23:1-4, Ezek. 34:1-10), and it's not surprising that First Peter would draw on the image: recall the story in John 21, where Jesus instructed Peter to "feed my sheep/lambs" no less than three times.

Likewise, the author instructed his fellow-elders to "tend the flock," using a word that means "to shepherd." It is an active verb, suggesting vigorous involvement rather than distant supervision. The imperative verb "to shepherd" is plural, but the word for flock is singular, so it's unclear if the writer had in mind a group of elders who led separate house churches, or if he thought of a council of elders with responsibility for all the churches in northern Asia.

The word for "exercising your oversight" is *episkopuntes*, the root of our word "Episcopal." As the early church developed, the word came to mean "function as a bishop," but that sense is probably not present here.

Elders were to serve willingly, "not under compunction," suggesting that the position was largely a volunteer responsibility. Elders were not to abuse the power inherent in their position (v. 3), but to serve as good examples of Christian behavior. Since elders would have charge of church finances, collections for the poor, and so forth, there might be a temptation to profit improperly from the position. So, 1 Peter reminds elders not to use their position "for sordid gain," but to serve willingly and eagerly. Their reward would come "when the chief shepherd appears," and they would "win the crown of glory that never fades away" (5:4).

---

Likewise, "younger" members were to respect the leadership of experienced believers. As with family relationships, all were to live in humble submission to one another, remembering that "God opposes the proud, but gives grace to the humble" (5:5, a quotation from the Greek translation of Prov. 3:34).

The writer's reference to humility led him back to the theme of faithful living in a difficult world. He brought his missive to a forceful conclusion with a string of imperative verbs: "humble yourselves," "cast your cares on God," "discipline yourselves," and "resist evil" (5:6-9). The closing words include a comforting promise of future hope for those who would follow his advice (5:10-11).

Let's look more closely. Faithful living requires a healthy measure of humility. Believers adopt modest attitudes not because they feel worthless, but because they understand their place in the larger scheme of things:

"Humble yourselves, therefore, under God's mighty hand, that he may lift you up in due time" (5:6).

"God's mighty hand" is a common Old Testament metaphor for God's power to deliver (Exod. 13:3, Deut. 26:8, 1 Kgs. 8:42, Neh. 1:10, Ps. 136:12, among others). First Peter addressed people who may have been forcibly humbled by the mighty fist of Rome. Involuntary submission is degrading, but humble believers can be confident that God's "mighty hand" will hold them firm and ultimately lift them up. "In due time" translates the word *kairos*, which describes "the appropriate time," in God's time.

Humility before God does not imply going about on our knees or wearing sackcloth. Mainly, it's about putting our trust in God rather than relying on our efforts alone. "Cast all your anxiety on him," Peter said, "because he cares for you" (5:7). The encouraging words were probably drawn from Ps. 55:22a (LXX 54:23): "Cast your burden on the LORD, and he will sustain you."

The notions of being humble and entrusting one's cares to God are closely connected. Holding on to our problems and worries points to a prideful belief that we can go it alone – or to a lack of belief that God can be of help. In contrast, entrusting our cares to God is a sign of both humility and faith.

The author's advice does not suggest that we blithely ignore the pressures, debts, or illnesses that may confront us and simply assume that God will take care of everything. It is our worries we are to turn over to God – not our responsibilities. We cannot expect God to make our apologies or pay our bills or improve our physical fitness, but we can look positively to God for help and hope as we do those things, and we need not waste energy worrying about them in the meantime.

As the disciples "cast their cloaks" on the colt for Jesus to ride on his triumphal entry to Jerusalem (Luke 19:35), so Christ's followers are to cast our cares on God as we walk through difficult times but toward ultimate triumph.

The importance of trusting God in times of trial exists through the ages. Some readers will remember Charles A. Tindley's touching hymn, "Leave It There," written in 1916. The song's verses sing of troubles associated with poverty, illness, enemies, and aging, each one leading to the chorus "Take your burden to the Lord and leave it there." **[Speaking from experience]**

**Speaking from experience:** When Charles A. Tindley wrote the hymn "Leave It There," he spoke from experience. Tindley was born in Maryland in 1851. As the son of a slave father and a free mother, he was considered free, but still lived among the slaves.

After the Civil War, Tindley moved to Philadelphia and found work as a manual laborer, carrying bricks. He sought to educate himself with the help of friends and tutors, studying Hebrew and Greek by correspondence. In time he was accepted for ordination by the Methodist Episcopal church by examination rather than by degree, and was assigned a series of small charges before becoming pastor of Bainbridge Street Methodist Episcopal Church in Philadelphia, where he had once attended and served as the unpaid sexton.

Under Tindley's leadership, the church grew from 130 members to a multi-racial congregation reported to have numbered more than 10,000. The church moved to larger facilities in 1906 and was renamed East Calvary Methodist Episcopal Church. After his death, members honored Tindley by rechristening the church as "Tindley Temple."

Though often called "the Prince of Preachers," Tindley also wrote hymns, including "I'll Overcome Some Day," a version of which became popular in the 1960s as the Civil Rights anthem "We Shall Overcome Some Day."

When Tindley wrote the words of "Take your burden to the Lord and leave it there," he spoke from the experience of having overcome significant obstacles.

## Steadfast faith
### (5:8-9)

First Peter calls for readers to trust God in times of need, but not to imagine that life can be lived without effort. Wise believers should discipline themselves and stay alert, for "Like a roaring lion your adversary the devil prowls around looking for someone to devour" (5:8).

The words for "be sober" ("discipline yourselves" in the NRSV) and "keep alert" (literally, "stay awake!") were often used together, especially by writers who thought of themselves as living in the last days, urging others to be faithful until the end.

Like other early Christians, the author believed that an evil foe lurked behind the many temptations and cruelties of this world, opposing the righteous and advocating evil. The word for "adversary" is a technical term for a legal opponent in court, but it could be used in the general sense of "enemy."

"Devil" translates "*diabolos*" (the root of our word "diabolical"). Its root meaning is something akin to "slanderer." *Diabolos* is the word typically used in the Septuagint (a Greek version of the Old Testament) to translate the Hebrew term *ha-sâtân* ("the accuser"). In the Hebrew Bible, with only one late exception (1 Chron. 21:1), the word *sâtân* always appears with the definite article (*ha*), as a title rather than a personal name. The accuser was not believed to be an evil power who opposed God, but one of the "sons of God" who served on the heavenly council. His charge was to observe human activity and report wrongdoing (see Job 1:6-7), as a heavenly "district attorney." [**Accuser or inciter?**]

By the first century, however, many Jews had come to think of *ha-sâtân* as a demonic power that sought to pervert God's purposes by tempting people to do evil. Over time, the *diabolos* came to be thought of as a rebellious angel who had been given temporary dominion in the world, but who would be defeated by Christ (John 14:30, 1 John 5:19).

The lion-like nature of evil will not only bite us, but also can ruin us (the word for "devour" can also mean "overwhelm"). Believers are urged to be alert for this roaming lion and to "Resist him, steadfast in your faith, for you know that your brothers and sisters in all the world are undergoing the same kinds of suffering" (v. 9). Paul also called on Christians to resist and stand fast against the "wiles of the devil" (Eph. 6:10-13), and James encouraged his readers to "submit to God" and "resist the devil," promising

**Accuser or inciter?** In the Hebrew Bible, the *sâtân* appears more commonly as an accuser than as a tempter (the serpent in Genesis 3 was not associated with the devil in the Old Testament). The primary exception is 1 Chron. 21:1, in which the accuser is said to have incited David to take a census of the people of Israel.

That unusual story is parallel to 2 Sam. 24:1, which says that the LORD (Yahweh) was angry at Israel, "and he incited David against them," instructing him to take a census. How can it be that one story says God incited David, and another says *sâtân* told him to do it?

The books of Chronicles were written several hundred years after the books of Samuel and Kings. The writer was apparently uncomfortable with the idea that God would incite David to do something and then punish him for it, so the later writer either assumed that God assigned the task to the heavenly accuser, or imagined that *sâtân*, apart from God, inspired the census.

that "he will flee from you" (Jas. 4:7). Temptation has many names and guises: believers must be on guard.

The temptations we face are not only those of a moral or corrupt nature, but also the endemic sins of a greed-based society that values self-gratification more than healthy community. The first step in overcoming temptation is to recognize it for what it is, and the first step in enduring tribulation is to recognize its temporary nature. Those who stand firm in their faith and in company with other Christians will find the strength to endure.

Readers may note the similarity of 1 Pet. 5:6-9 and Jas. 4:6-10. Both quote Prov. 3:34 ("God resists the proud but gives grace to the humble"), and both encourage their readers to resist the devil and to humble or submit themselves to God, trusting that God would lift them up.

### True strength
### (5:10-11)

First Peter concludes with a reassuring promise of God's intention to deliver and strengthen God's people. Verses 10-11 are a powerful benediction, a promise that God will bless those who are enduring trials and will "restore, support, strengthen, and establish you."

The piling up of four active verbs that are near synonyms makes for an emphatic statement. The word for "restore" means "to supply what is needed" or "to mend what is broken." The term translated as "support" can also mean "to make firm," or "confirm." Like the next verb in the series, it could also mean "to strengthen." The end result, found in the final verb, is that believers may become established, firmly grounded in their faith. Does that sound like us? [**Last words**]

The author's promise of divine deliverance does not preclude suffering or hard times, but counsels confidence nonetheless. Difficult days are an integral part of human life, but in the shadow of trouble, those who follow Jesus can rest assured that we serve a mighty God who can lift us up. We will be tried, we will suffer pain, we will be wounded in this life, but the restoring power of God is strong and provides what we need to endure.

### The Hardest Question
### Can we blame trouble on the devil?

Some readers will remember the late comedian Flip Wilson, who hosted a variety show during the 1970s. Wilson was known for portraying various characters, including an outspoken and self-focused woman named Geraldine Jones, who steadfastly refused to accept responsibility for any fault or failure. Whether it was buying an extravagant dress or partying too hard, her trademark excuse was "The devil made me do it." (Some of Wilson's sketches are still available on YouTube, such as this one: http://www.youtube.com/watch?v=5kaiLcwHXB4.)

Wilson didn't own a trademark on the phrase, however. The debut album of political rapper Paris was named for its title song, "The Devil Made Me Do It," and any number of others – whether flippantly or seriously – have blamed their actions on irresistible demonic influence.

But does the devil make us do anything? Are the temptations we face as individuals and as a society imposed by an external source, or do they derive from our internal desires?

The notion that "the devil made me do it" may go back to Genesis 3 and the story of how Eve and Adam ate from a forbidden tree following a conversation with a wily serpent. Readers commonly think of this as a story about temptation, and it is – but the primary temptation is from within. The serpent in the story (portrayed not as

---

**Last words:** The lectionary text does not include vv. 12-14, but we note that the final conclusion of the letter reflects personal touches. It was reportedly written by Silvanus, who also may have delivered it. Its purpose was "to encourage you and to testify that this is the true grace of God." Greetings are also sent from "your sister church (literally, "she who is") in Babylon." In the first-century Christian community, "Babylon" was commonly used as a cryptic name for Rome, which was the author's most likely location.

The reference to "my son Mark" contributed to an early tradition that Mark became a disciple of Peter, and that Mark's gospel preserves Peter's memories of Jesus. Since both Luke and Matthew depend on Mark for much of their material, this possibility is not insignificant.

The encouragement for believers to greet one another with a kiss of love and to live in peace are meaningful reminders of what will happen if the church takes Peter's advice seriously.

an evil being, but as the cleverest of God's creatures) didn't say "Here, you should eat this fruit," but mainly raised the question of whether God had really forbidden it and denied that Adam and Eve would die if they ate from it.

Eve's temptation came from within: "So when the woman saw that the tree was good for food, and that it was a delight to the eyes, and that the tree was to be desired to make one wise, she took of its fruit and ate; and she also gave some to her husband, who was with her, and he ate" (Gen. 3:6). When confronted by God, she blamed her behavior on the serpent.

Whether we think of it as the influence of our culture, our friends, or a personal devil, there are many ways in which we may be confronted with options good and bad, but the temptation to sin grows from our own desires. We can't blame excessive drinking on our peers, a penchant to overeating on Mom's good cooking, or general laziness on the appeal of the Internet.

We've noted above that the letters of 1 Peter and James have many similarities, including a warning to watch out for the devil, but both Peter and James put the responsibility for resisting evil in our hands. Peter commands us to stay awake and focused. James reminds us that the heart of temptation is within: "But one is tempted by one's own desire, being lured and enticed by it" (Jas. 1:14).

This is true whether we think of selfish tendencies of individuals or societies. Consider ills such as racial or gender-based prejudice, economic disparity, and unequal opportunity that plague our society and make it less than it could be. They do not arise from satanic influence, but from human greed. People make selfish or harmful choices because they can, not because the devil made them do it.

In his discussion of this text, Richard B. Vinson notes that the evil Peter personifies as a "roaring lion" has many shapes and dimensions, and he raises helpful questions: "What shape does the lion take in your community – racism, unfair wages, inadequate housing? What can you and your congregation do to resist?" (*1-2 Peter, Jude*, Smyth & Helwys Bible Commentary [Smyth & Helwys, 2010], 248).

# Seventh Sunday of Easter

## Fourth Reading
## John 17:1-11

# The Lord at Prayer

*And this is eternal life, that they may know you, the only true God, and Jesus Christ whom you have sent. (John 17:3)*

Sometimes we come to the edge of something big and feel a deep need for prayer, even if we don't know what to pray for or about. We might think of the hours before a wedding, a long overseas trip, the first day of a new job, or a final exam at the end of a long semester. We may feel certain it's what we want and confident that everything will go well, but still just uneasy enough to feel the need for a serious prayer.

Imagine how we would feel if the big event on the horizon was our own public humiliation and execution, a voluntary action to save our friends. Can we even imagine such a thing? If we could, we might understand something of how Jesus felt on the night before his arrest, when he felt the need to pray for himself, for his disciples, and for all who would come after them.

### Looking forward…
### (vv. 1-3)

John 17:1-26 is often described as Jesus' "High Priestly Prayer." The author does not speak of Jesus praying in the garden of Gethsemane, as do Matthew and Mark, but inserts a lengthy farewell discourse between Jesus and the remaining disciples after Judas departed from their final meal together. Mark and Matthew imply that Jesus prayed at great length in the garden – so long that the disciples kept falling asleep – but they mention only a few words of the prayer: "My Father, if it is possible, let this cup pass from me; yet not what I want but what you want" (Matt. 26:39, Mark 14:36).

John does not speak as if Jesus prayed at great length, but focuses on traditions related to his conversation with

> **A common approach:** Gail O'Day has pointed out that farewell speeches, as a genre, typically ended with a prayer. Moses' final speech to the Israelites, for example, concluded with a hymn of praise to God (Deut. 31:30–32:47) and a lengthy blessing of the people (Deuteronomy 33). In the apocryphal book of Jubilees, speeches attributed to Moses and Noah end with prayers (Jub. 1:19-21, 10:3-6). Jewish apocalyptic writings included multiple examples of farewell discourses that concluded with prayers. Thus, the convention would have been familiar to the author of Fourth Gospel and to his readers. (Gail O'Day, "John," vol. 9, *The New Interpreter's Bible* [Abingdon Press, 1995], 787.)

the disciples in those last hours. The first part of the discourse focused on words of comfort and instruction (13:1–16:33) in which Jesus spoke to his disciples. The final part was a prayer (17:1-26) in which Jesus spoke to God in the disciples' hearing, interceding for his followers in a "priestly" fashion. [**A common approach**]

Jesus began the prayer with a request for himself (vv. 1-8), then shifted to a prayer for his disciples (vv. 9-19) and for future followers who would come after them (vv. 20-26). Scholars outline the prayer in different ways, but whatever structure we adopt, it is important to note that the entire prayer exudes dimensions of past, present, and future. There was a sense in which Jesus' "hour" had already commenced, was continuing, and would come to have eschatological significance. Intercessions that appear to address the present disciples in vv. 6-19 may also apply to all future followers. Despite its varied emphases, the prayer exhibits a repetitive theme: that the Father, the Son, and believers might live in unity.

The final hour: On Jesus' statement that "The hour has come," G.R. Beasley Murray has written: ". . . it is the event to which the whole life and mission of Jesus has moved (contrast 2:4; 7:6, 8, 30; 8:20 with intimations of the arrival of the hour in 12:23, 27-28, 31-32; 13:1, 31). The petition, 'Glorify your Son that the Son may glorify you,' strikes the keynote of the prayer" (John, vol. 36, Word Biblical Commentary [Zondervan, 1987], 296).

When we look at the first verse, it's hard to imagine the queasy feeling Jesus must have had in his stomach as he looked heavenward and prayed "Father, the hour has come; glorify your Son so that the Son may glorify you, since you have given him authority over all people, to give eternal life to all whom you have given him" (vv. 1-2).

"The hour has come," Jesus said. His arrest would take place before dawn, with a long day of unimaginable pain and an agonizing death on the cross to follow. He could not have looked forward to it, but he knew that it was time. [The final hour]

What did Jesus mean by asking God to "glorify" him? That seems out of character for one who was humbly and unselfishly on the road to an ugly but voluntary death. We normally think of seeking glory as a negative thing, as a narcissist seeking to puff up his or her reputation in search of "vainglory."

Jesus' context was different. Though one with God from the beginning (John 1:1), Jesus had voluntarily set aside heavenly glory to come to earth in the form of a man, reveal the Father, and suffer for the sake of all people.

Jesus knew he would soon die and return to the glory of his heavenly throne. In his incarnation as a human, Jesus prayed to God as Father, seeking assurance that in the coming days his mission would be accomplished, his sovereignty would be established, and the kingdom of God would be born on earth. Then all could recognize God's work and those who had come to know eternal life could glorify God, giving honor where honor was due.

Jesus' prayer reflects an earlier statement. After watching Judas leave the upper room, knowing that his fate had been set in motion, Jesus spoke of his glorification as a *fait accompli*: "When he had gone out, Jesus said, 'Now the Son of Man has been glorified, and God has been glorified in him. If God has been glorified in him, God will also

glorify him in himself and will glorify him at once'" (John 13:31-32).

Glory, in this context, means much more than praise or honor. As the author tells it, Jesus connects his glorification with the fulfillment of his mission in granting eternal life, which he defines in a surprising fashion: "And this is eternal life, that they may know you, the only true God, and Jesus Christ whom you have sent" (v. 3).

This clearly seems to reflect language of the church, as it's unlikely that Jesus would have referred to himself as "Jesus Christ." What is expressed may seem surprising to some: the author has Jesus affirm that the essence of eternal life is not the promise of lazy days in heaven, but the ability to *know God*. In Hebrew thought, "to know" suggests far more than intellectual comprehension: it is to know God by experiencing God's presence, a personal relationship of communion with God. Only through Jesus the Son can we come to know the fullness and the glory of God, who is the source of our life both now and through eternity, however that is understood.

## Looking back…
## (vv. 4-8)

In v. 4 we can detect a subtle shift. Jesus had spoken of himself in the third person in v. 3, but now switches to a first person address. Except for the near-repetitive request for a return to glory in v. 5, vv. 4-8 come across as a final report of what Jesus had done in his earthly life and ministry.

"I glorified you on earth by finishing the work that you gave me to do," Jesus said, "So now, Father, glorify me in your own presence with the glory that I had in your presence before the world existed" (vv. 4-5). [Glory]

And how had Jesus glorified God? In his words, "I have made your name known to those whom you gave me from the world. They were yours, and you gave them to me, and they have kept your word" (v. 6). To "make God's name known" implies a full revelation of God's character, which Jesus had delivered through both his actions and words.

We should note that "those you have given me" does not refer to predestination or "the elect," as some readers might surmise, or even to all believers. This part of Jesus' prayer was focused on the disciples, whom God had chosen and "given" to Jesus to learn from him and to serve him. They had proven faithful in receiving God's

> **Glory:** Jesus' prayer calls to mind Paul's description of Jesus' humility and glory in Phil. 2:5-11, words that may have been part of an early hymn:
>
> "Let the same mind be in you that was in Christ Jesus, who, though he was in the form of God, did not regard equality with God as something to be exploited, but emptied himself, taking the form of a slave, being born in human likeness. And being found in human form, he humbled himself and became obedient to the point of death— even death on a cross. Therefore God also highly exalted him and gave him the name that is above every name, so that at the name of Jesus every knee should bend, in heaven and on earth and under the earth, and every tongue should confess that Jesus Christ is Lord, to the glory of God the Father."

teachings through Christ, to the point of accepting the mind-boggling premise that Jesus had come from God into the world (vv. 7-8).

The gospels often portray the disciples as stubborn, hard-headed, and slow to learn, but they *had* learned. They had taken Jesus' teachings to heart, accepted him as Lord, and "kept his word," seeking to live as he had taught them.

We who call ourselves "Christian" claim to be modern-day disciples. Have we taken Jesus' teachings as seriously? What evidence of that is apparent in the way we conduct our lives? Does our living bring glory to God?

## Looking out for others…
### (vv. 9-19)

With the disciples on his mind, Jesus prayed not for the world in general, but for the disciples in particular, "asking on their behalf." The disciples belonged to God, he said, but had been given to him (v. 9). As a result, "All mine are yours, and yours are mine; and I have been glorified in them" (v. 10).

The thought that Jesus had been glorified through the disciples brings us to thoughts of their mission. As Jesus had revealed to the disciples the true nature and desires of God, the disciples would be appointed to carry that message to the world so others could come to experience God and have eternal life. In this, Jesus' direct prayer for the disciples was indirectly a prayer for all who would benefit from their ministry.

Although Jesus remained present with his disciples as he offered this prayer, he knew that would soon come to an end. Having made a final commitment to his coming passion, Jesus thought of himself as already gone from the world, leaving the disciples behind (v. 11a). Thus, he prayed for God to protect them – not so much from danger or threats from the outside, but from divisiveness that might hinder their mission: "Holy Father, protect them in your name that you have given me, so that they may be one, as we are one" (v. 11b).

Jesus went on to acknowledge that the disciples would face opposition from the world "because they do not belong to the world, just as I do not belong to the world" (v. 14). Jesus did not ask that the disciples be granted supernatural security from human opponents, but from evil influences that could disrupt their unity and impair their mission in the world (v. 16): "As you have sent me into the world," Jesus said, so "I have sent them into the world" (v. 18). Jesus' work was holy work, sanctifying work. As the disciples patterned themselves after Jesus, they would also "be sanctified in truth" (v. 19).

When we think about our present church family, or other churches we have known, when did the church have its best days? When has it been least effective? What characterized the days of growth? Were more troubling days due to human opposition from outside the congregation, or from internal discord that sidetracked its mission?

It's no surprise that Jesus' primary prayer for the disciples was "that they may be one." Surely believers could profit from praying for Christian unity, not only in our congregations, but also in our communities. Too many of us, for too long, have accepted racial lines, denominational divides, and ethnic exclusivism as par for the course, though they are bound to hinder Christ's mission in the world.

What practical things can we do to come closer to Jesus' desire that we all be one?

### The Hardest Question
### If Jesus was also God, how could he
### pray to the Father?

Both children and adults may struggle with this conundrum: If Jesus really was one with the Father, how could he pray to the Father as a separate entity? Perhaps the best answer we can give is to take note of the context:

Jesus prayed to the Father during his time on earth, when he voluntarily surrendered some of the prerogatives of divinity and lived as a human being. In speaking of Jesus' incarnation, the author of Hebrews said: "Therefore he had to become like his brothers and sisters in every respect, so that he might be a merciful and faithful high priest in the service of God, to make a sacrifice of atonement for the sins of the people" (Heb. 2:17).

Theologians speak of Jesus as being both fully human and fully divine, but while on earth the emphasis was on his human side. The word "incarnate" means "in human form." We have no way of knowing what it was like to be Jesus as an eternal deity who voluntarily chose to lead a self-limited life as a fully human person. Jesus needed food and water just as we do. He grew tired and needed sleep. He could be frustrated and cranky, or relaxed and funny. Jesus experienced every aspect of what it means to be human, including the need for quiet time and the need for prayer.

The story of the Transfiguration offers a glimpse of what Jesus' full communion with God might look like. Toward the end of his ministry, in a dark mountain glen with three of his disciples, Jesus threw off his human appearance and was transformed so that his clothes became brilliant and his face shone like the sun. Moses and Elijah, in some sort of glorified bodies, came to talk with him, then the presence of God descended in a bright cloud, so that the disciples fell to their faces in fear. In that setting, Jesus did not kneel and pray before the presence of God. Rather, a voice came from the cloud, addressing the disciples: "This is my Son, the Beloved; with him I am well pleased; listen to him!" (cf. Matthew 17, Mark 9, Luke 8).

But the Transfiguration was an exceptional moment. During most of Jesus' earthly life he lived fully as a human who learned to obey his parents, become skilled at a trade, and live as a Jew. He learned to read the scriptures, to recite the *Shema*, to observe the festivals, and to pray.

At times, Jesus prayed as a part of Jewish worship. At times, he prayed for God to work through him in healing or helping others. Sometimes, Jesus' prayers appeared to be for the benefit of others, that they might learn of God through overhearing his prayers. At other times, as in today's text, Jesus prayed both for himself and for his disciples to have the strength to do what needed to be done.

That Jesus prayed while on earth does not imply continued subservience to the Father: we think of Jesus, after his resurrection and ascension, as a full participant in the divine fellowship of the Triune God. We cannot begin to understand that reality, but one might suspect the persons of the Trinity do not pray to each other.

While on earth, Jesus prayed to the Father as a natural expression of his identity as a person of faith who needed to seek God's presence, power, and comfort. His prayers also served as an instructive example to his followers. If Jesus needed to pray, how much more do we?

# Day of Pentecost

## First Reading
## Acts 2:1-21*

# A New Spirit

*And suddenly from heaven there came a sound like the rush of a violent wind,
and it filled the entire house where they were sitting. (Acts 2:2)*

Church tradition places special emphasis on a variety of special or holy days during the year. Occasions such as Christmas and Epiphany may fall on any day of the week, but two related biblical events – Easter and Pentecost – always fall on Sunday. Easter took place on the first day after the Passover Sabbath observed by Jews, and Pentecost (from the Greek for "fiftieth") took place seven weeks and one day after the Passover Sabbath, which initiated the Feast of Weeks.

Many Protestant churches do not observe Pentecost, but those that follow the liturgical calendar typically drape the pulpit or communion table with red. Ministers wear scarlet stoles, and congregants are often encouraged to wear something red.

The color reminds worshipers of the tongues of fire that marked the Holy Spirit's indwelling presence in the lives of those who experienced the first Christian Pentecost. It is a day for celebrating the amazing gift of God's Spirit.

### A mighty wind
### (vv. 1-4)

The story is familiar but worth a closer look. First-century Jerusalem was a cosmopolitan city with residents from many different countries. During the Feast of Weeks, the population swelled with Jewish pilgrims who flocked to Jerusalem to celebrate the festival. Called *Shavu'ot* in Hebrew, the festival was to take place 50 days after the Passover Sabbath: seven weeks (a "week of weeks," giving rise to the name "Weeks") plus one day (Lev. 23:15-22).

The Greek word for "fiftieth" was *pentecostos*, hence the term "Pentecost."

The Feast of Weeks was originally a harvest festival, a time to bring a sheaf of grain from the "firstfruits" of the winter wheat, but it also came to be associated with the giving of the law at Sinai, which some rabbis calculated to have taken place 49 days after the Israelites left Egypt.

The story begins with "When the day of Pentecost had come" (NRSV), but the word translated "had come" could also mean "was fulfilled," an expression that suggests more than a date on the calendar. Jesus began his ministry by saying "the time is fulfilled" (Mark 1:15, using a related word), and he had spoken earlier of prophecies concerning the coming of the Spirit being fulfilled (Acts 1:4-5, 8).

The previous chapter speaks of 120 followers of Jesus who had gathered in the upper room of a large house as they contemplated the meaning of Christ's ascension, heard Peter speak, and chose Matthias to replace Judas as the 12th apostle (1:12-26). Perhaps we are to imagine the same setting when v. 1 says "they were all together in one place."

During that morning meeting, Luke says, "suddenly from heaven there came a sound like the rush of a violent wind, and it filled the entire house where they were sitting" (v. 2).

The "violent wind" was apparently experienced more as sound than fury. The NRSV's "rush of" (NET "blowing") translates a verb that normally means "bringing" or "carrying." The whistling sound did not indicate the movement of air as much as the arrival of something remarkable.

---

*This text is used for Pentecost in Years A, B, and C.*

**The power of the Spirit:** In scripture, the coming of the Spirit enables the faithful to do something for God that they could not do in their own strength. God took some of the Spirit that formerly had rested on Moses alone and put it upon judges appointed to assist him (Numbers 11). The Spirit of God led Balaam to bless Israel, though he had been paid to curse them (Numbers 24). The book of Judges declares that the Spirit of Yahweh came upon Othniel (3:10), Gideon (6:34), Jephthah (11:29), and Samson (13:24; 14:6, 19; 15:14), empowering them to lead Israel to victory over their enemies. The same was true of Saul (1 Sam. 11:6), though the Spirit also departed from him (1 Sam. 16:14). When the Spirit of Yahweh came on David in a mighty way, however, it was "from that day forward" (1 Sam. 16:13).

The Spirit inspired the prophets to preach (2 Chron. 20:14, 24:20; Isa. 61:1; Ezek. 11:5) and enabled God's people to do what they could not do alone (Zech. 4:6). Jesus had promised his followers that, after his ascension, he would send the Spirit to empower them for witness (Acts 1:8). With Acts 2:4, Jesus' promise was fulfilled: the Spirit had come.

While the empowering presence of God's Spirit appears commonly in the Bible, however, it is not accompanied by tongues prior to Acts 2:4, where it appears to have a clearly evangelistic purpose. Although ecstatic tongues speaking became popular in the early church, it also appears to have become an end in itself, leading Paul to both endorse the practice and to express caution about it (1 Corinthians 14).

That something, we will learn in v. 4, was the Holy Spirit. In another sign of the Spirit's presence, tongues of flame appeared and hovered over the heads of all who were gathered there (v. 3). Ordinarily, one would think that a sudden wind would blow out small flames: this wind blew them in.

Both wind and fire were familiar symbols of the divine presence. Yahweh appeared in both storm and fire at Sinai (Exod. 19:16-19), and thundered against the Philistines, sparking a military rout (1 Sam. 7:10). God appeared to Abraham as a smoking firepot and a flaming torch (Gen. 15:17), to Moses in a burning bush (Exod. 3:2), and to Israel in a pillar of fire (Exod. 13:21-22).

For the faithful Jews-turned-Jesus followers, the imagery would have been clear: the sound of the storm wind and the appearance of fire could indicate nothing less than the very presence of God in the room with them.

Author Luke understood the presence of God to be in the form of the Holy Spirit (v. 4), sent in fulfillment of Jesus' promise (1:8). [**The power of the Spirit**]

In a further sign of the Spirit's presence, the gathered believers began to speak "in tongues." In Greek, the same word (*glossa*) is used for the tongues of flame and the other tongues with which they spoke, clearly suggesting that there was a spiritual component to the speech. The KJV and NIV11 preserve the wordplay by translating *glossa* as "tongues" in both places, but "languages" (as in NRSV and NET) is a better translation, since the following verses indicate that people from other lands heard them speak in their own languages.

## Bewildering speech
### (vv. 5-13)

With v. 5, Luke shifts the scene from events inside the room to a crowd that had gathered outside. People walking or living nearby apparently heard the same "sound like the rush of a violent wind" that had filled the house, and they came to see what the excitement was all about. If they could have seen the flames reportedly hovering over the people inside, they might have been even more amazed that the building was still standing.

The text identifies members of the crowd as "devout Jews from every nation under heaven living in Jerusalem" (2:5). "Every nation under heaven" is probably a hyperbole designed to parallel the evangelistic call to "all nations." Even so, people from many nations would no doubt have been represented.

The question is whether these were pilgrims or permanent residents. While we often imagine thousands of pilgrims, including internationals, flocking to the city, Luke says the "devout Jews" in question were "living in Jerusalem." The verb he used (*katoikountes*) is a present active participle from a root that means "to dwell." It was commonly used to indicate a permanent residence, but pilgrims to the city could have been "dwelling" in rented rooms.

In either case, "devout Jews" would have preferred to lodge in near proximity to the temple, which may also be implied here.

Luke does not locate the building, but the size of the crowd gathered outside (from whom 3,000 were baptized, according to 2:41) suggests that it must have been on the edge of a large public square or some other open space, possibly near the outer courts of the temple.

Luke provides no details about how the diverse multitude was able to hear the newly in-spirited persons as

**Rushing in, rushing out:** The closest thing I have ever experienced to Pentecost took place in August of 1971, during the annual meeting of missionaries in the country of Indonesia. I was a student summer worker, tasked with keeping about 25 teenage missionary kids occupied for the 10-day event. As the sessions went on, the adult missionaries became increasingly caught up in a Spirit-infused revival.

The youth met in an upstairs room normally used as a bar. One memorable morning, the students asked how they could experience the effusion of love and excitement they had seen in their parents. At a loss, I suggested that they pray. The youth went to their knees, and soon were overcome with a strong sense of the Spirit's presence. Laughter and hugging and praise broke out as the youth seemed overcome by the Spirit – and the first thing they wanted to do was run and tell their parents, who were holding a business meeting at the time. My efforts to hold them back were fruitless: they could not wait to rush from that upstairs room and invade their parents' meeting.

I suspect the disciples who experienced the original Pentecost may have had a similar desire to rush outside and proclaim the good news of what had happened. After all, the purpose of the Spirit's coming was to empower and embolden their witness "to all nations." It happened that representatives from nearly all the known nations were right outside, living in Jerusalem.

they spoke in languages that every person present could understand. Did the empowered believers rush from the building to mingle with the crowd and testify to Christ's mighty works? Did some of the group stand on steps or a raised platform? Peter reportedly addressed the entire crowd while standing with the other 11 disciples, apparently in view of those gathered (2:14). [**Rushing in, rushing out**]

The people expressed bewilderment, not so much at what the disciples said, but that they could understand what was said, since the speakers were known to be from Galilee, where Jesus had called his first disciples (vv. 6-7).

Galileans were known for their distinctive regional accent (see Luke 22:59), yet on the Day of Pentecost, people throughout the international audience heard them speaking in their own native languages.

Scholars and others have long debated whether the miracle that day was one of speaking or of hearing. Were the disciples given the ability to speak (and presumably understand) a known language, or were they uttering

some sort of heavenly language that their audience could miraculously understand? The text could lend itself to either interpretation, but the plainer sense suggests that they were speaking known languages.

Modern field workers on mission in non-English-speaking countries often spend the first two years of their assignments in language school, learning to communicate with the people they hope to reach. Because of Pentecost, the first wave of missionaries apparently required no such preparation.

Note how Luke combines the observations of many people into what appears to be a single speech as he lists the nations represented that day. Though from different parts of the world, members of the crowd apparently shared a Jewish heritage – but not the same response. Though "all were amazed and perplexed" by the events, wondering what it was all about (v. 12), "others sneered and said, 'They are full of new wine'" (v. 13).

Some interpreters see evidence in v. 13 that the disciples were speaking in *glossolalia*, or unknown tongues, and that some could understand it, while it sounded like gibberish to others. It's also possible that people could have been overhearing other foreign languages that they did not understand, which could also have sounded like nonsense. Cynically, they accused the speakers of being drunk.

## An insightful sermon
### (vv. 14-21)

Peter was generally the most outspoken of the disciples, so it's not surprising that he offered a quick response, forcefully addressing the crowd as "You men of Judea and all who live in Jerusalem" and challenging them to "listen to what I say" (v. 14).

Charges of drunkenness could easily be dismissed, as Peter said it was only 9:00 a.m. (v. 15, "the third hour," counted from about 6:00 a.m.). Wine often accompanied evening meals but was not commonly consumed in the morning. Those who were speaking in new languages were not inebriated by spirits, but inspired by the Spirit.

Peter spoke as if his listeners should not be surprised by what they saw. Quoting a familiar scripture, he described the miraculous movement of the Spirit as nothing more than the fulfillment of Joel's ancient prophecy that a time would come when God would pour out his Spirit on *all*

**David and the Messiah:** As Peter continued his sermon, he tailored his remarks to his audience of "devout Jews," who should have been familiar with the scriptures he quoted. Peter offered a quick summary of Jesus' death and resurrection, with which everyone in the city should have heard about, insisting that all had happened according to God's plan (vv. 22-24). He then interpreted Christ's resurrection in the light of scripture, quoting Ps. 16:8-11 (vv. 25-28). The psalm, traditionally attributed to David, speaks of one who was "not abandoned to Hades," a "Holy One" not left to "experience corruption" (v. 27).

The psalmist spoke in the first person, but David was clearly dead and buried, so Peter argued that he must have been prophetically speaking about a descendant who would escape death and be recognized as the Messiah (vv. 29-31). Jesus had fulfilled that role, Peter said, being raised by the Father and having poured out the Spirit in a way the people of Jerusalem could both see and hear (vv. 32-33).

Finally, Peter quoted yet another curious claim from the Psalms. In Ps. 110:1, also commonly attributed to David, the psalmist declared "'The Lord said to my Lord, 'Sit at my right hand, until I make your enemies your footstool.'" David must have been speaking of a future messiah, Peter insisted, proclaiming that Jesus should be understood as the fulfillment of David's messianic prophecy (vv. 34-36).

people, so that people of every race and gender and age would experience God's Spirit and express their faith through prophecy (vv. 17-18).

Peter reminded his hearers of how Joel had indicated that the day would be marked by signs in the heavens and on earth – signs much like those that had accompanied Christ's death on the cross (vv. 19-20). Likewise, he pointed to Joel's prediction that such an event would throw open the gates of heaven, so that "everyone who calls on the name of the Lord will be saved" (v. 21).

Our text ends at v. 21, but Peter's sermon continued through v. 36 as he quoted psalms attributed to David. Peter argued that David had predicted the coming of a messiah and called him "Lord," which would connect back to the closing line of the quote from Joel, that "everyone who calls on the name of the Lord shall be saved."
**[David and the Messiah]**

As we celebrate Pentecost today, we need not expect to experience wind and flames, for the Spirit of Christ has not left the earth and does not need to be "prayed down" again. Pentecost remains a reminder of the power

and importance of our witness, however. The Spirit is still active in the lives of those who seek to see and respond to the world as Jesus did, leading us to show love and grace in such surprising ways that others may still be amazed.

## The Hardest Question
### Every nation under the heavens – really?

How are we to understand the list of nations represented in Acts 2:8-11? First, we note that Luke's dialogue is clearly an artificial construct. Luke has combined questions raised by various persons and presented the whole as a group query.

Is there a particular significance of the nations on the list, some of which rarely appear elsewhere in scripture? While 2:5 says devout Jews "from every nation under heaven" lived in Jerusalem, 15 places are included in vv. 8-11. Some of the terms suggest ethnic groups rather than nations, and they do not comprise "every nation under heaven."

Scholars have suggested that Judea (listed fifth) and "Cretans and Arabs" (listed last) are later additions. Jerusalem was located in Judea, so it doesn't seem necessary to put it in a list of people who would be surprised to hear their own language. Also, some early church fathers appear to have quoted from a version of the text that had "Armenia" in place of "Judea." The reference to "Cretans and Arabs" appears to be tagged on to the end, and out of place with the geographical sweep of the other nations.

If we remove Judea, Cretans, and Arabs as later additions, we are left with an original list of 12 nations, reminiscent of the 12 tribes of Israel and the belief that God's Spirit would restore Israel. In listing the nations, Luke moved from east to west. Parthia, Media, Elam, and Mesopotamia were all well to the east of Jerusalem. Cappadocia, Pontus, Asia, Phrygia, and Pamphylia were located north and west. Egypt and Libya were south and west, while Rome was even further west.

Luke's list of internationals does not comprise all the nations of the world, but serves as a representative list that indicates peoples everywhere. Christ had promised to send the Spirit, which would empower the disciples to be witnesses "in Jerusalem, in Judea and Samaria, and to the ends of the earth" (Acts 1:8).

# Day of Pentecost

## Optional First Reading
## Numbers 11*

# A Spiritual Assist

*But Moses said to him, "Are you jealous for my sake? Would that all the LORD'S people were prophets,*
*and that the LORD would put his spirit on them!" (Num. 11:29)*

An optional first reading for Year A recounts one of the more curious stories from Israel's wilderness traditions. It comes from a section of Numbers that appears to rely wholly on the Elohistic source, though some consider it a separate tradition. [The Elohist]

The assigned text, which is fine for liturgical reading, should be fit into the larger context for the sake of a more detailed Bible study. Hence, we will review all of Numbers 11.

The connection with Pentecost Sunday is clear, as vv. 24-30 include an account of the Spirit falling on certain elders of Israel, resulting in prophetic speech.

Most of the first 10 chapters of Numbers, along with Exodus 19–40 and all of Leviticus, have their literary setting at Sinai/Horeb, where the descendants of Jacob, newly freed from Egyptian slavery, reportedly entered a covenant with God, received a catalog of laws and rules to live by, and constructed an elaborate tabernacle following divine instructions given to Moses.

### A rough start
### (vv. 1-9)

With Num. 10:11, the lengthy encampment at Sinai came to an end, the cloud of God's presence lifted from the tabernacle, and it was time to move on. By the end of ch. 10, they had traveled only three days before the people began to complain.

According to the text, God became frustrated with the people and sent fire to torch some of the outlying tents, leading the people to complain to Moses, who pleaded for Yahweh to extinguish the flames, and they diminished. [Taberah]

The "rabble" among the people then grumbled about the food again, criticizing the bland manna that God provided, and wishing aloud for the "good old days" in

> **The Elohist:** The Documentary Hypothesis, dismissed by some scholars but largely considered valid, proposes that the Pentateuch is a heavily edited document in which four primary sources have been combined. Clues to the identity of the sources are found in which name they use for the deity (generally Elohim vs. Yahweh), favored vocabulary (e.g., Sinai vs. Horeb for the same mountain), grammatical style, and particular interests.
>
> The Yahwist source, probably the oldest, appears to have originated in Judah. It refers to God as Yahweh, has a vernacular style, and favors southern tribes.
>
> The Elohist writings probably originated in the Northern Kingdom. They refer to God as Elohim and show more interest in the northern tribes.
>
> The Deuteronomistic source, which comes mainly from the late seventh century in Judah, uses characteristic vocabulary in and a stodgy style in emphasizing Israel's covenant (and conditional) relationship with God.
>
> The Priestly source, much of which comes from a later date, refers to God as Elohim prior to the revelation of the name Yahweh in Exodus. It is written in a formal and repetitive style, and it focuses primarily on ritual matters related to worship and cultic purity, of special concern to the priests.

---

*Numbers 11:4-6, 10-16, and 24-29 is used as the reading for Proper 21 in Year B.

> **Taberah:** Numbers 11:1-3 is one of many etiologies or "explaining stories" found in the Old Testament, especially in the Pentateuch. Most of them purport to explain the etymology of place names by relating them to events that took place there. In this case, "the place was called Taberah, because the fire of the LORD burned against them." *Tav'erah* is derived from the third person, singular form of the verb *bā'ar*, "to burn."

Egypt when they had meat to eat, and roots such as garlic and onions to spice up their cooking (vv. 4-6).

Manna, described in vv. 7-9, was reportedly provided by God as food for the wilderness. It was ground or beaten into a cake-like dough and boiled, according to the text, and tasted like olive oil.

## A stressed-out prayer
### (vv. 10-15)

God responded with anger, and so did Moses (v. 10). Like a mother who has heard one whine too many, Moses felt the need to vent, and unleashed his pent-up tension at God, who had put him in charge of the obdurate Israelites.

"Why have you treated your servant so badly?" he asked. "Why have I not found favor in your sight, that you lay the burden of all this people on me?" (v. 11). Leading Israel had become more of a curse than an honor, a thankless job that was weighing Moses down with more unappreciated responsibility than he cared to remember.

Using a bold metaphor, Moses accused God of being like a mother who gives birth to children but then turns them over to a wet nurse for daily care and even breast-feeding (v. 12). Would we dare to pray so boldly? It was Moses who had to listen to the people's rude appeal for meat, but he had no idea how to find such provisions (v. 13). Moses had led the people for many tension-filled weeks, and he had reached the end of his rope: "I am not able to carry all this people alone, for they are too heavy for me," he complained (v. 14).

If this were not enough, Moses added: "If this is the way you are going to treat me, put me to death at once – if I have found favor in your sight – and do not let me see my misery" (v. 15).

Moses' bold entreaty reminds us of Elijah's painful prayer in 1 Kgs. 19:4, of Jeremiah's broken complaints in Jer. 15:10 and 20:14, of Job's plaintive plea in Job 3. The burden of spiritual leadership can be overpowering. The same sensitivity that enables God's chosen leaders to guide others with compassion may also make them prone to depression when their wards turn against them or refuse to follow their leadership.

## A double-edged answer
### (vv. 16-23)

God heard Moses' prayer with patience and compassion. God did not condemn him for being honest and expressing his legitimate frustration, but offered a practical two-pronged response.

First, God instructed Moses to gather 70 others to assist in leadership, promising to take some of the spirit with which he had blessed Moses, and to put it on those who would help to share the load (vv. 16-17).

Second, God told Moses to instruct the people to get ready, because they would soon eat meat for a full month and become so stuffed that it would come out of their noses and they would become sick of it (vv. 18-20).

Moses responded with skepticism, asking how he could find a month's worth of meat for 600,000 people, but God responded that divine power had no limit (literally, "Is Yahweh's hand shortened?"). God would respond, and Moses would see for himself (vv. 21-23).

God expressed anger, but not at Moses. Moses was guilty of nothing but offering an honest prayer. God is big enough and wise enough to hear with patience what gnaws at our insides. God respects an honest prayer that comes from the heart, however disrespectful it may appear to be, far more than any pious platitudes that gloss over our true feelings.

God did not grant Moses a reprieve from his position of leadership, but promised to provide 70 deputies to assist him.

Moses' experience reminds us that God respects an honest prayer more than a pretty one, an appeal from the heart more than a recitation from the head. When our stress load gets as high as Moses experienced, even honest yelling is appropriate.

---

**Which tent?** The wilderness traditions appear to preserve stories of two different tents, both called the "tent of meeting" at times, which is confusing to readers.

According to Exod. 33:7-11, Moses set up a "tent of meeting" outside the camp. The tabernacle, whose construction was said to begin in Exodus 36, was also called the "tent of meeting" (Exod. 39:32, 40; 40:2; et. al.). It is described in Num. 2:17 as being located in the center of the camp, with three tribes arranged on either side.

Numbers 11 consistently refers to Moses and the elders meeting at and around a tent of meeting that was *outside* the camp, more in keeping with the tradition of Exod. 33:7-11.

---

### Response No. 1
### (vv. 24-30)

God's twofold promise, according to the narrator, was then fulfilled. Moses relayed God's message to the people, then chose 70 elders from the people and arranged them around "the tent." **[Which tent?]**

"Then the LORD came down in the cloud and spoke to him," the narrator says, "and took some of the spirit that was on him and put it on the seventy elders" (v. 25a). The presence of the Spirit had a visible and vocal effect: "… when the spirit rested upon them, they prophesied. But they did not do so again" (v. 25b).

The description leaves us puzzled. What does it mean that "they prophesied"? Did they all respond in unison, with the same words, or did each speak separately? Did their "prophecy" consist of proclamation, or praise, or prediction? In the Old Testament, prophets were people who received messages from God and then spoke on God's behalf.

We are also left to wonder why the elders prophesied once, but not again. Was their initial prophecy intended only as a sign of endorsement by the Spirit, an activity that would not be required in their function of helping Moses bear the load of leadership? Was the cessation of their prophecy an indication that any future pronouncements should come from Moses alone? The narrator does not say.

The report of v. 26 is equally perplexing: Eldad and Medad, two men who had not been among the 70 elders chosen for the tabernacle ceremony, also received a divine visitation. "The spirit rested on them," the text says, even though they had not "gone out to the tent, and so they prophesied in the camp."

The story does not specify that they continued to prophesy when the others had stopped, but it implies it. The tabernacle ritual with its attendant prophecy from the 70 had apparently ended, but the participants were still in place when "A young man ran and told Moses, 'Eldad and Medad are prophesying in the camp'" (v. 27). The verb for "are prophesying" is a participle that suggests continuing action.

Joshua, who served as Moses' top aide and had been among the chosen 70, took offense at what he considered to be an act of presumption. Apparently believing that Moses alone was authorized to speak for God, he implored Moses to put a stop to it (v. 28).

Moses could also be very sensitive when anyone challenged his leadership, so his generous response is surprising: "Are you jealous for my sake? Would that all the LORD's people were prophets, and the LORD would put his spirit on them!" (v. 29).

Moses had learned that he should be open to other voices in the camp, and he was apparently willing to believe that God's inspiring spirit was not limited to the chosen few who had surrounded the tabernacle. The gift of God's spirit to others did not diminish God's presence with Moses.

### Response No. 2
### (vv. 31-35)

God's second response to Moses was that the people's complaint about the lack of meat would come back to haunt them. Verse 31 reports that Yahweh stirred up a westerly wind that "brought quails from the sea and let them fall beside the camp." The quantity of quail is staggering and clearly hyperbolic: reportedly the land amounting to several miles (a day's journey) on all sides of the camp was covered with three feet of quail.

The people greedily went after all they could gather, working through the night and day with no one picking up less than 10 homers, or more than 60 bushels each. They then spread them around the area (v. 32), perhaps hoping to dry or cure the meat for preservation.

God had promised enough meat to last for a month, but "While the meat was still between their teeth, before it was consumed, the anger of the LORD was kindled against the people, and the LORD struck the people with a very great plague" (v. 33).

Modern readers might wonder if the sickness came from parasites in the quail or from meat that had spoiled from too much time in the sun, but for the narrator it was all God's doing, and it is not an appealing picture. The people complained about the lack of meat, so God stuffed them full and then made them so sick that many of them died.

The story comes to an end with an etiology, naming the place Kibroth-hattavâ, or "graves of the ones who craved" (*qivrôth hattavāh*, v. 34). Those who survived may have been glad to leave the place behind and journey on to Hazeroth (v. 35), one of many places from the wilderness traditions that cannot be identified.

The text is a reminder to be appreciative of the blessings we have, whether in the form of material provision or spiritual leadership. When we share our gifts with others rather than constantly seeking more, the work of God in the world can only grow.

## The Hardest Question
### How many people were there?

The book of Numbers is so called because it begins with a census of the people in chs. 1–4, described again in ch. 26. The census included only males age 20 and upward (1:2-3), and reportedly counted 603,550 men, not including the Levites (2:32). That would lead to an unlikely total of more than 2,000,000 Israelites roaming through the desert.

The number is clearly a hyperbole, intended for effect, perhaps based in part on a later census at the height of Israel's expansion. Based on the archaeological record, estimates for the population of the entire land of Canaan supported during the late Bronze Age rarely exceed 100,000 inhabitants.

Scholars have sought to deal with the problem in a variety of ways, the most common of which is to note that the word meaning "thousand" (*'elef*) sometimes appears to be used as a reference to "clans" or military "platoons" of considerably less than 1,000. So, if there were 600 clans rather than 600,000 men, for example, and we imagine as many as 100 persons per clan or extended family, the number would be closer to 60,000 – still an incredibly difficult number of people to lead, manage, and provide for in a wilderness area even if they had no livestock to feed and water.

In any case, the exact number of people is beside the point: the narrator intends to show that the people could not have survived without God's miraculous intervention – and that they should have learned from God's ongoing care.

## Second Reading
## Psalm 104*

# To Follow Jesus, Receive the Spirit

*When you send forth your spirit, they are created; and you renew the face of the ground. (Ps. 104:30)*

Pentecost Sunday is often observed with happy celebration and the color red. Red stoles on robes, red paraments on the pulpit furniture, red clothing and even red shoes recall the flames associated with the gift of the Holy Spirit as recounted in Acts 2. [**Pentecost**]

While we normally think of the Holy Spirit in the context of the New Testament, the Hebrew Bible often speaks of persons being empowered by God's spirit to do special work or to deliver a message from God (Judg. 3:10, 6:34, 11:29; 1 Sam. 10:9-13; Isa. 61:1-3; Ezek. 11:1-10; Mic. 3:8).

The spirit was also considered to be the animating presence within all people. Today's text offers poetic insight into that ancient Hebrew concept.

### The God who creates
### (vv. 1-26)

It is helpful, in overview, to read Psalms 103 and 104 together. They appear side by side for a reason: both psalms begin and end with "Bless the LORD, O my soul." While Psalm 103 commemorates God's mighty acts of salvation, Psalm 104 celebrates God's initial and ongoing acts of creation.

Psalm 104 is awash in metaphor, not unlike other imaginative attempts to describe creation in Genesis 1 and 2, Job 38–42, and Psalm 8.

The psalm suggests a progression not unlike the familiar story found in Genesis 1: God creates the heavens first (vv. 2-4), then the earth and sea (vv. 5-9), followed by animals, plants, and people (vv. 10-26). Other elements of

> **Pentecost:** The word "Pentecost" has Greek and Latin roots, meaning "fiftieth." On the Jewish calendar, Pentecost falls 50 days (seven weeks and a day) after Passover. That was when ancient Israel celebrated the harvest festival known as the Feast of Weeks, also called *Shavuot*.
>
> It was during this festival season, following Christ's resurrection, that the Holy Spirit descended upon Jesus' followers who were gathered in an upper room in Jerusalem.
>
> For this reason, the church celebrates Pentecost on the seventh Sunday after Easter each year – the 50th day when both Sundays are counted.

creation are scattered throughout (springs, vv. 10-13; the mountains, v. 18; the moon and sun, v. 19; even darkness, v. 20).

In Gen. 1:1–2:4a, God appears distant and creates by speaking alone, but here God is portrayed in much more personal or anthropomorphic terms, as in the second creation story, Gen. 2:4b-25. The psalmist describes God as being "clothed" with honor and majesty, and "wrapped in light" (vv. 1b-2a). God stretches out the heavens like a tent and sets beams for the heavenly abode above the cosmic waters (vv. 2b-3a). God uses the clouds as a chariot and rides on the wings of the wind (v. 3b, cf. Ps. 68:4, 33).

Like a wise builder, God makes the foundations of the earth firm, then covers its surface with water before setting the sea's boundaries (vv. 5-9).

Everything needed for life is attributed to divine causation: God makes springs to flow, causes grass to grow, and provides plants that humans can use to make bread, wine, and oil (vv. 14-15).

---

*This text is used for Pentecost in Years A, B, and C.*

In beautiful, lyrical fashion, the psalmist credits God with putting the moon in place to order the annual calendar, even as the sun's light and the darkness of night set the daily rhythm of life (vv. 19-20). [**Calendar**]

Creatures of the land (including humans) and the vegetation that supports them are featured in vv. 10-23.

Today's lectionary text, starting at v. 24, begins with an expression of awe at God's magnificent work and the incomparable wisdom required to create such an amazing world and fill it with living creatures (v. 24).

The poet then shifts to the sea, noting that it is also teeming with life, from "creeping things innumerable" to "living things both small and great" (v. 25). Humans are there, too, albeit in ships, along with "Leviathan that you formed to sport in it" (v. 26).

Leviathan has a mixed reputation in scripture. In some texts, Leviathan is a fearful seven-headed sea serpent,

**Leviathan:** In Canaanite mythology, Leviathan was a giant seven-headed serpent that lived in the sea and did battle with the gods. Some biblical texts also regard Leviathan as a multi-headed sea monster who either has been or will be defeated by Yahweh:

Isa. 27:1 – "On that day the LORD with his cruel and great and strong sword will punish Leviathan the fleeing serpent, Leviathan the twisting serpent, and he will kill the dragon that is in the sea."

Ps. 74:14 – "You crushed the heads of Leviathan; you gave him as food for the creatures of the wilderness."

Similar imagery is found in Daniel, where four beasts emerge from the sea, and in Revelation 13, where a seven-headed monster comes from the sea.

The entire chapter of Job 41 is devoted to a lengthy description of the powerful and dangerous Leviathan, whom no man can conquer – only God.

In Psalm 104, the psalmist is so intent on emphasizing God's majesty that even the mighty Leviathan is portrayed as a giant creature that sports in the sea, not a threat to the deity, but part of God's creation.

a symbol of the forces of chaos that God had to overcome in creation. [**Leviathan**]

Here, however, Leviathan is portrayed simply as a great sea creature, a part of God's good creation, that plays in the sea. Ancient mariners would have seen the occasional whale or giant squid, which may have contributed to stories of Leviathan.

### The God who provides
### (vv. 27-30)

With vv. 27-30, the psalmist turns from the theme of creation to provision: the same God who has created all things also sustains them.

"These all look to you to give them their food in due season" (v. 27) refers not just to the sea creatures of vv. 25-26, but to all animal life, including humans, who gather the bounty of good things that come from God's hand (v. 28).

This does not discount the work humans do in tilling the ground, sowing seed, and caring for the plants as they grow (v. 23), but the ancients understood that crops needed rain if they were to thrive. They believed that rain was the product of heaven's benevolence, and drought the result of divine displeasure.

The Old Testament includes several stories in which God directly causes rain to fall or withholds it to produce a time of drought (1 Kings 17–18, for example, in which Elijah announced when God was withholding rain and when it would fall again).

Israel's neighbors credited certain of their gods with controlling the weather. These included Hadad among the Syrians and Baal among the Canaanites. Images of Baal typically have him striding forward with his right arm raised, holding a thunder club, while his left hand holds a stylized spear representing a lightning bolt.

God provides more than rain for daily sustenance, however. The psalmist believed that life itself is due to God's favor, for the breath that enlivens all living creatures comes from God. "When you take away their breath, they die and return to their dust," the psalmist declared, but "When you send forth your spirit, they are created ..." (vv. 29b-30a, NRSV).

With this reference to God's spirit, we have the text's closest connection to Pentecost. The Hebrew term translated as both "breath" and "spirit" in vv. 29-30 is *ruach* (ending with a hard "h" sound, as in "loch"). The same word can be translated as "breath," "spirit," or "wind."

In this context, it is the breath of life. The sending forth of God's spirit creates life and renews creation: the word for "they are created" is the passive form of the same word used in Genesis 1 for God's creative activity (*bār'a*).

In contrast, when God "gathers their breath" (a literal translation), living things die and return to "their dust," a reminder of their pre-created state.

The imagery recalls the creation story in Gen. 2:4b-25, in which God is also described in near-human form, actively creating: "then the LORD God formed man from the dust of the ground and breathed into his nostrils the breath of life; and the man became a living being" (Gen. 2:7). A different word for "breath" is used there, but the concept is the same.

The continuation of that story also testifies that death involves a return to the ground, "for out of it you were taken; you are dust, and to dust you shall return" (Gen. 3:19).

The psalmist saw God's spirit as the source of life, but the Hebrews also believed people could be blessed with the Spirit in exceptional ways, gaining a special closeness to God or unusual abilities. When Israel was in need and God called out strong leaders such as Othniel or Gideon to deliver and lead them, it was said that "the spirit of the LORD" (*ruach-Yahweh*) came upon them (Judg. 3:10, 6:34).

When Samuel anointed young David as the next king of Israel, the "spirit of the LORD came mightily upon David from that day forward," even as "the spirit of the LORD departed from Saul" (1 Sam. 16:13-14).

When prophets spoke in God's behalf, it was believed that "the spirit of the LORD" inspired them (1 Kgs. 22:24, Ezek. 11:5, Mic. 3:8). When Isaiah spoke of a coming servant of the Lord in language that would later be applied to Christ, he emphasized that "the spirit of the LORD" would be upon him (Isa. 11:2, 61:1).

In all these texts, the word is the same as in Ps. 104:29-30, but it implies more than life-giving breath. God's spirit can also provide wisdom, discernment, leadership, or surprising power.

## The God who empowers
### (vv. 31-35)

Reflecting on the creative, sustaining, life-giving power of God brings the psalmist to celebrate God's enduring power over creation (vv. 31-32). It also inspires a pledge that he will sing praise for as long as he possesses God's life-giving spirit: "I will sing to the LORD as long as I live; I will sing praise to my God while I have being" (v. 33).

While v. 34 continues the poet's joyful acclamation, the first half of v. 35 comes as a bitter surprise, so jarring that the lectionary skips over it in the day's reading. Finding a text difficult is no reason for ignoring it, however.

At the very end of his paean of praise to God, just before the closing benediction, the psalmist injects: "Let sinners be consumed from the earth, and let the wicked be no more" (v. 35a).

The malediction may be surprising, but it is not entirely out of place. The poet is so high on God's creative and caring power that he wants to see God praised by all means possible, including his own meditations (v. 34).

The poet appears so overcome with gratitude that the thought of anyone rejecting God's way leaves him thinking that such persons don't deserve to have God's life-giving spirit. Thus, he prays, "let the wicked be no more."

This may seem extreme, but we remember that the psalmist writes in poetic language. It is a negative way of emphasizing his positive message that God, as creator and sustainer of all life, is worthy of perpetual honor and praise.

We are unlikely to join the psalmist in wishing that all sinners would cease to exist, and not just for fear that we and our family and friends might be numbered among them.

Even so, we could profit from joining the psalmist in his meditation upon God's amazing and ongoing gifts to humankind. If we believe that God is responsible for the wonders of the natural world and for all life – including ours – then we certainly have cause to join the psalmist in praising God for as long as we live, repeating the same words that began the psalm: "Bless the LORD, O my soul. Praise the LORD!"

In Hebrew, the last words are "Hallelu-yah." How often do we find time for praise?

## The Hardest Question
### Is there anything akin to Pentecost in the Old Testament?

Psalm 104 speaks of God's spirit as the source of life, and we noted other texts in which God's spirit could also be thought of as a special sign of God's favor and as a source of power or prophetic inspiration.

There are a few instances in the Hebrew Bible in which the spirit of God is said to have sparked ecstatic experiences not entirely unlike the one experienced in Acts 2.

Numbers 11:24-29 recounts a time when God told Moses to choose 70 elders, take them outside the camp, and station them around the tent of meeting. God promised to take some of the divine spirit that rested on Moses and put it on them so they could assist him in leading the people. "Then the LORD came down in the cloud and spoke to him, and took some of the spirit that was on him and put it on the seventy elders; and when the spirit rested upon them, they prophesied. But they did not do so again" (Num. 11:25). Surprisingly, however, the spirit also fell on two men inside the camp who were not among the 70, and they began to prophesy.

A more detailed encounter with the spirit is seen in the experience of Saul, Israel's first king. In 1 Samuel 10, after the prophet/priest Samuel anointed Saul and told him he was to be the next king, Samuel predicted that Saul would encounter a band of musical prophets, a group of traveling ecstatics who typically sang, played instruments, and danced themselves into a holy frenzy.

Samuel told Saul to fall in with the band of prophets and follow their lead. "Then the spirit of the LORD will possess you," Samuel said, "and you will be in a prophetic frenzy along with them *and be turned into a different person*" (1 Sam. 10:6). The change in Saul did not wait for his encounter with the prophets, however. The writer says that "As he turned away to leave Samuel, God gave him another heart…" (1 Sam 10:9).

The encounter appears to have been designed to affirm the great potential that God had placed within Saul, and to encourage him. Saul followed Samuel's instructions. When he met with the prophets, "the Spirit of God possessed him," and he fell into a frenzy along with the other prophets (1 Sam. 10:10). As he opened his life to the working of God within, Saul was given a new heart and a new spirit.

Saul's participation in the frenetic activity of the prophets may or may not have involved speaking in tongues (we know very little about their activities), but it was so uncharacteristic of him that the event became a byword among the people: when someone would do something out of character, others would say "Is Saul also among the prophets?" (1 Sam. 10:12).

The spirit of God came upon Saul at other times, transforming him into a charismatic leader who could do great things (1 Sam. 11:6ff). He had at least one more frenzied encounter with the prophets, though the spirit's purpose there was to divert Saul from his intention of killing David (1 Sam. 19:23).

Saul's experience suggests that the presence of the spirit in this extraordinary way was not automatic: after Saul fell short of expectations, God led Samuel to anoint David as the future king. The spirit of Yahweh then came upon David "from that day forward," but departed from Saul and was replaced by "an evil spirit from the Lord" (1 Sam. 16:13-14).

While modern believers may struggle with this notion, the ancient Hebrews had no difficulty attributing a good or evil spirit to the same God who could use spiritual means to effect either positive or negative change in a person.

The New Testament concept of the Holy Spirit varies in some ways, but its roots are deep in Hebrew thought. Those who gathered in the upper room in Acts 2 were Jewish believers who knew these stories of people who were overcome by God's spirit. As they opened their hearts fully to God and were overcome by the empowering presence of the Holy Spirit, they had no problem attributing its source and its ecstatic effects to God – though some in the crowd accused them of being drunk.

# Day of Pentecost

## Third Reading
### 1 Corinthians 12:1-14

# One and Many

*For just as the body is one and has many members, and all the members of the body,*
*though many, are one body, so it is with Christ. (1 Cor. 12:12)*

Do you consider yourself to be "gifted"? The word gets thrown around a lot, especially in schools, where children as young as first graders may be assigned to programs or classes for the "gifted and talented." While the intent is to help students reach their potential, programs that identify certain people as "gifted" also have the potential of causing others to feel distinctly *un*gifted. Resentment and dissension can result.

A similar problem arose long ago in the ancient city of Corinth, where those who identified themselves as most gifted appear to have been guilty of spiritual pride, and those with less obvious giftedness thought of themselves as second-class Christians.

The gifts were thought to be inspired by God's spirit, making this text an appropriate epistle reading for Pentecost.

### A spiritual church
### (vv. 1-3)

Paul had an up-and-down relationship with the Corinthian Christians, extending over a period of many years. In earlier chapters, Paul dealt with problems of factionalism, immorality, settling grievances, family life, slave-holding, and eating food that had been offered to idols. [**Paul and the Corinthians**]

In chs. 12–14, Paul moved to the hot-button topic of "spiritual gifts." His argument can be summarized briefly: the primary evidence that a Christian is truly "spiritual" is not *glossolalia* ("speaking in tongues"), but loving service.

"Now concerning spiritual gifts" (v. 1a) uses the word *pneumatikōn*, which can be either neuter or masculine, and appears alone. There is no word for "gifts" in the verse, so it

---

**Paul and the Corinthians:** It may be helpful to remember some highlights (and lowlights) in Paul's ongoing relationship with the church in Corinth.

Paul first visited the important city of Corinth and founded the church during his second missionary journey (Acts 18:1-18, c. 50–51 CE). The letter we know as 1 Corinthians was written from Ephesus during Paul's third journey, but it presupposes an earlier letter dealing with immorality in the church (1 Cor. 5:9). Some scholars think a fragment of this earlier letter has been preserved as 2 Cor. 6:14–7:1, which deals with immorality and doesn't really fit into its present context.

After sending the first letter, Paul heard from a group in the church he identifies as "Chloe's people" (1:11), and also received a letter from Corinth (7:1). He responded with the letter we call 1 Corinthians, apparently dealing with the issues raised by Chloe's people in chs. 1–6, and by the letter he had received in chs. 7–16 (cf. 7:1, 7:25, 8:1, 12:1).

The Corinthians responded to Paul's letter with some hostility, requiring him to make a "painful visit" from Ephesus to the church (2 Cor. 2:1). After returning to Ephesus, he wrote a strongly worded letter and sent it by Titus (2 Cor. 2:3-9, 7:12). Parts of this "severe letter" may be preserved in 2 Corinthians 10–13, which is harsher than the conciliatory tone of the surrounding text.

Paul was still burdened for the Corinthians when he left Ephesus. He hoped to meet Titus in Troas and learn how the letter was received, but he did not find Titus there, and moved on to Macedonia (2 Cor. 2:12). There he met Titus, who reported that the Corinthians had accepted the letter with grace and had been reconciled to Paul (2 Cor. 7:5-16). Paul then wrote 2 Corinthians to express his joy and to encourage the church at Corinth to raise a worthy offering for the poor in Jerusalem (2 Corinthians 9).

> **Tongues among the pagans:** Tongues speaking was a feature of some ancient cults or mystery religions, though it was more common among priests than worshipers. At the famed oracle at Delphi, a specially chosen priestess called "the Pythia" responded to questions by going into a trance and uttering unintelligible words, with attendants on hand to interpret. It was believed that the message had been given by the god Apollo.

could possibly be translated as "spiritual persons" or "spiritual things/gifts." Since the context relates to expressions commonly associated with the concept of spiritual gifts, however, translators generally choose that option.

In other places, Paul refers to spiritual gifts with words such as *diakonia* ("services"), *energēmata* ("workings"), and often *charismata* ("gifts"). Today those who emphasize spiritual gifts (especially "speaking in tongues") are commonly called "charismatics" or "Pentecostals." The fastest growing Christian movements in the world are in the Global South, and they are largely charismatic in character. For this reason, if nothing else, we should give attention to Paul's comments on the subject.

The serious concerns expressed in the letter suggest that a misunderstanding or overemphasis on tongues had led to division in the church. Some apparently claimed that speaking in tongues was a necessary sign of the Spirit's presence.

Paul disagreed. He insisted that the manifestation of tongues was not proof of the Spirit, and reminded his readers that many of them had once worshiped idols, which were incapable of speech (v. 2). Some of the pagan cults and mystery religions also practiced *glossolalia*: one can experience religious ecstasy and speak in tongues without knowing the true god. [**Tongues among the pagans**]

The proper test of one's speech – or at, least, the *source* of one's speech – lies in its content. Thus, Paul turned to another argument: no one claiming to have the Spirit of God would curse the name of Jesus, but would rather confess Jesus as Lord (v. 3). The point is not that Christians are incapable of mouthing the words "Jesus is cursed" – Paul would have spoken them as he dictated the letter – but that one inspired by the Spirit of God would not (indeed, *could not*) wish Jesus to be cursed.

## An energized church
### (vv. 4-11)

The issue of spiritual gifts had caused division and strife at Corinth, but Paul knew the Spirit promotes harmony rather than discord. "Now there are varieties of gifts, but the same Spirit; and there are varieties of services, but the same Lord; and there are varieties of activities, but it is the same God who activates all of them in everyone. To each is given the manifestation of the Spirit for the common good" (vv. 4-7). [**A Trinitarian reference?**]

In vv. 8-11, Paul lists several such ministries, but clearly does not intend for it to be a comprehensive list. Other "lists" of spiritual gifts are found in scripture (Rom. 12:6-8, 1 Cor. 12:27-28). All of them are different, and none of them are exhaustive. This list contains nine areas of "giftedness." Some commentators suggest that they are listed in descending order of importance.

The first two "gifts" are closely related: the ability to speak with wisdom (*sophía*) and knowledge (*gnōsis*). Paul had pointed (sometimes sarcastically) to the Corinthians' love of wisdom in chs. 1–4, contrasting their love of earthly eloquence with the deep wisdom that comes from God.

Literally, Paul speaks of the "word" (*logos*) of wisdom and of knowledge. Since the context has to do with speaking, however, Paul's intent is probably the "utterance" (NRSV) or "message" (NET) of wisdom and knowledge spoken by Spirit-empowered believers.

Whether Paul meant to suggest different things by "wisdom" and "knowledge," or simply doubled up the same thought for emphasis, is not clear. Typically, we

> **A Trinitarian reference?** Paul's comments in vv. 4-7 may reflect an early Trinitarian understanding. To the *Spirit* Paul attributes varieties of gifts, while he says the *Lord* (Jesus) assigns the diverse "services" requiring these gifts (or "ministries" – the word is *diakonia*), and *God* distributes the power to perform them ("activates" comes from the Greek *energēmata*: one could translate it as "energize"). Paul spoke about one God in different terms, and about the various ways that God works among us, but still acknowledged one God, who calls all believers to one purpose. There is no "one" gift above all others or prerequisite to others: all believers are gifted, and all are to use their gifts for the good of the whole.

think of wisdom as reflecting the mature and insightful use of knowledge. While knowledge may indicate no more than the accumulation of information, wisdom suggests the ability to employ knowledge in appropriate ways and at the proper time.

"Faith" in v. 9 is not faith that leads to salvation, for Paul is speaking to persons who are already believers. Rather, he speaks of the kind of faith that stands firm in times of crisis, enables the believer to give spiritual service in all circumstances, and inspires others with its staying power.

The pairing of "faith" with the gift of "healing" does not necessarily imply "faith healing," or the notion that healing is available for those who have sufficient faith. Jesus healed people who had expressed no faith at all. Paul believed that God had blessed other persons with gifts of healing that went beyond ordinary medical skills. Some modern believers claim to have experienced miraculous healing, too, but this has never been the norm. Christians should not doubt their faith if they pray for healing and do not receive it.

The term translated "miracles" (v. 10) is *dunameis* (the root word of "dynamite"), also translated as "mighty works." We can only guess at what some of these displays of power might have been. Such manifestations were thought to be signs of God's new age breaking in upon the world (cf. Gal. 3:5).

"Prophecy," a gift attributed to persons such as Agabus (Acts 11:28, 21:10f) and the daughters of Phillip (Acts 21:9), was thought of as the ability to declare the word of God for a given situation – not just the ability to predict the future.

Paul's readers believed that demonic spirits could also inspire prophetic speech, however. Acts 16:16, for example, speaks of a slave girl Paul had met in Philippi. A "spirit of divination" would reportedly prompt her to prophesy, a "gift" that her owners exploited, charging fees for her services as a fortuneteller.

For this reason, since there was a temptation to fake prophetic gifts, it was important that some persons be gifted with the "discernment of spirits" so that the church could determine if a would-be prophet's words came from God, or from another source.

The gifts listed in vv. 9-10 are all things that contribute to the welfare of the community, so we may expect Paul's concluding mention of "various kinds of tongues" and "the interpretation of tongues" to be understood in a similar context: spiritual gifts are designed for the benefit of the church rather than the enhancement of individuals.

It is notable that Paul put tongues and their interpretation at the bottom of the list, as if they were the least important, though they may have caused the most controversy. In 12:27-31, which also speaks of several spiritual gifts, he again lists tongues and the interpretation of tongues last.

What did Paul mean by "various kinds of tongues"? Some suggest that he may have had in mind the ability to speak actual languages not previously known to the speaker (as in Acts 2:6ff), along with the kind of ecstatic utterances that cannot be understood apart from the presence of one with the gift for "interpretation of tongues." Others note that each individual is unique, and so any person who speaks in unintelligible tongues would do so differently.

If everyone with the "gift of tongues" spoke in the same way, others could learn the language. Ecstatic utterances, however, were thought to be of a different nature.

No matter what the outer manifestation, Paul concluded, there is one Spirit at work to energize all believers with the presence and the power of God's grace gifts. The gifts are allotted "to each one individually just as the Spirit chooses," but their purpose is communal, to build up the church in unity and love.

## A united church
### (vv. 12-14)

Paul clarified his intent with the familiar and memorable illustration of the church as a body with different parts that must work together if the body is to function properly (vv. 12-27).

Today's text includes only the first three verses of Paul's extended metaphor, but they are sufficient to introduce the concept. "For just as the body is one and has many members, and all the members of the body, though many, are one body, so it is with Christ," he said (v. 12).

Paul went on to extend the metaphor, speaking of feet, hands, ears, and eyes; along with parts that are more or less respectable or honored (vv. 15-25). The different members are part of a single body, and thus experience suffering or honor together, not separately (v. 26).

The Spirit is the source of gifts in all their variety, but also the force that unifies members' giftedness and other differences in service to Christ. The church in Corinth included men and women, Jews and Gentiles, free citizens and slaves, but all belonged to the same body, baptized in and sustained by the same Spirit of God (vv. 13-14).

The complex nature of our bodies is self-evident. Every organ, bone, nerve, and artery serves the larger whole, and the failure of any one part leads to diminished health or ability. Both individuals and churches are part of the body of Christ, which functions best when all the parts are not only present and accounted for, but also working together.

## The Hardest Question
### What is "the body" to which Christians belong?

Paul's metaphor of the one body having many parts that need to work together comes with a bit of a surprise. Scott Nash has noted that one would expect that Paul was thinking of the church. After all, he was writing to a divided church in which some members did not want to associate with other members, or thought themselves better than other members, or imagined that they did not need certain members (*1 Corinthians*, Smyth & Helwys Bible Commentary [Smyth & Helwys, 2009], 363).

It would seem natural, then, that Paul's metaphor of a single body made of many interdependent parts would be a reference to the church. The surprise is that Paul looks past the church to which he was writing and applies it to Christ: "For just as the body is one and has many members, and all the members of the body, though many, are one body, so it is with Christ" (v. 14).

This suggests, Nash says, that Paul's use of body language implied something more substantial than a metaphor, for Paul goes on to say in v. 27 "Now you are the body of Christ and individually members of it." In vv. 4-11, Paul emphasizes that all are brought into the body ("baptized") by the Spirit, and all "drink" of the Spirit. Thus, Nash suggests, "Paul's point is that entrance into the body of Christ involves a complete saturation of the Spirit, inside and out" (p. 363).

Paul's metaphor, then, is bigger than the church at Corinth, or of any association of churches, or any denomination. It is to the "body of Christ" in its earthly representation that we belong, a body that includes apostles, prophets, and teachers, along with various functions with which persons could be enabled: mighty works, healing, service, leadership, and tongues (v. 28; in this list, as in vv. 4-11, tongues are last on the list).

This is the way God intended it to be. Different persons blessed with different gifts serve different functions, and all are part – not just of their local church, but of the body of Christ. Working together with mutual respect will make for a happier and more functional church, but it is all in service to Christ.

# Day of Pentecost

## Fourth Reading
### John 20:19-23*

# A Disciple We Can Like

*A longer version of this text, John 20:19-31, is the reading for the Second Sunday of Easter in Year A. A study is included in this volume at that point.*

## Optional Fourth Reading
## John 7:37-39

# A Pentecostal River

*On the last day of the festival, the great day, while Jesus was standing there, he cried out,*
*"Let anyone who is thirsty come to me, and let the one who believes in me drink." (John 7:37-38a)*

Pentecost: Christians observe it every year, some more avidly than others. Catholics, mainline denominations, and other liturgical traditions switch their paraments and pastoral stoles to red, often with embroidered doves or flames to symbolize the Holy Spirit. Male pastors may wear red neckties, and women clergy may break out red shoes. It's generally a happy day.

For churches on the charismatic end of the spectrum, Pentecost can be even more special. Worshipers may feel moved by the Spirit to stand, raise their hands, shout, dance, or even speak in tongues. Like the psalmists, their worship is punctuated with vocal praise and bursts of applause, unlike those who believe Hab. 2:20 should apply to modern worship: "the LORD is in his holy temple; let all the earth keep silence."

Jews also celebrate Pentecost, though on the day before, seven weeks and a day from the second day of Passover. Greek speakers called it Pentecost (meaning "fiftieth") because it was held on the 50th day after Passover.

Observant Jews anticipate the arrival of Pentecost by counting the days, even as Christians may count the days of Advent, or from Ash Wednesday to Easter. Jews don't use the term "Pentecost," but rather *Shavu'ot*, meaning "weeks." The festival, also called "Firstfruits," once celebrated the spring harvest of winter wheat (Exod. 34:22). Israel's traditions combined an agricultural holiday with a historical memory: rabbinic calculations in the Talmud claim that God gave the law to Israel on Mt. Sinai exactly 49 days after the first Passover celebration.

So, while Jews memorialize the giving of the law on Pentecost, Christians commemorate the giving of the Holy Spirit.

### Living water
### (vv. 37-38a)

The setting of our present text, from John, is also during a festival, though it was not *Shavu'ot*, but *Succoth*, otherwise known as the "Feast of Booths" or "Tabernacles." That festival occurred in the fall, shortly after the solemn Day of Atonement (*Yom Kippur*). It also combined agricultural and historical elements, celebrating the fall harvest while also commemorating Israel's 40 years of wilderness wandering,

---

**John, Jesus, and Festival:** The Fourth Gospel asserts that Jesus visited Jerusalem at least four times during his active ministry, and most of his teachings are centered there. The first visit coincided with Passover (2:13), and the second with a festival that is unnamed (5:1). The third visit is the one in our text, during the Feast of Tabernacles/*Succoth*. John 10:22 suggests that Jesus was still in Jerusalem when the festival of Dedication (Hanukkah) rolled around, in midwinter. Jesus' final visit, described in John 12–19, occurred during the Passover festival.

In contrast, the synoptic gospels (Matthew, Mark, Luke) portray Jesus as spending most of his ministry in Galilee, and place him in Jerusalem only during the last week of his earthly life. None of the gospels claims to offer a full biography of Jesus, however, and some describe the same teachings taking place in different settings. Observant Jews traveled to Jerusalem for the festivals as often as they could, so it is likely that Jesus made more than one visit to the city during his ministry.

when the people lived in tents. In Jesus' day, Jews would build temporary shelters and camp out in them during the week-long festival. [John, Jesus, and festivals]

Much of John's gospel centers around Jesus' visits to Jerusalem, all of which coincided with Jewish festivals, which faithful Jews sought to celebrate in Jerusalem when possible. The early part of John 7 locates Jesus in Galilee as the feast of Booths/*Succoth* drew near. His brothers urged him to go on to Jerusalem, but Jesus knew it would be dangerous for him, so he insisted that they go without him. "I am not going to this festival, for my time has not yet fully come," he said (v. 8). Later, however, Jesus decided to go, "not publicly but as it were in secret" (v. 10). After overhearing much conversation and debate concerning him, Jesus gave up his attempt at anonymity: at midweek he went to the temple and began to teach (v. 14).

People listening to Jesus expressed astonishment that he could teach so forcefully without being a trained rabbi, but Jesus insisted that his teaching had its source and authority in God, not the synagogues (vv. 15-18). He accused those who had criticized him for healing on the Sabbath of hypocrisy, noting that they circumcised on the Sabbath (vv. 19-24).

He and the crowd also sparred over whether he should be understood as the Messiah. Jesus did not claim the title outright, but he insisted that people who knew his earthly background didn't understand who had sent him. Some sought to arrest Jesus, "but no one laid hands on him, because his hour had not yet come" (vv. 25-36).

Today's text again finds Jesus in the temple, this time on the last day of the festival. If his prior teachings had not created a stir, this one would: "…while Jesus was standing there, he cried out, 'Let anyone who is thirsty come to me, and let the one who believes in me drink'" (vv. 37-38a).

Theologians and exegetes have long debated the proper translation of this sentence, and whether Jesus or the believer then becomes the source of "the river of the water of life." Whatever the interpretation, the clear intent remains the same: Jesus invited all who were spiritually thirsty to come to him and drink, and the act of "drinking" from Christ is connected to belief. In other words, Jesus recognized the human longing for spiritual wholeness and extended an invitation for people to quench their thirst through him, observing that only believers would take advantage of the offer.

The story of Jesus and the woman of Samaria reflects a similar thought. When Jesus offered her "living water," she did not understand. He then explained, "Everyone who drinks of this water will be thirsty again, but those who drink of the water that I will give them will never be thirsty. The water that I will give will become in them a spring of water gushing up to eternal life" (John 4:13-14).

The Fourth Gospel also records Jesus speaking of himself as the bread of life (6:35, 48), or the light of the world (8:12, 9:5). His choice of water as a metaphor in this context was probably linked to a symbolic water ritual that accompanied the Feast of Weeks. Tractate *Sukkah*, from a collection of rabbinic writings known as

**Libation and celebration:** The water ceremony included both celebration and humor. According to *Sukkah* 4:9, as the priest prepared to pour water from the cask into the bowl on the altar, it was customary for the people to shout "Raise your hands!" in recollection of a priest who had accidentally poured all of the water on his feet, and "all the people pelted him with their citrons."

Celebrants were expected to carry with them four species of plants, including citrons, a type of citrus fruit.

Daily ceremonies during the Feast of Booths also included the lighting of four giant candelabras in the women's court, using olive oil for fuel and torn scraps from the priest's worn-out clothing as wicks. "Pious people and men of [great] deeds" would light torches and dance before the candelabras in celebration as "the Levites [would play] with lutes, and harps, and cymbals, and trumpets, and countless musical instruments, upon the fifteen steps which descend into the women's court, corresponding with the fifteen songs of ascents in the Psalms, that upon them the Levites would stand with their musical instruments and sing." The temple was on a high knoll, and the candelabras were reportedly so bright that "there was not a courtyard in Jerusalem that was not illuminated by the light of the place of [water] drawing" (excerpts from *Sukkah* 5:2-4).

On the next day, as Jesus had continued to teach, he chose to use the metaphor of light: "I am the light of the world. Whoever follows me will never walk in darkness but will have the light of life" (8:12).

(Quotes from the Mishnaic tractate *Sukkah* are taken from the Sefaria website, at http://www.sefaria.org/Mishnah_Sukkah.5.1?lang=bi, where they appear in both Hebrew and English.)

the Mishnah, describes an impressive water drawing and libation ceremony performed each day of the festival. A golden flask containing three measures of water was drawn from the Pool of Siloam, which was fed by Jerusalem's primary water source, the Gihon Spring. As the flask of water was brought into the city through the Water Gate, priests would announce its coming with three ceremonial blasts from the *shofar* (an instrument made from a ram's horn), blowing a *tekiyah* (a long blast), a *teruah* (a broken, toccata blast), then another *tekiyah* (*Sukkah* 4:9).

When the water cask was paraded into the temple, a priest would ceremonially carry it up the steps of the large altar, where there were two large bowls (whether of silver or pottery is a matter of debate), one for wine offerings, and one for the water ritual. As the congregation watched, the priest would pour a measure of the water into the bowl. The water would then spew out through two small openings near the bottom, creating a fountain effect as the water washed over the altar.

The ceremony must have been imposing and accompanied by exuberant praise, for *Sukkah* 5:1 adds: "Anyone who has never seen the rejoicing at the place of [water] drawing, has never seen rejoicing in all his days." **[Libation and celebration]**

### The coming Spirit
### (vv. 38b-39)

The latter part of v. 38 presents a conundrum, for it claims to quote scripture ("As the scripture has said"), but there is no Old Testament equivalent to what follows: "Out of his heart/side shall flow rivers of living water." As noted above, some interpreters take this as a reference to the believer, while others think the reference is to Jesus.

Most translations say the river of living water will flow "from his heart," but the word used is *koilía*, which normally means "belly," though it could also be used as a reference to one's insides in general. Some interpreters take it as a general reference to the body: NET has "From within him shall flow rivers of living water."

Others suggest that the quotation may have been shaped by the author's belief that when a Roman soldier pierced Jesus' side with a spear during the crucifixion, "blood and water came out" (John 19:34).

While water is the topic, the real subject is the Spirit, for which the "water of life" is a metaphor. When we come to v. 39, there's no question about who is speaking, as the narrator adds an obvious editorial comment: "Now he said this about the Spirit, which believers in him were to receive; for as yet there was no Spirit, because Jesus was not yet glorified."

The NRSV translation is unfortunate, as a casual reader might take it to mean that the Spirit did not yet exist. A better reading is "for the Spirit was not yet, for Jesus had not been glorified." Some ancient copyists added "not been given" in hopes of clearing up any misunderstanding. The point is that while Jesus was still physically on earth, the Spirit had not yet come upon believers. Only after Jesus' crucifixion, resurrection, and ascension – when he had been fully "glorified" – would the Spirit be given to the church.

The memorable Pentecost experience described in Acts 2 became the fulfillment of Jesus' promise that those who came to "drink from" him would receive the Spirit in abundant and overflowing ways.

All believers are invited to have a "Pentecost experience" of sensing the presence of Christ's Spirit within. Tongues aren't required: only thirst, and belief.

### The Hardest Question
### Where does the period go?

The proper translation of John 7:37-38 is one of the most debated texts in the New Testament, not because any of the words are unclear, but because we can't be sure where the period – or periods – should be placed. Many early Greek manuscripts did not use punctuation, sometimes making it difficult for translators to know the proper relationship between words, phrases, or even clauses.

In this case, most modern translations, including the NRSV, follow a reading that was popular among early church fathers from the East. This reading puts a period after "drink," so that we have "Let anyone who is thirsty come to me, and let the one who believes in me drink. As the scripture has said, 'Out of the believer's heart shall flow rivers of living water.'" This assumes that it is Jesus who quotes the scripture, referring to the believer who drinks. The NRSV inserts the word *believer's* in the last phrase in place of the Greek "his," so the reader will know that the translators see the believer as the one who has rivers of living water flowing from him.

Another option is to put a period after both "me" and "believes in me," as in a footnote to the NIV11 version: "Let anyone who is thirsty come to me. And let anyone drink who believes in me. As Scripture has said, 'Out of him (or them) will flow rivers of living water.'" This reading also presumes that it was Jesus who made the comment about scripture, so that the one from whom living water flows is the believer.

An optional translation, favored by many Western church fathers and a number of modern exegetes, would put a single period after "believes in me," creating a poetic couplet in chiastic form: This gives the reading: "If anyone is thirsty let him come to me, and let him drink who believes in me. Just as scripture says, 'Out of his heart shall flow rivers of living water.'" This translation presumes that the statement about scripture in v. 39b, like the obvious comment in v. 40, was made by the narrator, rather than Jesus. In this case, we would presume that the rivers of living water would flow from the side of Christ rather than the believer, which many believe is a more accurate view. As J. Ramsey Michaels has noted, "It is more natural to think of Jesus than of individual Christian believers as the source or wellspring of the life-giving Spirit of God" (*John*, Understanding the Bible Commentary Series. [Baker Books, 2011], 138).

The problem is compounded by the fact that there is no Old Testament scripture that says "Out of his heart shall flow rivers of living water," so the quotation is only a vague allusion, and we can't be sure where it's from or what its original meaning might have been. One text that associates water with an individual is Prov. 4:23, which warns, "Keep your heart with all vigilance, for from it flow the springs of life." Proverbs 5:15 counsels the wise to draw from their own cisterns and wells. Both proverbs, from the wisdom school, probably have to do with trusting one's wisdom and avoiding negative influences, and could hardly relate to the present text.

Other Old Testament texts portray God as the source of both physical water and spiritual succor. Exodus 17:1-6 speaks of water flowing from a rock during Israel's journey from Egypt to Sinai. Psalm 78:16 recalls the event, saying "He made streams come out of the rock, and caused waters to flow down like rivers" (likewise Ps. 105:41).

Ezekiel's vision of the new age speaks of a river of living water flowing from the temple in God's new kingdom (Ezek. 47:1-11), while the prophet Zechariah spoke of a coming day when a fountain of cleansing water would erupt in Jerusalem (Zech. 13:1) and a river of living water would flow from Jerusalem to both eastern and western seas (Zech. 14:8).

Isaiah 44:3 speaks of God pouring out water on a thirsty land, and Isa. 55:1 rings familiar: "Ho, everyone who thirsts, come to the waters; and you that have no money, come, buy and eat! Come, buy wine and milk without money and without price."

Such similar texts as we can find, then, favor the image of God/Christ as the source of water, rather than the believer.

# Index of Lectionary Texts
## Year A, Volume 2

CPSIA information can be obtained
at www.ICGtesting.com
Printed in the USA
JSHW040819040922
29881JS00001B/1